AGAINST RACISM

W.E.B. Du Bois, 1950s

W. E. B. Du Bois

AGAINST RACISM: UNPUBLISHED

ESSAYS, PAPERS, ADDRESSES,

1887–1961

BY W.E.B. DU BOIS

EDITED BY HERBERT APTHEKER

THE UNIVERSITY OF MASSACHUSETTS PRESS

AMHERST, 1985

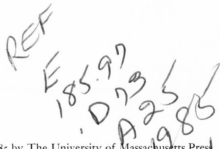

Copyright © 1985 by The University of Massachusetts Press
All rights reserved
Printed in the United States of America
Second printing

Library of Congress Cataloging in Publication Data
Du Bois, W.E.B. (William Edward Burghardt), 1868–1963.
   Against racism.

   Includes index.
   1. Racism—United States—Addresses, essays, lectures.
2. United States—Race relations—Addresses, essays, lectures.
3. Afro-Americans—Addresses, essays, lectures.
I. Aptheker, Herbert, 1915–   . II. Title.
E185.97.D73A25 1985   305.8′00973   84–16173
ISBN 0-87023-134-0

This publication has been supported by the National Endowment for the Humanities,
a federal agency which supports the study of such fields as history, philosophy,
literature, and languages.

Except where noted, all photographs are from the archives of the University
Library, University of Massachusetts at Amherst, and grateful acknowledgment is
made for permission to use them.

To Leone Stein
with love from
Fay and Herbert

Contents

Illustrations

Introduction

After publication of W.E.B. Du Bois's selected correspondence, in three volumes, and of his *Education for Black People* and *Prayers for Dark People*, there remained a significant number of papers, essays, and addresses that had never seen print. With the publication of this book, I believe that the consequential manuscripts in the collection he charged me with editing in 1946 and left in my custody in 1961 now have been made available.

Included is a major effort of about thirty thousand words in which Du Bois offered his views on the position of Afro-American people in the mid–1930s, and on the relationship of the New Deal to that position, and made suggestions for an innovative strategy in the struggle for freedom.

These papers clearly trace Du Bois's dramatic political development from a generally conservative orientation to a more and more liberal and then, in his final two decades, an increasingly radical outlook. Always present, however, was an implacable detestation of racism; the volume's title reflects his historic and courageous stand on this central issue in U.S. and modern world history.

Several aspects of Du Bois's fabulous career are illuminated in these papers. These include important material on his estimate of Booker T. Washington and his role not only in the National Association for the Advancement of Colored People (NAACP) but also in the Niagara Movement and in helping plant the seeds of what became the National Urban League. Some of the papers convey moving insights into aspects of his character—notably his long essay on the great art galleries of Europe and his early analysis entitled "The Spirit of Modern Europe." In these writings as a group Du Bois shows his restraint, courtesy, extraordinary energy, and transparent honesty. There are occasional flashes of things which appear nowhere else in his published writings. Startling, for example, in light of the impression conveyed in other works that racism hardly touched his childhood, is the sentence in an 1890 paper written for a Harvard class in English: "In early youth a great bitterness entered my life and kindled a great ambition."

Du Bois consistently emphasized not only the racial aspect of Black oppression but also, beginning about 1904, its class features. He also was keenly aware of the national qualities in the Afro-American experience. Here we find him giving attention to all three elements and often to their interrelationships.

Certain historical hypotheses, only now being developed, appear in these pages—for example, the relationship between slave resistance and the bourgeois-democratic movements in Europe, and the suggestion that racism was relatively absent in the early colonial period and was provoked by ruling elements as an instrument for maintaining power.

Du Bois comprehended the significance of Black people's political power potential; he insisted upon what later generations called "Black power." He also emphasized the basic character of economic power and devoted the final thirty years of his life to spreading understanding of that reality, while noting, again, the interpenetration of economic and political strength.

Sometimes Du Bois's prophetic powers are breathtaking. An instance is his suggestion in a 1944 speech delivered in Haiti of what became known, in the Kennedy years, as the "Alliance for Progress." His uncompromising 1946 critique of what was soon called the Cold War, his urging of a policy of anticolonialism and antimilitarism, and his rejection of antiSovietism fell on hostile ears among the NAACP leadership and cost him his job. These positions, together with his pioneering opposition to nuclear weapons—which almost led to his imprisonment—point in these final years of the twentieth century to paths which it may well be essential to take if we are not to terminate human existence before the century's close.

The reader will observe an absence of material from the period just before the First World War to 1935, terminating Du Bois's first connection with the NAACP. This gap reflects not omissions by the editor but rather a lack of significant unpublished papers for these years.

The latter fact is explained by the ocean of published work Du Bois produced in that generation: books like *John Brown*, *The Quest of the Silver Fleece*, *The Negro*, *Darkwater*, *The Gift of Black Folk*, *Dark Princess*, and *Black Reconstruction;* writings in and editing of the *Moon*, the *Horizon*, the *Brownies' Book*, and the *Crisis*; weekly newspaper columns in the 1920s and 1930s; and scores of articles in such periodicals as the *New Republic*, *Nation*, *Journal of Negro Education*, *Current History*, the *World Tomorrow*, *Foreign Affairs*, and *American Mercury* and in the newspapers including the *Times*, *Post*, *Sun*, *World*, and *Herald-Tribune* in New York City. Because he had these outlets, and others, available, nothing consequential seems to have remained unpublished (except correspondence, of course), even from the astonishingly prolific Du Bois.

All manuscripts are published in their original form with rare exceptions. Words added by the editor are bracketed. The ampersand is spelled out; typographical errors are silently corrected. Slips in dates also are corrected—for example, Du Bois's placing of Booker T. Washington's 1895 Atlanta speech in 1896. Errors in rendering names are corrected: Warbasse, not Barbasse; Arthur Helps, not Samuel Helps; Theophilus G. Steward, not Stewart; and the like. No substantive changes have been made without specific notice to the reader.

In the index the reader will find complete names of people mentioned by Du Bois.

From time to time, in the years necessary to the completion of this volume, assistance has been kindly offered to me by Malcolm Call, Debra Holiday, Dr. Doris G. Marquit, Hugh T. Murray, Jr., and Dr. Roger E. Rosenberg. Leone Stein was Director of the University of Massachusetts Press for most of the time during which the book was being prepared, and her assistance went far beyond the limits of duty.

Fay P. Aptheker was an essential partner in the Du Bois project from its beginning shortly after the Second World War, and remains so as its completion approaches.

Neither Dr. Du Bois nor his wife, Shirley Graham Du Bois, lived to see the present stage of the effort; but they supported it as long as they did live, and their devotion and trust made perseverance imperative.

Herbert Aptheker
September 1983

The Public Career of W.E.B. Du Bois
(23 February 1868–27 August 1963)

1883–85   Serves as western Massachusetts correspondent for T. Thomas Fortune's *New York Age* (later *Globe*); also occasionally contributes to the *Springfield Republican*.

1884   Graduates from high school in Great Barrington as valedictorian; speaks on Wendell Phillips (who has recently died).

1885–88   Attends Fisk University, Nashville, Tenn., receiving B.A.; teaches in country school during two summers.

1887–88   Performs as chief editor of the *Fisk Herald*.

1888   Enters Harvard as a junior.

1890   Graduates, B.A., cum laude, in class of 300; attracts national attention with commencement address, "Jefferson Davis: Representative of Civilization."

1891   Delivers paper entitled "The Enforcement of the Slave-Trade Laws" at annual meeting of the American Historical Association, held in December in Washington, D.C.

1892   Receives M.A. (history) from Harvard.

1892   Wins Slater Fund Fellowship for Graduate Study Abroad.

1892–94   Does graduate study, mostly in history and economics, at University of Berlin; travels extensively in Europe.

1894–96   Teaches Greek and Latin at Wilberforce University, Ohio.

1895   Receives Ph.D. (history) from Harvard.

1896   Publishes *The Suppression of the African Slave Trade to the United States of America, 1638–1870*, Harvard Historical Studies no. 1 (New York: Longmans, Green).

1896–97   Is assistant instructor in sociology, University of Pennsylvania (but teaches no classes!).

1897   Spends summer in Farmville, Va., studying Black population.

1897–1910   Serves as professor of economics and history, Atlanta University.

1897–1911   Organizes annual Atlanta University Studies of Negro Problems; edits the annual publications.

1898   Publishes "The Negroes of Farmville, Virginia: A Social Study," *U.S. Department of Labor Bulletin* 3 (January): 1–38.

1898–99   During summers studies Black farmers' conditions in Georgia and Alabama.

1899 Publishes "The Negro in the Black Belt," *U.S. Department of Labor Bulletin* 6 (May): 401–17.

1899 Publishes *The Philadelphia Negro: A Social Study*, Publications of the University of Pennsylvania: Series in Political Economy and Public Law, no. 14 (Boston: Ginn and Co.).

1900 Acts as secretary, First Pan-African Conference, London.

1901 Publishes "Negro Landholder of Georgia," *U.S. Department of Labor Bulletin* 6 (July): 647–777.

1902–4 (various periods during summers): Studies conditions of Black rural populations in the South, especially Georgia and Alabama.

1903 Publishes *The Souls of Black Folk: Essays and Sketches* (Chicago: A. C. McClurg and Co.).

1904 Publishes "The Negro Farmer," *U.S. Bureau of the Census Bulletin* 8: 69–98.

1905–6 Edits the *Moon*, a weekly issued in Memphis, Tenn. (Only two issues are known to exist. That issued 23 June 1906 was no. 30; perhaps two or three additional numbers appeared.)

1905–10 Is main founder and general secretary of the Niagara Movement.

1906 Publishes "The Negro Farmer," in U.S. Twelfth Census, *Special Reports: Supplementary Analysis and Derivative Tables*, pp. 511–79.

1907–10 Founds and edits the *Horizon*, a monthly published in Washington, D.C.

1909 Publishes his biography *John Brown* (Philadelphia: George W. Jacobs and Co.).

1909 Participates in New York City meeting which leads to founding in 1910 of the National Association for the Advancement of Colored People (NAACP).

1910–34 Serves as member of Board of Directors of NAACP and as director of Publicity and Research.

1910–34 Founds and edits the *Crisis*.

1911 Participates in First Universal Races Congress, London.

1911 Joins the Socialist party.

1911 Publishes *The Quest of the Silver Fleece: A Novel* (Chicago: A. C. McClurg and Co.).

1912 Resigns from Socialist party; supports Woodrow Wilson for president; helps organize first major Black breakaway from the Republican party.

1913 Joins editorial board of the *New Review*, a socialist-oriented monthly magazine issued in New York City.

1915   Publishes *The Negro,* Home University Library, vol. 91 (New York: Henry Holt, 1915).

1915   Leads nationwide, partially successful, effort to boycott theaters showing *Birth of a Nation.*

1917–18   Supports U.S. entry into World War I; fights against maltreatment of Black troops; leads in effort to enroll Black officers; heads massive Silent Protest Parade (1917) down Fifth Avenue in New York City against lynching and jim-crow.

1919   With Martha Gruening, investigates and exposes sources of East St. Louis pogrom.

1919   Investigates in Europe for NAACP racist treatment of Black troops; acts as chief organizer of the modern Pan-African movement.

1919   Attends first conference of the modern Pan-African movement, in Paris.

1920   Helps expose atrocities of U.S. occupation in Haiti.

1920   Receives Spingarn Medal from NAACP.

1920–21   Founds and edits the *Brownies Book,* a monthly magazine for children.

1921   Publishes *Darkwater: Voices from within the Veil* (New York: Harcourt, Brace and Co.).

1921   Chairs Second Pan-African Congress, London, Brussels, Paris.

1923   Chairs Third Pan-African Congress, London, Paris, Lisbon.

1923   Accepts appointment by President Coolidge as special minister and envoy extraordinary for the United States at the inauguration of President Charles D. B. King of Liberia; visits other parts of West Africa.

1924   Publishes *The Gift of Black Folk: Negroes in the Making of America* (Boston: Stratford Co.).

1926   Makes first and extensive (six weeks') visit to Soviet Union.

1926   Forces resignation of Fayette McKenzie, the last white president of Fisk University, as culmination of his leadership for several years of effort to democratize Black universities.

1927   With Alain Locke, leads so-called Harlem Renaissance; founds Black theater—the KRIGWA players—in Harlem.

1927   Chairs Fourth Pan-African Congress, New York City.

1928   Publishes *Dark Princess: A Romance* (New York: Harcourt, Brace and Co.).

1930   Publishes two Blue Books, issued by Haldeman-Julius in Girard, Kans.: *Africa: Its Geography, People and Products* (no. 1505), and *Africa: Its Place in Modern History* (no. 1552).

1930–33   Tries to democratize NAACP and, in response to impact of the depression, to introduce economic cooperatives in Black communities, as a step toward Black self-sufficiency.

1933   Teaches summer course called "Karl Marx and the Negro" at Atlanta University.

1934   Resigns from the NAACP and the *Crisis*, having failed in efforts at transformation.

1934–44   Serves as professor and chairman of Department of Sociology, Atlanta University.

1935   Publishes *Black Reconstruction: An Essay toward a History of the Part Which Black Folk Played in the Attempt to Reconstruct Democracy in America, 1860–1880* (New York: Harcourt, Brace and Co.).

1936   Makes extensive journey around the world, including Nazi Germany, the USSR again, China, and Japan.

1939   Publishes *Black Folk Then and Now: An Essay in the History and Sociology of the Negro Race* (New York: Henry Holt and Co.).

1940   Publishes *Dusk of Dawn: An Essay toward an Autobiography of a Race Concept* (New York: Harcourt, Brace and Co.).

1940–44   Founds and edits *Phylon*, a quarterly published at Atlanta University.

1943   Organizes First Conference of Negro Land-Grant Colleges.

1944   Makes extended visits to Haiti and Cuba and gives several public lectures.

1945   With Mary McLeod Bethune and Walter White, serves as consultant to U.S. delegation at founding of the United Nations, on behalf of the NAACP; seeks, vainly, to persuade delegation to adopt anticolonial position.

1945   Presides at Fifth Pan-African Congress, Manchester, England.

1945   Publishes *Color and Democracy: Colonies and Peace* (New York: Harcourt, Brace and Co.).

1945   Oversees publication of *Encyclopedia of the Negro: Preparatory Volume with Reference Lists and Reports* (New York: Phelps-Stokes Fund), of which he was chief of several editors.

1947   Edits and presents to the United Nations an NAACP appeal against U.S. racist discrimination.

1947   Publishes *The World and Africa: An Inquiry into the Part Which Africa Has Played in World History* (New York: Viking Press).

1948   Resigns from NAACP as a result of his opposition to cold war policies of Washington.

1948   Becomes co-chairman (with Paul Robeson) of the Council on African Affairs.

1949   Helps organize International Cultural and Scientific Conference for World Peace (the so-called Waldorf Conference); participates in World Peace Congress in Paris; participates in International Peace Congress held in Moscow.

1950   Chairs Peace Information Center; helps lead national campaign to ban the atomic bomb.

1950   Becomes the candidate for U.S. senator from New York on the American Labor party ticket; receives 210,000 votes.

1950–51   Is indicted under the McCormick Act as an "unregistered foreign agent"; arrested, tried, acquitted.

1952   Publishes *In Battle for Peace: The Story of my 83rd Birthday* (New York: Masses and Mainstream).

1957   Publishes *The Ordeal of Mansart*, vol. 1 of a trilogy, *The Black Flame* (New York: Mainstream).

1958–59   Makes journeys around the world, with notable visits to the USSR and the People's Republic of China.

1959   Publishes *Mansart Builds a School*, vol. 2 of *The Black Flame* trilogy.

1961   Publishes *Worlds of Color*, vol. 3 of *The Black Flame*.

1961   Joins the Communist party of the United States.

1961   Accepts President Kwame Nkrumah's invitation and goes to Ghana as head of editorial board to produce an Encyclopedia Africana—first projected by Du Bois in 1909 and surfacing again in the 1930s but never eventuating.

1963   Becomes a citizen of Ghana; suggests a march in Ghana in support of the August March in Washington.

1963   In July, one month before his death, publishes his edited book *An ABC of Color* (Berlin [GDR]: Seven Seas Publishers).

1963   On 27 August, the day of the great Washington March, dies in Accra; buried there after a state funeral.

This calendar arrangement necessarily omits whole areas of Du Bois's public life. Between 1897 and 1961 he published hundreds of articles in nationally and internationally circulating magazines, including essays written for Belgian, French, German, Chinese, and Russian audiences. He contributed weekly columns to several newspapers, among them the *Amsterdam News*, the *Chicago Defender*, the *People's Voice*, the *Chicago Globe*, *Freedom*, and the *National Guardian;* these columns, which began in the 1920s, were especially numerous in the 1930s and continued, with fair regularity, through the 1950s. He wrote introductions and forewords to more than a score of volumes and contributed chapters to dozens of works edited by others, including various encyclopedias and dictionaries.

Du Bois published many poems, some of which—notably *A Litany at Atlanta* (1906)—have been widely anthologized. He wrote and produced pageants which were seen by thousands of people in New York City, Philadelphia, Washington, D.C., and Los Angeles. He may justly be called the father of the Afro-American intelligentsia, and in his correspondence and personal encounters he inspired and guided three generations of poets, dramatists, novelists, musicians, and actors, as well as scholars.

Du Bois testified several times before governmental bodies, usually at hearings dealing with questions of education, racism, and disarmament. And he wrote numerous pamphlets, especially in his leadership roles against racism and war and nuclear weaponry.

Du Bois's honors were numerous: fellow and life member of the American Association for the Advancement of Science; member of the National Institute of Arts and Letters; Knight Commander of the Liberian Order of African Redemption; recipient of the International Peace Prize and the Lenin Peace Prize; and holder of honorary degrees from Fisk University, Howard University, Atlanta University, Wilberforce University, Morgan State College, University of Berlin, Charles University (Prague), Moscow University, and the University of Ghana.

AGAINST RACISM

1887-1900

An Open Letter to the Southern People (1887)

While at Fisk University in Nashville, Tennessee, Du Bois drafted this open letter. It was written in ink and signed by him as the editor of the student paper, the Fisk Herald; *this affiliation dates the manuscript, since Du Bois held the editorship in 1887.*

Considering the place and the time, and the audience explicitly addressed, the letter is militant, though Du Bois would later combat with great vigor its formulation about "social equality." Of special interest is the reflection of Du Bois's prophetic powers, particularly in the sentence "The South will not always be solid, *and in every* division *the Negro will hold the balance of power." Notable, too, is an incident described here to which, so far as I know, Du Bois never again referred: "You can therefore faintly imagine my surprise when the President of the Tennessee State Temperance Alliance introduced me to his sister in company with a number of White gentlemen."*

Du Bois's opposition to hard liquor—it did not extend to wine or beer— went back to the teachings of his mother; he seems never to have imbibed whiskey.

Dear Friends:

Perhaps the real significance of the recent defeats of Prohibition in Texas, Tennessee, and Georgia you have not fully considered.[1] Though the causes no doubt were many, the chief it is certain was that the Negroes as a rule voted against the amendments in direct opposition to a majority of the whites. The question naturally arises, why did they do this? As a Negro and a Prohibitionist who labored in the cause, I wish to answer this query.

For twenty-five years you have more than intimated that there is little in common between White and Black in the South. Socially we have been Patrician and Plebian; financially, Capitalist and Laborer; politically, Democrat and Republican. This was perhaps natural when four millions of slaves were

1. In 1887 the legislature of Tennessee submitted to popular referendum a proposed constitutional amendment prohibiting the manufacture and sale of alcoholic beverages. It was rejected, 145,000 to 117,000. The Texas legislature did the same thing that same year; there the proposal lost, 222,000 votes to 129,000. In Fulton County, Ga., which includes the city of Atlanta, a vote on the question of prohibition that was taken in November 1887 resulted in 5,100 against and 4,000 in favor. It is relevant to note that the national convention of the Women's Christian Temperance Union was held in Nashville, Tenn., in 1887. See Ernest H. Cherrington, *The Evolution of Prohibition in the U.S.* (Westerville, Ohio: American Issue Press, 1920), pp. 229–32.

made the equals of their one-time masters, but now the consequences are rapidly transcending all such excuse. The Negro has at last come to consider that whatever is for the benefit of the White man is for his detriment. Nor is it strange he should jump at such a conclusion; a blind prejudice has too often heaped injustice of the grossest kind upon him; the rights dearest to a freeman, trial by his peers, a free ballot, a free entrance into the various callings of life, have been ruthlessly wrested from him in multitudes of cases. Arguing him into an inferior being you have forced him into the gallery, the hovel, and the "Jim Crow" car; arguing his ignorance have rendered nearly seven millions of people practically voiceless in politics; in the face of this you have refused his children equal educational advantages with yours, because, forsooth, we do not pay as many taxes.

But in spite of all affirmation to the contrary there is a vast community of interests between us. We are mutually interdependent as the recent campaigns have clearly shown. You saw that without the Negro vote Prohibition would fail. You therefore wisely changed your tactics. You appealed to us earnestly; you showed what drink was doing for the race; you pointed to our wives and children and urged the need of homes and education; you even for a time laid aside long-cherished prejudices; White and Black mingled in the same audiences and listened to orators of both races. Socially you have been used to placing us little above your horse or dog. You can therefore faintly imagine my surprise when the President of the Tennessee State Temperance Alliance introduced me to his sister in company with a number of White gentlemen. This was a small thing, but such *small things*, you know, do not often happen south of Mason and Dixon's line, and it serves to show the revulsion of feeling during the campaign. Perhaps never before was the Negro so generally recognized by you as a man. Nor was the appeal, so cordially made, wholly without effect. The large majority of intelligent Colored men, the students of Fisk, Atlanta, Clark, and other schools, responded to the call and worked nobly for the cause.

But the vast majority of the Negro race, thanks in great measure to your own lack of foresight, are not intelligent. The stone which the builders rejected had at length become the head of the corner. The short-sighted policy which refused us education and oppressed us with caste prejudice recoiled upon its strongest advocates. The wages of prejudice was distrust. The great mass of ignorant voters looked upon Prohibition with suspicion simply because those who hitherto had seldom deigned to ask their votes or to argue with them on political matters, were suddenly so very anxious for their suffrages. They saw, as an old Negro said to me, "A heap too many dimocrats on dis yere ding!" They could not see how a measure which was to be beneficial to you would not in some way curtail their liberties. They were not in the habit of making nice distinctions between moral and political questions, and their suspicions were strengthened by the very advances on your part. "Wy," remarked a Colored man to me on Election day, "Reckon dese you white wimmen 'ad be' round coaxon niggers for votes, ef dar wa'nt suthin' back o'all dis?" And I had to acknowledge it *was* an unusual sight!

Thus the Negro was in a quandary. He stood like some mighty Samson faintly realizing his strength and looking with distrust upon the Delilah who had once shorn him of his liberties, and had since shown little affection for him. It wanted little to turn the scale, and that little the subtle insinuations of demagogues soon supplied. His own suspicions were strengthened, and arguments all too plausible easily presented themselves. If you spoke of the evils of intemperance, he pointed to the evils of Caste; if you urged the need of homes, he could tell how often he had been cheated out of his; if education was your argument, he could tell how in his own district the Colored school had been cheated out of its share of the free-school fund, or how many Southern Congressmen opposed the Blair bill.[2] Convinced of such reasoning, the rank and file of the Negro people voted against Prohibition and caused its defeat.

Now comes the moral. Our interests are one. This fact you by many actions have hitherto seemed to deny to such an extent that the ignorant mass of my own race think there is no common bond, that we are in direct opposition. Education is one way of helping to eradicate so monstrous a notion. Nor is the fact that such a belief exists to be lightly looked upon. It is not only contradictory to the national ties of human brotherhood, it is also fraught with the destiny of a nation. It is impossible that two races should peaceably inhabit the same country and entertain such opinions and practices.

This is one of the strongest and most conclusive arguments for a Blair bill; national aid to education is imperatively demanded. But even education will not wholly cure the evil unless you change your attitude toward us. The question of Prohibition may not have brought this as forcibly to your minds as to mine, but remember this is not the only question in which the best of you will need the aid of the Negro to settle for the right.[3] The South will

2. In 1881 Senator Henry W. Blair of New Hampshire introduced a bill which would have appropriated millions of dollars yearly for a decade for the purpose of eliminating illiteracy. Expenditure was to be supervised, however, by the federal government, not by the states; this provision ensured opposition from southern members of Congress which defeated the effort. The Blair bill remained a live question for many years; Du Bois ended an editorial in the *Crisis* (March 1911) with the words "Revive the Blair Bill!" Incidentally, this same Senator Blair introduced a resolution in 1887 calling for federal prohibition.

3. At the World's Temperance Convention, meeting in London in August 1846, Frederick Douglass "attacked the temperance movement in the United States for its failure to make provision for the Negro in its ranks and to concern itself with his bondage. The speech was apparently cut short by the presiding officer." Quoting John A. Krout, *The Origins of Prohibition* (New York: Alfred A. Knopf, 1925), p. 217.

not always be *solid*, and in every *division* the Negro will hold the balance of power. Great questions are before your country, great evils are gnawing at the foundations of your policy, and the question comes plainly, will you have them settled by fellow-citizens who have the welfare of the Nation at heart, or, by cherishing a foolish prejudice, will you have them settled by those whom *you* have made to feel that the best interests of the Nation are *not* their best interests. It is a dangerous thing to have seven million of citizens in the heart of the country even distrust you, much less hate you.

The North and South have long been felicitating each other on the returning good feeling between them; but the bonds that unite two sections of a great country are nought beside those that unite neighbor to neighbor, citizen to citizen, Black to White, in this Southland. Let us then, recognizing our common interests (for it is unnecessary to speak of our dependence upon you), work for each other's interest, casting behind us unreasonable demands on the one hand, and unreasonable prejudice on the other. We are not foolish enough to demand social equality or amalgamation, knowing full well that inexorable laws of nature regulate and control such movements. What we demand is to be recognized as men, and to be given those civil rights which pertain to our manhood. I might name many ways in which your policy toward us could be broadened to our mutual advantage in the end, but such is not my purpose; it is not against particular acts that I inveigh, but against the spirit that prompts them: it is not that I care so much about riding in a smoking-car, as the fact that behind the public opinion that compels me to ride there, is a denial of my *manhood*. Against *such* a sentiment laws or force *cannot* avail. It lies *wholly* with you. If you *correct* this evil you will find that in the future, as in the past, you will have in us staunch friends in sunshine and storm; if you do *not* the breach can only widen, until a vast throng of fellow-citizens will come to regard each other as natural foes.

Harvard (1887–92)

In the office of the registrar of Harvard University is a folder with the title "Du Bois, William Edward Burghardt A.B. 1890"; this folder contains detailed information about Du Bois's work at Fisk and at Harvard, with some incidental information about his high school career at Great Barrington, Massachusetts.* It opens with a letter from Du Bois dated 29 October 1887, written from Fisk and addressed to the secretary of Harvard University.†

* I gratefully acknowledge the research assistance of Malcolm L. Call on this point.
† This letter is given in the *Correspondence*, 1:6.

Dear Sir:

I am a Negro, a student of Fisk University. I shall receive the degree of
A.B. from this institution next June at the age of 20. I wish to pursue at
Harvard a course of study for the degree of Ph.D. in Political Science after
graduation. I am poor and if I should enter your college next year would
probably not be able to raise more [than] $100 or $150. If I should teach a
year and then enter I could earn enough to pay my expenses for a year.
I wish your advice as to what I had better do. You can see by the catalogue
I shall send herewith what our course of instruction is here. I can furnish
satisfactory certificates of character and scholarship from the President and
Professors of Fisk, and from Western Massachusetts where I was born, and
graduated from the Public Schools.[1] I am also Editor of the Fisk Herald.
As I said I wish your advice as to whether I had better teach a year or two
or come immediately after graduation. I expect to take the special field of
Political Economy.

I am, Sir,

Yours,

W.E.B. Du Bois

1. Perhaps in response to a suggestion from Harvard, Du Bois did present "certificates of scholarship and character," and these are in the Harvard folder. A. K.
Spence, a professor of Greek and French and also a dean at Fisk, wrote to "Whom
It May Concern" on 16 March 1888 that Du Bois was "an apt scholar" and indeed
"one of my best." He added that he was certain young Du Bois was worthy of
any efforts that might be expended to further "his advancement."

Frank A. Hosmer, head of the Great Barrington High School, wrote on 9 April
1888 that Du Bois, whom he had known from boyhood, possessed "sterling character"
and displayed "high scholarship." Hosmer thought Du Bois had "the capacity and
the earnest desire to be a man of usefulness in the world" and merited all possible
assistance.

The Reverend Erastus M. Cravath, president of Fisk, in a letter dated 10 April
1888 and addressed to "The Faculty of Harvard University," stated that Du Bois
had "maintained a high rank in all branches of study" and that he had "an unusually
quick, active mind." Cravath urged that Du Bois be granted a scholarship so that he
might attend Harvard.

Similar letters of unqualified recommendation came from the Fisk professors of
German (H. F. Bennett), of Latin (H. C. Morgan), and of mathematics (Herbert
H. Wright). Professor Frederick A. Chase, of the department of physical science at
Fisk, wrote a six-page letter to the secretary of Harvard College in order to "add
a few remarks" to those made by President Cravath. He detailed Du Bois's work in
botany, physiology, astronomy, chemistry, and geology and noted that in all Du Bois
"maintained a 'first grade' in scholarship." He added that although Du Bois might
convey "the impression of being conceited," he performed "faithful work"; Chase
believed that with proper guidance "he would develop into an earnest and hard
working student."

Across the top of Du Bois's letter was written, presumably by its recipient:
"Ought not to come without suff^t means to carry through a year or nearly
so. Might apply for Price Greenleaf aid, if strongly recom^d by Faculty of Fisk."

Presumably as a result of Du Bois's letter, he was sent a form for applying
for admission to Harvard College, which he returned filled out and signed
but not dated. He noted that Fisk had "no regular method of marking class
standing" and stated that he had attended Great Barrington High School
"4 years as an undergrad, 1 yr. as a post-graduate." In the space calling for any
teaching experience he wrote: "In Public Schools of Tenn., during summers
of '86 and '87, in common English branches. Have also done some miscellaneous
tutoring in the sciences to a small extent, while in college." As to the class
he desired to enter, Du Bois wrote: "Senior, (if not possible, Junior)."

Attached to this application, in Du Bois's handwriting, was a detailed record
of his work at Fisk University. Each page of this record carries on it the
seal of Fisk, apparently by way of authentication.

English Composition

Rhetoric, A. S. Hill, with Appendix, 100 hrs.
Class Rhetoricals, weekly, *Public Rhetoricals,* annually
On Editorial staff Fisk Herald, monthly college paper, 3 yrs., last year as
Editor-in-chief

English Literature

English and American Literature, Shaw, 85 hrs.
Rolfe's *Shakespeare,* Hamlet, 18 hrs.

Latin, Studied 6 yrs.

Latin Composition, Jones, 30 hrs.
Caesar, Gallic War, Bks. I–IV
Cicero, Orations, 4 against Cataline, Pro Archia & ½ of Pro Marcello
Vergil, Elogues, and Aeneid, Bks. I–VI
Horace, Odes 4/5 of those Chacer Stuarts ed., 2 epodes, 3 satires, 3 shorter
epistles, and the Ars Poetica
Tacitus' Agricola
Livy, XXIst Bk.

German, 190 hrs.

Woodbury's New Method
Worman's 1st Deutsche Luch.
Translation and conversation
Wilhelm Tell, Schiller, Acts I–II

The graduating class at Fisk University in 1888; Du Bois, seated at left, is here twenty years of age. The young man graduating with Du Bois is L. H. Tindall of Aberdeen, Mississippi; the women are Miss L. A. Bowers of Galveston, Texas, Miss Maria Benson of Nashville, Tennessee, and Miss Mary Stewart of Oswego, New York.

Speakers at Harvard commencement, 1890; Du Bois is seated at right.

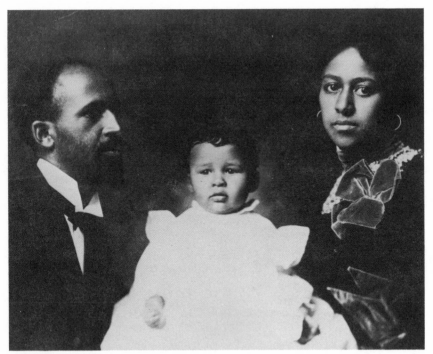

Du Bois and his wife (née Nina Gomer of Cedar Rapids, Iowa) and their son, Burghardt, whose early death is described in the classic Souls of Black Folk *(1903). The photograph was taken, probably late in 1895, in Xenia, Ohio, locale of Wilberforce University, where Du Bois was then teaching. Du Bois carried this photo, with his own likeness excised, on his person for many years.*

French, 190 hrs.

Analytical Reader and Elementary Grammar, Keetels
Worman's 1st French book
Grammaire Francais, Worman
French Testament
Translations and conversations
Studies of French Literature, 40 hrs.

Greek, Studied 5½ years

Greek Composition, Jones, 30 hrs.

Xenophon, Anabasis, Bks. I–IV { Boise & Freeman's Selections from Greek Authors

———, Memorabilia, 19 pp.
Plato, Phaedo, 12 pp., *Thucydides*, 40 pp., Bk. I
Study of Greek Literature, by lectures and use of translations of works of
Sophocles, Aeschylus, Euripides..., 30 hrs.
Herodotus, selections, 10 hrs.
Demosthenes, De Corona
Homer, Iliad, I–II
Sophocles, Antigone
Another Greek Tragedy (The name of which is not yet announced. We
shall read this in about 25 hrs., by the aid of literal translations.)

Philosophy

Science of Mind, Bascom, 75 hrs.
Logic, McCosk, 72 hrs.
Moral Philosophy, Fairchild, 11 weeks @ 5 hrs.
Logic of Christian Evidences, Wright, 38 hrs.[1]
Natural Theology, discussions, 38 hrs.

Political Science

Political Economy, Jevons (abridged), 15 hrs.
Political Economy, Wayland-Chapin, 105 hrs.

---

1. In *Dusk of Dawn: An Essay toward an Autobiography of a Race Concept* (New York: Harcourt, Brace and Co., 1940), Du Bois recalled that "the book on 'Christian Evidences' which we were compelled to read, affronted my logic." He went on: "It was to my mind, then and since, a cheap piece of special pleading" (p. 33). It is just as well that young Du Bois did not convey this view in his Harvard application!

Politics, Nordhoff, 30 hrs.[2]
Development of New England Towns, Adams (pamphlet), 10 hrs.

History

U.S. History, Barnes, Brief, 100 hrs.
Outlines of History, Swinton, 50 hrs.
History of England (I never took a text-book on this subject, but have read
carefully *Macaulay's*[3] and *Knight's* histories.)
Ancient History, Smith's History of Greece (smaller), 25 hrs.
Leighton's History of Rome, 25 hrs.
New Testament History, Smith, 38 hrs.

Mathematics

University *Algebra*, Davies, 85 hrs., Greenleaf's Elementary, 100 hrs.
Wentworth's *Geometry*, complete, 115 hrs.
Conic Sections, *Trigonometry* and *Mensuration*, in Peck's Manual of Geometry
TC, pp. 189–304, 70 hrs.
Surveying, Bellows & Hodrinan, 100 hrs., practice with instruments and
plotting included

Physical Science

Physics, Norton, 50 hrs., with experiments before class
Natural Philosophy, Norton, 85 hrs., with experiments before and by class
Physiology and Hygiene, Brown, 45 hrs.
Human Body, Martin, 50 hrs.
Boch-Steger models in physiology, 10 hrs.
Astronomy, Lockyer, 65 hrs., practice with 3 in. telescope

Natural History

Botany, Wood, 55 hrs. Herbaciam required, 50 specimens. (I collected 125
specimens.) Daily analysis of specimens.

2. In *Darkwater: Voices from within the Veil* (New York: Harcourt, Brace and Co.,
1921), Du Bois referred to the influence upon him of "that excellent little high school
text book, 'Nordhoff's Politics,' where I first read of politics" (p. 151). The book was
Charles Nordhoff's *Politics for Young Americans* (New York: Harper, 1875); possibly
Du Bois studied it both in high school and at Fisk.

3. In his posthumously published *Autobiography* (ed. Herbert Aptheker [New
York: International Publishers, 1968]), Du Bois told of seeing Macaulay's *History of
England*, in five volumes, in a Great Barrington bookstore. He was then in his
second year of high school, "and I wanted it fiercely." He bought it on installment
(unusual at that time), paying twenty-five cents a week and actually owning it at
Christmas, probably 1882. Writing almost eighty years later, he declared that the
set "still stands in my library" (p. 87).

Zoology, Genncy's Elements, 25 hrs. (dissection of small specimens)
Minerology, Dana's Manual of Minerology & Petrography, 30 hrs., with blow
pipe analysis
Geology, Dana's New Text book, 65 hrs., with field work

Chemistry

Chemistry, Eliot & Storers' Elements, 85 hrs.
Laboratory practice, 40 hrs.

Miscellaneous

E. L. Trouvelot's Astronomical Drawings, 10 hrs.

*To make attendance at Harvard possible, Du Bois required scholarship
assistance. On 30 March 1888 he signed an application form that incorporated
the following information, requesting a grant of $250 from the Price Green-
leaf Fund; the grant was approved.*

*In response to a question concerning what the applicant could count on
during 1888–89, Du Bois wrote:* "I think I can raise about $200, but I am
not positive now."

Previous education: "I have always stood well in my classes as my cert. will
show."

Plan of study at Harvard College: "I wish to study for A.B., giving special
attention to the sciences and philosophy."

Profession in view after graduation: "I shall take a post-graduate course,
probably in philosophy, for Ph.D."

Special reason for wishing to enter Harvard College: "I have finished the
course of one of the new southern institutions and wish to enjoy the advantages of an older and broader institution. I had not hoped to be able to do
this on account of limited means until I saw the advertisement of this aid." [1]

*Several further applications from Du Bois, for 1889, 1890, and 1890–91, are in
the archives at Harvard. One, signed by Du Bois and probably submitted*

1. Attached to this application were two documents. One, dated simply March 1888,
was signed by James T. Burghardt (Du Bois's uncle) "to certify he is unable of
himself, or with such aid as I can give him, to meet the necessary expenses at Harvard
College." The other was from Paul F. Eve, M.D., of Nashville, Tenn., dated 7 April
1888 and stating that Du Bois "is physically and mentally sound, capable of hard
study, and strong enough to lead a life of active usefulness."

College records show that Du Bois also received a Matthews Scholarship, in
October 1889.

early in the spring of 1890, was addressed to Harvard's Academic Council and sought appointment "to a Lee, Goodwin, *or* Bromfield Rogers *fellowship."*

I have devoted most of my college work to Philosophy, Political Economy, and History, and wish after graduation to study in the graduate department for the degree of Ph.D. I wish to take the field of *social science* under *political science* with a view to the ultimate application of its principles to the social and economic advancement of the Negro people. I wish to spend the first year at Harvard and one or more years at some European institution. I propose to take the advice of the proper professors as to the exact method of study, which I have not as yet determined.

Respectfully yours,
W.E.B. Du Bois '90

P.S. I wish this application to take precedence of my application for a scholarship.[1]

Harvard's Commencement Day in 1890 fell on 25 June. The proceedings were unprecedented: the commencement orator for the class was a Black student. Perhaps for this reason, and because of the presence of Mrs. Grover Cleveland, wife of the former president, the ceremony at Sanders Theatre was unusually well attended.

The Nation, *in an editorial, stated that when Du Bois was called, "a slender, intellectual-looking mulatto ascended the platform." When he bowed "to the President of the University, the Governor of Massachusetts, the Bishop [of the Episcopal Church] of New York, and a hundred other notables, the applause burst forth heartily, as if in recognition of the strange significance of his appearance there." Du Bois, the writer added, "handled his difficult and hazardous subject with absolute good taste, great moderation, and almost contemptuous fairness" (3 July 1890, pp. 14–15).*

Du Bois was given ten minutes. His manuscript was written in ink and took something under the allotted time to deliver—a practice Du Bois followed throughout his life.

1. An undated note, signed by Albert Bushnell Hart, then assistant professor of History, follows this application in the Harvard archives: "Mr. Du Bois has done very good work in American History, and shows distinct ability. I consider him a good candidate for a scholarship."

JEFFERSON DAVIS AS A REPRESENTATIVE
OF CIVILIZATION

Jefferson Davis was a typical Teutonic Hero; the history of civilization
during the last millenium has been the development of the idea of the Strong
Man of which he was the embodiment. The Anglo-Saxon loves a soldier—
Jefferson Davis was an Anglo-Saxon, Jefferson Davis was a soldier. There
was not a phase in that familiarly strange life that would not have graced
a mediaeval romance: from the fiery and impetuous young lieutenant who
stole as his bride the daughter of a ruler-elect of the land,[1] to the cool and
ambitious politician in the Senate hall. So boldly and surely did that cadaverous
figure with the thin nervous lips and flashing eye, write the first line of the
new page of American history, that the historian of the future must ever see
back of the war of Secession, the strong arm of one imperious man, who
defied disease, trampled on precedent, would not be defeated, and never
surrendered. A soldier and a lover, a statesman and a ruler; passionate, ambitious and indomitable; bold reckless guardian of a peoples' All—judged by
the whole standard of Teutonic civilization, there is something noble in the
figure of Jefferson Davis; and judged by every canon of human justice, there
is something fundamentally incomplete about that standard.

I wish to consider not the man, but the type of civilization which his life
represented: its foundation is the idea of the strong man—Individualism
coupled with the rule of might—and it is this idea that has made the logic
of even modern history, the cool logic of the Club. It made a naturally brave
and generous man, Jefferson Davis—now advancing civilization by murdering
Indians, now hero of a national disgrace called by courtesy, the Mexican
War; and finally, as the crowning absurdity, the peculiar champion of a people
fighting to be free in order that another people should not be free. Whenever
this idea has for a moment, escaped from the individual realm, it has found
an even more secure foothold in the policy and philosophy of the State. The
Strong Man and his mighty Right Arm has become the Strong Nation with
its armies. Under whatever guise, however, a Jefferson Davis may appear as
man, as race, or as nation, his life can only logically mean this: the advance
of a part of the world at the expense of the whole; the overweening sense
of the I, and the consequent forgetting of the Thou. It has thus happened,
that advance in civilization has always been handicapped by shortsighted
national selfishness. The vital principle of division of labor has been stifled
not only in industry, but also in civilization; so as to render it well nigh
impossible for a new race to introduce a new idea into the world except by
means of the cudgel. To say that a nation is in the way of civilization is a

1. This was Sarah Knox Taylor, daughter of General Zachary Taylor. She died
three months after the marriage.

contradiction in terms, and a system of human culture whose principle is the rise of one race on the ruins of another is a farce and a lie. Yet this is the type of civilization which Jefferson Davis represented: it represents a field for stalwart manhood and heroic character, and at the same time for moral obtuseness and refined brutality. These striking contradictions of character always arise when a people seemingly become convinced that the object of the world is not civilization, but Teutonic civilization. Such a type is not wholly evil or fruitless: the world has needed and will need its Jefferson Davises; but such a type is incomplete and never can serve its best purpose until checked by its complementary ideas. Whence shall these come?

To the most casual observer, it must have occurred that the Rod of Empire has in these days, turned towards the South. In every Southern country, however destined to play a future part in the world—in Southern North America, South America, Australia, and Africa—a new nation has a more or less firm foothold. This circumstance, has, however, attracted but incidental notice, hitherto; for wherever the Negro people have touched civilization their rise has been singularly unromantic and unscientific. Through the glamour of history, the rise of a nation has ever been typified by the Strong Man crushing out an effete civilization. That brutality buried aught else beside Rome when it descended golden haired and drunk from the blue north has scarcely entered human imagination. Not as the muscular warrior came the Negro, but as the cringing slave. The Teutonic met civilization and crushed it—the Negro met civilization and was crushed by it. The one was the hero the world has ever worshipped, who gained unthought of triumphs and made unthought of mistakes; the other was the personification of dogged patience bending to the inevitable, and waiting. In the history of this people, we seek in vain the elements of Teutonic deification of Self, and Roman brute force, but we do find an idea of submission apart from cowardice, laziness or stupidity, such as the world never saw before. This is the race which by its very presence must play a part in the world of tomorrow; and this is the race whose rise, I contend, has practically illustrated an idea which is at once the check and complement of the Teutonic Strong Man. It is the doctrine of the Submissive Man—given to the world by strange coincidence, by the race of whose rights, Jefferson Davis had not heard.

What then is the change made in the conception of civilization, by adding to the idea of the Strong Man, that of the Submissive Man? It is this: the submission of the strength of the Strong to the advance of all—not in mere aimless sacrifice, but recognizing the fact that, "To no one type of mind is it given to discern the totality of Truth," that civilization cannot afford to lose the contribution of the very least of nations for its full development: that not only the assertion of the I, but also the submission to the Thou is the highest individualism.

The Teuton stands today as the champion of the idea of Personal Assertion:

the Negro as the peculiar embodiment of the idea of Personal Submission: either, alone, tends to an abnormal development—towards Despotism on the one hand which the world has just cause to fear, and yet covertly admires, or towards slavery on the other which the world despises and which yet is not wholly despicable. No matter how great and striking the Teutonic type of impetuous manhood may be, it must receive the cool purposeful "Ich Dien" of the African for its round and full development. In the rise of Negro people and development of this idea, you whose nation was founded on the loftiest ideals, and who many times forgot those ideals with a strange forget-fulness, have more than a sentimental interest, more than a sentimental duty. You owe a debt to humanity for this Ethiopia of the Outstretched Arm, who has made her beauty, patience, and her grandeur, law.

In his Autobiography *(p. 144), Du Bois related that in an English course he took in his junior year at Harvard (1888–89), he permitted his antiracist feelings to get the best of his grammar and style and thus was given a failing grade on a paper he submitted. This was a unique experience in Du Bois's educational career; "I went to work at my English," he wrote, and managed a barely passing final grade. The course, English C, was a required one entitled "Forensics," taught by the philosopher, Josiah Royce with two assistants, Ernest L. Conant and George P. Baker, Jr.*

To further polish his mastery of the English language, Du Bois chose to take English 12 in his graduate year at Harvard, 1890–91. This was an English composition course and met three times a week, under Professor Barrett Wendell, with Jefferson B. Fletcher as assistant.

Several of the exercises Du Bois wrote for this class survive. One, entitled "My Room," written on 18 October 1890, is published in full in the Auto-biography *(p.134). Another, written on 3 October 1890, is quoted in part in that book (p. 145); Du Bois there stated that Barrett Wendell liked its last sentence: "Out of 50 essays, he picked this out to read to the class."*

Among the surviving essays, eight are published below in full for the first time. The seventh in the series, "The American Girl," is surprising for its tone. Precisely what events in the life of the twenty-three-year-old Du Bois prompted it we cannot know; its harshness—even cruelty—is most unusual in his writings.

SOMETHING ABOUT ME (3 OCTOBER 1890)

For the usual purposes of identification I have been labeled in this life: William Edward Burghardt Du Bois, born in Great Barrington, Massachusetts, on the day after Washington's birthday, in 1868. I shall room during the present twelve-month at number twenty Flagg Street, Cambridge. As to who I really am, I am much in doubt, and can consequently give little reliable information from casual hints and observations. I doubt not that there are many who could supply better data than the writer. In the midst then of personal uncertainty I can only supply a few alleged facts from memory according to the usual way. I believe there was nothing unusual about my birth. I "point with pride" to no long line of distinguished ancestors—indeed I have often been in a quandary as to how those revered ones spent their time. From this circumstance I naturally prefer men, other things being equal, who have no grandfathers. My boyhood seems, if my memory serves me rightly, to have been filled with incidents of surprisingly little importance, such as brooks with stones across, grass, and gate-posts. In early youth a great bitterness entered my life and kindled a great ambition. I wanted to go to college because others did. I came and graduated and am now in search of a Ph.D. and bread. I believe, foolishly perhaps but sincerely, that I have something to say to the world and I have taken English twelve in order to say it well.

AUTUMN LEAVES (5 OCTOBER 1890)

I notice from my window that the leaves on the little elm opposite have begun to turn. Those in the middle are yet quite green, and hardly so dull or dusty as one might imagine from the character of the street. In the outer leaves, however, one can see the first signs of death. Below, the leaves are flecked with yellow spots, some vivid and pretty, some dull and rusty. As the eye mounts higher and higher, the spots become more frequent, the yellow more vivid, till at last at the very tip of the two little branches that shoot highest, the leaves have been transformed into one mass of gold, which glistens against the pale blue of the sky. How beautiful is this glory of death, so beautiful indeed that we scarce dare to ask a resurrection—a beginning, after so grand an end.[1]

VALUE (5 DECEMBER 1890)

In the course of a little thinking on Economic subjects I have come to some conclusions on the subject of Value which I am going to try to express. Why are we willing to pay a high price for some things and not for others, even when the low priced thing is the most useful? For instance, why am I

---

1. A comment, probably by Jefferson B. Fletcher, has been added in ink: "Painstaking—Commonplace."

willing to pay a dollar for a bushel of potatoes while I wouldn't give a cent for a bushel of air? Surely the air is more necessary to life. Well I think this is the reason: in order to get potatoes I shall under any circumstances have to give up the gratification of some other wants as love of ease and the like; in other words I must labor. Now the value of anything is the comparative worth I set on certain gratifications which I must sacrifice, in order to enjoy the gratification in question. Or to state the same thing more abstractly: wants conflict, i.e., in order to satisfy one you must sacrifice others, and value is the measure of the conflict of wants. In getting air almost no want is sacrificed, ergo air is valueless. To get potatoes, however, means hoeing under the sun; ergo, potatoes are valuable.[1]

[UNTITLED] (6 DECEMBER 1890)

I used to boast that I never had been cheated out of any money. I don't now. I was coming from Chicago to Boston once to make my first visit. It was night and I was sleepy, and I didn't have a sleep-car berth for weighty reasons. We stopped at Syracuse some time along the middle of the night, and I was politely awakened by a gentleman. He was a small, young fellow, with ordinary clothes, ordinary face and ordinary carriage. He was very sorry to disturb me but he wanted, you know, to send off some money by the train and he had a number of small bills. Could I accommodate him by giving him a twenty dollar or two ten dollar bills for them? Yes? He was so obliged—going to Boston? Charming town Boston—well acquainted— wrong change? A thousand pardons, how careless. Let's see two, four, seven, nine—here a dollar more, then. Very much obliged—must get his overcoat— goodnight. And the train moved away. When I came to my sense I found I had exchanged twenty dollars for ten.

STREET-CAR STRATA (15 DECEMBER 1890)

A street-car ride to Boston on a pleasant morning is quite a treat. By varying the time by a few hours you can get almost any sort of company you wish. If you start at six, you go with big-fisted laborers, carrying dinner-pails, and looking stolid. If seven be the hour you meet clerks and shop-girls, who may look a little sleepy, but are quite jolly withal. At eight, the bookkeepers and upper ten of the lady clerks, typewriters, and the like, surround you. They are more reserved, do not smile for fear of smashing some rule of etiquette, and generally carry a mysterious little frilled bag. At nine o'clock

---

1. Comment: "Seemingly obvious [and] Lengthy."

you will meet the business men, or at least see signs of them behind the row of morning papers. They are large-stomached important personages, who read the stock quotations, and skip "foreign news." Yesterday I went on a ten o'clock car, and met still another world: they were my ladies of the house going shopping; good-sized, well-dressed, decent looking individuals in pairs for the most part, and possessed seemingly of illimitable powers of conversation. It would be interesting and instructive to spend the day on street-cars.[1]

CONNECTED (6 JANUARY 1891)

The check I received just before Christmas was very opportune, but the dear fellow who sent it had actually forgotten to sign it. So I sent it back and started home with about two dollars in my pocket, and haunted by the fear that some untoward accident might leave me worse than penniless. There are more interesting situations than a night ride on a screeching train through a snow storm. On and on we went, peering out at the flickering lights hurrying past, or sometimes catching the dim outlines of a little town. I arrived at Pittsfield. Could I connect for West Stockbridge? No. Good heavens if I paid a hotel bill, I wouldn't have money enough to get home! O these railroads, these * * *.[1] O, I can connect after all—well and good. I connected.[2]

THE AMERICAN GIRL (10 APRIL 1891)

When I wish to meet the American Hog in its native simplicity; when I wish to realize the world-pervading presence of the Fool; when I wish to be reminded that whatever rights some have I have none; when I wish, by a course of systematic vulgarity, to be made to forget whatever little courtesy I have, when I wish to be doubly sure that the man lied who asserted that men's dead selves would furnish steps enough for a rise in the world: when I wish any of these things I seek the company of the American girl.

Let me partially describe her. Her method of dressing (and you can guess why I begin here), could only be tolerated by those who had seen no other. Her bonnet is selected with a supreme indifference to size or shape of head, convenience of carriage, or harmony of effect; her corsets can usually be traced in beautiful outline "fore and aft." Her dress never varies from her neighbors' no matter how much she may vary, and her shoes have no connec-

1. Comment: "Observant. Specific. Interesting, Style a little heavy."
1. The asterisks are in the original.
2. Comment: "Disconnected. Weak."

tion with the size of her feet. Her face has generally three or four stereotyped expressions. It is apt to be more shrewd than intelligent, arrogant than dignified, silly than pleasant, and pretty than beautiful. Her carriage is always that compromise between a hop, skip, and a jump, which has come to be the distinctive mode of female locomotion. At the very pinnacle of this girl's character stands a horror of being "mannish," which generally means a constitutional aversion to the use of commonsense. Next comes an ingrained idea that all the courtesy, politeness, and consideration of the world is her own peculiar property and she is always disposed to serve a process on the wretch who keeps anything back. She is always suspicious, but against no one as much as herself, and woe to the little female unintroduced who comes beneath the eyeglass of my bedizened and bustled lady of the blear eye. Finally she has a more or less definite idea of certain rights which she has lost and with her usual consistency taboos her sisters who have taken the rational method of demanding them, because they are "mannish, you know."

How shall we cure this eye-sore?

"Who would be free, themselves must strike the blow."

When my lady wishes to cultivate her brains instead of her nose let her, first: Emancipate herself from the rule of the Ribbon. Secondly, get an education on something else beside the piano; and lastly, go to work.[1]

DEBATING CLUB (10 APRIL 1891)

I went to a "young men's congress" last night. It was an ideal affair. Mr. Smith of Arkansas was always jumping to his feet with a "Mr. *President.*" Mr. Jones of Washington was always interrupting him with a point of order, while Mr. Sims, who invariably forgot whence he was, occupied the floor every fifteen minutes with a "question of privilege"; this generally turned out to be a disquisition on some question which had little to do with the universe much less the subject on hand. The "speaker" got angry every ten minutes, thumped the table, made sarcastic remarks about "gentlemen," and invariably put the main question before the amendment. O it was rich—almost, I fancy, as Reed's own.[1]

1. Comment, probably by Fletcher: "The taste of this is questionable. Certainly, too, such a method would repel many readers who might by an ironical and duly restrained expression of the same line of thought be brought far towards agreement with you. Rudeness rarely pays. Rudely truculent." Another hand, probably that of Wendell himself, added: "Well-criticised. Such truculence as yours is thoroughly injudicious. Nothing could more certainly induce an average reader to disagree."

1. Comment: "Realistic. Amusing." The reference in the last line is to Thomas B. Reed (1839–1902), a Republican member of Congress from Maine and Speaker of the House, 1889–91 and 1895–99, whose "Reed Rules" helped further Republican party measures.

The paper entitled "Contributions to the Negro Problems" was written in ink and undated. My guess is that it was composed sometime in 1891, when Du Bois was a graduate student at Harvard, and perhaps offered at a seminar directed by Professor Albert Bushnell Hart. Of particular interest is Du Bois's suggestion that "historical evidence . . . tends to prove that there was at first comparatively little race prejudice between whites and blacks"; this view is gaining more and more credence in the present period.

CONTRIBUTIONS TO THE NEGRO PROBLEMS

We are getting now far enough from the [Civil] War and its memories to take a more unprejudiced interest in the position of the Negro people in the United States. Probably few questions have been discussed with such an unblushing disregard of facts as those surrounding the presence of the race in America: take, for instance, the matter of color—prejudice; it has again and again been said that the repulsion between the whites and blacks is instinctive and that while some illicit and irregular amalgamation has taken place, yet this amalgamation is so exceptional in its character as merely to prove the rule.

When however we carefully investigate this matter we find that history may teach us much. Everyone knows that the intimacy between the races during slavery, in personal relations and human sympathy was very great. It has generally been assumed, however, that this intimacy of daily life was a growth from an initial feeling of repulsion, and that the fixed relations of the slave regime allowed a large but limited growth of sympathy between the races. Historical evidence does not support this view, but on the contrary tends to prove that there was at first comparatively little race prejudice between whites and blacks in early colonial times, and that the prejudice only appeared after a long period of artificial fostering by the laws of the land. Take for instance this curious legislation of the colony of North Carolina in 1723; it is entitled "An Act for an additional Tax on all free Negroes, Mulattoes, Mustees, and such Persons, Male and Female, as now are, or hereafter shall be, intermarried with any such Persons, resident in this government."

I. "Whereas complaints have been made by divers Freeholders and other Inhabitants of this government, of great numbers of free Negroes, Mulattoes, and other Persons of mixt Blood, that have lately removed themselves into the government, and that several of them have intermarried with the white Inhabitants of this Province; in contempt of the Acts and Laws in those cases made and provided:

II. *Be it therefore Enacted* . . . That all free Negroes, Mulattoes, and other Persons of that kind, being mixed Blood, including the Third generation, who are, or hereafter shall be, Inhabitants or Residents in this government, both Male and Female, who are of the age of twelve years and upwards, shall, from the Ratification of the Act, be deemed and taken for tithables, and as such each and every of them shall, yearly, pay the same levies and taxes as the other Tithable Inhabitants do, and shall, and are hereby made liable to pay the same yearly to such Person or Persons, in such manner and at such Times and Places, and to be subject to such Fines and Penalties, as in and by an Act, entitled *An Act, for making the Sum of Twelve Thousand Pounds . . . and for regulating the Taxes;* which the other Inhabitants of this Province, being Tithables, are obliged and subject to.

III. *And be it further Enacted . . .* That from and after the Ratification of the Act, any white Person or Persons whatsoever, Male or Female, Inhabitants of this government, or that may or shall remove themselves hither from other Parts, that now is or hereafter shall be, married with any Negro, Mulatto, Mustee or other Person being of mixed Blood as aforesaid, shall be, and are hereby made liable to the same Levies and Taxes as the Negroes, Mulattoes and other mixed Blood as herein above is expressed; and it is the one Intent and Meaning of this Act, that all and every of the aforesaid Tithables removing themselves into this government, shall pay the levy and Taxes assessed for the year they come hither providing they come before the Tenth Day of June in that Year."

Collection of the Public Acts of Assembly of N.C. (Newbern, 1751), 1723, ch. 5, pp. 56–57 Act of 1741 §13 punished intermarriage of Black & White by a fine of £50 proclamation money on the white. §14 Minister or Justice marrying these fined same amount.

Iredell, 1799, pp. 68, 69[1]

Fortunately, those appointed fellows at Harvard were required to make written reports at the end of the year's grant. Du Bois reported to the Faculty of Arts and Sciences, on 23 March 1891, concerning his first year of graduate work (he would gain his M.A. in June 1891); he was reappointed to his fellowship for the year 1891–92.

My work for the year 1890–91 has been divided into two parts:
I. One-half my time has been spent in special research in History 20e: my subject has been the Suppression of the African Slave Trade in the United States (including colonial times). I have attended chiefly to the legislative phase, and have made a collection of all the colonial laws suppressing, or in

1. James Iredell, ed., *Laws of the State of North Carolina, 1715–99* (Raleigh: By the author).

any way restricting, the traffic from 1638 to 1788. I have collected and transcribed, with exact references to authorities, one hundred and forty-six such laws, arranging by colonies and indexing each. I then took up the period of national legislation and have made a similar collection of all the acts and propositions introduced into Congress from 1789 to 1830, using the Journals of both Houses, and the Annals and Debates; I have collected about one hundred of these. To finish this work I have the periods of 1787–89, and 1830–70 to go over, besides the foreign relations and secondary authorities. I intend to make this material the basis for my doctor's thesis in 1892 or 1893. For the character of my work I refer, by permission, to the directors of the Seminary, Drs. Hart and Channing.[1]

II. The other half of my time has been divided between Political Economy 2, Roman Law, History 21, and English 12. In *Political Economy 2*, I have followed the work of the regular course and done some outside work on the wages question; in *Roman Law* I have taken the regular course, paying especial attention to the law of slavery; in *History 21*, I have taken up early German institutions and am reading Waity's *Deutsche Verfassings-geschichte*, and the chronicle of Gregory of Tours; I have read a text of the Sabine Law, Tacitus's Germanic, and several critical works on the Family, land-holding, etc. In all these courses I have taken the regular examinations, and refer to the records for the character of the work done.[2]

If reappointed to a fellowship I propose to pursue the following course of study next year: to write a thesis on the Suppression of the Slave Trade on the basis of the material which I shall have finished collecting by the end of this year; to pursue such additional courses in History and Economics as shall fit me for the doctor's degree in Political Science. Just what courses these will be I have not yet determined but shall take advice on the matter.

Respectfully submitted,
W.E.B. Du Bois

Du Bois reported on his work to the Faculty of Arts and Science again in 1891–92; this statement was undated but was probably submitted in the spring of 1892.

1. History 20e, a seminary (or seminar) in American History, was conducted by Albert Bushnell Hart and Edward Channing. It met each Monday morning from 7:30 to 9:30 and also every alternate Monday evening "for the presentation of papers and discussion of topics." A reading knowledge of French and German was presumed. Du Bois's grade in this seminar was A.

2. The records show the following grades: English 12, taught by Barrett Wendell and Jefferson B. Fletcher, B; Political Economy 2, taught by Frank W. Taussig and John G. Brooks, A; History 21, taught by George Bendelari, B (the subject was early Medieval institutions and a reading knowledge of German and Latin was required); Roman Law, taught by William Schofield, B.

Gentlemen

I desire to report on my course of study for the academic year 1891–92, as holder of the Henry Bromfield Rogers Memorial Fellowship; and also to apply for appointment to a fellowship for the year 1892–93.

My work for this year has been as follows:

Seminary in American History

History 28, European History (½ course)

History 29, English History (½ course)

History 30, Federal Government (½ course)

History 31, Constitutional Law (½ course)

Political Economy 3, Sociology

History 9, (2nd Hlf. yr.) English Constitutional History

Private work in Modern European History, and International Law.[1]

Something over half my time has been spent on my research work in the American History Seminary. At the end of last year I had nearly finished the collection of my material. The first half of this year I spent in the arrangement and classification of this material, the perfection of my bibliography, and in the search of secondary literature. I prepared a paper at this stage, which was presented to the annual meeting of the American Historical Association, at Washington.[2] I then began the writing of my thesis for the doctor's degree in Political Science, entitled "The Suppression of the African Slave Trade in the United States of America, 1638–1890." The first draft of this was finished and in the hands of Professor Hart, 28 March, 1892. The final draft with appendices will be ready by the required time, May 1.

Outside this I aimed to arrange my work so as to fill in the general field in which I am studying. My course was chosen under advice, and has been regularly followed incident only to some interruptions during the writing of my thesis. My course has lacked definiteness mainly because I have been unable to get a precise statement of the requirements for the degree in my case. My study this year has been aimed to remedy this, and to concentrate

1. The graduate records of Du Bois for 1891–92 show that he received an A for the American history seminar; B for History 28, taught by William Macvane and Edward Channing, treating modern French and German history; A— in History 29 on modern British constitutional history, with the same teachers as History 28; A— for History 30, taught by Hart, which concerned itself with an analysis and history of the U.S. federal government; and B for History 31, taught by Macvane, which dealt with U.S. and English constitutional law. Political Economy 3, taught by Edward Cummings, treated the development of the modern state and its social function; rather mysteriously the records show the grade for Du Bois in this case to be "absent."

2. Du Bois's paper was published as "The Enforcement of the Slave-Trade Laws," in the *Annual Report of the American Historical Association, 1891* (Washington, D.C., 1892), pp. 163–74). It evoked favorable commentary in several nationally circulated periodicals.

my work. The question of my presenting myself for examination for the degree is under advisement.

Besides the regular courses in which I registered, I have during the second half-year attended the lectures in History 9 regularly,[3] and have done some outside reading in modern European history, such as Fyffe, etc., and in International Law (Hall).

I desire to continue my study another year. I wish to study in the general field of Political Science and in the special field of modern history, paying particular attention to the origin and development of social problems of the day. This course, both for general and special work, I can best pursue, I think, in one of the European universities. My ability to do this will depend on my receiving a fellowship.[4]

I therefore desire to apply for appointment to a Rogers or Parker fellowship, or for any other form of aid that will enable [me] to carry out this plan, during the year 1892–93.

Respectfully submitted,
W.E.B. Du Bois

A Novel Idea (7 December 1892)

In Berlin Du Bois wrote what he called "Plot for a Story." Beneath this phrase appeared the words of a suggested title: "Shattered Ideals," with a line subsequently drawn through "Shattered."

A young man (X) born in Gt. Barrington, Mass., U.S.A., loves a little playmate. Early left an orphan, he goes into business in Boston at the advice of his sweetheart's father. His business (dry goods) prospers and he enlarges. Just as it becomes necessary to hire a typewriter for the position a colored girl (Z) applies for the position; he hesitates but takes her on trial. His white

3. History 9 was taught by a Dr. Gross; it treated the constitutional history of England to the sixteenth century.

4. In 1892 Du Bois was awarded a Slater Fund Fellowship for Graduate Study Abroad. He tells the story of winning this fellowship in his *Autobiography*, pp. 150–53. With it he studied at the University of Berlin from 1892 to 1894 and also traveled widely in Europe. In June 1895 Harvard granted him his Ph.D. For his letters and reports during those years, see *The Correspondence of W.E.B. Du Bois*, ed. Herbert Aptheker, 3 vols. (Amherst: University of Massachusetts Press, 1973–78), 1:5–29.

clerk girls object but he promises to keep her strictly in the office and they somewhat unwillingly assent. Z proves valuable aid, he makes money, but fails in health. Finally he goes to Gt. Barrington to woo his child love but she has outgrown her youthful fancy and kindly but firmly refuses him. Grieved and hurt he returns to work, but nearly breaks down. By Z's faithful work and kindly care he partially recovers, and in his gratitude determines to defy public opinion, marry Z and become a merchant king by developing the South American trade. To his surprise Z refuses him, saying that while she highly respects him she can never love a white man, & that moreover the alliance would be most unfortunate for both. She then tells him of her plans: she was born in the South and attempted teaching but she saw the need of a leading aristocracy to raise her people. This she thought could be begun by her if she were wealthy. Stanley's work turned her attention to Africa and she thought she could help civilize Africa, raise the American Negro and make money by embarking into African trade. She had carefully studied trade & sought to make capital at typewriting. He promises to further her plans, but his health again failing a trip to Europe is advised. Here in solitude & study his old thirst for knowledge & old ideals revive. He sees the cheapness of American democracy. He determines that the last hold of Romanticism is in Africa & that he will be a crusader. Trade, solitude & study can there go hand in hand and there Z can surely marry him. Meantime the head bookkeeper of his store marries & he orders Z installed in her place at increased salary; his clerks strike & he orders colored clerks. His customers object—his business fails. He rouses himelf; returns & plunges into business. He finds that he must dismiss his Negresses & hire white girls; they refuse to come unless Z goes—he cannot afford to keep her as typewriter and must dismiss her. The little sum she has saved keeps her while she seeks another position which she finds not, & at last in despair takes a position as servant-girl. His business revives—his bookkeeper falls in love with him and he marries her. As he spends a summer at Narragansett Pier with wife and children, the head waiter speaks of his wife accidentally—she comes in sight with her baby boy—it is Z. They look and part forever.

Celebrating His Twenty-fifth Birthday (1893)

On 23 February 1893 Du Bois celebrated his twenty-fifth birthday. He prepared a program for the birthday eve and the birthday itself and then a record of its fulfillment and of the contemplation it inspired in him.

1868–1893
Berlin, Germany, Oranienstrasse No 130A.

•   •   •

PROGRAM
for the
Celebration of my twenty-fifth birthday

•   •   •

Birthday-eve

7–9 Music   10½–12 Letters to Grandma Mabel
9–10½ Plans   12 Sacrifice to the Zeitgeist
                                              Mercy—God—work

•   •   •

Birthday

•   •   •

7–8–9½ Breakfast—old letters   6–7 Seminar
        Reflection   Parents   7–8 Supper (Greek wine, cocoa,
                         Home   Kirchen, oranges)
        Poetry   Steal Away   8–10 Year Book
        Song   Jesus Lover of my   10–12 Letters to C. B. Carrington
                Soul   Florence
                America
9½–11 A Wander
11–1 Art
1–3 Dinner
3–6 Coffee in Potsdam

W.E.B. Du Bois

This programme was very pleasantly carried out. I arose at eight and took
coffee and oranges, read letters, thought of my parents, sang, cried, etc. (O
yes, the night before I heard Schubert's beautiful Unfinished Symphony,
planned my celebration and room, wrote to grandma and Mabel and had a
curious...[1] ceremony with candle, greek wine, oil, and song and prayer.
Then I dedicated my library to mother. Then I wandered up to the reading
room; then to the art gallery; then to a fine dinner with Einderhof over a
bottle of Rudecheimer and cigarettes. Then went to Potsdam for coffee and
saw a pretty girl. Then came back to the Seminar; took a wander, supped
on cocoa, wine, oranges and cake; wrote my year book and letters—and now
I go to bed after one of the happiest days of my happy life.

Night—grand and wonderful. I am glad I am living. I rejoice as a strong

1. One word illegible. This whole manuscript was not easy to decipher, and it is
possible some words are rendered incorrectly.

man to run a race, and I am strong—is it egotism—is it assurance— or is
[it] the silent call of the world spirit that makes me feel that I am royal and
that beneath my sceptre a world of kings shall bow. The hot dark blood of
that forefather—born king of men—is beating at my heart, and I know that
I am either a genius or a fool. O I wonder what I am—I wonder what the
world is—I wonder if Life is worth the striving—I do not know—perhaps I
never shall know: but this I do know: be the Truth what it may I will seek
it, on the pure assumption that it is worth seeking and Heaven nor Hell,
God nor Devil shall turn me from my purpose till I die.

I will in this second quarter century of my life, enter the dark forest of
the unknown world for which I have so many years served my apprenticeship—the chart and compass the world furnishes me I have little faith in—
yet, I have none better—I will seek till I find—and die. There is a grandeur
in the very hopelessness of such a life—life? and is life all? If I strive, shall
I live to strive again? I do not know and in spite of the wild *sehnsucht* for
Eternity that makes my heart sick now and then—I shut my teeth and say
I do not care. *Carpe Diem!* What is life but life, after all. Its end is its greatest
and fullest self—this end is the Good. The Beautiful its attribute—its soul,
and Truth its being. Not three commensurable things are these, they are three
dimensions of the cube. Mayhap God is the fourth, but for that very reason
incomprehensible. The greatest and fullest life is by definition beautiful,
beautiful,—beautiful as a dark passionate woman, beautiful as a golden
hearted school girl, beautiful as a grey haired hero. That is the dimension
of *breadth*. Then comes Truth—what is, cold and indisputable: that is *height*.
Now I will, so help my Soul, multiply breadth by breadth, Beauty by Truth
and then Goodness, strength, shall bind them together into a solid whole.

Wherefore? I know not now. Perhaps infinite other dimensions do. This
is a wretched figure and yet it roughly represents my attitude toward the
world. I am striving to make my life all that life may be—and I am limiting
that strife only in so far as that strife is incompatible with others of my
brothers and sisters making their lives similar. The crucial question now is
where that limit comes. I am too often puzzled to know. Paul put it at
meat-eating, which was asinine. I have put it at the (perhaps) life-ruin of
Amalie which is cruel.[2] God knows I am sorely puzzled. I am firmly convinced that my own best development is now one and the same with the best
development of the world and here I am willing to sacrifice. That sacrifice
is working for the multiplication of Youth × Beauty and now comes the

2. I am guessing that Amalie was the German young woman with whom Du Bois had
a close relationship and who wished to marry him and return to the United States
with him. Du Bois in his *Autobiography* notes the situation—without mentioning any
name—and indicates that he opposed the idea for fear of the difficulties it would
mean for the biracial couple.

question how. The general proposition of working for the world's good becomes too soon sickly sentimentality. I therefore take the work that the Unknown lay in my hands and work for the rise of the Negro people, taking for granted that their best development means the best development of the world.

This night before my life's altar I reiterate, what my life...[3]

I remembered how when wandering in the fields I chose the realm of Mind for my territory and planned Harvard and Europe. My loves—O my loves, how many and how dear, she is the beautiful whom I worshipped, Ollie the lonely,[4] Dicky the timid, Jenny the meek, Nellie the wavery child. Then came a commencement when hundreds applauded—Nell carried my diploma— and then I left for the Northwest,[5] then came Harvard—scholarships, high marks, Boylston prizes when Cambridge applauded, Commencement when the Harvard applause awoke echoes in the world—then Europe where the heart of my childhood loosed from the hard iron hands of America has beat again in the great inspiring air of world culture. I only know Germany—its Rhine or memories, its München or Gemutlichkeit, its Dresden or Art, its Berlin with its music and militarism. These are the five and twenty years of my apprenticeship.

These are my plans: to make a name in science, to make a name in literature and thus to raise my race. Or perhaps to raise a visible empire in Africa thro' England, France or Germany.

I wonder what will be the outcome? Who knows?

I will go unto the king—which is not according to the law and if I perish —I PERISH.

Harvard in Berlin (November? 1892)

The American contingent of student exiles, two hundred strong, have scarcely settled down to their year's work although Christmas, and a German Christmas at that, is in sight. Our vocabulary is yet a most delightful conglomeration of unintelligible "Deutsch," and unintelligent English. Nevertheless light is gradually breaking in dark places, intricate jungles of sounds become passable, and strings of gutturals [are] resolving themselves into clear ideas. Our Berlin academic halls, too, are getting hard and solid, losing that sort of etherial sheen which, to the fresh American, envelopes everything European.

3. Pages 8–10 of the original manuscript are missing.
4. The reading of this word is uncertain—perhaps "lovely" is intended.
5. Meaning Fisk University in Tennessee; note the erroneous geography.

German universities used to have a way of opening whenever the various students and professors thought best. These delightful days are now past and by the law of the land lectures begin somewhat more promptly, generally about the last week in October.

To be a bit chronological, the first ordeal of the student is to matriculate— a ceremony of no mean proportions in Berlin. I remember we used to make certain sarcastic remarks over Harvard "red tape," but it was because we had not seen the deeper crimson of the Berlin quality. I consumed three mortal hours (one of which was my lunch hour) in the process of getting my name on the official rolls of the university. There we shivered and waited, outside the mystic room 33, the Americans spending their time in discovering each other, talking shop, and—football. Here I learned my one infallible rule for picking out an American in a German crowd. Look at his feet—the two styles of shoes have absolutely nothing in common.

Finally about 12 o'clock (my entrance card said 10) there came a rush, and a hundred or more students sallied out of the holy of holies, and a like number crowded in, myself among them. It was a large room, with high ceiling, and a row of four windows on one side in the deep recesses of which stood busts of Berlin's famous professors. The center of the room was occupied by chairs, in which the students seated themselves; at the upper end was a long table about which perhaps a dozen officials were grouped. Near the left end was the present year's *rector magnificus*, the widely famous Rudolf Virchow, doctor of medicine, laws and philosophy, city councillor and member of the Reichstag. He is a meek and calm looking man, white haired and white-bearded, with a kindly face and pleasant voice. At smaller tables ranged before the windows, were the deans of various faculties.

The method of procedure was thoroughly and, I think I may say, painfully, German. First the chief secretary at the side of the magnificent rector was invested with the pile of gymnasium diplomas and passports we had surrendered in the ante-room. Then he slowly read out the names, and as a student heard his name he disentangled himself and approached the table. Recognizing with some difficulty my Germanicized name I presented myself with some trepidation at the bar. The stiff secretary (it's quite the thing to be stiff in new Germany) with my help more clearly deciphered my name, ascertained under which faculty I wished to study, firmly declined to examine any of my sheepskins, and passed me over to the rector: rector Virchow smiled benignantly, made some remark as to my faculty, and after filling out the blanks with some remarkably poor writing, presented me with a large 24 × 18 inch sheet of paper: this stated that a certain...[1] had in the general goodness of his heart endowed the present Mr. Virchow with various powers;

1. Illegible word in the original; probably a reference to some title for the kaiser.

among these was that of making me (who was described with some infelicity of phrase as a "most ornamented young man") a legalized and licensed Berlin student. This was well printed, on fair paper, and I shall, eventually, have it framed.[2] Armed with this I was introduced to magnificent No. 3, who wrote my name in a ponderous and sinister looking volume, together with an unnecessarily large amount of elicited information as to my previous history and the personnel of my ancestors. I was then shoved on to secretary after secretary: this one furnished me with another diploma for my particular faculty; that one with a card.[3]

The next filled this out with my name and number. Meantime I was getting weary of this prolonged ceremony and very full of suggestions for improvement; also hungry. I was still gently urged on—a bit more willingly now as I had almost completely encircled the table and felt morally certain that much further progress would necessitate architectural changes in the room. The last official after prolonged calculation relieved me of fifteen marks, and added to my load of sorrow a rich and varied assortment of literature, comprising among other things, rules and regulations (O, world-book!) library commands and demands, blanks for the questor, recipes against moral turpitude, etc., etc. Before and behind me the line of students continued the dead march, in a manner that strongly reminded me of Mr. Armour's Chicago hog parlors. Nor was the end yet; with the easy German contempt of time I was now piloted to the dean of the Philosophical faculty, to whom I laid siege being armed with enough signed and sealed printed matter to have enabled me to achieve brilliant social success anywhere west of Buffalo. Down my name went again, and down went another autograph on my diplomas. Well, he was the last man: I gave a polite little sigh of relief, and—was informed that I must now resume my seat, wait till the whole line behind me were through, when the rector would hold a hand-shaking. Being peaceful and law-abiding I sat down; if I had the ability to have told a straight lie, I don't know what I might not have attempted. I am quite certain that many of the German students disappeared and escaped with honor. As it was I lingered, and, finally, all being duly labelled and ladened, the rector arose and addressed a few words of fatherly advice—something about being good and studying,

2. If he did the result seems not to have survived among the Du Bois Papers. In 1980, when I was a visiting professor at Du Bois's University of Berlin (now Humboldt University), I made copies of all documents pertaining to him in the university archives. These now are on deposit with the Du Bois Papers at the University of Massachusetts Library in Amherst. Among them are papers showing registration and others tabulating the courses he took and the professors with whom he studied.

3. At this point Du Bois drew a "facsimile, exact size" of this card, which students were required to have with them at all times. Deciphering it is difficult; hence it is omitted.

etc.,—and then we all filed passed him, bowed, shook his hand, and departed to give room to the next hundred lambs. So great was the labor necessary to becoming a full-fledged Berlin student.

The next business before me was that of finding a room—a work of more than ordinary difficulty in an unknown tongue. There are numbers of American students who come to Germany and go into American boarding-houses, talk and walk with Americans, and leave having missed the true poetry of student life. Imagine a Harvard student boarding at Young's and spending his leisure in Newton!

The correct Berlin method is to hire a nook in a flat, from three to five stories up. There with pipe and beer, coffee and black bread, he lives not like a king, but as a free and easy viking bound to the student world by his kneipes (drinking bouts), his societies, and—possibly—his lectures. The student quarter of Berlin—so far as a distinctive quarter can be assigned them—is the old Latin quarter. In an ordinary city this would be the slums, but Berlin being an extraordinary city with no visible proletariat, this quarter is merely narrower and darker than the rest of the Berlin world. Here you can hire a comfortable room for $5 to $10 a month. Morning coffee costs perhaps $1.30 per month extra, and heat 7 or 8 cents a day. O yes, I must not forget to say that boot-blacking is thrown in and the most impecunious student may always have a faultless polish.

My room is roomy and four flights up, with books, papers, and *her* picture —of course! There is the wardrobe and bureau with mirror to match, lounge and table, screened bed and commode, and a ponderous institution called a stove. I am devoutly awaiting the advent of a domestic Bismarck, who shall make some compromise and transfer the wild and seething heat of the German feather-bed covering to the coldly placid and beautiful tile stove. My floor is uncarpeted, my walls are but scantily adorned—in fact this is not the shadow of a Harvard dormitory room, and yet I live in remarkable freedom and contentment and feel somewhat disposed to sneer at the effeminate luxuries beyond the sea.

My coffee with two fat rolls and butter, I take at eight. About ten I follow the example of my fellow Germans, I stalk through the academic halls reflectively munching a sandwich to ward off starvation. I find the custom much better for study than [word illegible]; ah! how often have I groaned in a nine o'clock recitation under the weighty exuberance of a Memorial breakfast! Germans are compelled to dine at 12, because their language calls the meal "mittags-essen" [midday meal] while "dinner," which could come at six is—*ach weh!* French. We all dine in restaurants. I generally pay about 21 cents including beer and tip. Coffee comes again at 3, and my *abendbrot* [supper], I take in my room from my private larder—my landlady warming the tea. Thus my total expenses, including theater once or twice a week, a symphony now and then, and other good music galore, together with various other recreations, cost me about $200 a term or $400 for the year. If more economically minded, I might make this $300.

A Woman (22 May 1893)

She stood beside me way up in the amphitheatre of the Court Theatre of Berlin—dark-clothed with curled black-brown hair down her back. Not pretty to know—for her features were angular, her hands large & her figure ordinary. She was tho' strangely human & when she turned her great eyes on me I knew not what they said—a third beseeching, a third haughty, a third bold. I watched her furtively at the opera—it was Wagner's Götter-dammerung, beautiful but fearfully "langweilish" and suddenly I can see her eyes were all full & running with tears. She saw I was looking and swallowed a sob & stared straight at the stage. I wondered who she was all alone at a Wagner opera—evidently she didn't understand it. She was neither lady or bred. She disappeared in the crowd afterward & I saw her no more. Poor child—one of sorrows of Berlin.

The Art and Art Galleries of Modern Europe (1896?)

This address originally was delivered at Wilberforce University under the sponsorship of its Athletic Association, probably in 1896. Later, perhaps in 1898, it was delivered at Augusta, Georgia. The original manuscript contains inserted and altered words appropriate for the latter locale, but reprinted below is the text as used in Wilberforce.

I purpose tonight to tell you something of the Art and Art Galleries of Modern Europe, not from the standpoint of the artist or art critic, but from the standpoint of one who loves beautiful things and whose good fortune it has been to give a passing glance at many of the great art collections of the modern world.

We who take interest in the training of men believe steadfastly and conscientiously in the full rounded development of man. We believe that there can be no sturdy moral growth without deep intellectual training; and we believe too that there can be no true lasting moral worth and mental development without healthy physical life; and we believe that all exceptions to these propositions merely prove the rule. But these three factors of life are not coordinate; the physical development of man is not an end in itself but a means to an end; the great underlying life principle which conserves life for the sake of those great ends which make life worth living. Therefore tonight the Athletic Association asks you to listen not to a dissertation on physical culture but rather to a talk on one of the three great ends of living for the attainment of which healthy muscular manhood is the first prerequisite.

Three things in life beckon the human soul: the Good, the True and the Beautiful. We hear of the good every day—hear of it so much in fact that we sometimes become deaf from very hearing and forget that simple goodness is the end of all moral strife; and that it is just as impossible to be a Christian and be bad, as it is to be full and empty at the same time. Again we hear much of the True; the object of our being here in school, the object of all right training, the object of all science is to search out and make known the real Truth about the world we live in. But there is a third something—a third dimension in life without which we cannot truly live: it is the Beautiful. Goodness is a matter of the Will power, Truth, a matter with which the mind deals; but the heart and the emotions deal with the Beautiful.

We immediately see how inexpressibly broad a field we have here, how infinitely varied in aspect and product and with what tact and delicacy it must be cultivated and fertilized. It is always extremely difficult to teach young people to give proper attention to the beautiful things of life, to realize that the object of all life is to make the universal beautiful; so to use the Good, that we may realize the Beautiful in the True. And yet it is a problem how to bring this central fact before the many varieties of character which are represented here.

The first place of such training is of course the home—the picture books of early years, the paintings in the parlor, the decorations of the bedroom, the mother's Sunday clothes—all these are the materials out of which the youth must form his ideals of what is beautiful. How important then are the little decorations of home, and how easily can a hideous combination of colors, or a tawdry picture make a man an aesthetic idiot for life. Unfortunately we as a people are just beginning to build our homes and consequently many of us have missed the vast educational power of beautiful surroundings in childhood. These must train themselves by the study of beautiful things in after life. For this purpose the first great art school is Nature: here at Wilberforce we are surrounded by an art gallery which treasures countless masterpieces, and yet there are dozens of us who will go through this coming Springtide and see nought but dirt and water—unmindful of the glory of the sunsets beyond the western meadows, unmindful of the daily panorama of sun, and clouds and sky.

Thus far I have attempted to bring to your minds the fact that the Beautiful is one of the great ends of life and that we can train ourselves to appreciate the beautiful things in life and even discover beauties hidden to untrained hearts. One gallery of the beautiful I have said is the world about. I now come to the second great reservoir of the Beautiful, which we call Art: Art is beauty created by man; it is something of which a human soul conceives, a human hand executes and all human hearts everywhere acknowledge beautiful. Take for instance a little flower. If I ask you why it is beautiful you could not tell me—it simply is beautiful; it raises pleasing sensations—a sort of mental satisfaction almost indescribable. Again take another work of Art—a great building. I remember sailing along a blue rushing river, once, when suddenly rounding a bend, two dark and mighty towers seemed to shoot into the air, capping a wilderness of graceful fretwork and mighty buttress, standing there in that calm August day like twin giants. It was the Cathedral of Cologne. Why was it beautiful? "If eyes were made for seeing, then beauty is its own excuse for being." [1] And yet some reasons one may give as to why it was beautiful. Was it not because of the thoughts it raised in me? The awe, the wonder, the feeling of strength, the lust of creative manhood, and yet withal the sweet symmetry of life?

Take a wonderful painting, is it beautiful because it imitates a beautiful thing? Possibly, but if so it is no more than is a photograph, not a work of Art. A real masterpiece of art is beautiful in proportion to what it creates, to the emotions it raises in the hearts of its beholders. Let me illustrate. At the National Galleries in Berlin there hung once a picture. It was a strange weird thing in grey and blue with great long-necked swans sailing down a river. We had all viewed it when the young lady of the house, who was a wee bit strong minded, expressed her opinion and said, "Why that picture is simply absurd—who ever saw swans with necks like that?" But one of those present said: That makes no difference—suppose no such swans ever did exist; so long as the artist succeeds in embodying a great idea, in creating a beautiful thing, is not his object accomplished? Is an artist a mere photographer of chickens' heads? No: Art does not imitate nature, but nature imitates art. Or to put it better both strive toward one vast Ideal, the infinite beauty of the other world.

If then true art is to be measured by our own emotions, how necessary it is that those feelings be capable of responding to the highest, that the nature of the beholder be so nicely attuned that it responds to the lightest touch and most subtle harmony of the work of Art. Let me illustrate: suppose we have two pictures: a mere chromo, the other is an excellent work. What is the difference? Perhaps some of you would not see any difference—if so it would merely mean that your aesthetic nature—your perception and appreciation of [the] really beautiful—is in sad need of training. Some of you must instinctively feel that these paintings are of different degrees of merit and yet could not give a reason; finally a few of you could immediately say:

1. Du Bois quotes Emerson, "The Rhodora."

the masterpiece is cunning in execution—in light and shade, in harmonious colors, in careful painting. The other is inharmonious and blaring; the masterpiece has unity of idea. It is not that it exactly imitates ship and sea—one who had never seen either would get the same idea of strength and beauty. On the other hand, the other picture is overdone—the underlying idea is evident but it is too broadly and crudely brought out—there is none of that nice suiting of means to end which is so important.

If now you have some conception of what the Beautiful in life is, of how nature and Art strive to create beauty and what a masterpiece of Art should be, let us now ask how are beautiful things preserved from the rust and decay of earthly life? We know that Nature preserves itself through continual renewal, helped and hindered by the hand of man. We see for instance how God strives to keep our fine campus beautiful and how some of the students strive to make it ugly; how the eternal beauty of Nature refuses to be covered by the hideous neglect of our ravine and by the heaps of nastiness we dump into it for the sake of unsightliness and disease. But I am not to speak of the preservation of the beauties of Nature—though it were indeed a fruitful theme—but rather of the preservation of works of Art.

I suppose that not one half of the thousands of people that visit Chicago or New York know that there are art galleries there—of those who know it, few visit them—fewer study; and yet here is a little attempt to preserve a few beautiful things. That is what an art gallery is and whenever you go to Chicago, to New York, to Philadelphia, and Boston—go to the art galleries, not rushing through pell-mell, but go sit down and look at a beautiful picture a half hour each week. It is an education, soul training which nothing can surpass. Then remember when you see these galleries, that these are but faint echoes of the great galleries of the world, where the masterpieces of the world's greatest artists are hung. The galleries of the World's Fair [in Chicago, 1893] were wonderful and yet even there not a single one of the world's greater masterpieces of art were hung. Only in Europe can we study the art of the world.

There are in Europe today ten great collections of works of Art, which I will name in the order of their fame: The Louvre which occupies that mighty series of palaces in Paris situated at the head of the greatest avenue in the world; the great collection of Rome centers in the palaces of the Vatican near the greatest cathedral, St. Peter's. Third, the famous collection in the Pitti and Uffizi palaces at the lovely city of Florence in the valley of the Arno. Fourth, the great collection at the Zwingen in Dresden, Germany. Fifth, the galleries of the Alto and Neue Pinakothek at Munich; sixth, the collections of the strangely beautiful sea city of Venice. Seventh, the fine new galleries at Vienna. Eighth, the great Dutch collections at Amsterdam. Ninth, the National Museum at London opposite Trafalgar Square. Tenth, the collections at Antwerp, Belgium. Of these I have visited all except that at Antwerp. Besides these ten greater collections, there are numberless minor collections each one larger and more important than anything we have in America: for instance, the collections at Berlin, Madrid, Naples, Frankfurt, Milan; at Cassel, Düsseldorf, St. Petersburg, etc. All of these I have seen except those at Madrid and St. Petersburg.

First now, I want to tell a little about the history of the more famous of these collections and then something of their arrangements, etc.; finally I shall take up a few of the great masterpieces. Let us take for instance the great Munich gallery. It has been formed by the union of three collections of pictures. First [were] those collected in the 16th and 17th centuries by the early Electors of Bavaria who encouraged such great masters as Albrecht Durer, and such art centres as Nuremburg. Second the great collections of Düsseldorf were during the wars following the French Revolution carried bodily to Munich to keep them from going to Paris; 3rd, when the monasteries and churches were suppressed at Cologne in 1805-1810 the great paintings were taken to Munich, so that today we have here a vast collection of 1,400 pictures arranged in 12 saloons and 14 cabinets and housed in a magnificent hall called the Alto Pinakothek. So the celebrated Dresden gallery was begun about 1750 by Augustus III, King of Saxony; while the collection of Italians dates back to the Renaissance. Thus you see these collections of pictures are not mere chance things collected in a day or a decade, but are centuries old, intertwined with the history of the nations, fostered by loving care and standing today as great monuments to European civilization.

Whose works, now, are enshrined upon these great altars erected to the Infinite Beauty of the world? Perhaps many of you know the names of the world's greatest artists, but lest some do not I am going to name twelve great masters—and every one of you should learn their names: Michael Angelo, Titian, Raphael, Phidias, Leonardo, Corregio, Murillo, Rubens, Rembrandt, Velasquez, Van Dyke, Durer.

Let me tell just a bit of each one of these: Michael Angelo was born in Tuscany, Italy, 1475 and died in 1564. He was a born artist and under the patronage of the Medici in Florence executed many noble works. I never tired while in Rome in gazing at his ceiling in the Sistine Chapel and his famous statue of Moses with beard and horns you all know. Raphael was born at Urbino, Italy in 1483 and died at Rome in 1520. He is universally considered the greatest of Italian painters if not of the world's artists. His masterpieces are copied the world over: that pretty little round picture of the Madonna and the child and St. John, which you so often see, hangs in the galleries of Florence; the wonderful canvas of the Transfiguration is at Rome, and others of his strangely beautiful conceptions of the Christ child are at Munich. Titian is the great master of color and is also an Italian. His masterpieces are in Venice and Florence. Phidias was the great Greek sculptor who adorned the Parthenon and taught the carver of the Venus of Milo. Leonardo was an-

other Italian, the first great pioneer of the Renaissance and modern painting—
a universal genius. Corregio, Murello and Velasquez are Spaniards whose
works are chiefly in Spain although Murello's celebrated little beggars are at
Munich. Rubens and Van Dyke are Belgians and their paintings, especially
Rubens', are all over Europe and among the best known in the world. These
may be seen at Dresden, Munich, Antwerp and Vienna. Rembrandt is the
great Dutch master of light and shade, the wonderful yellow light of whose
pictures has been the despair of imitators. Albrecht Durer is the great German
painter born in quaint Nuremburg in 1471 and his house I have seen, still
standing—a careful conscientious pioneer in German art.

Let me now call your attention to certain great masterpieces of art; the
Venus of Milo, by Praxiteles, the Moses of Michael Angelo, the Sistine
Madonna by Raphael, the Cathedral of Cologne of Meister Gerard, the
Descent from the Cross by Rubens, the tribute money by Titian, the Beggar
Boys by Murillo, the Night Watch by Rembrandt, and the portrait of
Charles I by Van Dyke. I shall begin with the Cathedral of Cologne, the
most magnificent Gothic edifice in the world. I then pass from architecture
to sculpture and from sculpture to painting.

Here is a picture of the Cathedral of Cologne.[2] Look at it and as you look
let it grow larger: let the bold cruciform structure swell beyond the little
confines of this room and of this building—imagine a vast structure three
times the length of this building, three times its width, and three times its
height with two mighty towers, the highest in Europe, 512 feet in height or
twice as high as two buildings like this set on end one on top of the other.
The original foundation stone was laid on the 14 August 1248 and from that
time it has slowly grown through the centuries, now desecrated by war,
now honored by kings until at last October 15, 1880, the first Emperor of
Germany and his prince and First Bismarck celebrated the completion of the
vast work. As a result we have not one of those tawdry eyesores which meet
American eyes as the result of the expenditures of millions, but a beautiful
harmonious symphony in stone every part of which goes to embody a great
and otherwise inexpressible conception of the beautiful. The blazing marble
of Milan's fretted cathedral is wonderful, Westminster Abbey is venerable,
Notre Dame is historical, but Cologne is grand.

. . .

From the desire to decorate great monuments of architecture like this first
arose in the ancient world the branch of art known as Sculpture. Let us then
turn to the Venus of Milo by Praxiteles, replicas of which you have all seen.
This is probably the most famous single statue in the world and stands today
in the galleries of the Louvre at Paris. Starting from the Arc de Triumphe,

2. Du Bois supplied the auditors with cards illustrating the works he described.

that bold monument built to the glory of the First Napoleon, you sweep down the broad magnificent avenue of the Champs Elysees. Coming at last to the Tuileries, you pass the works of marble statuary and pass groups of gay and polite Parisians until at last you approach great piles of buildings in the graceful renaissance architecture and passing by wings and through quadrangles you enter the famous galleries of the Louvre—without doubt the greatest art collection of the world. There, in a little room as large as perhaps one of the parlors and hung in black velvet, stands a single marble statue, armless and maimed, nicked and disfigured, yellow with age and yet with all one of the most perfect works of Art which the perfect Greek world has handed down to the 19th century. The statue was probably the work of the great Greek sculptor Praxiteles and lay buried for centuries in the little island of Melos in the Mediterranean, and was finally exhumed in 1820, and brought to France. Fortunately no one has been allowed to spoil this masterpiece by attempting to restore its lost parts. Through all its obvious deformity its beauty still shines. It is a full length figure larger than life representing Venus the Goddess of Love or the Wingless Victory; "grandly serious, and almost severe"—the simple drapery resting on the hips and displaying the perfect symmetry of the massive beautiful frame and the whole conception has that mysterious dignity and unapproachableness which is the genuine expression of the divine. A great critic has said:

> This is the only statue of Aphrodite handed down to us which represents her not merely as a beautiful woman, but as a goddess. The form is powerful and majestic, and yet instinct with an indescribable charm of youth and beauty while the pure and noble expression of the head denotes the goddess's independence of all human requirements and the calm self sufficiency of her divine character. The fact that this beautiful work, notwithstanding its great excellence, is not one of those which have been extolled by ancient authors, affords us an approximate idea of the beauty of those lost masterpieces which formed the great marvel of antiquity.

The statue was found in 1820 by a peasant in the island of Melos, now Milo, at the entrance to the Greek archipelago, and sold for $1200 to the French Government.

I have coupled with this another masterpiece of ancient sculpture—the Victory of Samothrace. This figure, found in 1863, was originally erected in memory of a naval victory won by Demetrius Poliorcetes about 305 B.C. The much mutilated statue represents the goddess on the prow of a vessel, in the act of sounding the signal for battle upon her trumpet. In dignity of conception and in the masterly handling of the voluminous drapery, this sculpture is perhaps the finest extant work of early-Hellenistic art.

There is something more, however, in both these statues than their overmastering grace and beauty: it is the story they tell of the Greek ideal of healthy womanhood. These are pictures of women, strong, tall, muscular, with that peculiar grace and rhythm which comes from unharnessed freedom of movement. The modern world has almost lost that ideal of beauty. Look at the waists of these women—manifestly graceful and yet a modern dress-maker could not clothe them. We have put before us all sorts of unhealthful looking deformities, called fashion plates and so perverted has modern taste become that a natural strong and healthy woman is almost ashamed because she is not delicate and fragile and swan-like. Notice the foot on the Venus of Milo—broad, strong and made for walking. She could not get a decent shoe in the state of Ohio. Does this not teach us something? It surely tells us that if the young women of the Negro race wish to be really beautiful and happy, it is not mere beauty of face or length of hair that they must cultivate, but that health, strength, and symmetry of form which simply cannot be had by following the prevailing fashions of dress and which is beyond all the most beautiful thing about a human physique.

The works of architecture with statues like these and like the Laocoon group embellished in Grecian times are still among the world's greatest build-ings, as for instance the Parthenon, pictures of which you have often seen. After the Greeks no masterpieces of sculpture appear for a thousand years; then the Italians through their great genius, Michael Angelo, produced numerous great works. One of these is his statue of Moses. A few copies of this with the picture of the master I am distributing. Michael Angelo was born in Italy in the wonderful 15th century and was a youth of 17 when Columbus discovered America. A prince found him playing among the stat-uary of his gardens and taking him to his palace, educated him in art, until he became as sculptor, painter and poet, the greatest of the great artists of his day. His record of work is wonderful, he carved this statue of Moses, he made a statue of David, painted the great picture of the last judgment and built the Church of St. Peter's at Rome. No man before ever put so much poetry in stone: here sits the man who walked and talked with God, the tables of the divine law in his hands, the great beard coiled and wound in his fingers, the horns of superhuman power on his forehead and the eyes dreaming away toward the Promised Land which he never saw.

• • •

After the Greeks had come to the making of statues apart from buildings, they soon began to paint their statues and color them from life; this through the Greeks and Romans led insensibly to the art of painting—an art which reached its finest development in the 16 and 17th centuries of the modern world. I suppose if any artist were asked to name one picture which all things considered was justly entitled to be called the most famous in the world he would answer: the Sistine Madonna by Raphael, which today stands in the gallery of Dresden, Germany. This is an altar piece first painted for a church

at Piacenza, Italy about 1515, and purchased in 1753 for $45,000—a ridiculously
small sum compared with its worth today. The picture is eight feet high
and six feet wide and represents the Virgin and Christ Child, the saints Sixtus
and Barbara and two cherubs. Let me read Professor Springer's criticism
of the Picture: "A curtain has just been drawn back and the Virgin issues as
it were from the depths of heaven, awe-inspiring, solemn, and serene, her
large eyes embracing the world in their gaze. The idea of the sudden revelation
of a hitherto concealed mystery could not be more effectively expressed.
Below are two cherubs, pictures of naive innocence; at either side two saints
contrasted in age and sex, expression and movement, supplementing each other
with admirable effect. Sixtus commending himself to the virgin's mercy—
and the beaming face of Saint Barbara represents the joyful enthusiasm of the
redeemed." I have spent many minutes watching this picture and I do not
think that I can ever forget the large misty eyes of the Mother of God as she
steps upon the clouds with the Wonderful Child in her arms.

The Assumption by Titian is an immense picture hanging in the gallery at
Venice, near the square of St. Mark's. I used to imagine that the Avenue
Champs Elysees in Paris was but a glorified image of that moon beam road
to the stars which we have all seen through our childish tears. And if it is,
then I can imagine no better ending for that celestial way than the Piazza of
St. Mark's at Venice, with the gilded domes and glistening turrets of the
marble church, the endless columns and galleries and brilliant shops and the
thousands of whirling doves which in this city of water find this their only
resting place. Near St. Mark's hangs Titian's masterpiece; it represents the
assumption of the Virgin Mary—surrounded by holy men and angels, she rises
toward God and no mortal mother ever had that look of divine happiness
which hovers on the lips of Titian's Madonna.

I have not been able to secure copies of this, the greatest of Titian's pictures, but I have brought you two specimens of his work, one of which, the
tribute money, is well known. The subject is a familiar one: the keen Jew-
hating-Roman and Roman tribune approaches the master and asks "Is it
lawful for Jews to pay tribute unto Caesar?" The master asks whose image
and superscription is on the penny and says "Render unto Caesar the things
which are Caesar's but unto God the things which are God's." The other
picture is the less known Madonna of the Rabbit. Titian, one of the world's
great artists, was an Italian like Raphael and Michael Angelo and lived at
the same time. At 10 years of age he went to Venice and studying art began a
brilliant and profitable life. His picture is among those distributed.

•   •   •

You will notice how much this golden age of Italian art deals with biblical
and religious subjects, the Christ and Mary his mother, the saints, prophets
and apostles. It is the glory of the Catholic church that she made beauty the

handmaid of religion and enriched the world with noble conceptions of goodness and purity. However there were soon men who began to see the beauty in every day life and to paint it—to look round on earth and sea and children and men and paint them in life. This began in the Flemish school of painters in little Belgium, with such masters as Rubens and Van Dyke. To be sure they painted subjects, like Rubens' wonderful Descent from the Cross, but they made the figures human and everyday so that one felt the touch of flesh and blood. Then by easy transition they painted portraits of men, like Van Dyke's great portrait of Charles the First, the king whom Oliver Cromwell beheaded. Rubens, who was born in Westphalia in the 16th century and educated partly in Italy, was a prodigious wonder and painted over 200 great paintings, some as large as a wall of this room. Van Dyke was a pupil of Rubens and especially celebrated for his portraits.

From Italy the study of beauty reached north to Belgium, and from Belgium to Holland. Holland is a curious bit of mud north of Europe stolen from the sea by a sturdy homely people. And there arose then a set of men who painted life as they saw it—every day themes and perhaps the greatest of the painters was Rembrandt. He was a miller's boy born at sleepy Leyden the same year that the English settled Jamestown; a good-hearted fellow, always in debt, always at work, painting his wonderful yellow lights. His largest and greatest work is the "Night Watch"—but you can get but faint idea of it from the black and white print. You should see it as I saw it in a burst of brilliant color, at the end of the long hall in the gallery at Amsterdam. It is 11 × 14 feet and it represents the assembly of a company of militia. Because of its energy and action and wonderful play of light and shade it is noted as one of the great pictures of the world. Rembrandt himself was a handsome young fellow and he knew it and often painted his own portrait. This specimen is by himself.

Finally painters even turned to the slums and the gutters to find the picturesque and striking and here is Murillo, the Spanish painter's celebrated beggar boys which the world has long admired.

·   ·   ·

I have of course described these pictures knowing that it would be hard for you to realize the beauty of the originals without seeing them. Nevertheless these outlines will help you and if you never see the pictures themselves you can, if you will, have in each of your homes copies of such great masterpieces; not cheap and vile caricatures, but real valuable copies which cost but little and are lasting sources of pleasure. These pictures I have used cost 1 cent each.

This brings me to urge in conclusion that you should early learn to appreciate and surround yourselves with beautiful things: "A thing of beauty is a joy forever." This has a deeper meaning than we imagine because we so misuse the word beautiful; but things of real lasting beauty: bits of china, graceful furniture, pretty wallpaper, neat dress, little pieces of statuary and above all beautiful pictures—these things will add enough to your lives to make even your sorrows curves of grace in a crooked world. Not in evil, not in idleness, not in sensuality, comes the real fulness of life; pedantry is not learning, extravagance is not art and yelling is not religion—but all life is one striving toward the Eternally Beautiful.

> Whichever lives and loves
> One God, one law, one element,
> And one far-off divine event
> To which the whole creation moves.[3]

On Migration to Africa (1897)

An undated and incomplete memorandum by Du Bois to Paul Hagemans (spelled "Hageman" in the original), the consul general of Belgium to the United States, stationed in Philadelphia,* is consequential and intriguing. It reflects Du Bois's serious interest in relations between Afro-Americans and Africans; it also anticipates Garvey's program—in its commercial aspects— as well as Du Bois's own Pan-African dream, which would, as he writes in this memorandum, see "the Negroes of the World unite for the uplifting of Africa."

Within the manuscript are two leads for its dating: first, Du Bois remarks that since the prohibition of slavery, in 1865, thirty years have passed; second, he suggests that the Belgian government take the recommended action "in collaboration with the American Negro Academy," which was begun in March 1897. Du Bois was a founding member of that academy; in December 1898 he was elected its second president to succeed the revered Alexander Crummell.

Du Bois lived in Philadelphia during much of 1897 as an "assistant instructor" in sociology at the University of Pennsylvania. Despite the title, he was hired not as a teacher at that all-white institution, but rather to serve as the author of a study of the Black community of Philadelphia—to be published as The

---

3. Du Bois quotes Tennyson, *In Memoriam.*

* Paul Hagemans (1853–1926) was appointed consul general in Philadelphia in December 1889; he served in that post until discharged, at his request, in May 1922. This information was kindly provided in a letter dated 9 June 1983 from Baron de Vleeschauwer, consul general of Belgium in New York City, to Dr. Roger E. Rosenberg of San Jose, California, my research assistant.

Philadelphia Negro *in 1899. He left in the autumn of 1897 to take up a post as professor of history and economics at Atlanta University.*

It is relevant to note that in 1897 H. Sylvester-Williams of Trinidad and T. J. Thompson of Sierra Leone, both then students in London, had established there the African Association. They seem to have acted at the suggestion of Alexander Crummell, then visiting London, and Crummell informed the academy about the new institution on his return to Philadelphia later in 1897.†

Belgium, as possessor of vast holdings in Africa, was one logical focus of Du Bois's attempt to locate a place in Africa that would welcome Black American emigrants. Hagemans had received recent publicity: because he was a founder of a commercial museum in Brussels, he had been consulted in the building of such a museum in Philadelphia. The latter was opened with much fanfare in 1897, no less a personage than President William McKinley officiating at the inaugural ceremonies.‡

For these reasons I surmise that Du Bois wrote this memorandum while living in Philadelphia, sometime in 1897.

The memorandum itself throws some light on the appearance, in March 1902, of a printed prospectus for the African Development Company, of which Du Bois was secretary. Available information on that rather mysterious company has been provided elsewhere.§

Memoir to Paul Hagemans, Esq., Consul-General of Belgium to the United States of America, on the question of the emigration of American Negroes to the Congo Free State.

Sir:

Of the sixty millions (54,983,890) of people inhabiting the United States in 1890, at least 7,470,040 and probably eight millions were of Negro blood. In one century these people with but little outside immigration and under a rigorous system of slavery have increased from a total of about 700,000 over 900%.

Until 1865 it is well known that the great majority of these people were slaves—and in that year they were liberated. The experiment of liberating 4 million slaves at a blow was in itself hazardous, especially when these slaves had been kept in systematic ignorance and dependence by law, had had their family relationships disregarded and their women debauched until at least 1/7 of them had white blood in their veins. But when in addition to all this

---

† See Alfred A. Moss, Jr., *The American Negro Academy: Voice of the Talented Tenth* (Baton Rouge: Louisiana State University Press, 1982), pp. 53–54.

‡ See Henri G. Bayer, *The Belgians, First Settlers in New York and in the Middle States* (New York: Devin-Adair Co., 1925), pp. 281–82.

§ H. Aptheker, *Afro-American History: The Modern Era* (Secaucus, N.J.: Citadel Press, 1971), pp. 148–49.

the government after a few years of desultory military protection left them
to their own devices, gave them not a single foot of land, not a single tool,
not a cent of money, scarcely the protection of the law, and only granted
the right of ballot which they were too ignorant to use—the result was
naturally a social problem of vast and threatening proportions. Thirty years
have elapsed since the beginning of this curious experiment and while it is
still too soon to look for decisive indications as to the final outcome we may
nevertheless seek for indications.

The first question would be what has been the result of emancipation on
the increase of Negro population? Has so great a change in condition [led]
to their destruction? The figures are as follows:

1790	757,208	% [increase]
1800	1,002,037	32.33
1810	1,377,808	37.50
1820	1,771,656	28.59
1830	2,328,642	31.44
1840	2,873,648	23.40
1850	3,638,808	26.63
1860	4,441,830	22.07
1870*	4,880,009	9.86*
1880	6,580,793	34.85
1890*	7,470,040	13.51

* Defective census

(There is a suspicion that the census of 1890 was defective in enumerating
the Negroes.) The unreliability of the censuses of 1870 and 1890 makes
careful deduction here dangerous, but certainly we can conclude that in the
midst of a moral, political, and economic revolution such as few races have
ever withstood, the American Negro has not only not lost ground numer-
ically but has steadily increased in numbers until today there are a million
more Negroes in the United States than there are inhabitants in the kingdom
of Belgium, and their rate of yearly increase since emancipation has been
considerably larger than that of Belgium.

The next question is that of the economic condition of the Negro. One
would naturally expect to find them very poor: They were unskilled, penniless
slaves emancipated without a cent. The first economic result of emancipation
was the parcellement of the large plantations in the cotton raising states and
the settling of the ex-slaves as [tenants?].[1] This was forced upon the landholders by the unconquerable aversion of the freedman to longer work as a

1. The manuscript is torn at this point.

laborer. The result of this revolution is shown by the reduction in the average size of farms in the south. More striking however are the statistics of property owners among Negroes. In 1860 a few free Negroes owned property but they were considerably less than 1% of the Negro population in 1890.

In these states we have more definite returns:

Of all the Negroes in the United States in gainful occupations there are engaged in

	Negroes [%]
Agriculture	57.2
Personal serving	31.4
Manufactures	5.6
Trade and transportation	4.7
Professions	1.1

Of all Negroes, 41.1 were in gainful occupations.

Of the intellectual status of the Negro it can be shown:

ILLITERACY

	Col. Pop. over 10	% illiterate
1860	———	90%?
1870	3,168,905	85.20
1880	4,085,571	75.00
1890	4,870,910	60.02

Colored school children in the United States 1894–5 (estimated) 2,723,720—in school (enrolled) 1,441,282 or 52.92%; daily attendance 856,322, or 59.41 of attendance; 27,081 colored teachers.

There are in [the] country 162 [schools] for secondary and higher education: 32 colleges, 73 normal schools, 57 secondary and high schools, in these: 1549 teachers, and 37,102 students.

MORALS

Thirty-three to each 10,000 Negroes are criminals. These statistics are somewhat [exaggerated] [2] by the fact that the standard of Justice in dealing with Negroes is different than that used in dealing with white and that especially in the south the petty thieving, etc., swells the Negro total.

The great fact however with regard to the moral conditions is the color prejudice in the United States. Partly this prejudice rests on a natural basis: the Negro has been a slave, he is still largely in menial employments, is largely ignorant and wields little influence in the higher walks of life: beyond this however is a settled prejudice versus the colored races. Large numbers of

2. The manuscript is torn at this point.

Americans do not believe the Negro capable of high civilization, want no social contact with him and seek consciously and unconsciously to close to him every path of advancement: in social life ten percent or less of Negro blood will absolutely debase any American; with but few exceptions he is shut out of first-class hotels and in many states out of theatres and in a few he must use a separate and inferior railway car. The professions of law and medicine are closed to him except among his own people; the avenues of trade and transportation are rendered very difficult for a Negro and even the trade unions discriminate whenever they dare. Every step of advance which the Negro has made and is making is thus taken in the face of an unreasoning and often half-conscious prejudice which renders it doubly difficult. As an example there was recently held in Cincinnati a public competition examination for appointment of a cadet to the National Naval Academy: the young man with seven and three-fourths white blood and one-fourth Negro blood won; then upon that rose a strong demand that he not be appointed. It is now threatened at the Academy that if he were [appointed] he will never be allowed to graduate because of his colored blood.

This treatment naturally embitters the life of the American Negro and at the same time spurs him on. He recognizes his inferiority in everything that goes to make up culture and yet feels his ability to overcome all this and take his stand among the nations of the earth; he feels himself an American of the Americans; he was among the first inhabitants of the land, he has toiled for the wealth of the country, he has fought in every war from that of independence to that of Emancipation and claims rightly that no constituent element of the country has a better right to citizenship than he. At the same time he recognizes the fact that his cause is after all the cause of the vast historic Negro race; and that Africa is in truth his greater fatherland; he has an intense interest in that land and although the fight for sheer existence in America has left him little or no time for reflection or active cooperation in African projects, yet he always feels that as the advance guard of Pan-Negroism the future development of Africa will depend more or less on his efforts. Hitherto this has been little more than a pious ideal. To be sure Liberia was settled by Negroes from America and we feel its kinship and yet many things connected with the settlement of Liberia are foreign to the American Negro of today. The trouble with Liberia was that anybody and everybody was encouraged to go: there was no proper preparation, no equipment of tools and capital, no proper idea of the country and climate— simply an indiscriminate invitation to the lazy, vicious, and ignorant to go to a land of milk and honey; the result was an emigration of elements of the American Negro least fitted to be colonists; the question now comes as to the emigration of American Negroes to the Congo Free State—is it feasible and if so is it desirable?

In the first place I do not hesitate [to state] that any general emigration of American Negroes to Africa is neither possible nor desirable; it is not possible for the Negroes as a body do not wish to go and the forcible expulsion of a nation of eight million would be simply impossible without civil war and an expenditure of not less than two and one-half billions of francs. Nor would such a wholesale emigration be desirable because the great mass of the American Negroes are not yet capable of making the skilled, intelligent colonists which the Congo Free State needs—they are fast progressing but still over one-half of them cannot read nor write; few of them are skilled laborers and few of them have reached such a training that they could safely be depended upon to develop a new country.

Nevertheless, it is I believe, both feasible and desirable, in the next five or ten years to start a small but steady stream of carefully selected classes of emigrants who could go to Africa knowing the conditions, equipped for meeting them and desiring to work to the credits of the Congo Free State, the American Negro, and themselves. For the accomplishment of this plan the first step would be the dissemination of knowledge of the history and conditions of the Congo Free State among American Negroes. As it is now we here know far more of Liberia and South Africa than of the Congo Free State and in those places there is little to attract the better classes of desirable colonists.

I beg to suggest therefore that the government of Belgium take steps to supply this information: it would, for instance, issue in English a booklet setting forth among other things:

> The history of the Congo Free State
> A description of the physical features
>   "   "   " its climate
>   "   "   " its natural resources
> The sort of immigrants needed
> The sort of tools an immigrant would need
> Amount of capital an immigrant would need
> The Method and route of immigration
> The legal and social status of American immigrants of the land

I would suggest that this work be done in collaboration with the American Negro Academy (an organization which represents a better class of educated Negroes) so as to avoid misunderstanding and bring it quickly to the notice of the best class of Negroes. This would be the first step and could be taken immediately. The next step should be bent towards encouraging some sort of commercial intercourse between the Congo Free State and the Negroes of the West Indies and of the United States. This would be the beginning perhaps of bonds that would eventually bind together and encourage the Negroes of the World to unite for the uplifting of Africa. How this could be brought about I cannot say at present but I shall give it my earnest thought. The planting of such seed, and the opening of friendly intercourse between the American Negroes and the authorities of the Congo Free State would I have no doubt lead to an [the manuscript breaks off at this point].

I am Sir,

Beyond the Veil in a Virginia Town (1897)

While studying the Afro-American population of Philadelphia, Du Bois observed that a considerable number had come north from Virginia, and from Prince Edward County in particular. He determined, therefore, to spend the months of July and August 1897 in the county seat, Farmville, where he of course lived with Black people.

One result was the publication of Du Bois's "The Negroes of Farmville, Virginia: A Social Study" in the U.S. Department of Labor Bulletin 3 *(January 1898): 1–38. Another result was this hitherto unpublished sketch, probably written late in 1897 or sometime in 1898.*

Midway between the memory of Nat Turner and John Randolph of Roanoke, beside the yellow waters of the Appomattox, lies a little town whose history winds about the falling of the stars in '32 and about "The Surrender." One would not call [Farm]ville a pretty town, nor yet has it the unrelieved ugliness of the west. There is a certain southern softness and restfulness not to say laziness about it that gives a charm to its sand and clay, its crazy pavements and "notion" stores. But the most curious thing about [Farm]ville is not its look—old brick mansions and tiny new cottages, its lazily rolling landscape and sparsely wooded knolls that beck and nod to the three-peaked ridge of the blue Alleghanies—the most curious thing about [Farm]ville is its Veil. The great Veil—now dark, sinister and wall-like, not light, filmy and silky, but every[where] a dividing veil and running throughout the town and dividing it: 1200 white this side and 1200 Black beyond the Veil.

You who live in single towns will hardly comprehend the double life of this Virginia hamlet. The doctrine of class does not explain it—the caste misses the kernel of the truth. It is two worlds separate yet bound together like those double stars that, bound for all time, whirl around each other separate yet one.

Two little boys are walking along the street. "Big execution in town today," says one; "white or colored?" asks the other. Two men are standing in the post office. "I'm running fifty hands in the foundry now," says one. "White or colored?" asks the other. Two countrymen urge their jaded mares across the Appomattox and up main street. "Big meeting at the county," says one;

"white folks or niggers?" asks the other. And thus it runs through life: the Veil is ever there separating the two peoples. At times you may not see it—it may be too thin to notice, but it is ever there. And we have added an eleventh commandment to the decalogue down here: you may have other Gods before Me, you may break the kill commandment and waver around the adultery but the eleventh must not be broken; and it reads: Thou shalt not cross the Veil.

Of the life this side the Veil you all know much; it is the twice told tale of country town life flavored with war memories, and a strange economic experiment, curiously influenced by the other world, but withal white like to Illinois or Connecticut in its business and gossip, its Church fairs and [word illegible] craze, its courting, marrying and dying.

But beyond the Veil lies an undiscovered country, a land of new things, of change, of experiment, of wild hope and sombre realization, of superlatives and italics—of wondrously blended poetry and prose.

The Spirit of Modern Europe (1900?)

Du Bois's second visit to Europe occurred during the summer of 1900, when he participated in the Negro exhibit at the Paris World's Fair and also in the Pan-African Conference held in London.

The paper given below was prepared probably in 1900 upon his return from Europe; it was offered before an all-Black audience in Louisville, Kentucky.

I propose to discuss with you tonight the trend and meaning of modern European civilization. I shall endeavor first to define for the purposes of the evening the meaning of the somewhat shadowy term, Civilization. I shall then endeavor to sketch for you in broad outline the concrete signs of culture in the aptly-called Culture-States, and to discover behind this picture the elements that combine to me the Spirit of Europe. I shall try to show how that spirit does and ought to affect the American Negro and the Negroes of this city.

The 19th century has wrought a vast revolution in human thought which some but dimly realize. In the 18th century a religion of individual worth, a crusade for the extinction of personal slavery and serfdom and a general revolt against excessive government led the thoughts of people to center almost exclusively upon the individual: individual freedom, individual development, individual responsibility all led inevitably to a doctrine which interpreted the whole universe in the terms of single men and induced even souls of exceptional capacity to regard their own personal salvation as the chief end of existence. This individualistic regime still wields vast power over minds today especially in the American business and social world. Nevertheless in the centres of European culture it has long since begun to give way before a larger idea. Men have begun to see that when 10, 100, or 1,000,000 individuals come to share their lives, to live together in cooperation, to constitute a village, a city or a state, there is in that aggregation something more than 10, 100 or 1 million single men: to this new something, it is not necessary to give a name, but it is necessary to remember that whenever men live together in political, social or other organization, that the organization itself has a life, a development and a meaning far transcending the individual lives that compose it. Just as the glory and interest of individual stars is heightened and illumined by the inter-relations of those stars which we call the solar system.

The spirit of the 20th century is not a negation of the individual but a heightening of his significance: he is regarded not as his own end and object, but chiefly as related to his fellow-men, as one link in a chain which is daily holding vaster weight.

You must realize what great changes of thought have accompanied such a revolution in human philosophy; the problems of yesterday were individual problems—the problems of today are social problems; we asked yesterday how shall we educate this child—we ask today how shall we educate this community. We asked yesterday how shall we save this human soul—we strive today to build races worth the saving—in all this the point of application still remains the individual mind and conscience, but the meaning, the horizon of the individual has swept far beyond his petty self.

It is my object tonight to bring before you, therefore, not the problems of individual life but the trend and meaning of the organized life of the greatest human organizations of the day. For this, the greatest study to which the human mind has yet attained, is in reality a view of the answer of mankind to the mystery of human existence. It is more than the discordant half-articulate answers of individual lives—it is the vast and eternal striving of myriads of lives blended into one varying but continuous whole, which embodies in itself the Ideas and Ideals which have guided and are guiding humanity.

It is these Ideas as expressed and exemplified in the organized life of mankind that we call Civilization—an expression whose vagueness is due not to any doubt as to its existence but to the imperfection of human life in its own expression and realization.

The civilization of the 20th century centres in Europe: in other words the organization of European states and their development for the last four centuries has been the pattern and norm of the civilization of the world. Some nations have to be sure stood apart, but in this century it can truly be said in Tokio and Hongkong—in Cairo and Cape Town—in Melbourne and Honolulu—in San Francisco and New York—as well as in London, Paris and Berlin that the civilization of the 20th century is European.

How manifest it is, then, that the man or the nation that would know itself, must first know the vast organization of which it forms a part. The sands swept onward by the whirling seas cannot consider alone their own internal constitution or the little differences of their individual pebbles—first, they must know whither they are being swept and why, and whence come the mighty waters, and what shore is hidden by the dark and sombre clouds beyond.

In a day then when the battle of humanity is being fought with unprecedented fierceness and when the brunt of that battle is about to fall upon the shoulders of a black nation which though larger than the Greek State is half shrinking from its high mission to dabble in the mud of selfishness, it is well to pause in our perplexity and critically study the path before us, the hillsides round us—the dark heaths behind, where broods Sorrow—cruel fellowship:

> "The stars she whispers blindly run
> A web is woven across the sky
> From out waste places comes a cry
> And murmurs from the dying sun."

II

I do not wonder that the Hordes of Atilla the Scourge of God swept across Hungary—for the great broad green and yellow fields are just fitted for sweeping and rolling winds. Almost the whole journey from Budapest eastward to Poland we wheeled across great fields glad with flocks and harvests, gliding sometimes for miles as straight as an arrow flies, then winding in great graceful curves. The rich well-watered country was even more picturesque than the towns. The peasants affected a dress as bright as the Italians with red petticoats and gaily colored kerchiefs. I saw some faces as dark as mine own among the men, with their wide flowing breeches, top boots and gaily ornamented jackets. The towns were generally built in rows down a long street always with walls of white plaster and thick roofs—neat and busy they looked with great barns, wide fields and one white guardian church in the central oval, with a half byzantine tower. At the end of the great Hungarian plains toward Russia rise suddenly the dark Tatra Mountains and beyond, the towers of the city of Cracow looked by no means unstately even on the gray day I entered the ancient capital of Poland. Not a pretty city and yet with remains of ancient greatness, historic monuments and above all—a Soul. The great square of the Ring-platz with its fine old Market House and Gothic Church is in the centre—the Church boldly decorated as if to emphasize the defiant Catholicism of Poland between the Russian Greek and the German Protestant.

I have brought you thus abruptly to the eastern edge of Europe in order that we may first see the Culture of Europe in its lowest terms. Poland today

is hardly a name and yet its spirit lives yonder within the carved portals of
the old University where I once sat with a young Polish student: 20,000,000
souls he told me still beat with the one idea of making Poland again one of
the great nations of Earth; he spoke of their literature, their language, their
oppression and their unconquerable will—and finally as we walked by the
Florian gate, the last relic of the ancient Polish fortifications, we looked
northeast and he spoke of the rise of that mighty race of the east, and the
day when the broad faced Slav, led by Russia, Poland and Hungary should
lead down the world a new civilization that would eclipse the German as the
Teuton overshadowed Rome. All this is not organization—Poland is not a
State, but she represents the disembodied idea of statehood—of race ideal, of
organized striving which some day must tell.

Let us now turn back toward that west Teutonic culture and look at the
capitals of a great nation—Vienna and Buda-pesth—two capitals, the very
phrase has an ominous sound and reminds us that after all Austria is by blood
no nation but a combination of curiously heterogeneous elements: German
and Hungarian, Bohemian and Pole, Roumanian, Servian and Gypsies have here
joined together in a agglomeration of races which is not matched even in
America and forming in some respect the vastest race problem on earth; and
yet amid disorganization and subjection, war and intrigue, prejudice and
hatred, Austro-Hungary stands and has stood for centuries as one of the most
magnificent organizations of human beings since Rome—a wearer of the Roman
eagles and the legitimate heir of the Holy Roman Empire.

No sweeter mountain scenery can exist than that which surrounds Vienna.
The bold line of distant hills which one sees from the companile of St. Marks
in Venice seems shy at first and glides away leaving only the flat, rich but
monotonous plain. Past Undine, however, we catch up with the great scarred
crags. We wind through valleys with Swiss boldness amid scenery whose
wildness is enhanced by the mysterious twilights, which, rising from the deep
cavernous ravine, overtake us on the very borders of Austria. Their grey
and yellow crags frown on us, green vales and green torrents border the
mountainsides and now and then some mighty peak piles its titanic bulk against
the sky and seems to shut us out from the Austrian world—but the cunning
engine glides around, up, down or straight into the earth, on galleries in
arcades, over rivers, until it finally with one last sigh lays us into the hands
of the imperial custom house officers. Another ride of mountain village and
dale but shut in by darkness and we enter one of the great world cities—
Vienna—a city wound with the history of the modern world. Here Marcus
Aurelius, the Roman Caesar, died: here Charlemagne placed the bounds of his
empire and here the great Rudolf of Hapsburg founded an empire that ruled
the world five centuries. Here reigned Maximilian the First who brought
together the Austro-Hungarian Empire, and against the Walls of Vienna
the terrible onslaught of the Mohammedan Turk beat in vain for entrance

to Europe. Around Vienna the intrigues and victories of Napoleon centered from Corsica to Austerlitz—and here, after the downfall of the great Tyrant, sat the famous congress which parcelled out the world and declared the African slave trade a stench in the nostrils of humanity.

What can one say that will convey an adequate idea of Vienna: its broad streets and majestic buildings, its theatres and cafes, its museums, and galleries, its palaces and art? All this cannot be told—it must be seen: I can however take from each city, as I pass, one element of its complicated and kaleidoscopic life and characterize it—an element which appears in all great centres of culture but which receives in this particular city some peculiar emphasis. If then in Vienna I choose an element of culture which in the civilization of Europe goes to make up its real Spirit I should select the element of *Knowing*, that systematic attempt to classify the facts of this multitudinous world, to draw its ends together; of that more indefinite but, too, more important, knowledge of human nature, which we call Science and Experience. We often ask why people today rush to cities: we moralize [why] thousands [would] rather starve in the dens of Whitechapel or the alleys of Louisville than be well fed in the rich valleys of Virginia or in physical comfort in Carolina. The response is clear: the riddle of human life is better answered in cities. Knowledge of human affairs is broader and deeper—the world instead of being bounded by bare hills and petty gossip spreads from sea to sea, leaps the ocean, sweeps the world and yet rests upon our breakfast tables! And men would rather *know* in discomfort than be ignorant in plenty. This is true in Atlanta, in Philadelphia, in New York but it is more true in Vienna. We have noise, and clatter and physical excitement on our streets, but the pulse of human cosmopolitan life that beats in a Vienna cafe, the delicate telegraphy which makes a Calcutta despatch throw the Austrian capital into violent pulsation and sympathetic argument—all this can only be really appreciated in a world city like Vienna. Then too men of Vienna who devote themselves to knowing—students, professors, journalists and Savants—have a place in life, a honor paid them—a recognition of the deep importance of their work which is calculated to make the over-worked American teacher a bit dissatisfied with his lot. There is too in a great city like this a deference to Truth as such—a hatred of a lie even if for truth's sake. An unclouded faith in a Path that leads to Truth though it pass across the little systems, and a crying to the timid world

> "Our little systems have their day
> They have their day and cease to be
> They are but broken lights of thee
> And Thou, O Lord, art more than they."

Let us turn away from Austro-Hungary and set our faces toward the Beautiful Land—Italy.

One day in the mid-morning of life I shot from the bosom of St. Gotthard into a valley smiling with chestnut trees, corn and ripening fruit, fringed with thick foliaged hills, and massive snowcapped mountains all silver and gold. On the one hand lay the strong and turretted castles of Belizona with their ancient walls, and on the other the brilliant green water of the green of Italian lakes. Farther on lay Lake Lugano—a bright blue green more deeply tinted than the sky and behind sloping ramparts of darker green, with rolling hills, dark rocks and a faint gleam of the Alps. Below lies a town with its yellow block-like houses and a winding railway to Milan; and all about a shimmer of sunshine and Italian sky. The stranger calls the land Italy but he who visits it calls it by its own name, *Italia*. Here the world darkens and brightens. Little black eyes and browned faces flash about you amid a brighter bluer world. Even dirt and poverty and unfathomed smells take on a careless ease and laughableness that put you to dreaming. Riding through corn, melons, olives, lazy men and pretty women, we came to a city of great squares and noble streets, Milan, in whose Piazza glistening in brilliant marble lace work—in tiny striving minarets and statues, in delicately traced windows and bold arches—stands a Cathedral; not so infinitely majestic as Cologne but more divinely beautiful—suited to Mary the Mother to whom it is built.

I remember the pale crimson light from its great windows in the choir, the faintly echoing voices of the chanting priests and the vast carved pillars in the aisles—and I remember no more beautiful thing. But we must hurry on past Yellow Turin, past Genoa on the sea, glistening in the moon light, past little Pisa with its leaning tower, to Rome. The Eternal City that sits at the gates of the Evening unconquerable and immortal, singing of a future as mighty as the past. I rode to Rome at night amid furtive glimpses of the wide Mediterranean, past old towns and storied towers to the gray walls of the ghostly city lying asleep beneath the dome of St. Peters. St. Peters looks on many Romes; on the busy openhearted enthusiastic Rome of today with its lively people, fine buildings, crowded thoroughfares and saucy urchins. Mingled with this new Rome and but half buried lies the Rome of the Popes, the Rome that was the center of the world empire founded by the mighty Hildebrand, extended by Innocent the Third and partially throttled by the great movement for Italian Unity. The massive temples of Catholicism like St. Peters, St. Johns and St. Pauls, fountains and avenues and coats of arms, all attest the past glory of the greatest spiritual kingdom of modern times; beneath papal Rome and covered with the dust of centuries, emerging at intervals in grey old ruins, beautiful columns, great arches and stupendous buildings, stands the Rome of the Emperors, the defiant remains of the greatest and most persistent of human governments.

Below this lies the more scanty crumbling remains of the Rome of the Republic: sleeping in some mouldy archway in the corners of the Forum, in subterranean passages, and looking like the mere skeleton of that early Rome which conquered the world by first conquering itself. How wonderful are all these mingled monuments to the eternity of human striving; the giant Coliseum, the sweeping aqueducts, the bath and lolling places, the tombs and the churches all echo mouldy myths and stirring deeds—until at last one seems to walk in a city of today with the creeping ghosts of other days around him—pale hands clasp him, whisperings come on the dust-laden breeze and he knows not whether Victor Immanuel or Caesar Augustus sits in the palace on Quirinal Hill.

And at last he sees that above and around all the dreamers of a dream city there rises the beautiful half-corporeal Rome of the Spirit of Rome—that Soul which soaring from ashes, flame and war, from crime and bigotry, above the ignorance of Goth, Vandal and hypocrite, kept the tradition of the Holy Roman Empire warm in the hearts of men, gave eagles to the world's escutcheons and title to Kaiser, Czar and Emperor, and above all conserved and handed down to the 19th century those monuments to Eternal Beauty—those miles of galleries and museums, those priceless libraries: wrought by the hand of God and the fingers of St. Thomas Aquinas, Raphael and Michael Angelo. Need I pause to say that the element of European civilization that Rome typifies is the Eternity, the Endlessness—the continuity of Human Organization? The history of the world is not a history of the death of nations, but of their lives—of the unquenchable fire of civilization kindled in Egypt, replenished by Greece, scattered burning by Rome, and gathered conserved and augmented in the furnace of Europe.

Let us turn our faces northward and passing by Florence and Venice, crossing the Alps we will pause a moment beside the massive walls of quaint old Nuremburg in South Germany. Here in the 15th century the ruling lord of yonder rambling castle became by the Grace of the Emperor Sigismund, lord of a barren track of cheerless sand in Northern Europe, called Brandenburg; let us follow the footsteps of the Margrave Frederick to his bleak northern home for his journey there was the beginning of a dogged strife against Nature and the Devil, unparalleled in human history: and this Frederick of Hohenzollern and his sons and his son's sons from Joachim to the Great Elector, from the first Frederick to the Great Frederick, and from the first Emperor of New Germany to the Emperor of today form an example of human pluck and perseverance, dogged determination and royal service, which prove their right to rule is divine. We Americans in the somewhat vulgar parade of a doubtful democracy often assume to poke fun at Germany—to call her mediaeval, and wonder at her submission to the antics of a despot. Our laughter too is generally in direct proportion to our ignorance of German history. We learn too little—far too little in our schools and libraries—of the story of this land: how led by a succession of men who were every inch kings this land has risen from a little ridiculed patch of sand to be the greatest power of central Europe. How against the laws of Nature and of man, in the teeth of its enemies and in spite of its friends—nay, above all, in the face of its own distrust in itself and apeing of others—it struggled on led by hero hands, fed by master minds and idealized by one Vast Ideal till it accomplished what men called impossible. And to crown these Impossibilities it built an impossible city in an impossible place and called this Impossibility, Berlin.

Berlin, sitting like some great hard island amid a floating sea of pines and sand, is not a pretty city like Florence, or gay like Vienna or storied like Rome: but one thing it is: it is the most carefully governed city in the world: a city virtually without slums and fireproof, with streets cleaned every day and quiet every night, ruled by the best of its citizens, for the least money possible, where ward politics are unknown and policemen represent law, order and decency; and above all and over all, where the child, the youth and the man are taught that Order is Earth's, as well as Heaven's first law. The average American may feel too much government in Berlin, may see too much bowing to position and official red tape and yet he is bound to acknowledge that the lesson of governmental authority which the new German Empire has given European civilization is perhaps the most valuable contribution of modern days.

Such a realization of high ideals costs something.

> "From Battle's night,
> Arose with might
> Like gleaming helm
> The German Realm."

Thus says the war monument at Augsburg on which a sorrowful young warrior stands sheathing his bloody sword while around sit winged Victory, Industry, Sorrow and Hope. Sorrow and victory in Germany but across the Rhine Sorrow and defeat.

Let us cross the Rhine passing Heidelburg castle—that the most human of ruins, and go onto the greatest of the world's cities—Paris. I say greatest advisedly, for there is not on earth a city comparable in *all* the things that make a great metropolis to the capital of France. The Ruins of Rome are more ancient but not more stately, Vienna in all things is but an echo of Paris, Berlin is more orderly because less cosmopolitan, Venice is more beautiful but less elegant and tasteful, London is larger but less imposing. In Paris alone have we combined a vast aggregation of human beings under a modern municipal government amid historic surroundings and clothed in an outward magnificence and grandeur unparalleled in history. The sweep of that one vast avenue from the Arch of Triumph to the Louvre through the Elysian Fields—that avenue which kings and emperors have trod and Genius and fashion made famous—with the Venus of Milo at one end and the memory of Austerlitz at the other—before that avenue the streets of the world pale into insignificance. Here is the centre of the aesthetic culture of the 10th century and from the brilliant cafes of the sweeping Boulevards go forth edicts more despotic than the decrees of Caesar, more haughty than the determination of Bismarck and more powerful than those of the Autocrat of all the Russians. The vast staircase of the Grand Opera of Paris leads where no other staircase in the world leads. The crowns bestowed by the 40 Immortals rank higher than any other honors of the learned world; the editors of the newspapers of Paris rule more people than Cyrus the Great—and the man or woman in the civilized world who has not at least a distant acquaintance with the language of the Parisians dare not claim a pretense of liberal culture.

What is then the secret of the preeminence of Paris—around what Idea has the culture of the modern world centred in this mighty Babylon of the 19th century? Not about any one idea we may be sure—not about any single group of ideas; and yet if I were to select from the Spirit of Paris, one element which as much as any other and more than many others tells the secret of her greatness, I would say: Freedom—the untrammelled liberty of the individual human will has been among the most conspicuous elements that have formed the metropolis of the modern world. We must not forget that that personal freedom which has become almost the axiom of modern times was once the exception. The majority of the human beings whom Horace met on the Via Sacra were slaves. The vast majority of the people of Athens were slaves. Then the axiom was that the highest good of the majority of men was to promote the Highest Good of the Best men. Wars and revolutions and a religion of deeper broader humanity changed this doctrine of slavery, to serfdom—a system which recognized some rights for the masses but vigorously denied that the object of the state was to promote the well-being of the ignorant peasant as well as that of the great noble. Here progress for a time was held back by the powerful arm of Louis the 14th, then in a whirlwind of blood and hatred such as the world had never seen, the French Revolution burst upon Europe rushing in one wild carnival from slavery to liberty—from liberty to license—from license to anarchy—from anarchy to Murder—from murder to despotism until finally after the most fearful orgies that ever disgraced civilization and after the most glorious victories that ever maddened a mad people, France from sheer breathlessness fell into the arms of a republic whose motto is Liberty, Equality and Brotherhood. And today no one city on earth affords to the human mind and taste greater freedom than Paris—a freedom at times dangerous, at times licentious, but a freedom that is free.

I shall never forget how the little boat that took me from Paris to London tossed upon the white capped billows of the channel under the rays of the pale moon. The cliffs of England lay veiled before, and behind dark France faded away. Like a fairy kingdom rose that wonderful island before me, unguarded save by the mighty ocean—

"Britannia needs no bulwarks
No towers along the steep

Her march is o'er the mountain waves
Her home is on the deep
With thunders from her native oak
She quells the floods below—
As they roar on the shore
When the stormy winds do blow
When the battle rages loud and long
And the stormy winds do blow." [1]

London is not one city but an aggregation of cities forming the clearing house of the British Empire—vast because the Empire is vast, busy with the work of the world, typifying in its own irregularity and endless labyrinth of ways, interests, amusements and cries, the heterogenous world it represents. Here is the center of the world's commerce, the bank of the world, from Melbourne to Rio Janiero—from South Africa to Iceland. Paris binds the cultured European world together, London binds the world cultured and uncultured, civilized and savage. The taste and elegance of Paris guide the aesthetic life of men but London clothes and feeds men, fills up the desert and makes the waste places of Earth sing for joy. The Spirit of London is Justice—that spirit which the austere Roman law described as the constant and perpetual determination to render every human being his due. England has failed in attaining the perfect realization of this ideal—who has not?— yet she has approached nearer than any people on earth. Why is it that an English bank note is worth more than solid gold? Because solid gold may be lost or stolen but an English promise to pay is never lost or broken. We rail at English business rapacity, at the greed of Lombard Street but just as long as Englishmen pay the honest debts better than the rest of the world, just as long as English woollens are all wool, English cutlery all steel, and English linen all flax—just so long wise men will let London rule the business world. No nation has treated subject peoples—black, white or yellow—with half the justice that England has—or has so widely recognized the broad bond of humanity under all climates and conditions. Can we then wonder that the vast gloomy city with its miles of granite, its hoarse roar and stolid tramp is the city of cities, where one feels that he has left the regions of the air and is walking on solid earth? That life is real, life is earnest.

And the grave is not its goal.

Our journey is done. I have dragged you thus headlong over Europe in order that I might make you realize that after all America is not the centre

---

1. Du Bois quotes Thomas Campbell, *Ye Mariners of England*.

of modern civilization. I have wearied you perhaps with sea and sky and
cities and mountains—but I have dwelt on these things that I might give you
a vivid picture of a real world and not mere empty description. On the other
hand, I have sought something more than the panorama of a holiday excursion
trip—I have sought to make you see back of the living, breathing life of these
other worlds the dominant vivifying ideas which make their civilization
European.

I want now to gather up these theoretical threads and to give a final answer
to the question—What is the spirit of modern Europe?

Europe today represents in her civilization five leading ideas: Continuity
of Organization, Authority of government, Justice between men, Individual
Freedom and Systematic Knowledge.

Continuity of Organization conserves the civilization of the past and makes
modern civilization possible: for what is civilization but the gathering and
conserving of the ideas of different men and peoples? The great Graeco-Roman
civilization borrowed and developed the culture of Africa and India and
Judea. The mass of barbarism that reeled down golden haired and drunk
from the blue north did not bring a new culture, did not quench the old, but
doffing its ignorance and idolatry and donning Christianity, and the civilization
it had well nigh destroyed, gave to that old Egyptian-Grecian-Roman civilization, through the Renaissance, a new birth into the world, which modern
Europe has nurtured to manhood. To conserve this culture it was necessary
that human society should never die and the eternal life of the organism of
which you and I form a part is the vastest realization of modern times. Here
is an eternity that must be conserved, must be striven for, must be made
broader and around the idea of preserving intact the institutions of society
from generation to generation from century to century modern Europe has
built its first wall.

The second idea of authority is an acknowledgement of the fact of human
inequality and difference of capacity. There are men born to rule, born to
think, born to contrive, born to persuade. To such as have special aptitude
or special training for special work the principle of authority declares
that they and not others should do that work; that tailors cannot build houses,
nor carpenters make shoes, nor shoemakers run electric plants. The principle
of authority declares that in the limited range of special ability or training
men should be rendered implicit obedience by their fellow men: that we
should bow to the rule of rulers, to the knowledge of students, to the skill
of artisans and to the righteousness of Christ and that the refusal to do this
is anarchy, revolution, ignorance and wickedness.

The third idea of European culture is Justice: that is the full free recognition of individual desert. It declares on the one hand that they who will
not support the pillars of civilization must be forcibly restrained from tearing
them down. This is its older and negative side: today justice also declares

that we must distinguish between those who will not support human culture
and those who cannot, and give moral training to the one and physical,
industrial and mental training to the other: and that, finally, there must be
in the distribution of this help and encouragement, no prejudice, no discrimination; it must reach all alike, rich and poor, high and low, good and bad,
black and white, Jew and Gentile, barbarian, Scythian, bond and free.

The fourth element of the Spirit of Europe is Freedom: not license, not
absence of bonds, not even in all cases, abolition of slavery, but the right to
choose the work of life according to individual bent and capacity, the right
to carry on that work untrammelled by ignorance, prejudice or deviltry and
the right to enjoy the unstolen fruit of striving—in short the Freedom to
choose that life—slavery to an Ideal which through the Truth shall make
you free.

The fifth element of European culture is Knowledge: woe to the coward
of the 20th century, who dare not know, for the spirit of the 19th has proven
that from the deep and modest search for Truth, neither Beauty nor Goodness
have aught to fear, and that the only way in which the world can advance
to higher culture, to more eternal Life, to more unquestioned authority—to
more impartial Justice and to more devoted Freedom, is by means of a
cultivation of Science, of that systematic knowing, in the future, with ever
greater doggedness, insight and determination, than in the mighty past.

In short, then, Europe today stands for a systematic and continuous union
of individual effort to promote Justice and Freedom by means of Knowledge
and Authority.

It may easily be said that this is after all the end and striving of all civilization,
no matter how imperfectly realized in particular societies. This is both true
and false: true that the same ideals which Europe today clearly recognizes
were more or less dimly seen in Egypt, Persia and Judea but it is false to think
that ever before in human history these ideals of society ever stood in such
clean light, or came so near realization. The inquiry therefore resolves itself
into a question of method: What is the method and means by which Europe
has attained its ends? The answer is the secret of the success of the culture
of modern Europe. It is the thorough recognition of the fact that no
army march faster than its rear guard, that the civilization of no community can outstrip that same community's barbarism, that knowledge is
measured by the amount of ignorance abroad in the land, that the culture
of every nation and city is measured by its slums. This idea of social solidarity
and social responsibility, this recognition of the fact that human life is not
an individual foot race where the devil takes the hindmost, is the central
idea of the 20th century and woe to the race or individual that does not
recognize its power.

Nevertheless the application of this idea is narrowed by sheer necessity:
England may recognize the Social Responsibility of the English nation for

every English man, woman and child: Germany for every German, France for every Frenchman but if the great Culture states should at a bound seek to assume Social Responsibility for all humanity—for China, India, Egypt and Central Africa, Borneo and the Fiji Islands, civilization would simply be swallowed up in Barbarism: the solution which Europe is going to give to this puzzling dilemma is the placing of the Social Responsibility of each race in the hands of that race and the allowing it with as little hindrance as possible to work out its own peculiar civilization. Thus the national and Race ideal has been set before the world in a new light—not as meaning subtraction but addition, not as division but as multiplication—not to narrow humanity to petty selfish ends, but to point out a practical open road to the realization in all the earth of a humanity broad as God's blue heavens and deep as the deepest human heart.

The modern theory of the world's races no longer looks upon them as antagonistic hatred-cultivating groups: the patriotism of the Italian does not preclude his honoring the Englishman. The race pride of the German did not suffer in bowing to the genius of the Slav. Races and Nations represent organized Human effort, striving each its own way, each in its own time to realize for mankind the Good, the Beautiful and the True. The German unites and strives in *his* way, and so long as they strive not *against*, but along *with* each other the results blend and harmonize into vast striving of *one humanity*

> One God, one law, one element
>   And one far off divine event
> To which the whole creation moves.

What lesson, has all this to us? What part in this striving has any new race like this we represent here tonight that comes upon the world's stage in the morning twilight of the 20th century: Is there still a place in the world for more striving, for more race Ideals, for a broader Humanity? And if there be what are the new races doing? Some are rising: yonder where the whiteness of the north first begins to soften into the dark yellow come the Japanese—working, suffering and fighting, bullied and imposed upon but striving—ceaselessly striving and already in the mighty struggle now going on the European world reckons with a new factor, a new nation—a new Race, a larger humanity. Farther on lie an historic people rich with history but long dead—but even there is heard the faint crying of a new birth, the signs of new activity, the rise of new ideas. China some day will follow Japan and the world of modern culture will be larger. Farther on the world darkens—dark brown faces are seen, the scattered remains of an ancient civilization appear and in the millions of India the world is listening for the sign of the new birth which the Queen's Jubilee gave warning of. At last come that mighty and mysterious people, sons of the night

"Whose visage is too bright
To hit the sense of human sight
And therefore to our weaker view
O'er laid with Black staid Wisdom's Hire
Black, but such as in esteem
Prince Memnon's sister might beseem
Or that starr'd Ethiop queen that strove
To set her beauty's praise above the sea nymphs."

The African people sweep over the birth place of human civilization, they dot the islands of the sea, they swarm in South America, they teem in our own land.

The students of Louisville are a part of the advance guard of the new people; the teachers of Louisville are training the minds and forming the ideals that are to aid and guide their onward marching.

These ideals differ in no respect from the ideals of that European civilization of which we all today form a part. And therefore our watch word today must be Social Solidarity—Social Responsibility: Systematic and Continuous union of our individual effort to promote Justice and Freedom among ourselves and throughout this land by means of knowledge and authority.

Here justice means absolute honesty of purpose and action. Young Negroes are today peculiarly tempted to impose upon the ignorance of their people, to prey upon their weakness, to flatter their vanity. You must rise to a higher ideal, knowing that a lie in tongue or deed is a deadly thing whether it be for or against us. Freedom means not the right to loaf and squander money on luxuries, not aimless enjoyment of life but rather the right to work, to delve, to struggle, to save, to sweat for God and that Truth that brought our fathers out of the House of Bondage. Knowledge means the trained capacity for comprehending the truth: in this world men who can do nothing, get nothing to do. And men who can and will do must know how and what to do. Young men and women who would serve the Negro race must bravely face the facts of its condition: the ignorance, the immorality, the laziness, the waste, and the crime. Finally authority means the recognition of the fact that all cannot lead because all are not fit to lead but that we must listen to the noblest not to the loudest, to the workers rather than to the talkers, to the Right and not to the Wrong.

Here are the paths which civilization points out and in these paths we must plod. With the unfortunate surrounding prejudice we have little concern. Beyond a quiet and dignified protest we can do nothing but await the action of time and common sense. Meantime however within our own ranks lies work enough—a people who are training up far more than their proportion of criminals—who are scattering disease and death, whose ignorance threatens the foundations of democratic government—such a people have a task before them calculated to keep their hands busy and their eyes open for a century to come.

We are puzzled at times as to just how to begin so colossal a work and yet as it seems to me the opening paths are before us: and they are for the masses good common school training and industrial education; for the talented few the best higher training that suits them. And this aristocracy of learning and talent—the graduates of Spelman, Atlanta, Howard, Fisk, and Northern institutions, are not to be trained for their own sakes alone but to be the guides and servants of the vast unmoved masses who are to be led out of poverty, out of disease and out of crime. It is a vast undertaking and yet a noble one—one in which we need all the divine faith of our mothers to cheer us in victory or in defeat

"For how can man die better
Than facing fearful odds
For the ashes of his fathers
And the temples of his Gods." 2

2. Du Bois quotes Thomas B. Macaulay, *Lays of Ancient Rome,* Horatius.

1900-1935

Postgraduate Work in Sociology in Atlanta University (1900)

Du Bois undertook his duties at Atlanta University in 1898. One of his tasks was to continue and to expand the university's Study of the Negro Problems, accomplished by annual conferences on selected subjects. The first and second conferences were held in 1896 and 1897; the third through the eighteenth (in 1913) were directed by Du Bois, and their proceedings edited by him.

The paper that follows—the original manuscript is incomplete—was delivered probably in the fall of 1900 before a gathering of Afro-American schoolteachers in Athens, Georgia. This, like the preceding essay, anticipates much of the thinking expressed in 1903 in Du Bois's classic essay "The Talented Tenth."

I propose to bring before this association tonight, a simple thesis of three propositions:

1st   That outside their school work teachers ought to study

2nd   That the present economic and social condition of the Negro is a fit subject of study

And finally that the Negro Conferences of Atlanta University furnish an opportunity for pursuing these studies.

The unfortunate thing about any system of education is that it must be more or less artificial—more or less removed from real life and consequently there ever lurks in our modern systems of training the danger that the transition from school to work, from preliminary training to real life shall be so sudden and so great that the subtle delicate connection between the two shall be lost forever and that which should have trained the youth for life may usher him into life worse than untrained.

None know better the truth of this statement than you—for I speak tonight to a score of graduates—to those who on one fair morning have seen the Mountains of the Lord—the transfigured world with its halo of hope and aspiration and noble achievement. To you the question comes with deeper meaning than to others—the question: Where now is the Vision splendid? Where now are the ideals of Commencement morning? It is the shadow of the answer to this question that ever throws a certain sadness over graduating exercises; that ever forces us to mingle with the chorus of congratulation and God-speed the sad minor of warning and fear; that places in every graduate's essay vague references to the beginning of work; the entrance into *real* life, the *end* of some fair morning.

Here then lies the danger of graduation: for real mornings do not suddenly but gradually change to noonday; real beginnings do not come to sudden pauses but lead step by step to realization. But in school life on the very threshold of the larger life comes a sudden, somewhat artificial change, a turning of the road, which is too apt to bewilder and mislead, so that the graduate of the Normal school and college must flounder about blindly for many a year and when he finds himself too often he has lost his youthful vision of life.

When therefore I ask of you as graduates of institutions of learning where are the ideals and aspirations of your school days, I am really saying to you: How far are you carrying out and fulfilling the preliminary training of youth? How far are you cultivating and developing that careful intellectual culture the elements of which you received in school? What have you done since graduation to make your commencement morning a real commencement of deep broad learning such as the few years spent in the best of colleges can do little more than briefly indicate? If you have done nothing—if you have allowed your intellectual life to be narrowed down to the daily treadmill of the school, the kitchen and the spring fashion,—if those higher broader studies which once awoke in you dim glimpses of a vaster world about you, have been allowed to struggle, fade and die, then you have fulfilled not the promise but the fears of that commencement morning.

And too many of us, far too many, have fulfilled those fears. We have caught in school a faint revelation of this wonderful universe that hangs beneath the stars. We have followed yonder road past brave cities and smoky mills and the seething throngs of men, till it dips beneath the sea; we have heard the deep and dark blue ocean roll against the shores of other lands, storied with song and the deeds of mighty men. We have raised the dead heroes of earth and listened to the tale of other days; we have glanced at the foundation of the world, have traced it whirling round the sun; we have sought to peer into our own souls and catch some echo of the mystery of life—and then suddenly we have turned our backs upon all the wealth and rich promise of this vision of life, and have seated ourselves for a life work without study, without thought, without intellectual breadth or scientific curiosity, without books and periodicals, with a simple sordid program of dress and bread and butter—to a life that is lifeless and a culture that is dead.

I have not come to rail at the man or woman who after some glimpse of liberal culture has thus narrowed his life. I know too well the temptations that lead to it and the necessities that force the young with so dark a life; it is a hard thing to be thoughtful among the thoughtless, to be readers among a race of talkers, to find time for study and culture when it is so hard to earn a decent living. And yet one must, unless the Negro people have a cultured aristocracy whose learning is deeper than a lot of high-sounding titles and silly degrees, and broader than the ability to make speeches, it cannot survive.

The duty of making themselves such an aristocracy lies today preeminently
in the hands of the Negro teachers: they alone as a class have had the requisite
elementary training and they alone have some leisure time. They must constitute
themselves a class civilized in the 19th century meaning of the term—broad
in learning, accurate in scholarship, diligent and unceasing students, keeping
in close touch with the best culture of the day and satisfied with no accomplishment which is below the highest standards of the age. Today let us
frankly acknowledge we have no such class of persons. Here and there we
may find isolated cases—but a class united in plain living and high thinking,
who are capable of bringing to bear upon the solution of the Negro problem
trained scholarship and cultured judgment, such a class the Negroes of the
U.S. have not yet evolved and until they do we need not—cannot—look for
the final solution of the greatest problem of humanity.

And the creation of this class does not call so much for more schools and
colleges as it does for determination on the part of graduates from present
institutions. So long as these graduates succumb to the temptation to ape the
extravagant dressing and living of the leaders of the White south; so long as
they try to rise by showing off and by practicing the arts of demagoguery
among these simple-minded people or so long as they let their efforts to earn
bread and butter utterly absorb and choke the intellectual life—so long will
culture and civilization fail where it is most needed.

I have taken this somewhat elaborate method of emphasizing the fact that
it is the business of graduates to study and to study beyond the narrow requirements of the elementary school curriculum which they teach. Otherwise
graduation has no significance. They must carry out the work of intellectual
development which the best school can only begin. The truly educated man
is he who has learned in school how to study and in life what to study. His
commencement morning was in truth the commencement of his education.
And this he can do—in spite of sordid surroundings in the absence of all
incitements to self-culture, in spite of the demands of home and school and
work, he can—you can leave time for self cultivation and self development—
for the realization of some of the high ideals of your youth—you can do it
because others have done it and above all because you *must:*

> So near is grandeur to our dust
> So near is God to man
> When duty whispers low Thou must
> The youth replies *I can.*[1]

Granting then that every truly educated person must have and take time
to carry on careful earnest study along with his work, the next question is
what subject of study shall he choose. *One* subject rather than *many* he *must*

1. Du Bois quotes Emerson, "Voluntaries."

choose because no one's life can compass the realm of human learning. Every day we see men specializing more and more—seeking more and more carefully not to know it all, but to know one thing thoroughly—to be master of one small subject. Herein lies the secret of modern civilization—the division of employments, the specialization of thought and effort. The particular subject of your study depends on many things: on your occupation, your surroundings, your natural bent. It would be natural for a primary teacher to become interested in child psychology and to do something more than the dilettante work laid down in school journals. Country teachers have especial opportunity for botanizing, city teachers for history and social studies; while each one of us has special aptitudes and inclinations which will open this or that path to our efforts.

But one fact there is which binds us together with an interest deeper than life and broader than whim or surroundings: and that is that we are of one descent, children of a common sorrow, and joint heirs to the same hard heritage and by the token of the black blood of our fathers there is and must be one subject above all others of eternal interest to us and that is the condition and place of the Negro in the modern world. We have, to be sure, been surfeited by shallow unintelligent discussions of this matter until we at times almost wish we might let the matter rest. But we cannot: to English-men England must have perennial interest—must centre their thoughts and aspirations, must consciously or unconsciously be the goal of all their thinking and striving. The centre of a Frenchmen's world must be that vast myriad-minded nation that tragic history, those beautiful cities which the world calls France. And so to us there is and can be but one thought and one vast effort—the salvage of the Negro problem.

And yet in spite of this clear fact, it is alarming to think how little we are studying the problem which we must solve. We talk of it—rather too much, perhaps; we theorize about it assuming such facts as please us; we carelessly take it for granted that every Negro is born with an intimate and careful knowledge of the situation and destiny of his nine million fellows and that to procure any desired information it is only necessary that he should open his mouth. And yet no sooner is such a statement made than its absurdity is apparent. How many of us realize the enormity of this problem? How many of us know that there are today as many Negroes in the U.S. as there were Englishmen in England in the time of Elizabeth and half as many as there are Spaniards in Spain today? How many of these millions have those people met who write essays on the problem? And of those few hundreds which they have met, what do they know as to their condition, struggles and their particular problems? What are people thinking of, who jumble into one bunch and treat as one unvarying mass the Negroes of Athens, Ga. and Yazoo City, Miss.—the Negroes of New Orleans and Philadelphia, of South Georgia and California, of Texas and New York? The very fact that we do this shows with what careless ignorance we are attempting the solution of the greatest problem of the century. We must stop such slipshod methods and confess that, *first* we ourselves know little, very little of the real condition of the Negro people and that *consequently* we must study that condition, minutely, faithfully and intelligently. If stones are worth microscopes and steam engines, time and brains—if grass is worth trained experience and scientific knowledge, surely nine millions of human beings are worth some discriminating intelligent attention from those who are eager to discuss them.

[I am] passing by the historical and scientific aspects of this strange assembly of social phenomena, and wish to touch on one of the many problems here presented, one which is of peculiar significance to us as teachers: This is the problem of earning a living: the question as to how the scores of young people whom we are annually sending forth from our schools are going to be able to earn their bread and butter in a respectable way. It is nothing strange or unusual that this economic problem should be the question of questions for the Negro in the opening years of the 20th century. It is the logical fruit of slavery and always where there are freedmen there must be poverty. The struggle for bread must be hard and the condition of survival is such economic cooperation as will furnish wages suited to the wants of the new laborer. We see this problem of poverty all about us in the south: on the one hand growing intelligence, increasing skill and willing strength, on the other hand a rich land with its abundant resources only half-developed and its riches wasted every day—and yet in the midst of all this, poverty, idleness and crime. Here is work to be done, here are workers who might do it and yet the scores of workers are idle and much of the work undone.

What does this mean? It means that the fault lies in the organization—in the whole social situation and that unless we thoroughly understand and carefully study the delicate and intricate relations of this great group of men we shall not know how to train the heads and hands of the freedmen's sons to develop the rich resources of this land. Here then lies a field of study of peculiar interest to the teacher—the question of the economic situation and possibilities of the Negro; the most pressing of the numerous Negro problems.

Thus far I have sought to say that it is the imperative duty of all and particularly of teachers to pursue along with their work some definite course of study. Next I have sought to point out that among the many courses of study which one might pursue none is more important than that which has for its object the thorough understanding of the Negro problem and especially of the present pressing problem of work. It is my final task to say something of the especial manner in which the teachers of Georgia may cooperate in a systematic study of the subject indicated.

You will of course understand that I do not wish for a moment to seem to

say that the study of social problems is the *best* study for all of you to pursue—
I say merely that under the circumstances of our situation here it is of peculiar
interest and value. Nor again do I say that the only method of effectively
studying the Negro problem is through cooperation with the Atlanta Conference; but I do say that in unity there is strength and that only by continuous
systematic effort covering wide areas and conducted according to the best
scientific knowledge of the day, can we hope finally to gain such a knowledge
of these social problems as will guide the statesman, the philanthropist and
the patriot. Such a centre of systematic effort the Annual Negro Conference
at Atlanta University aims to be and as such needs widespread interest and
trained workers. The study of society as it is carried on today is a slow and
difficult task. No sociologist claims to present in his science any such
finished system of laws and measurements as chemistry or astronomy. It is
rather a great field of study where careful observers are daily counting,
measuring and searching—gathering the data which another age will systematize and interpret. To realize how intricate and multitudinous these facts are
we have only to look about us. What is the real difference between the
man that walked the deserts of Arabia 3000 years ago and the citizen of
New York: the greatest difference lies neither in clothing nor culture but
rather in their relations to their fellow men. The nomad Arab is bound simply
to a few score individuals by ties of blood—herein lies his love, his ambition,
his simple striving; he works for them alone and knows none others save
as enemies. But the citizen of New York is bound to the whole world by ties
of commerce, work, thought and ideals. He toils for India and India toils for
him; he works for Africa and Africa works for him; he thinks the thoughts of
London, fears with Paris, and hopes with Vienna. He is part of one great
throbbing whole which we call modern civilization. The vast and intricate
relations of men—the mutual efforts and the subtle spirit of that Mother Age
in whose bosom we were nurtured—it is this mighty subject of human cooperation in modern society that the essence of sociology seeks to study. It has not
yet thoroughly comprehended and it does not pretend that it has. It has
discovered no great or startling laws of human action and may never do so—
but it has collected a mass of material of supreme interest and value; and
of such a nature that no modern thinker who is interested in the condition and
destiny of human beings can afford to ignore its methods and results.

The Atlanta Conference seeks to apply to the study of the Negro problem
the methods of sociological inquiry which the trained experience of the world
has found most successful, and it seeks to interpret the results in the light
of similar data obtained by students the world over. For the carrying out of
this work we need trained workers; we need in every city and town in the
south a group of intelligent cultured Negroes trained in social observation
and in the most accurate methods of social measurements. With such a set of

machinery we could *know* instead of *guess*, we could replace spasmodic experiment with united purposeful action, we could repel wild assertion with sober fact; in time we could take the first step which a civilized people must take before all others—the step toward understanding a social problem before they seek to solve it.

It may seem to you at first a very easy thing to carry out such a program. I speak feelingly and from some experience when I say it is not. Out of all the millions known to be interested in the American Negro, you would be surprised to know how difficult it is to get the cooperation of a few hundred in the collection of accurate facts. When we send out 500 letters from Atlanta University, we count ourselves fortunate if 150 of the persons addressed take the trouble even to reply; and of these 150 replies perhaps not more than fifty send replies worth the making. Enjoying as I am the hospitality of Athens, I shall refrain from saying how many letters I sent here last year asking for a little information not difficult to obtain before I received a reply. Suffice to say that in order to get the information as to Negro merchants collected by the Atlanta Conference last year we sent out no less than 2500 communications and fully 1500 of these we have still to hear from. Furthermore the sort of information which we can ask for is seriously limited by the fact that our correspondents are largely untrained and unaccustomed to the careful accurate work required in such inquiries.

For this reason we are hoping that as the years go by larger and larger numbers of graduates who feel that they ought to continue systematic study will take advantage of the opportunities for post-graduate study offered by Atlanta University and that they will particularly become interested in the department of History and Sociology of which the Atlanta Conference forms a part. We offer no special inducements for such students outside the opportunity to study under guidance and the satisfaction of knowing that mental development did not stop with commencement morning. If the department should grow there is the possibility of a summer school in social questions and a wide and valuable development. Here then is the need—here is the opportunity.

We need first to arouse among the thinking class of Negroes an interest in study for its own sake; we need to turn this interest not entirely but to some extent toward the study of the Negro problems and finally the Atlanta Conference would like to feel that it could rely on the teachers of Georgia for prompt, careful and intelligent cooperation in spite of the fact that this will cost time, trouble and effort. And especially do we want increasing numbers of these young people to use their spare time in making themselves trained observers and valuable workers.

Only by such unpaid and gratuitous efforts shall we emerge into the light. We continually [manuscript ends].

First Meeting of Persons Interested in the Welfare of the Negroes of New York City (1903)

Dr. Wallace Buttrick, secretary and executive officer of the General Education Board, wrote Du Bois from New York City on 31 December 1902: "By request of Mr. W. H. Baldwin, Jr., I beg leave to inform you that a private conference regarding the condition of the Colored people will be held at Mount Olivet Baptist Church, 161 West 53rd Street, New York City, on Sunday afternoon, January 4, at four o'clock." *

Though Du Bois's specific suggestions—spelled out hereafter—were not implemented, this meeting was a forerunner of the National Urban League, as its historian pointed out.† Baldwin was president of the Long Island Rail Road, and his widow, Ruth Standish Baldwin, was to be the main founder of the league eight years later.

On January 4, 1903 at 4 o'clock in the afternoon a number of gentlemen met at Mount Olivet Church, 161 West 53rd St., New York to discuss means of bettering the condition of the Negroes of this city. There were present:

Mr. W. H. Baldwin, Jr.	Dr. Wallace Buttrick
Dr. Felix Adler	Mr. Horace Denning
Dr. C. T. Walker	Mr. W. E. B. Du Bois
Dr. W. H. Brooks	Rev. Mr. R. G. Boville
Dr. W. L. Bulkley	Mr. J. E. Garner
Rev. Mr. C. S. Morris	Mr. S. R. Scottron[1]

Letters of regret at their inability to attend were received from Mr. Robert Ogden, and Mr. George Foster Peabody.

Mr. W. H. Baldwin Jr. was made chairman and Mr. W. E. B. Du Bois, secretary.

Mr. Baldwin stated that this meeting grew out of a general desire to help Northern Negroes as well as Southern by means of the philanthropic movements of the day. He called on Dr. Adler who expressed the desire of the prime movers in this enterprise to know first more of the condition of the Negroes, their number, housing facilities, opportunities for work, etc., in order that it would be plainer what help could best be given.

---

* This letter is in the Du Bois Papers, University of Massachusetts, Amherst.

† Nancy J. Weiss, *The National Urban League, 1910–1940* (New York: Oxford University Press, 1974), pp. 20–21.

1. Of these participants, Felix Adler was the Ethical Culture leader; C. T. Walker, minister of the host church; William Brooks, Black pastor of St. Marks Methodist Episcopal Church, New York City; and W. L. Bulkley, first black principal of a predominantly white school in the New York City system.

Dr. C. T. Walker thought the chief obstacles which the Negroes encountered were the difficulty of securing work and the fact that the rents charged for homes were higher for Negroes than for whites.

Rev. Mr. C. S. Morris spoke also of the difficulty of securing work and especially emphasized the discrimination in rents. He himself is paying $29 a month for a house for which the former white tenant paid $19. In general the Negroes, he said, paid from $3–$5 more a month than whites.

Rev. Dr. Brooks spoke of the crowded condition of Negro tenements, the lodging system which helps pay rent, and the general diversity and intricacy of the Negroes' problems.

Mr. Garner said that in his business of general house-cleaning he met much opposition from trade-unions on technical matters in which he thought color prejudice played a great part. He thought a Negro trade school was needed.

Mr. Scottron touched on the history of Negro schools and of the teaching of manual training in the old Mulberry Street school. He thought a manual training school for janitors and laundresses was necessary.

Dr. Bulkley thought that the great necessity was to give the Negroes a knowledge of the opportunities about them and urge them to attend the established trade schools rather than to attempt a separate school on racial lines.

Mr. Du Bois pointed out the peculiar history of Negroes in such cities as New York; every time they had pressed forward and raised themselves they had been deluged by migration of less advanced fellows from the South and race prejudice made no distinction between better and worse elements. He urged the establishment of a kind of social settlement for Negroes as follows:

A PROPOSED SOCIAL SETTLEMENT

1. Location   The social settlement here proposed is designed especially to meet the peculiar needs of cities in the North with a large Negro population, as, say, New York, Boston, Philadelphia or Chicago.

2. Object   The object of this settlement is to seek to bring about such an adjustment between the life of the segregated Negro group and that of the larger city as will gradually lead to the making of the Negro into an integral part of the city life in educational and social activities.

3. Methods   The settlement under the direct leadership of educated Negroes of ability, and in close cooperation with the white leaders in philanthropy shall aim to establish itself as a physical center for movements affecting the betterment of the Negro, for the gathering of careful information concerning his needs and condition, and for furthering effective cooperation among all established agencies which seek his good.

The settlement shall avoid becoming either a church or a school. It shall not aim usually to set up distinctively racial institutions but shall rather direct Negroes to the best institutions already established.

In lines where for various reasons there is a manifest demand for institutional work the settlement shall take up the work until better agencies are found: it should thus become at present a center for lectures and distinctively secular entertainments, a center for properly regulated public amusements, a center for athletic exercises, etc.

Above all such a settlement should recognize that personal friendship, continued and effective, is the main-spring of social help. And it should attempt to use friendship to help the weak and unfortunate and to find enlarged opportunity for Negroes of ability and desert.

The settlement should be a common meeting ground for the best elements of both races and seek to promote mutual acquaintance and understanding.

The settlement should be as far as possible a central meeting point for all enterprises and organizations designed for the betterment of the race; it should be a clearing house for the local race problem, acting as a directory and adviser in matters of almsgiving, education, religion, and work.

4. Preliminary Steps The first preliminary step toward the establishment of such a settlement should be a thorough study of the Negro in New York City by means of an inquiry involving a house to house visitation.

Such a study should be modelled on the Philadelphia study except that the published report should be smaller and more popular in style while the larger results should be kept on file for reference.

The house to house inquiry should cover a number of typical districts, and include at least 30,000 Negroes. A canvass of such a group thoroughly done would cost from $1000 to $1500 for canvassers; to this must be added the cost of tabulating the material and collecting general statistical and historical matter, which would cost about $1000 more. To this must be added the salary of the director for overseeing and preparing the report and the cost of publishing the printed report. The total cost would probably be from $3000 to $4000. The Philadelphia investigation cost $5000.

After the publication of the report a board of trustees for the settlement should be established, a proper site and building secured and the difficult work of selecting a proper director and residents begun.

Lecture in Baltimore (December 1903)

The locale, month, and year of this manuscript are stated in the original. Its form suggests that these pages were used as notes or guides for a lecture or possibly several lectures. The paper, however, represents a very clear and forceful expression of Du Bois's basic position and its opposition to that of Booker T. Washington.

The industrial schools with all their money and popularity are today reaching but a few thousand pupils out of three millions, so far as effective trade teaching is concerned. Not one Negro child in three is today receiving a common school training or has any chance to receive it; and there is not a single adequately endowed and reasonably equipped Negro college in the United States.

How are we to obtain these great educational aids?

First, we must have teachers.

Second, we must have money.

How are schools of any sort established? By furnishing teachers. Given properly equipped teachers your schools are a foregone success. Without that I don't care how much you spend on buildings and equipment, the schools are a failure. It is here that the Negro colleges like Atlanta University show their usefulness. Nearly two thirds of our graduates teach. They are manning the high grades of the public schools of the South from Carolina to Texas and it is our contention that the teachers of an untaught people need especially vigorous training. That no public school system can be maintained that does not rest upon the normal school and the college for the training of teachers and teachers of teachers. If this is true of the public schools, it is just as true of the industrial schools. The graduates of Atlanta University are today teaching in over twenty industrial schools, for such schools need something more than skilled workmen as teachers, they need trained intellects as well as hands, and if the college-bred teachers were withdrawn from the Negro industrial schools today nearly every one of them would close their doors.

It is worse than thoughtlessness for a nation to give all its countenance and support to common and industrial schools and neglect the institutions which make the very existence of these common and industrial schools possible, and yet in the very face of this obvious fact the few effective colleges of the South are literally starving for their support and have to undertake a regular and costly propaganda to teach an intelligent nation that brick buildings full of children and hammers do not teach themselves—thus without souls and brains industrial schools and all other schools are flat and fearful failures.

Then too the general educational system of the South needs money; the South is simply unable to cope with her problems of popular education, and when to this is added a wide unwillingness, born of race prejudice, the results demand and demand imperatively national aid to Southern education.

The problem of the slave trade was intricate, difficult and perplexing, if you will, but strangely simple. Oh well, it was answered: if you are seeking moral levels that over-reach men if—but this is a practical question; are they not better off and so the argument glided. And just so it is today with the vast problems left as a heritage from this shameful past. Here sits the same vast simplicity: is it right to let the physical peculiarities of a human being stand between soul and soul? You may dress a query in a thousand forms and complete with a hundred problems, and yet the simple query stands and will stand: shall you measure men according to their manhood or according to their race and color? And above all, those who themselves suffer from the caste proscription of America must themselves especially refuse to give up those great principles of right and justice without which we shall never become a great people. The principles are three in number: first the right to vote, civic equality and the right to know. It is the basic principle of modern democratic government that no group of people can be trusted with the destinies of another group—that in the hands of every free citizen must be placed the ballot not as an ornament, not as a luxury, but as a defense against the unscrupulous and thoughtless, and a guarantee of liberty and justice. Without the right to vote there is no real freedom and no chance for free development. The ignorant may be temporarily curtailed in their rights till they gain intelligence, but only the ignorant. The Southern movement for disfranchisement has been not against ignorance but against black men, and it has been accompanied by a determined effort to curtain rather than broaden the education of Negro children. It is our duty to oppose it, to use every honorable means to prevent its accomplishment, and refuse absolutely to follow or countenance any movement or man who apologizes for, or belittles the significance of this monstrous crime against a struggling people.

The second principal to which we must cling is the principal of equal civil rights. As Americans we must strive lest America become a land of caste. Self respect and equality of opportunity depend on decent treatment of black men in those institutions conducted by the state, for convenience of the public—equal accommodations on the railroads, equal protection of the laws, an absence of discrimination in work and wages—these things will not come without effort. The man that supinely sits down and gives up the rights of manhood or even goes so far as actually to protest that he doesn't want them, that he has a sincere liking for the jim crow cars and a fascination for lynch laws—such men do not deserve American citizenship. In the long run men and nations get what they sincerely and earnestly demand; we will get the same if we have the courage, courtesy and manhood to stick to our principles and not go moving after false gods.

Thirdly, the Negro must have educational opportunities. There has been no more disgraceful episode in the history of the Negro in America than the way in which during the last ten years we have given up the demand for the thorough education of our children. A propaganda for industrial training is in itself a splendid and timely thing to which all intelligent men cry God speed: they that walk in darkness, my friends, need shoes; compasses they must have to guide their going and a knowing of the winding ways; but above all they that walk in darkness need the light—the uplifting presence of morning on the Hills of God, the whistling of birds in the upland corn beneath the showering sunlight, the flare of the flaming sword of that dread angel who keeps the way of life.

But when it is coupled by sneers at Negro colleges whose work made industrial schools possible, when it is accompanied by the exaltation of men's bellies and depreciation of their brains, then it becomes a movement you must choke to death or it will choke you.

A Proposed Negro Journal (April 1905)

An important component of Du Bois's life was his editorship of magazines: the Moon *(1906–7), the* Horizon *(1907–10), the* Crisis *(1910–34), the* Brownies Book *(for children, 1921–22), and* Phylon *(1940–44). All sought, in one way or another, Black liberation, and Du Bois always found that getting the necessary funds was a highly difficult matter.*

His correspondence shows that very early in the twentieth century he began serious efforts to establish a journal;* among those he approached for financial help—in this case without success—was the banker Jacob Schiff, who contributed to Tuskegee and was to contribute for many years to the NAACP. Letters exchanged between the two men, in April 1905 have been published.† In one, dated 13 April, Du Bois remarked that he was enclosing "some notes" elucidating his ideas concerning the projected magazine. These notes are published here.

1. *The Need of it*
The present is a very critical time for the American Negro and for the darker races in general. It is not simply a question of individual ability but of group cooperation to initiate forward movements in culture and social reform and to repel unjust attack. To stimulate this cooperation wide self-knowledge within the race, of its own needs and accomplishments, is demanded; and certain ideals, racial and cultural, must be brought home to the rank and file. A proper Journal would be the first step toward these ends.

---

* See, for example, Charles Waddell Chesnutt to Du Bois, 27 June 1903, in the Correspondence, 1:56–57.

† Ibid., 1:108–10. (On p. 108 a letter of 4 April 1905 is incorrectly dated 14 April.)

2. *Attempts to supply the Need*

The first Negro periodicals in America appeared over 50 years ago in the shape of small weekly sheets. Since then thousands of small papers of this sort have sprung up and died. Today there are, approximately:

    1 quarterly magazine
    2 monthly magazines
   10 newspapers, weekly, with more than local circulation.
 200 local weeklies.

The quarterly magazine is a church periodical; it is not well edited, and has little readable matter. Its circulation is probably not much over 500 paying subscribers.

The monthly magazines are the *Colored American* of N.Y., formerly of Boston and the *Voice of the Negro* of Atlanta. The latter has perhaps 5000 paying subscribers, the former possibly 2000. They are fairly good periodicals of the ordinary sort but they lack (a) careful editing on broad lines, (b) timely, readable articles, (c) an efficient news service, (d) good illustrations, (e) modern aggressive business management.

The larger newspapers have from 1000–4000 subscribers. They lack especially an efficient news service. They clip from daily papers and have a few correspondents.

Nearly all these ventures were started with little or no capital, largely by enthusiastic but half-educated men and they are not able to give the readers what the readers are demanding in most cases.

3. *Character of Journal Proposed*

I propose to establish a monthly Journal on the order of *Harper's Weekly* or *Colliers*, but smaller in the number of pages and probably in size of page—at present I have in mind a 24-page Journal 10 x 9 inches. This Journal is to be:

(a) A literary digest of fact and opinion concerning the Negro in particular and all darker races.

(b) A compendium of the News among these people gathered by staff correspondents in the larger cities and centres of the U.S. and in the West Indies, West and South Africa, etc.

(c) Interpretation of the current news of the larger world from the point of view of the welfare of the Negro.

(d) Short, pertinent and interesting articles.

(e) Illustrations attempting to portray Negro life on its beautiful and interesting side. Above all the Journal should be cast on broad intelligent lines, interpreting a new race consciousness to the modern world and revealing the inner meaning of the modern world to the emerging races. It should rise above narrow interests, personal likes or dislikes and seek above all practical united effort toward ideal ends.

4. *Chances of Financial Success*

There are in the United States 3,562,387 Negroes 10 years of age and over who can read and write. At least 200,000 of these are today subscribing for one or more Negro Journals—usually a small local weekly with "patent" inside and a couple of columns of local news. Probably another 100,000 read these papers and a large additional number could be induced to read and to look at pictures if the proper Journal were at hand.

This brings two problems: (a) What sort of paper do Negroes want? (b) How could such a paper be gotten into their hands? The first problem is one of editing; it can not be answered off-hand but the experience of the past proves that interesting news attractively and briefly told and good pictures can be made a vehicle for much teaching and inspiration. The problem of business management is more difficult. It must be worked out on the lines of a class periodical for a peculiar people who are not used to modern advertising methods. The problem is hard but not insoluble. By combining a knowledge of modern publishing methods with a knowledge of the Negro people a man may hope for success here and in time for a possible circulation of 50,000–100,000.

With this circulation advertisers could be interested along certain lines.

Out of the business once established could grow various enterprises in publishing: supplementary reading for Negro schools, text-books, works of Negro authors, etc.

Negro writers and artists could be encouraged to write of themselves and depict the things nearest to them and thus to speak more naturally and effectively than they usually do.

5. *Capital Invested*

Realizing this need of a periodical I have for many years sought to establish it. I could not raise the capital myself; my salary is $1200 on which I support myself, wife and child and carry an endowment life insurance of $5000. (Penn Mutual). I could not easily raise capital among Negroes for most of them are poorer than I. Moreover they would want quicker returns than I could promise.

I determined, however, to begin with my own savings and then seek further aid. Together with Mr. Edward L. Simon, a graduate of the college department of A.U. [Atlantic University] and a competent printer, I formed a copartnership in March 1904. We bought out the Job printing plant of W. J. Yerby (since moved to 350 Beale St.), 163 Beale St., Memphis. Insert card. In this business we have made the following investment:

Cost of plant	$250.00
New Type	559.74
One (1 horse power) electric motor	50.00
1 Whillock cylinder press	1650.00
1 Job Press (7 × 11) in exchange	45.00
1 perforating machine	25.00
Fixtures, improvements, etc. about	150.00
	$2734.74

We have paid in, in cash $1600, beside reinvesting all profits for the year. The receipts for local Job work the first eight months were:

April & May	$310.55
June	238.30
July	187.03
August	145.30
September	96.40
October	134.30
November	231.30
Total	$1343.28

This is in a city of 49,910 Negroes with one rival Negro shop and numberless white shops. A detailed statement of the year's work is in preparation. Mr. Simon has managed the plant entirely, receiving a salary of $60 a month. The cylinder press has just been installed and on this we have paid only part, giving notes for about $1000, which we expect the job work to pay for within a year or 18 months.

We are at present housed in a rented building, which we have leased for 5 years @ $40 a month. We use the first floor and cellar and sub-rent the second floor for $22 a month.

6. *Capital Needed*

For the publication of a 16 pp. paper 10 × 9 inches (the size of the N.Y. *Life*) we estimate as follows on an edition of 5000:

Composition 16 pp.,	$22.10
" 4 pp. of cover	8.00
Make-up of forms	5.00
Press work	9.50
" on Cover	4.00
Binding, etc.	23.00
Paper 15 Reams 60# @ 6¢	48.00

Paper 2½ Reams 120# @ 6¢	15.00
Ink	3.00
Total cost, one issue	$137.60
" " 12 issues	$1651.20

An edition of 10,000 would cost about $2900. A 32-page Journal would cost about $5000 for 10,000 copies.

Our present plans include expenditures about as follows:

Expenses of manufacture of Journal and mailing, one year	$4,000
Salaries, 4 men, one year	4,000
Additional equipment needed (including a small linotype typewriter, etc.)	2,500
Pay for staff correspondence, contributors, etc.	1,500
	$12,000

To this must be added rent and repairs, replacement of material, expenses of travel and advertisement, etc.

To offset this there is the income of the job office, and subscriptions and advertisements.

We think that a capital of $10,000 in addition to the nearly $3000 already invested would enable the enterprise to start with good prospects of success.

Garrison and the Negro (December 1905)

Du Bois was the main founder, in July 1905, of the Niagara Movement, which gave organized expression to the opposition to Washington's Tuskegee machine. Among the earliest events sponsored by that movement were celebrations hailing the life of William Lloyd Garrison, held in December 1905 to mark the centenary of his birth.

For the occasion Du Bois drafted, in ink, his views of Garrison's relevance to the time.

Several times a feeling has been voiced that the Negro American is not always appreciative of the great efforts which men and associations have from time to time made in their behalf. True it is that recently the note of complaint among colored men in this land has drowned out the voices of thanks and gratitude and the watchword in the black world is certainly agitation and censure rather than praise.

On the other hand, nothing is more significant than the spontaneous outburst everywhere throughout the land of a desire and determination to celebrate the 100th anniversary of the birth of William Lloyd Garrison. These celebrations will usually be local church and school affairs but the movement is general and the spirit behind it notable. No people are more appreciative of kindness to them or sacrifice in their behalf than colored people. And when it is exhibited in the wonderful devotion and sacrifice of a man like Garrison, the desire to acknowledge it is well nigh universal.

On the other hand, there is a feeling today among Negroes that certain *classes* of men are more *desirous* of making the Negro problem one of alms-giving and charity rather than of manhood and manhood rights. To this they are righteously opposed and when in good faith some earnest workers in this great field point to the columns of figures showing the money spent for Negro Churches and schools there prevails among colored people along with all their thankfulness a spirit which a widely read Negro paper has recently voiced:

> For all time, charity, which neither pauperizes nor patronizes heaven's unfortunates, but gives itself with its gifts, all praises and thanks are due. But chilling, unfeeling, vaunting pretension, masquerading in the mantle of charity, deserves neither respect nor consideration. The neediest prefer to bear the ills of want and wretchedness rather than be the miserable objects of prying pity or condescending curiosity which proffers alms today, that it may defer justice and fair play tomorrow; which comes, if ever, only to keep the word of promise to the ear and break it to the hope.

Such words and such a feeling must be respected. It contains the germs of manhood, self-respect and self hope. The period of universal Negro charity is passing—slowly to be sure, all too slowly—but passing. When then these millions turn to celebrate the birth of a great and good man who gave not his money (for he had none) but himself to their cause, what wonder it is that they make the meetings an occasion of consecrating themselves to the carrying out of the principles Garrison advocated rather than of mere eulogy. The words therefore of the following "Garrison Pledge of the Niagara Movement" are of especial significance, as they are to be widely used in this celebration.

THE GARRISON PLEDGE OF THE NIAGARA MOVEMENT

Bowing in memory of that great and good man, William Lloyd Garrison, I, a member of the race for whom he worked and in whom he believed, do consecrate myself to the realization of that great ideal of human liberty which ever guided and inspired him.

I hereby pledge myself to fight for freedom: freedom of speech, freedom of thought, freedom to vote, freedom to enjoy public conveniences and freedom to associate with those who wish to associate with me.

I propose to enter this great moral battle with head up like a man saying as he said:

"I will be harsh as truth and uncompromising as Justice."

"My reliance for the deliverance of the oppressed universally is upon the nature of man, the inherent wrongfulness of oppression, the power of truth, and the omnipotence of God."

My cause is a holy cause.

"Opposition cannot weary it out; force cannot put it down; fire cannot consume it. It is the spirit of Jesus who was sent to bind up the broken-hearted, to proclaim liberty to the captives and the opening of the prison to them that are bound; to proclaim the acceptable year of the Lord and the day of vengeance of our God." Its principles are self-evident; its measures rational; its purposes merciful and just. It cannot be diverted from the path of duty, though all earth and hell oppose.

I will remember that "The success of any great moral enterprise does not depend upon numbers" and that "It is possible that a people may bear the title of freemen who execute the work of slaves." Therefore:

"I solicit no man's praise."

"I fear no man's censure."

Our trust for victory is solely in God. We may be personally defeated—but our principles, never.

I am in earnest.

I will not equivocate.

I will not retreat a single inch.

And I will be heard.

A million men behind such a pledge will not let the spirit of William Lloyd Garrison die.

The New Negro Church (1917?)

A good summary of Du Bois's views towards the Black church—constant throughout his life—is offered in a paper that he donated to the Library of Yale University.* The manuscript is undated, but its first paragraph makes clear that it was written either in 1917 or 1918; the particular occasion for which it was prepared is not known.†

---

* The file number is box no. III, folder no. 51.

† For Du Bois's views on religion see also H. Aptheker, " W.E.B. Du Bois and Religion: A Brief Reassessment," *Journal of Religious Thought* 39 (Spring–Summer 1982): 5–11.

It is painfully true that White Christianity has in the twentieth century been curiously discredited. First, it is faced by the fact of the World War. Here in the twentieth century of the Prince of Peace the leading nations representing His religion have been murdering, maiming and hurting each other on a scale unprecedented in the history of Mankind. Again, into the White Church of Christ race prejudice has crept to such an extent it is openly recognized and in the United States at least it is considered the natural and normal thing that white and colored people should belong mostly to different organizations and almost entirely to different congregations. Finally in the white church an obvious and open segregation has taken place so that a poor man in some of the great churches of the north would be as great an anomaly as a black man in the Methodist Church South. These facts do not impugn Christianity but they do make terrible comment upon the failure of its white followers.

On the other hand, the colored church of Christ has certain things of which it may rightfully boast. It is a democratic church; a church where the governing power is largely in the hands of the mass of membership, where everybody is courteously welcomed even if the application of a white person might cause astonishment, and where the attempts to organize aristocrat and exclusive congregations have been curiously unsuccessful as compared with the enormous success of the great churches of the [white] people.

This success of the colored Christian church calls, however, for no "Holier than thou" attitude. As colored people we have not yet been faced by the kind of temptation that has led white people astray. We have no human beings in our power to despise. We have little wealth to tempt us to aristocracy, and we have so near to us the example of what prejudice and hatred can do that most of us have been well warned.

On the other hand, there are many faults and dangers: First of all the kind of sermon which is preached in most colored churches is not today attractive to even fairly intelligent men; we have gotten into the widespread habit of letting preachers talk to us without giving them any attention because we assume that most of the things they say are not worth attention.

The theology of the average colored church is basing itself far too much upon "Hell and Damnation"—upon an attempt to scare people into being decent and threatening them with the terrors of death and punishment. We are still trained to believe a good deal that is simply childish in theology. The outward and visible punishment of every wrong deed that men do, the repeated declaration that anything can be gotten by anyone at any time by prayer. Especially is the colored church failing by its dogmatic hypocrisy in relation to amusements:—While church members and nearly all decent people dance and play cards and go to the theatre under certain circumstances, the church continues to pretend that these things are always absolutely and eternally wrong. At the same time it seldom punishes or seeks to punish those of its members who indulge in them. Lastly, the colored church finds itself continually in the treadmill of its economic lack of vision: It builds a church edifice, works hard to pay the mortgage interest, follows this by a series of tremendous rallies to pay off the principal and burns the mortgage. By that time the church is old and either needs repairs or a new church. When the new church is built the same circle is gone over again.

In the first of these dangers what must the new Negro Church do? It must make its sermons a regular source of real information. It must give the people Knowledge. It must inspire them with high ideals of good deeds, and not simply entertain them or scare them or merely yell at them. Especially must the new Negro Church take a consistent stand on amusements. It must discourage excesses and immorality, but it must cease to condemn every person who dances under any circumstances, every person who sees a play of Shakespeare and every person who sits down with his friends for a game of eucre. It is absolutely impossible to class all dancing, entertainment, and the playing of games with debauchery and lewdness; all attempts to do this are bound to be flat failures.

Again, the method of recruiting persons to church membership should be changed. It is not necessary to carry on our present method of periodical revival with the hiring of professional and loud-mouthed evangelists and reducing people to a state of frenzy or unconsciousness in order to get them into the church. A regular campaign carried on every month in the year, quietly and seriously among reasonable people will bring to the aid of the church a much better class of membership than present methods attract.

Above all, the business activities of the new Negro Church must be more systematic. The same methods that procured and paid for the church home can buy and pay for homes of the church members. Buying clubs and co-operative effort can reduce the cost of living for the church members and for the church neighborhood. More systematic effort can be made for obtaining employment for colored folk and for encouraging enterprises that will employ them. The burden of educating its children even through high school and college should rest upon every Negro church.

Above all, the church must take an unbending stand on the matter of character. It seems almost inconceivable that today so many churches and ministers and so many good church members actually sneer at good men and good deeds and honest action. They seem to want the world to believe that dipping a man into a pool of water is more important in the sight of God than inducing him to keep his body clean and pay his honest debts and refuse to spread malicious gossip. Clean straight-forward character, honest unbending unselfishness must be the product of the Negro Church if it is to survive; and this coupled with a helpful business program and a sane attitude toward amusements will characterize the New Negro Church.

Du Bois at the Paris Exposition, spring 1900. He was responsible for what was called the Negro Exhibit—displays of books, art objects, and inventions by Afro-Americans. For his discharge of this responsibility he was given the gold medal of the exposition.

*This photograph was taken in
1907, probably in connection with
the third annual meeting of the
Niagara Movement, of which
Du Bois was general secretary.*

*Participants in the third annual meeting of the Niagara Movement, held in
Boston in 1907. Observe that women constitute nearly half of the delegates.*

NAACP-*sponsored Silent Protest Parade against lynching, marching down Fifth Avenue in New York City, 1917. Du Bois is second from the right in the second row, carrying a cane.*

Du Bois on one of his regular annual lecture tours, here in Boley, Oklahoma—one of the several all-Black cities in that state—in 1920.

Du Bois during his remarks on receiving the Spingarn Medal, summer 1920, at Atlanta, Georgia.

Miscegenation (January 1935)

Late in 1934 Victor Robinson, M.D., *wrote to Du Bois several times, stating that he was preparing an* Encyclopedia Sexualis *and asking Du Bois to contribute an essay on miscegenation. Du Bois had already published a brief essay stressing the need for more preventive medicine in the* Medical Review of Reviews, *issued in New York City and edited by this Dr. Robinson (January 1917, 23:9).*

On 10 January 1935 Du Bois sent Robinson the requested essay from Atlanta University; for reasons unknown, however, it was never published.* The bibliographical notes Du Bois appended to this essay were abbreviated and uncorrected; they have been completed and corrected here.

The truth as to the mixture of races is difficult to study because of the opinions and desires of people and of their deep-seated prejudices. The leading European nations of today, being generally convinced of their superiority to other types of men, are opposed in theory to racial inter-mingling as tending to degrade their stock. Beneath this, and supporting the conviction, are decided economic advantages based on the use of colored labor as an exploited caste, held in place by imperial military and naval expansion.

When back of all this one seeks scientific reasons, the path is singularly difficult. First of all, there is the basic question: What is a race? Usually we think of three main races, but Blumenbach found 5, Agassiz 8, Huxley 11, Haeckel 12, Topinard 18, Crawford 60, and Gliddon 150.

The matter is not really of great importance. As Von Luschan says:

"The question of the number of human races has quite lost its raison d'etre, and has become a subject rather of philosophical speculation than of scientific research. It is of no more importance now to know how many human races there are than to know how many angels can dance on the point of a needle. Our aim now is to find out how ancient and primitive races developed from others, and how races have changed or evolved through migration and interbreeding..." (Professor Felix Von Luschan in "Anthropological View of Race," *Inter-Racial Problems,* 1911, pp. 16, 21, 22.)

Taking the conventional divisions of mankind into black, yellow and white, we can place no hard and fast dividing line between them. They fade insensibly into each other; and when we take into account other characteristics, such

---

* The correspondence with Robinson was in the papers Du Bois turned over to me in 1961, but a copy of the essay itself was not. Mr. Richard Newman, of the Garland Publishing Company, obtained this essay and very kindly supplied me with a copy.

as head-form, bony structure, hair form and bodily measurements, the confusion is almost complete. The inevitable conclusion is as Ratzel says: "There
is only one species of man, the variations are numerous, but do not go deep."
Deniker adds: "Where the genus homo is concerned, one can neither speak
of the species and variety nor the race in the sense usually contributed to
these others in zoology."

Broadly speaking, we mean by Race today, not a clearly defined and scientifically measured group, but rather "a great division of mankind, the members
of which, though individually varying, are characterized as a group by a
certain combination of morphological and metrical features, principally
non-adaptive, which have been derived from their common descent." (p. 397.
Hooton, *Up from the Ape.*)

It is conceded that the present main races and their numerous subdivisions
also often called races, arose from the intermingling of more primitive groups.
Reuter says:

". . . Ever since the existing human species diverged into its four or five
existing varieties or sub-species, there has been a constant opposite movement
at work to unify the type. Whites have returned southwards and mingled
with Australoids, Australoids have united with Negroids, and produced
Melanesians, and Papuans; and these, again, have mixed with proto-Caucasians
or with Mongols to form the Polynesian. The earliest types of white man
have mingled with the primitive Mongol, or directly with the primitive
Negro. There is an ancient Negroid strain underlying the populations of
Southern and Western France, Italy, Sicily, Corsica, Sardinia, Spain, Portugal,
Ireland, Wales and Scotland. Evidences of the former existence of those
negroid people are not only to be found in the features of their mixed
descendants at the present day, but the fact is attested by skulls, skeletons,
and works of art of more or less great antiquity in France, Italy, etc. . . .
There are few Negro peoples at the present day—perhaps only the Bushmen,
the Congo-Pigmies, and a few tribes of forest Negroes—which can be said
to be without more or less trace of ancient white inter-mixture." (p. 15,
The Mulatto in the United States, Reuter.)

The modern problem of race intermixture arises when the intermingling
of racial groups as they are at present constituted, is considered. These groups
are in no case pure races. They have been built up through indiscriminate
inter-breeding throughout past ages, and as Haddon says: "A racial type is
after all but an artificial concept." Whatever the origin of these races may be,
nevertheless today mankind is obviously divided into various groups widely
different in appearance and degree of culture. How far are these group at
present intermingling, what is the future of such cross-breeding, and what
will be the physical and cultural results? First, it must be remembered that
even at present racial types are not static but are growing and developing
entities.

Modern Italians, Frenchmen, Englishmen and Germans are composites of the broken fragments of different racial groups or sub-groups. Interbreeding has broken up ancient races and interaction and imitation have created types with uniformities in manners, languages and behavior. World-wide communication has tended to miscegenation on a broad scale.

What has been the result in modern times? Can we look upon this intermingling as the unfortunate meeting of superior and inferior stocks? Von Luschan, as quoted above, says:

"Fair and dark races, long and short-haired, intelligent and primitive, all come from one stock. Favorable circumstances and surroundings, especially a good environment, a favorable geographical population, trade and traffic, cause one group to advance more quickly than another, while some groups have remained in a very primitive state of development; but all are adapted to their surroundings according to the law of the survival of the fittest. One type may be more refined, another type may be coarser, but if both are thorough-bred, or what we call good types, however they may differ, one is not necessarily inferior to the other."

This question of innate racial differences is a difficult one. Ratzel says:

"It may be safely asserted that the study of comparative ethnology in recent years has tended to diminish the weight of traditionally accepted views of anthropologists, as to racial distinctions, and that in any case, they afford no support to the view which sees in the so-called lower races of mankind a transition stage from beast to man."

Spiller says: "It is not legitimate to argue from differences in physical characteristics to differences in mental characteristics. The physical and mental characteristics in a particular race are not either permanent or modifiable only through ages of environmental pressure, but rather marked changes in education, public sentiment, and general environment, even apart from inter-marriage, materially transform physical and mental characteristics in a generation or two. The status of a race at any particular moment or time offers no index to its innate and inherited capacities. It is important to recognize that civilizations are meteoric in nature, bursting out of obscurity only to plunge back into it. . . ." (*Inter-Racial Problems*, G. Spiller, pp. 35, 36, 38.)

Boas, speaking particularly of the alleged inferiority of Negroes, says:

"An unbiased estimate of the anthropological evidence so far brought forward does not permit us to countenance the belief in a racial inferiority which would unfit an individual of the Negro race to take his part in modern civilization. We do not know of any demand made on the human body or mind in modern life that anatomical or ethnological evidence would prove to be beyond the powers of the Negro . . .

"In short, there is every reason to believe that the Negro, when given facility and opportunity, will be perfectly able to fulfill the duties of citizenship as well as his white neighbor. It may be that he will not produce as many great men as the white race, and that his average achievement will not quite reach the level of the average achievement of the white race; but there will be endless numbers who will be able to out run their white competitors, and who will do better than the defectives who we permit to drag down and to retard the healthy children of our public schools." (Franz Boas, *The Mind of Primitive Man*, pp. 272, 273.)

Scientific opinion at present tends to admit that the Negro is not inferior in any essential character of mind; and is approximately equal to other races in his ability to acquire culture.

Hankins almost alone of current anthropologists tries to prove that physical differences must mean mental differences. But even he acknowledges that racial differences are of degree and not of kind, and that races may be inferior to others, in some respects, and superior in other respects. (E. H. Hankins, *The Racial Basis of Civilization*, p. 322.)

The average reader, particularly since the advent of Hitler, will be tempted to agree with Hooton:

"So much nonsense has been talked about 'race' that many pessimists are inclined to regard it as little more than a slogan of mass snobbery bellowed by propagandists or piped by anemic pleaders for an aristocratic regime long obsolete and vanished." (Hooton, *Up From the Ape*, p. 501.)

What has been the cultural result of racial intermingling? The effect of the growth of national consciousness and imperial rivalries has been an attempt to prove that all modern culture derives from an Aryan or Nordic race and that degeneration and relapses from cultural standards have been the result of racial mixture. This theory was first stated in its extreme form by Count Joseph A. Gobineau in the middle of the 19th century; and his thesis has been expanded and continued by H. S. Chamberlain in Germany, and Grant, Gould, Stoddard and McDougall in America. Recently, the theory has received singular emphasis on the part of Hitler and his Nazis.

Historical criticism, however, and anthropological research, do not support this thesis. It has been shown, for instance, that race mixture among the Romans was more frequent in earlier Roman history than later, and that Nordics like the golden-haired Commodus and the blue-eyed Nero were much more despicable than Trajan and Hadrian, whose descent was doubtful. The decline of Rome was certainly social and economic, rather than racial. Indeed, it is a tenable thesis to declare with Schneider, that at least some race mixture is a prerequisite to the greatest cultural development. Egypt, Babylon, and all Western Asia show great race mixture. Mayo-Smith says "that there has never been a state whose population was not made of heterogeneous ethnical elements," and Von Luschan says:

"We all know that a certain mixture of blood has always been of great advantage to a nation. England, France and Germany are equally distinguished for the great variety of their racial elements. In the case of Italy, we know that in ancient times and at the Renaissance Northern 'Barbarians' were the leaven in the great advance of art and civilization; and even Slavic immigration has certainly not been without effect on this movement."

In Spain, there was great mixture of blood: Venetians, Carthaginians, Romans, Visigoths, Vandals, Jews, Arabs and Moors. With the Moors came a considerable infusion of Negro blood. The mixture of Danes and Eskimos has made a superior race of mixed bloods. The population of South America is composed of Indians, whites and Negroes with a large class of persons of mixed blood from all three elements in varying proportions.

Lacerdo says of the half-breeds of Brazil that they have given birth down to our time to poets, painters, sculptors, distinguished musicians, magistrates, lawyers, eloquent orators, remarkable writers, medical men and engineers, who have been unrivaled in their technical skill and professional ability.

"The co-operation of the mulattoes in the advance of Brazil is notorious and far from inconsiderable. They played the chief part during many years in Brazil in the campaign for the abolition of slavery. I could quote celebrated names of more than one of these mulattoes who put themselves at the head of the literary movement....

"It was owing to their support that the Republic was erected on the ruins of the empire." (p. 381. *Inter-Racial Problems*, G. Spiller.)

In modern European history there have been many instances of distinguished mulattoes, such as Pushkin of Russia, and the Dumas of France. Also, among the mixed European Asiatic group in India and Java, there have been several artists and men of distinction.

While the general effect of inter-mixture of blood is fairly manifest, and exceptional mulattoes and other mixed bloods are well-known, there is little in the line of actual scientific study and measurement of mixed-bloods upon which to base conclusions. Von Luschan says: "We are especially ignorant as to the moral and intellectual qualities of half-castes."

There have been few thorough-going studies of mulatto groups. Two outstanding studies are by Professor Eugen Fischer and Carolyn Bond Day. The study by Fischer is of the Rehoboth community of south-west Africa (*Die Rehobother Bastards und das Bastardierungsproblem bein Menschen*, Jena, 1913). This consists of the descendants, some 150 in number, through five or more generations, of the hybrid offspring of a group of trek Boers and Hottentot women, and includes the offspring of a number of unions with members of the parent races.

Professor Fischer finds these people "a strong, healthy and fruitful people, taller than either parent race, i.e., they show a common indication of hybrid vigour. Physically there is no predominance of heritage from either race, but the inheritance of facial characters and colour is described as alternate, and in spite of the three groups there is no special tendency for the inheritance of facial characters and colour is described as alternate. Psychologically, the most important observation is that the Hottentot mentality predominates; there is neither European energy nor steadfastness of will."

Carolyn Bond Day's excellent study of 2,537 mulattoes shows a healthy, moral and virile group, fully a part of their modern cultural environment. The Editor, E. A. Hooton, says: "I cannot see that these data afford any comfort to those who contend that miscegenation between Negroes and whites produces anthropologically inferior types." There is no adequate study of crime, disease and delinquency among any large group of mixed bloods.

The bitterest protest and deepest resentment in the matter of inter-breeding has arisen from the fact that the same white race which today resents race mixture in theory has been chiefly responsible for the systematic misuse and degradation of darker women the world over, and has literally fathered millions of half-castes in Asia, Africa and America. At the same time, whites have stigmatized and sneered at their own children, and in most cases, refused to recognize or support them; nor has this system been wholly the sexual incontinence of the dreg of white society which so often represents the advanced nations in their contact with backward nations. In a large number of instances, the best blood of the upper-class whites has been also widely represented.

Today, the moral and physical problems of race mixture are tense and of present interest chiefly in Germany, South Africa and the United States. In West Africa, the West Indies and South America, the racial mixture which is going on does not disturb the community and is not, therefore, a social problem. In Germany, Hitler's renaissance of anti-Semitism is simply a part of the general resentment and suffering in Germany because of the results of the war, and of the Treaty of Versailles. Of the great gift made by Jews to German culture during the last thousand years, there can be absolutely no dispute. On the other hand, it is also indisputable that present economic rivalry and racial jealousy give Hitler and his followers a whip today to drive the German people into clannish and cruel opposition to their Jewish fellow citizens.

In South Africa, the intermingling of races went on until the ascendency of the Boers stiffened racial solidarity and built a wall against the advance of the natives. The colored group in Cape Colony and Southwest Africa form an isolated and suppressed mass without full political freedom or fair economic opportunity.

In the United States, the question of racial inter-mixture is one that has caused the most intense feeling and controversy. And yet, singularly enough, it has been given a minimum of scientific study. Franz Boas says:

"I think we have reason to be ashamed to confess that the scientific study of these questions has never received the support either of our government or of any of our great scientific institutions, and it is hard to understand why we are so indifferent toward a question which is of paramount importance to the welfare of our nation. The anatomy of the American Negro is not well-known; and, notwithstanding the oft-repeated assertions regarding the hereditary inferiority of the mulatto, we know hardly anything on this subject. If his vitality is lower than that of the full-blooded Negro, this may be as much due to social causes as to hereditary causes. Owing to the very large number of mulattoes in our country, it would not be a difficult matter to investigate the biological aspects of this question thoroughly. The importance of researches on this subject cannot be too strongly urged, since the desirability or undesirability of race-mixture should be known. Looking into a distant future, it seems reasonably certain that with the increasing mobility of the Negro, the number of full-bloods will rapidly decrease; and since there is no introduction of new Negro blood, there cannot be the slightest doubt that the ultimate effect of the contact between the two races must necessarily be a continued increase of the amount of white blood in the Negro community." (Franz Boas, *The Mind of Primitive Man*, pp. 274, 275.)

As is usual in such cases, the greater our ignorance of the facts the more intense has been the dogmatism of the discussion. Indeed, the question of the extent to which whites and blacks in the United States have mingled their blood, and the results of this inter-mingling, past, present and future, is, in many respects, the crux of the so-called Negro problem in the United States. In the last analysis most thinking Americans do not hate Negroes or wish to retard their advance. They are glad that slavery has disappeared; but their hesitation now is to how far complete social freedom and full economic opportunity for Negroes is going to result in such racial amalgamation as to make America octoroon in blood. It is the real fear of this result and inherited resentment at its very possibility that keeps the race problem in America so terribly alive.

This, instead of encouraging scientific study of the facts of miscegenation, hinders and makes it difficult. Men hasten to express their opinions on the subject without being willing to study the foundation upon which such opinions are based.

Historically, race mixture in the United States began far back in Colonial days. Many white women of the indentured servant class married slaves or free Negroes. Much confusion arose in the fixing of the legal status of the issue of such marriages and laws began to be passed forbidding the marriages largely because of their economic results. An indentured servant marrying a free Negro legally became free, and the child of a slave by a free white woman was according to American law also free. Travellers, like Branagan, and De Warville, cite several cases involving inter-marriage between Negroes and respectable white people. Bassett says that in North Carolina many of the free Negroes were children of white women by Negro men. On the other hand, the larger part of this inter-mingling naturally resulted from the association of slave owners with their female slaves. Then, as a free Negro and a mulatto class began to multiply, numbers of white men supported mistresses and raised families of mulatto children.

In some parts of the South, especially Louisiana, a type of polygamy arose in institutional form. Negro and mulatto girls became the mistresses of white men by regular arrangement. They were supported and families of mulatto children were reared. If the man married a white woman, the colored mistresses were sometimes deserted. Often, but not always, without provision for their support. In many other cases, the white man supported both a white and a colored family, and two sets of children. The free mulatto girls, from families of wealth and culture, often contracted such unions. Besides this more regularized form, the keeping of Negro mistresses was common in the South.

The attempt to study the size and growth of the mulatto group through the United States Census has not been very successful. In 1930, no compilation was made and there were no figures before 1850. In four censuses, between 1850 and 1890, the mulatto population was counted. No count was made in 1880, and in 1900, the attempt was given up probably because the plan in 1890 to make a distinction between persons of different degrees of white and Negro blood was officially acknowledged to have been a failure. In all the census figures, the method of ascertaining the presence of Negro and white blood is left almost entirely to the judgment of the enumerator. The census of 1920 says:

"Considerable uncertainty necessarily attaches to the classification of Negroes as black and mulatto, since the accuracy of the distinction made depends largely upon the judgment and care employed by the enumerators. Moreover, the fact that the definition of the term 'mulatto' adopted at different censuses has not been entirely uniform doubtless affects the comparability of the figures in some degree. At the census of 1920 the instructions were to report as 'black' all full-blooded Negroes and as 'mulatto' all Negroes having some proportion of white blood. The instructions were substantially the same at the censuses of 1910 and 1870; but the term 'black' as employed in 1890 denoted all persons 'having three-fourths or more black blood,' other persons with any proportion of Negro blood being classed as 'mulattoes,' 'quadroons,' or 'octoroons.' In 1900 and in 1880, no classification of Negroes as black or mulatto was attempted, and at the censuses of 1860 and 1850 the terms 'black' and 'mulatto' appear not to have been defined."

With these explanations, the figures for mulattoes in the United States, according to the census, are as follows:

Continental United States Negro Population

Census Year	Total Negro	Black	Mulatto	Per cent Mulatto
1850	3,638,808	3,233,057	405,751	11.2
1860	4,441,830	3,853,467	588,363	13.2
1870	4,880,009	4,295,960	584,049	12.0

1890	7,488,676	6,337,980	1,132,060	15.2
1910	9,827,763	7,777,077	2,050,686	20.9
1920	10,463,131	8,802,577	1,660,554	15.9

These figures are of doubtful validity. There is, for instance, no reason to think that the mulatto population decreased by 400,000 between 1910 and 1920. I said in 1906: "From local studies in all parts of the United States, covering about 40,000 colored people, I found 17,000 blacks, 15,000 brown, and 6,000 yellow and lighter," and that "I was inclined to think from these specific studies and wide observation throughout the nation that at least one-third of the Negroes of the United States had recognizable traces of white blood." T. Thomas Fortune, earlier than this, estimated that not more than 4,000,000 of the 10,000,000 in the country were of (pure) Negro descent. These estimates have recently been supplemented by the studies of Herskovits. He says that:

"In the American Negro today, we find represented the three principal racial stocks of the world: African, Negroes, Caucasians from Northern and Western Europe, and Mongoloids; that is, American Indians from Southeastern North America and the Caribbean Islands.

"From groups studied at Howard University, in Harlem, New York City, and in a rural community in West Virginia," Herskovits concludes that:

Class	Number of Individuals	Percent of Total
Unmixed Negro	342	22.0%
Negro and Indian	97	6.3%
Negro and White	798	50.8%
Negro, White and Indian	314	20.9%

"When, therefore, we speak of American Negroes, we speak of an amalgam and not of Negro in its biological sense. The American Negro is forming a definite physical type with a variability as low as that of the populations from which it has been derived, and perhaps lower. They are a homogeneous population despite the fact that they are greatly mixed." (M. J. Herskovits, *The American Negro.*)

The census estimate of 85% pure Negro is not correct. There is a large infiltration of Indian blood in the Negro race, amounting, perhaps, to 29%. (M. J. Herskovits, *Anthropometry of the American Negro*, p. 279.)

No other careful studies of mulatto physique have been made, although Atlanta University (Publications No. 11) brought together much interesting data. Most American students have the curious habit of studying Negroes in America indiscriminately without reference to their blood mixture and calling the result a study of the Negro race. This method invalidates much of the anthropological and psychological data collected during the World

War. There were some efforts to distinguish between degrees of white blood but usually these were based crudely on mere skin color.

Assuming, then, that most recent measurements and tests of American Negroes are studies mainly of mulattoes with a minority of full-bloods, we have these results: The measurements of physique have been summarized by W. M. Cobb. He declares that the American Negro "is forming a type intermediate between the parent Negro, white and Indian stocks in those superficial traits which are differential race characters. . . .

"In fundamental bodily characters and developmental patterns, the American Negro is identical with other types of modern man." (W. M. Cobb, "The Physical Constitution of the American Negro.")

In the psychological tests, results are equally indeterminate. Strong, Phillips, Yerkes and Brigham, are sure that intelligence tests prove the inferiority of the Negro race, while Herskovits, Reuter, and Bagley disagree. Much depends on how the tests are given and by whom. Also, there has been some suppression of results. Louisville, Kentucky has never published her results of the intelligence tests for white and colored children. The charge comes from responsible circles that the results did not "come out right." One may fairly conclude with M. S. Viteles of the University of Pennsylvania:

"From among these varied conclusions it is possible for anyone interested in the problem of Negro-white differences to choose one which best suits his particular bias. The varied character of the findings themselves and the difficulties of interpretation suggest extreme caution in generalizing on differences between the Negro and the white." (p. 175. *The American Negro*)

With regard to the educational achievements of Negro and mulatto children, Charles H. Thompson of Howard University concludes:

"That the doctrine of an inherent mental inferiority of the Negro is a myth unfounded by the most logical interpretation of the scientific facts on the subject produced to date." (p. 208. *The American Negro*)

There long persisted a legend born of slave propaganda that people of mixed blood were less fertile than the parent stocks. Davenport and others declare that there is no support for this notion. There is no lack of fecundity in Negro-white crosses nor deficit viability. It is not generally true that hybrids between whites and blacks are relatively infertile. Some such hybrids show an especially high fecundity.

So much for our knowledge of the extent of race mixture in the United States, and of its physical results. Its social results are in violent dispute. As a matter of theory, McDougall does not believe in mixing widely different stocks, and makes the general statement that "the soul of the cross-bred is, it would seem, apt to be the scene of perpetual conflict of inharmonious tendencies." Hertz points out that this same argument was used against the inter-mingling of the blood of Roman patricians and plebeians; and of course the real conflict comes in the environment of the mulatto and not in his soul.

An illegitimate or even a legitimate child, uncared for and uneducated, in conflict with his surroundings and untrained by his parents, may easily become a degenerate criminal, torn by inner contradiction; but this does not probably arise from his blood and physical descent, but obviously from his environment.

In general, the achievement of American mulattoes has been outstanding, so much so that many writers, like Reuter, have declared that the whole extraordinary accomplishment of the Negro race in America has been due to its mulatto leadership. This is a palpable exaggeration, and overlooks leaders like Sojourner Truth, Dunbar, Roland Hayes and Robert Moton. But certainly the number of outstanding Americans of mulatto blood is considerable, including as it does Frederick Douglass, Booker Washington, Henry O. Tanner, the artist, and Charles W. Chesnutt, the writer.

The real problem of miscegenation in America is not a question of physical possibility. That has been proven by many centuries of inter-mingling. Nor is it a question of its possible cultural results in individual cases, since the mulattoes have not only produced a number of exceptional men, but have in many instances formed normal, progressive groups. Nor is there any doubt but that continued residence of white and black people together in this country over a sufficiently long term of years will inevitably result in complete absorption, unless strong reasons against it, in place of mere prejudice, are adduced. There is, however, a very grave problem as to how fast and under what conditions this amalgamation ought to take place, and equally it may be questioned if separate racial growth over a considerable time may not achieve better results than quick amalgamation. It is here that the nation needs the guidance of careful and unbiased scientific inquiry.

If a poor and ignorant group amalgamates with a large and more intelligent group, quickly and thoughtlessly, the results may easily be harmful. There will be prostitution and disease, much social disorganization, and the inevitable loss of many human values by both groups. The lower group will tend to lose its self-respect and possibility of self-determination in its eagerness to reach the standards of the higher group; and it may disappear as a separate and more or less despised entity. The higher group will tend to lower its standards, will exploit and degrade the lower group, and fall itself into crime and delinquency, because of the ease with which it can use the lower group. It will try to protect itself by caste regulations, and refuse the lower group protection for its women by anti-marriage laws, and in turn lose respect for its own legislation in its fear of the other group. All this will lead on to the dangers of lawless caste, race hatred, and war. On the other hand, if by encouraging mutual respect and evenhanded justice, the two races can possibly readjust their social levels until they attain essential equality in well-being and intelligence, then either amalgamation will take place gradually and quietly by mutual consent, or by equally peaceful methods the groups will seek separate careers or even separate dwelling places, either in the same or different lands.

BIBLIOGRAPHY

As has been said, any person with mind made up in regard to miscegenation can find a strong body of literature to support his belief whatever that belief may be. If one believes that miscegenation is wrong and harmful, one may base one's conclusions on these books:

Gobineau, Joseph Arthur de. *The Inequality of Human Races*. Translated from the French editions of 1853–55 by A. Collins. London: Heinemann, 1915.

Chamberlain, Houston Stewart. *The Foundations of the Nineteenth Century*. Translated from the German by John Lees. London and New York: John Lane, 1912.

Grant, Madison. *The Passing of the Great Race*. New York: Charles Scribner's Sons, 1916.

Gould, Charles W. *America: A Family Affair*. New York: Charles Scribner's Sons, 1920. Rev. ed., 1922.

McDougall, William. *The Group Mind: A Sketch of the Principles of Collective Psychology, with Some Attempt to Apply Them to the Interpretation of National Life and Character*. New York: G. P. Putnam's Sons, 1920.

Stoddard, Lothrop. *The Rising Tide of Color against White World-Supremacy*. New York: Charles Scribner's Sons, 1920.

Liberal anthropologists and students of race can be studied in the following books:

Haddon, Alfred Cort. *The Races of Man and Their Distribution*. New York: Frederick A. Stokes Co., 1910.

Sergi, Giuseppi. *The Mediterranean Race: A Study of the Origins of European Peoples*. 1901. Reprint. Atlantic Highlands, N.J.: Humanities Press, 1967.

Deniker, Joseph. *The Races of Man: An Outline of Anthropology and Ethnography*. London: Walter Scott Pub. Co., 1901.

Ratzel, Friedrich. *The History of Mankind*. Translated from the German by A. J. Butler. New York: Macmillan Co., 1896.

Fischer, Eugen. *Die Rehobother Bastards und das Bastardierungsproblem bein Menschen*. Jena: Gustav Fischer Verlag, 1913.

Seligman, C. G. "Anthropology." In *Encyclopaedia Britannica*, 14th ed. 2:41–50. 1929.

Hankins, Frank H. *The Racial Basis of Civilization: A Critique of the Nordic Doctrine*. New York: Alfred A. Knopf, 1931.

Reuter, Edward Byron. *The Mulatto in the United States; Including a Study of the Role of Mixed-Blood Races throughout the World*. Boston: R. G. Badger, 1918.

———. *Population Problems*. Philadelphia: J. B. Lippincott, 1923.

————.*The American Race Problem: A Study of the Negro.* New York: Thomas Y. Crowell Co., 1927.

Hooton, Earnest A. *Up from the Ape.* New York: Macmillan Co., 1931.

Davenport, Charles Benedict. *Heredity of Skin Color in Negro-White Crosses,* with appendix of field notes chiefly by Florence H. Danielson. Washington, D.C.: Carnegie Institution, 1913.

Viteles, M. S. "The Mental Status of the Negro." *Annals of the Academy of Political and Social Sciences* 140 (November 1928).

The following books will be deemed by some to be unusually favorable to the Negro race, and backward races in general.

Day, Caroline B. *A Study of Some Negro-White Families in the United States,* with foreword and notes by E. A. Hooton. Cambridge, Mass.: Peabody Museum of Harvard University, 1932.

Spiller, G., ed. *Papers on Inter-Racial Problems Communicated to the First Universal Races Congress, London, July 26–29, 1911.* London: P. S. King and Son; Boston: World's Peace Foundation, 1911. New ed., with introduction, by H. Aptheker. New York: Citadel Press, 1970. [Du Bois notes particularly the following contributions from this volume:]

Brajendranath Seal. "Meaning of Race, Tribe, Nation," pp. 1–13.
Felix von Luschan. "Anthropological View of Race," pp. 13–24.
Alfred Fouillée. "Race from the Sociological Standpoint," pp. 24–29.
Gustav Spiller. "The Problem of Race Equality," pp. 29–39.
Earl Finch. "The Effects of Racial Miscegenation," pp. 108–12.
Jean Baptist de Lacerdo. "The *Metis,* or Half-Breeds of Brazil," pp. 377–82.

Herskovits, Melville J. *The American Negro: A Study in Racial Crossing.* New York: Alfred A. Knopf, 1928.

————. *The Anthropometry of the American Negro.* New York: Columbia University Press, 1930.

Finot, Jean, *Race Prejudice.* Translated from the French by Florence Wade-Evans. London: Archibald Constable Co., 1906.

Boas, Franz. *The Mind of Primitive Man.* New York: Macmillan Co., 1911.

Du Bois, W.E.B. *Health and Physique of the Negro-American.* Atlanta University Studies, no. 11. Atlanta, Ga., 1906.

Cobb, W. Montague. "The Physical Constitution of the American Negro." [Du Bois gives no date or other information concerning this article. It is likely that it was a then-unpublished paper by a well-known Black physician who was a friend of Du Bois's. Cobb had an article entitled "Physical Anthropology of the American Negro" published in the June 1942 issue of the *American Journal of Physical Anthropology* and one entitled "Physical Anthropology and the Negro in the Present Crisis" in the September 1942 *Journal of the National Medical Association* (34:181–87).]

1936

The Negro and Social Reconstruction (1936)

One of Du Bois's major unpublished works was prepared in response to a mimeographed request from Alain Locke, dated 1 February 1935, that Du Bois write on "Social Reconstruction and the Negro." The suggested length was about thirty-five thousand words, and the deadline was set as the end of May 1935. The proposed booklet was to be one in a series issued by Associates in Negro Folk Education, funded by the Carnegie Corporation and, later, by the Rosenwald Fund.

Du Bois agreed, submitted the manuscript on time, under the title "The Negro and Social Reconstruction," and was paid the stipulated sum of $240 ($40 was for secretarial help). Unusual delay followed; finally, in May 1936, an edited version of the manuscript reached Du Bois. It did not altogether please him. He noted that his arguments had been "toned down" but accepted some of the editorial suggestions and made a few corrections of his own. He returned the manuscript on 22 May 1936, stating, "It is now in the shape I would like to have it published."

Locke responded, in a letter dated 30 May 1936, "I can assure you of reasonably prompt printing now." He added, "The MS will be printed substantially as is" and suggested that Du Bois leave the proofreading to him. Locke did state that a section Du Bois called "Basic American Creed," upon which he had worked long and hard, was to be omitted, on the grounds that it was "direct propaganda." *

Du Bois left on a world tour of several months' duration in June 1936. While he was gone—and Locke knew he was gone—Locke wrote him (11 November 1936) that it had been decided not to publish his effort. Shortly after he returned Du Bois sent Locke a two-sentence letter, dated 4 February 1937, the heart of which was: "May I ask you to return my manuscript at your earliest convenience?"

●　●　●

If we examine the correspondence as a whole, the manuscript itself, and the other booklets in the series,† it is clear that the essential reason for the

---

* The exchange between Locke and Du Bois is in the *Correspondence*, 2:78–86. The "Basic American Creed" is in Du Bois's *Dusk of Dawn*, pp. 319–22.

† From 1936 to 1942 nine booklets were published in what was called the Bronze Booklet series. There were two by Locke on art, another by him on music, two by Sterling Brown on fiction and poetry and drama, one by Ralph Bunche (*A World View of Race*), one by Eric Williams on the Caribbean, one by Ira De A. Reid on education, and a final one by T. Arnold Hill, of the National Urban League, replacing Du Bois's work and called *The Negro and Economic Reconstruction*.

inordinate delay in handling this manuscript and the clumsy, not to say impolite, manner of its rejection (after it had been paid for) was the feeling that Du Bois's views were too radical, too challenging, too unusual.

These views, and Du Bois's insistence on fighting for them, basically explain his leaving the NAACP *in 1934. Du Bois expounded his attitudes briefly in the* Crisis *during his closing months as its editor, and elaborated them in an essay in* Current History *entitled by the editors "A Negro Nation within the Nation" (June 1935, 42:265–70). But the fullest exposition of his views are in "The Negro and Social Reconstruction," published herewith as he himself approved it in 1936. The List of Works Cited has been added for the convenience of the reader.*

INTRODUCTION

In considering the problem of industrial depression and unemployment, it is natural to think of the Negro population of the United States simply as one part of the problem according to its numbers. Further thought, however, will modify this. First of all, because this population of twelve millions is but two generations removed from chattel slavery, it naturally has a greater percentage of poverty, dependency and delinquency and impaired physical health. This would immediately make the problem of relief and economic salvation more difficult in its case. The situation is further complicated by the fact that this portion of the American population has never been considered as an integral part of the nation, neither in industry nor in political and civil rights. Consequently, there is added to the economic problem a social problem of aims and ideals. If this part of our population is to be "restored" to prosperity, just what is the status to which it could be restored, or ought to be restored? What place should it be conceived of as able to occupy in the future United States, or permitted to occupy in accordance with public opinion?

These problems have always faced the American Negro in different guise, and it is the object of this booklet to consider by what special planning, past and present, the Negro and his friends have sought to gain for him an assured status in the United States.

CHAPTER I   VIOLENCE AND MIGRATION

The first effort to counteract violence is naturally violence in return, which means war, rebellion, or revolt. The Negro slave, seized in Africa between 1442 and the middle of the nineteenth century, fought for freedom against attacking black tribes or white slave raiders. The cost in life was very large and it was Stanley's estimate that for every slave actually captured by raiders four human beings were left lying dead in the villages.

Once captured and brought down to the coast, there was little chance for revolt on the slave ships, although some cases occurred.

Landed in the West Indies, the earliest slaves immediately sought to escape. "The Negroes were not docile like the Indians and were evidently considered as most dangerous people." (Helps, *Spanish Conquest*, Volume IV, page 372. Quoting from Ley.)

Energetic measures for curbing slave revolts took place from the earliest times. They consisted, first, in so mixing the Negroes on plantations by tribe and language that communication between them was difficult; by severe laws against conspiracy or attempts toward uprising; by subduing the war-like customs and freedom by hard, manual toil. The Christian religion was eventually used very successfully to induce submission and contentment.

The plan, therefore, to gain freedom through violence was pretty well curbed in the slaves that came to the American continent through the West Indian tutelage. Nevertheless, the plan of revolt was never wholly abandoned as is shown by the testimony of the slave codes. These codes were cruel and severe and give definite evidence that the American slaveholders were afraid of conspiracies among their slaves.

The actual revolts among American Negroes, from 1619 to 1863, were few in number, although there were a great many scares and rumors of conspiracies which spread panic for a time and then afterward were systematically minimized. The truth seems fairly clear, that every decade in the South there was some attempt somewhere of slaves to organize and escape their status by armed resistance, but the organization of the slave patrol held these attempts down to a few which were really dangerous. The slave patrol was an organization which included not simply the comparatively small numbers of slave-holders, but enlisted the interest of the mass of poor whites, so that actually the slaves were outnumbered by the whites, save in certain localities; and there it was possible to bring in wide outside assistance in a comparatively short time. Of course, all the arms and ammunition were in the hands of the whites. Moreover, the humanity of some slaveholders and the personal attachment of kind-hearted slaves, nearly always resulted in the betrayal of plots in order to save a particular white family.

A form of violence for the indirect purpose of achieving freedom by proving patriotism was the participation of Negroes in the various wars fought by the United States. Even in Colonial times, some Negro troops were used and it is well-known that the first violence of the Revolutionary War was led by a Negro, Crispus Attucks. A thousand or more Negroes fought on the colonial side during the war and several hundred among the British under Governor Dunmore. Negro sailors were prominent in the War of 1812.

What was really the largest and most successful slave revolt came at the

time of the Civil War when all the slaves in the vicinity of the invading armies
left the plantations and rushed to the army and eventually some 200,000
ex-slaves and Northern Negroes joined armies of the North, in addition to
a much larger number of laborers and servants. It was this revolt of the slaves
and the prospect of a much larger movement among the 4,000,000 other slaves,
which was the real cause of the sudden cessation of the war.

Long before the spasmodic efforts at revolt ended in armed slaves helping
to put down secession, other and more successful plans had been tried. Broadly
speaking, they involved the running away of individual slaves and of gangs
and, in the case of free Negroes, migration to Canada, the West and Southwest
and to Africa, and to other destinations overseas.

How large a number of slaves escaped, it is impossible to say. Judging from
the growth of the Negro population in the North and the complaints of the
slaveholders, it must have been considerable. There were at least 100,000 and
possibly 200,000 fugitives from slavery, representing a loss of at least $25,000,000
capital invested in slavery and perhaps twice that sum. This was the economic
loss that spurred secession.

The union of Negroes and Indians for resistance to the whites was long
feared in the United States. Negro slaves took refuge among the Indians in
Virginia in 1787 and about the same time began to escape among the Indians of
Carolina and Georgia. The two races intermarried, making return of the
fugitives difficult, as the Indians refused to surrender their Negro-Indian
children. After the Revolutionary War and the War of 1812, Americans
accused the British of conniving at the escape of Negroes by means of their
Indian allies.

Georgia from 1789 to 1813 accused the Creek Indians of encouraging the
running away of slaves. The Creeks were attacked by Andrew Jackson and
defeated in 1814, but in 1815, 1,000 Georgia Negroes took possession of the
former British fort and together with the Creeks threatened the South. The
Spanish refused to destroy the fort, but Jackson moved against it in 1816 and
wiped it out with great barbarity. Then came the so-called Seminole wars,
which were raids to secure fugitive slaves and drive out the Indians.

Gradually, as the slave controversy increased, the chains of the slaves were
drawn tighter and the free Negroes of the North found themselves in a more
precarious position. Plans for migration beyond the borders of the United
States began to mature. Indeed, from the earliest times, the thought that the
Negro population of the United States would eventually be repatriated in
Africa was widespread among whites and also among Negroes.

The Civil War stopped thoughts and plans for emigration for many years,
although there were small internal movements of freedmen from Carolina to
Florida, from the Gulf states to the Southwest and from Virginia to the South
in search of better working conditions and free land. When the Negroes
began to pour in on the Union Army, Abraham Lincoln proposed to carry

out his own long cherished plan of colonization. He consulted foreign countries and secured an appropriation of $100,000 from Congress in 1861 and a further appropriation of $500,000 in 1862. He favored compensated emancipation in the Border States on condition that the Negroes should move beyond the limits of the country.

It was not until the withdrawal of Federal troops in the South in 1876 that widespread plans of migration from the South to the North took place. There had been some migration of freedmen from the South immediately after the war, but the difficulty of getting work in the North and the prospect of greater freedom in the South held this to a minimum. The terrorism of the Ku Klux Klan and the forced disfranchisement of the Negroes in 1875 and 1876 led to widespread plans for migration into the West and particularly into Kansas.

Discussion and Reading

1. How could black Africa have defended itself against European slavetraders?
2. Did the slaves have a right to revolt?
3. Did the American Colonization Society want to send all Negroes to Africa?
4. Did the Negroes help win the Civil War?
   (Consult Helps' *Spanish Conquest*, Volume 4; Bryan Edwards' *History of the West Indies*, 4th Edition, Volume I, Appendix, and Volume 4; T. G. Steward, *The Haitian Revolution;* Du Bois, *Black Reconstruction.*)

Discussion Questions

What opposition did the Negro offer to his subjection to slavery—in Africa—in colonial America—in pre–Civil war days?

How was that opposition and defense broken down and off-set?

Was the Negro always submissive, and what was his attitude toward war —revolt—violence?

What outlets did American conditions allow the Negro for his desire for freedom and independence? Did the Negro have special motives and incentives for engaging in war and military service? How was this related to his own desire for freedom?

What was the Negro's war record, in the Revolutionary War, in the War of 1812, in the Civil War?

What effect did his direct and indirect participation in the Civil War have upon the outcome of the slave cause?

References

Edwards, Bryan. *History of the West Indies*—Volume 1.

Du Bois, W.E.B. *Black Reconstruction.*

Helps, Arthur. *The Spanish Conquest.*

Steward, T. G. *The Haitian Revolution.*

Woodson, C. G. *The Negro in Our History*, Chaps. II & III.

Woodson, C. G. *The Story of the Negro Retold*, Chap. II.

CHAPTER II   POLITICAL POWER

The Civil War sent through the Negro population a new thrill and vast hopes for emancipation and progress. These hopes were nourished by the promises held out to Negroes when they fought in the ranks and in labor for the Northern armies. They came to seeming fruition in the Reconstruction Legislation of 1867. Not until these gains were blasted by the reaction of 1876 did the Negro masses again take up their old weapon of migration to any great extent.

From 1867 to 1876 Negroes placed their whole hope of full emancipation and economic security upon their political power. This was of course putting the cart before the horse. Their political power could only have been permanently sustained by economic security—ownership of land, control of some capital and education. They sought education and began to get it through their establishment of the public school in the South. Thaddeus Stevens and Charles Sumner and others tried to give them peasant-proprietorship and they themselves sought this through legislation in South Carolina and elsewhere. But the power of the Southern landholders and capitalists hindered this and these efforts were reinforced by Northern capital; this economic combination ruined the political as well as the economic hopes of the Negroes.

Between 1876 and 1890, political power gradually dwindled until the Negroes were practically disfranchised and unrepresented in Congress, the state legislatures, city councils and the county administrations. In addition to this, their loss of political power went to increase the political power of Southern capital which established a vast "rotten borough" called the "Solid South," and threw the whole democratic balance of the nation out of gear.

Meantime, political organization, chiefly within the Republican Party, tried to restore the ballot, achieve legal defense and new civil enactments. The Republican Party of the various Southern states consisted during this period almost exclusively of Negroes, which meant that they had some right to share in and direct the distribution of Federal appointments to office. In the North, the support of the Negro voters helped to keep the Republicans in power for many years after the Civil War.

The annual conventions, therefore, of the Republican Party became centers of the fight for restoring Negro political and civil rights. In all the national conventions from 1876–1900, the Negro delegates from the South usually held the balance of power between contesting Republican candidates. But since they had back of them no effective voting population, men were able to secure the position of delegate by manipulation and bribery. For the most part, both colored and white delegates gradually came to be for sale to the highest bidder. Soon, the first solicitude of prospective candidates for the Republican nomination was to buy up the Southern delegates before the convention. Venal whites drifted into the party and controlled the Negroes; venal Negroes were easily induced to forget their higher mission in a scramble for money and place, and venal friends of candidates thus bought the presidential nomination. This bribery of Southern delegates at national conventions became an intolerable scandal and resulted not in any attempt to restore the ballot to the Negro masses, but rather in recognizing their disfranchisement by cutting down their representation in the councils of the Republican party; a situation which still obtains.

Co-incident with this has come a change in the party platforms. The Republican platforms from 1868 until 1900 invariably complained about the disfranchisement and civil disabilities of Negroes, but the party in Congress after 1896 made no attempt to follow up these provisions. In later years, less and less has been said about the Negro until lately only a perfunctory protest against lynching has been included in the party platform.

In the National Government for a long time, the Negro received important representation in the executive branch. Once Theodore Roosevelt was about to appoint a Negro as Treasurer of the United States, but was thwarted by the race prejudice of his Secretary of the Treasury. Collectors of Customs have been appointed in Charleston, New Orleans, and Atlanta in the earlier days, but no important Federal position has come to Negroes recently in those states. In Washington, the Registrar of the Treasury has usually been a colored man until quite recent times; and the Recorder of Deeds of the District of Columbia almost invariably. In recent administrations, it has been customary to appoint some prominent colored men as assistants in the District Attorney's office, and, under the New Deal, a number of advisory positions have been given to colored men of education and ability. One of the municipal judges of the District of Columbia is usually a Negro.

In 1900, it was claimed that there were 58 colored men in the higher Federal employ, including 11 in diplomatic and consular service and several Collectors and Postmasters. In the clerical service and the army, there were 15,868 Negroes. In 1912, 19,729 such positions were claimed, including 8,000 in the army and navy. In 1916 and 1924, the number of presidential appointments of Negroes decreased, but the colored Federal employees were reported to have increased to 51,882 in 1928. Most of these were in the Post Office Department. It was said that the Negroes, constituting 9.9% of the population in 1920, occupied slightly more than 9.1% of the positions in the Federal Executive Civil Service.

From 1871 to the present, 24 Negroes have sat in Congress, including 2 Senators. Most of these came during Reconstruction, but one Negro Congressman is still serving. In at least three other cases, there is no doubt but that colored men actually were elected to office, but were counted out.

In several Northern congressional districts, the Negro vote by 1924 had reached such a size that the possibility of a Negro representative was manifest. For this reason, the white congressmen from one district in Illinois and from one in St. Louis, became practically representatives of the Negro race and worked for such bills as the Negroes demanded, especially the anti-lynching bill. When Congressman Madden of the Chicago black belt died, a colored man, Oscar De Priest, was elected to succeed him in 1928 and re-elected in 1930 and 1932. He was defeated in 1934 by a colored Democrat named Mitchell, showing that the Democratic Party was compelled to take a colored candidate in order to defeat the Republicans. In 1928, in St. Louis, a colored candidate was defeated, but made a strong showing.

In the states, Negroes served in the legislature of Georgia until about 1910, but in most of the other Southern states they were eliminated by 1890. In the Northern states, they began to appear as members of the legislature about 1900. Illinois has usually 3 or 4 members of the Lower House and 1 colored Senator. There are usually one or two Negro members of the legislature in Kansas, Nebraska, Michigan, California, Missouri, Indiana, Ohio, Pennsylvania, West Virginia, New Jersey, and New York. Once or twice there have been members of the legislature in the New England states. Some of these legislators, like Harry Davis of Ohio, have made distinguished records. It was often said that had Davis been white, he would have been Speaker of the House.

There are no Negro municipal or local officials in the South, except a few notaries. In the North, there have been some important offices held. Chicago has had a Superior Court judge and there are 2 Superior Court judges in New York City. Massachusetts once had a judge and there have been colored police magistrates in several states. Some important commissionerships are held as in the Civil Service Commission and the Tax Commission in New York City and the Civil Service Commission of Cleveland, Ohio.

On the whole, however, while office holding by American Negroes has been creditable, it has been disappointing since it has mainly served to further the political, social, and economic position of a few individuals. They have seldom reached positions of real influence where they could take any decisive action to better the status of their people.

Finding that office-holding and affiliation with the Republican Party was disappointing in its results, the Negro lately attempted to divide his vote both for the President and for congressmen and members of the legislature so as to reward and punish friends and enemies. Negroes largely supported President Wilson in 1912 and he promised them "justice." A smaller number supported Cox and Davis in 1920 and 1924 and a larger number, Roosevelt in 1932. Negroes have also in considerable numbers supported the Socialists. The result of this split vote has been to give Negroes considerable influence in local municipal politics in certain cities like Boston, New York, and Chicago. Perhaps this municipal political power in the larger Northern cities is the greatest source of influence which remains to the Negro in politics, together with a considerable balance of power vote in the border states.

The greatest single triumph of Negro voters was the defeat of Parker of North Carolina for confirmation to the Supreme Court. He had been an opponent of Negro suffrage and was named by Hoover; but his record in regard to organized labor was bad and the influence of the labor vote and of the Negroes combined led to his failure to be confirmed.

The drive of Negroes for legislation through political power has had some measure of success. Appropriations for Howard University, for instance, were long limited and provided for by questionable legislative methods. In the 68th Congress, the appropriation was ruled out on the point of order and finally, in 1930, the legality of the appropriation was fixed by Act of Congress and Howard became assured of a Federal subsidy, with an initial appropriation of $1,249,000. The Federal appropriations for education have benefited the Negro, although he has been unsuccessful in his attempt to have them pro-rated according to his numbers in the population. The division has been left entirely to the states and has been notoriously unfair throughout the South.

In another direction, Negroes have succeeded in having laws defending their civil rights put on the statute books. The first case was the celebrated civil rights law of 1875 so long advocated by Charles Sumner, which was eventually emasculated by decisions of the Supreme Court in 1883 and 1913. State civil rights legislation guaranteeing the legal right of Negroes to service in public places have been enacted in 16 states since 1884:

Connecticut	1884 and 1905
Iowa	1884 and 1892
New Jersey	1884
Ohio	1884 and 1894
Colorado	1885
Indiana	1885
Illinois	1885
Michigan	1885
Minnesota	1885, 1897, and 1899
Nebraska	1885 and 1893
Rhode Island	1885
New York	1893, 1895, and 1913
Pennsylvania	1887 and 1935
Washington	1890
Wisconsin	1895
California	1897

A wave of "Jim-Crow" legislation, however, including disfranchisement and requiring separation in cars, street cars and education, swept over the South from 1890 to 1910 and Negroes could do little to oppose it. They did succeed, however, in confining separation in Maryland to local trains and to defeating separate car laws in Missouri and West Virginia.

On the other hand, the Negro has succeeded in some cases in keeping discriminatory legislation off the statute books. In 1913, after Wilson and the Democrats came to power and because of Jack Johnson's victory, a determined drive was made to spread laws against the intermarriage of Negroes and whites on the statute books of the Northern states. Anti-intermarriage bills were introduced in Congress and in California, Colorado, Illinois, Iowa, Kansas, Michigan, Nebraska, New York, Ohio, Pennsylvania, Washington, and Wisconsin. Only one passed when Nebraska strengthened an existing statute.

On the whole, however, the social and economic emancipation of the Negro race by means of the ballot has failed of any great success, but perhaps the failure has been no greater in the case of Negroes than it has in that of whites. It has simply made the fact more clear that without economic reconstruction political freedom and power is impossible.

Discussion and Reading

1. Could the Negro laborer have survived without the vote?
2. Which was of greater importance: the right to vote, or land ownership?
3. Was it fair to fight Southern corruption by cutting down the Negro vote in the Republican conventions?
4. Should Negroes hold office?
   (Consult Brawley, *Social History of the American Negro;* Woodson, *The Negro in Our History;* Merriam, *The Negro and the Nation.*

Discussion Questions

What were the main reasons for the loss of Civil Rights after they had been guaranteed to the Negro?

Can political freedom and power exist without some economic strength to support it?

Could the Negro laborer have held his gains during Reconstruction without the right to vote? Which was of greater importance; the right to vote or land ownership?

What measures did the Republican party take to protect Negro civil rights? At what time did the Republican party really desert the traditional policy of "protecting the Negro"? Was it fair to fight corruption in Southern politics by cutting down the Negro vote in the Republican conventions?

Did the Republican party desert its principles in acquiescing in the disfranchisement of the Negro? What was the effect on Southern political life and the effectiveness of democratic machinery?

What is the division of public opinion about the right of Negroes to hold public office? To what extent have Negroes held public office in American political life? Is that greater or less today than it has been in the past?

Reading References

Brawley, B. G.: *Social History of the American Negro.*

Merriam: *The Negro and the Nation.*

Woodson, C. G.: *The Negro in Our History*—Chaps. III & IV.

CHAPTER III   CAPITAL AND LABOR

During the sway of the Negro's plan of gaining full American citizenship by political power, and explaining and supplementing that effort from 1867 to 1930, came two other movements: one from 1896 to 1920 which sought firmly to integrate the American Negro into American industry as farmer, laborer, skilled artisan and capitalist; and the other movement from 1876 to 1930 which sought by agitation and legal defense to clear away race discrimination and allow untrammeled advance of black folk according to chance and ability. One plan was emancipation by labor power under capitalistic auspices and the other by appeal to legislation and democratic ideals.

Despite political power and legal defense and whatever might be accomplished by migration, it was evident from the first that economic power must underlie all efforts of the American Negro to establish himself. The fact was that the Negro was a poor and ignorant laborer, and his exploitation, which began in slavery, was not ended by emancipation. How, then, should he establish himself as an effective and decently paid laborer? The first clear and coherent plan to this end was presented by Booker T. Washington and enunciated in his celebrated speech at the Cotton States' Exposition, Atlanta, in 1895.

This occasion had been carefully planned before hand and was not at all a spontaneous event. William H. Baldwin, a young railroad executive and far-sighted industrial statesman, knew by personal experience Southern labor conditions. He was rapidly coming to the front, having been made President of the Long Island Railroad and slated for the presidency of the Pennsylvania System. He knew that Negro labor with proper training and treatment could be made effective and he and other industrialists also feared the new demands and growing organization of unionism among white craft laborers. As a firm believer in capitalistic exploitation, Baldwin thought that in the South there could be built up two laboring classes who would naturally supplement each other and together make for the economic development of the New South.

He wanted the black laborers trained in skilled industry. He wanted the white laborers well-paid, but curbed in their increasingly intolerant demand for a voice in industry. Here was the developing Negro race, increasing in intelligence, distressed by its partial deprivation of political power and civil rights and needing new incentives and practical ideals. Here, also, was an extraordinary man; a self-made Negro, trained at Hampton, who had been brought down to take charge of a small school in Alabama, started by a young colored woman named Davidson.

Mr. Washington was an opportunist, slow but keen-witted, with high ideals. He believed in political rights for people who could exercise them, but in the case of the Southern Negroes, he knew that the attitude of the white South was against their political activity and he, therefore, took the position that the Negro must first gain an industrial status before he could ask for the exercise of political rights. He knew that the Negro needed civil and social rights. No one suffered more than he from the existence of discrimination in schools, on the railroads, in hotels, and otherwise. But he believed that if the Negroes showed the people of the United States that they could advance despite discrimination, that the inherent justice in the nation would gradually extend to deserving Negroes the rights that they merited.

Above all, Mr. Washington had not the slightest doubt that the current organization of industry in the United States was normal and right; that capital was accumulated by thrift; that labor was rightfully bought and fed and that profits were rightly the result of buying the product of labor. He, therefore, proposed that the Negro take this path toward eventual equality, working hard and skillfully to earn a living, and beyond that to accumulate in the hands of the more thrifty and gifted individuals, enough capital to hire employees and make money. He expected that the black owners of property would thus gain recognition from other property-holders and gradually rise in the scale of society. As a first step toward this new capitalism, Washington especially stressed landholding, wide-spread peasant proprietorship and even large-scale farming among Negroes.

As a practical path toward these things, Mr. Washington's program included the giving up of political rights, at least temporarily; the giving up of agitation for civil rights; and the insistence upon training young Negroes for farming and industry through industrial schools and a vocational program of education. This plan, launched in 1895, and triumphant from that date until about 1910, was in reality an alliance with white capital and was rewarded by large contributions toward Negro education, especially to such schools as conformed to the Hampton and Tuskegee type. It was rightly regarded as a clever and far-sighted compromise which, if it would not solve, would at least peacefully postpone the solution of a baffling internal problem of race conflict. Mr. Washington, between 1900 and 1910, became one of the most popular men in America, in constant demand North and South, as a speaker, adviser

and referee. There resulted a new understanding between the leading elements
of the North and South with regard to the Negro. Agitation for voting was
frowned upon and skilled labor was encouraged. The Negro college, while
not entirely discouraged, was looked upon with some suspicion and careers for
Negro college graduates became difficult. To some extent, appointments and
opportunities of young Negroes were carefully censored and over a very
wide extent of [the] country referred for approval to Tuskegee.

As the white opinion of the land became unified behind Mr. Washington,
colored opinion began to become uneasy and suspicious. The best white
Southern opinion certainly supported Mr. Washington, but the politicians and
the rabble soon got out of hand. A wave of "Jim-Crow" legislation and
disfranchising bills swept over the South and border states from 1890 and
1910—at the very time when Negro political power and agitation had been
lulled to its lowest by the Washington compromise. Mississippi in 1890, South
Carolina in 1895, Louisiana in 1898, North Carolina in 1900, Alabama in 1901,
Virginia in 1902, Georgia in 1908, and Oklahoma in 1910 disfranchised Negroes
by adroitly drawn illiteracy and property tests.

The result of this was not on the whole encouraging. Evidently despite their
promises, the better white South could not protect the voteless Negro. Moreover, the attempt to set up a Negro labor class in rivalry to white laborers
led to increased race hatred and lawlessness in the South between white and
black labor. Separation of the races in travel had been made compulsory in
Tennessee, Florida, Mississippi, Texas, Kentucky, Georgia and Louisiana by
1891. It then paused, but a new wave of legislation began in 1898 and covered
South Carolina, North Carolina, Virginia, Maryland, and Oklahoma. Determined and repeated efforts were made in Missouri, West Virginia and
Delaware. Other laws and ordinances completed the program of racial caste
and convinced increasing numbers of Negroes that the only result of the
Washington compromise was going to be a permanent caste-system in the
United States acquiesced in and condoned by Negroes themselves.

In the North, results were no better. White labor inherited from before the
Civil War a fear of the competition of slave labor and of the competition of
the free blacks. They finally but grudgingly, encouraged them in separate
labor organizations and a Negro trade-union movement began and was headed
toward success when it became a part of the new political organization,
which swept the Negroes into Reconstruction.

After this, however, the craft unions began to exclude Negroes, but when
the new Knights of Labor were organized, earnest attempt was made to bring
the Negroes in. This, however, was stopped when the American Federation
of Labor, the organization of the skilled crafts, came into power in 1886. Most
of the constituent organizations excluded Negroes either openly or by secret
policy, so that the division between black and white labor gradually became
wider.

This triumph of the radical anti-Negro South, the continued prevalence of lynching and the anti-Negro labor policy in the North, greatly embarrassed Mr. Washington. He hated caste and lawlessness and wanted the best for his people, but he believed implicitly in his economic program and made the fatal mistake of trying to forestall criticism from Negroes and to disparage, if not to oppose Negro colleges. The result was an outburst of wrath and criticism led by the younger college-bred group which split the Negroes into two opposing camps.

Mr. Washington's work, however, was not all lost. It first was shown in the ownership of land. Negroes owned 97,458 farms in 1890. This number increased rapidly until it reached a total of 218,467 in 1910. Then forces over which Washington had no control manifested themselves and land ownership decreased to 181,016 in 1930, which meant a loss of at least 4,000,000 acres of land; and since 1930, nearly a million acres more have been lost. In other words, Negroes bought land just at the time when land ownership was losing its security, so that the Negro landholder was caught in the depression, which so overwhelmed the farmers of the world, that he could not by his unaided efforts hope to make economic improvement on Southern farms. The same difficulties in lesser degree faced the white farmer and the result was that the farm population moved to the city in large numbers and entered industry. Most of these migrants from country to city were white, but a large and increasing number were Negroes. Between 1910 and 1920, the center of the Negro population in the United States moved 19 miles North.

Negro farmers and farm laborers for this reason decreased from 56.6% to 36.7% of the working population from 1890 to 1930. On the other hand, Negroes in transportation, manufacturing and mechanical industries, and in business and clerical work, increased in the same period from 10.3% to 29.9%. But they did not become, as Washington had hoped, skilled workers and business leaders to any great extent. Manifestly, this was not merely the result of lack of skill or unwillingness to work. It was partly the result of race prejudice and partly a change in the whole industrial system of the nation and the age of which Booker Washington did not dream.

Discussion and Reading

1. Was Booker T. Washington's plan best for the Negro?
2. What was the real motive for Negro disfranchisement?
3. Does the future of the Negro lie on the farm?
   (Consult Washington, *Up From Slavery*; Du Bois, *Souls of Black Folk*; Johnson, *Negro in American Civilization*.)

Discussion Questions

What were the real motives back of Booker Washington's program for the Negro?

How did the Washington program serve the interests of the industrial capitalists? Was he in open collusion with capitalists or did he think that his plan was really in the best interests of Negroes?

What was Booker Washington's attitude toward segregation? toward voting? toward the necessity of cooperating with the better element in the South? toward Northern industry and philanthropy?

What were the practical effects of this program? Did Mr. Washington regret the set-backs?

Does the future of the Negro really lie, as he thought, in land-ownership, farming and trade labor? What handicaps have since developed along these lines in the path of the Negro's progress?

Reading References

Du Bois, W. E. B. *Souls of Black Folk.*

Johnson, Charles S. *The Negro in American Civilization.*

Nowlin, W. F. *The Negro in American National Politics.*

Washington, Booker T. *Up From Slavery.*

CHAPTER IV   AGITATION AND LEGAL DEFENSE

The disfranchisement of Negroes was clearly illegal and a nullification of the Civil War amendments. It therefore became after 1876 and down to our own day, a settled plan among Negroes to reassert their political power through systematic appeal on the basic questions of their legal status before the highest tribunals of the land. This was also buttressed by efforts at new legislation which would secure their civil rights. These efforts were carried on by individual action and group movements.

These groups and leaders were for the most part no clearer than Mr. Washington in their conception of fundamental economic forces and impending industrial changes. Essentially they were advocates of eighteenth century "laissez-faire" and "freedom" and traditional American free competition in work and wage but without a Color Line.

The earlier court cases which involved the interpretation of the war amendments were brought before the courts by officials or parties who had no particular interest in securing favorable decisions for Negroes. Thus, the Slaughter House cases of 1873 which emasculated the 14th Amendment; the decisions of 1876 which declared the Force Act of 1870 unconstitutional and denied the right of the Federal government to protect its own voters at the polls; and the decision of 1883 which destroyed the civil rights bill; all these cases were not brought by Negroes nor were the cases prepared primarily in their interest.

Unless now the Negro bestirred himself, a legal basis of color caste in constitutional law would be laid. Various conventions and organizations for protection of Negro rights had been held in the North before the Civil War; the conventions of 1830–1836 beginning in Philadelphia; national colored conventions which met in Troy, New York, in 1847, and in Cleveland, Ohio, in 1848; in Cincinnati in 1852. The movement culminated in a great meeting in Rochester, New York in 1853, which laid plans for industrial education and a National Negro Council. Here a dissenting group despairing of justice in the United States, called an Emigration Convention in 1854. In 1864, a National Convention of Colored Men was held in Syracuse, New York with Frederick Douglass as president.

Interest was now transferred to the South and the political and civil rights struggle there. It was not until after 1866 that the plan of national Negro organization was resumed, first, in the attempts to form a labor organization which resulted in national and state meetings from 1867 to 1871. A National Convention of Colored Men met in Louisville, Kentucky in 1883 and a National League was formed in Boston a little later.

In 1887, T. Thomas Fortune, editor of what is now the *New York Age*, issued an appeal for a national organization and repeated this in 1889. The so-called Afro-American League, afterward changed to Afro-American Council, met in Chicago with 21 states represented in January, 1890. J. C. Price was President and Mr. Fortune, Secretary. The League held another meeting in Tennessee and then died until Bishop Walters revived it in 1898. It met that year in September at Rochester and later in November in Washington.

The object of this organization was to investigate lynching, to test the constitutionality of discriminatory laws, to secure civil rights legislation, to promote migration from the South and to encourage organization. It met afterward annually for several years and practically died with a final meeting in St. Paul, Minnesota about 1900. Its weakness was that it consisted simply of an annual meeting without a continuous working organization. The result was that it did little more than meet, organize and pass resolutions.

In the year 1905, a new aspect came over the plans for American Negroes for social reconstruction. The new disfranchisement laws and the wave of discriminatory legislation, coupled with Mr. Washington's concessions, alarmed the colored people. Particularly the young colored college man began to fear the dictatorship of the Tuskegee machine and the difficulty of expressing even legitimate criticism. This opposition was crystalized by the jailing of Monroe Trotter in Boston for trying to heckle Mr. Washington during a speech at a colored church. This was going too far, and while Trotter was much more bitter and outspoken than was necessary, yet he did have a right to talk even though he criticized Mr. Washington. The result was that a call was issued in June, 1905, signed by 59 men from 17 states. In July 1905, 29 of these

men, representing 14 states, met at Niagara Falls and formed the Niagara
Movement. The movement grew and in 1906 held a significant meeting at
Harpers Ferry. The Manifesto which it sent out was plain and bitter:

> The men of the Niagara movement coming from the toil of the year's
> hard work and pausing a moment from the earning of their daily bread,
> turn toward the nation and again ask in the name of ten million the
> privilege of a hearing. In the past year the work of the Negro hater has
> flourished in the land. Step by step the defenders of the rights of American
> citizens have retreated. The work of stealing the black man's ballot has
> progressed and the fifty and more representatives of stolen votes still sit
> in the nation's capital. Discrimination in travel and public accommodation
> has spread so that some of our weaker brethren are actually afraid to
> thunder against color discrimination as such and are simply whispering
> for ordinary decencies...
>
> Against this the Niagara Movement eternally protests. We will not be
> satisfied to take one jot or tittle less than our full manhood rights. We
> claim for ourselves every single right that belongs to a freeborn American,
> political, civil, and social; and until we get these rights we will never cease
> to protest and assail the ears of America. The battle we wage is not for
> ourselves alone but for all true Americans. It is a fight for ideals lest this,
> our common fatherland, false to its founding, become in truth the land
> of the thief and the home of the Slave—a by-word and a hissing among
> the nations for its sounding pretentions and pitiful accomplishment...
>
> We do not believe in violence, neither in the despised violence of the
> raid nor the lauded violence of the soldier, nor the barbarous violence
> of the mob; but we do believe in John Brown, in that incarnate spirit of
> justice, that hatred of a lie, that willingness to sacrifice money, reputation
> and life itself on the altar of right. And here on the scene of John Brown's
> martyrdom we reconsecrate ourselves, our honor, our property to the
> final emancipation of the race which John Brown died to make free.

In 1907, the Niagara Movement developed organizational difficulties mainly
because Mr. Trotter, its guiding spirit, was not a good organizer, despite his
courage. The movement, moreover, met the opposition of influential white
opinion which at the time was backing Hampton and Tuskegee. A year later,
a lynching occurred at the home of Abraham Lincoln, and Wm. English
Walling and his wife, Anna Strunsky, visited the city. Walling wrote a fiery
article in *The Independent*, suggesting that something ought to be done to
finish the emancipation that Abraham Lincoln started. Mary White Ovington,
Oswald Garrison Villard, Charles Edward Russell and others suggested such
a conference to be held in New York on the hundredth anniversary of
Lincoln's birth. Thus the National Association for the Advancement of Colored
People was born. After this, the Niagara Movement held no further meetings.

There was no formal merger, but seven of its charter members became directors of the new organization. Thus out of the impulse of the Niagara Movement, the N.A.A.C.P. was formed and in November 1910 the *Crisis* first appeared as its organ.

> The National Association for the Advancement of Colored People seeks to uplift the colored men and women of this country by securing to them the full enjoyment of their rights as citizens, justice in all courts, and equality of opportunity everywhere. It favors and aims to aid, every kind of education among them save that which teaches special privileges or prerogative, class or caste. It recognizes the national character of the Negro problem and no sectionalism. It believes in the holding of the Constitution of the United States and its amendments, in the spirit of Abraham Lincoln. It upholds the doctrine of "all men up and no man down." It abhors Negro crime, but still more the conditions which breed crime, and most of all the crimes committed by mobs in the mockery of the law, by individuals in the name of the law.
>
> It believes that the scientific truths of the Negro problem must be available before the country can see its way wholly clear to right existing wrongs. It has no other belief than that the best way to uplift the colored man and best way to aid the white man to peace is social content; it has no other desire than exacting justice, and no other motive than patriotism. (First Annual Report, January 1, 1911.)

The work of the N.A.A.C.P. in the succeeding 25 years is well-known. Its greatest triumph has been in the field of legal defense of Negroes and Negro rights. With the help of the foremost legal talent of the nation, it has secured from the U.S. Supreme Court decisions which in principle establish:

1. Recognition of the validity of the 15th Amendment.
2. The unconstitutionality of the "Grandfather" clauses in Southern State constitutions.
3. The unconstitutionality of residential segregation laws and ordinances.
4. The right of Negroes to sit on juries.
5. The dictum that "due process of law" may be violated by the threat of mob violence.
6. The denial of the right of a state to segregate primary elections by race.

In addition, scores of individuals have been defended, and the most effective and sustained anti-lynching campaign in the history of the country has been carried out—though not yet to the successful passage of a Federal anti-lynching law.

Though the N.A.A.C.P. began through philanthropic aid from wealthy liberals, it became in its best years more and more of a Negro-supported effort.

Contrary to general opinion, the amount of money received from wealthy whites was small, and its withdrawal would have made little difference except at the start of the project. From 1912 to 1927 Negroes were making substantial advance along economic lines. It is no accident that Negro organization especially for self-improvement and defense was at its peak during that period. By 1928 the economic progress of the Negro was beginning to be slowed down by the depression. Philanthropic gifts to Negro education were lessened, the industrial rivalry of white and black labor increased and Negro organizations began to decline in strength as resources and revenues declined. The N.A.A.C.P. and *The Crisis* were no exception and faced declining income and support. This should not be interpreted as the Negro's unwillingness to fight discrimination and lynching. It was due primarily to the fact that the colored people, economically hard pressed, were unable to sustain the program financially, especially any needed expansion.

From 1910 until the depression, the N.A.A.C.P. was the most effective militant organization in Negro life and its success was unquestioned. Its history, however, laid bare two basic facts: first, white America, even though sympathizing somewhat with the difficulties and handicaps in the path of Negroes, was not ready to grant them anything like substantial equality; and secondly, the difficulties which faced the Negroes in the basic matter of earning a living were still so large and went so deep that the Negroes themselves did not have the power to make effective their demands for their rights.

Discussion and Reading

1. Was Booker T. Washington responsible for "Jim-Crow" legislation?
2. Why was not the Niagara movement more effective?
3. How far should the Negro seek freedom and equality through the courts? (Consult Donald Young, *American Minority Peoples*, Herbert Miller, *Races, Nations and Classes*, Stephenson, *Race Distinctions in American Law*.)

Discussion Questions

What started the Civil Rights movement among Negroes? Who were some of its leaders?

Did the civic and social treatment of the Negro improve or grow worse after 1874? What happened in 1877 to start a reaction?

What was back of disfranchisement and "Jim Crow" legislation in the South? How far did the movement spread and what forces checked it? Would it have gone further except for vigorous Negro agitation and resistance?

Was Booker T. Washington's program responsible for "Jim Crow" legislation? Did he approve of it?

Why was not the Niagara Movement more effective? What was the origin and the platform of the N.A.A.C.P.?

How far should the Negro rely on legal appeals and decisions in the fight for freedom and equality and civic justice? With what hope of success?

Reading References

Miller, H. A.: *Races, Nations and Classes.*

Skaggs: *The Southern Oligarchy.*

Stephenson: *Race Distinctions in American Law.*

Young, Donald: *American Minority Peoples.*

CHAPTER V [AND VI]   WORLD WAR AND DEPRESSION

The situation of the American Negro at the outbreak of the war seemed favorable. His higher schools were increasing in efficiency and the elementary school system in the South, while still bad, was improving. His political power, curtailed as it was, was increasing and beginning to be used with some intelligence in the North and in the Border States. Determined agitation was beginning to decrease noticeably the annual number of lynchings which had reached the astonishing total of 235 in 1892, and began now with some exceptions to fall below 75 a year.

The Negro press began to increase in efficiency and boldness. Negroes had taken prominent part in the great Races Congress held in London in 1911, and begun to visualize the problems of other groups. In the election of 1912, a considerable number of Negroes supported Wilson in an effort to divide the Negro vote and put the Democratic Party and the "Solid South" under obligations to the Northern Negro voter.

The outbreak of the World War did not at first greatly interest American Negroes. In 1914, 49 Negroes were lynched and the agitation to segregate Negroes in residential sections increased. Negro tenants were bombed in Philadelphia. A corporation was formed to segregate them in New York and the Smith-Lever Bill to assist education in the South went through without safeguards for Negro children. In North Carolina, a leading journal was offering prizes for essays on the segregation of Negroes on farms. In the 67th Congress, some 20 bills against Negroes were introduced and in September of 1915, the United States seized Haiti, the very year that Booker T. Washington died. There were 53 lynchings that year and the only favorable occurrence was the Supreme Court decision which overthrew the "Grandfather" clauses. St. Louis and Dallas, Texas, in 1916 decided to segregate Negroes. In May, a Negro was publicly burned in Waco, Texas, under circumstances of horrible brutality and in November, in South Carolina, a well-to-do Negro was publicly lynched for demanding the current price for his cotton.

In 1916, in the midst of a controversy between the Methodists as to whether or not they should get rid of Negroes in order to unite with the Methodist Church South, a migration of Negroes North began to take place. It was induced, first, because of an unusual demand for labor in the North due to the stopping of immigration by the World War. And, on the other hand, crop failures in the winter of 1915, together with the ravages of the boll weevil, decreased the demand for labor in the South. A mass of Negroes estimated between 250,000 and 500,000 for the year, began to move North.

In 1917, the United States entered the World War. During that year, a series of events exasperated the colored people. First, came riots and massacres: in July, the city of East St. Louis destroyed $400,000 worth of property, killed between 100 and 200 Negroes and drove 6,000 people out of their homes. In September, colored soldiers of the regular army and citizens broke out into a riot at Houston, Texas. In August, there was trouble at Chester, Pennsylvania and elsewhere on account of the invading Negro laborers.

The South began propaganda. They magnified the riots and bad conditions of labor; they stopped labor agents by requiring high priced licenses and they used violence in refusing to sell tickets and driving Negroes from railway stations.

Thus, when unexpectedly the United States was swept into the World War, a sudden crisis faced the American Negro. How far could a black man fight loyally for this country and why should he, in the face of disfranchisement and lynching? Persistent rumors of German propaganda among Negroes were flying here and there, perhaps with some small basis of fact, but little tangible result. It would be futile for Negroes to oppose the war and any suspicion of "disloyalty" on their part would be followed by increased discrimination and mob violence, visited particularly on their most helpless classes. On the other hand, there was in the very conduct of the war abundant chance to make this crisis in the national fortunes an occasion for bettering the Negro's condition. If, for instance, they were not included in the draft, this would be a denial of their American citizenship. If they could not be soldiers but only laborers, this would deny their manhood. If they could not be officers as well as soldiers, this would be an attack on their ability. The N.A.A.C.P. took leadership and fought for inclusion of Negroes in the draft and for volunteer Negro soldiers. Then the first difficulty came in the matter of officers for Negro troops.

The N.A.A.C.P. was immediately put in a curious dilemma. It had been agitating against all discrimination and it first asked for the admission of Negroes to officers' camps on the same terms as whites. This was peremptorily denied. Thereupon, the Chairman of the Association, abetted by some of the other officers, asked for a separate camp to train Negro officers and received in this plan the enthusiastic support of students of Howard University and other institutions. The result after some hesitation was that a camp was established at Fort Des Moines, Iowa and 700 Negro officers trained.

Then came further delay. According to the draft law, Negro and white troops were to be separated. Were these officers to lead Negro troops exclusively or were there to be white officers mixed with them? Were they to be in one division or interspersed among white troops? The final compromise, arranged with some hesitancy, was to form a division of Negro troops known as the 92nd Division with white field officers and Negro line officers. A second division, called the 93rd Division, was projected, but never actually functioned as a division.

Meantime, in the Draft, the difficulties of racial discrimination came up. In the South, despite widespread allegations that Negroes were physically inferior to whites and manifestly were poorer and more needed by their families, a larger percentage of Negroes were drafted than among whites. In the training of drafted troops there was a great deal of difficulty. In the North, single Negroes drafted, appearing in white camps, were refused or tossed about until they could be put in a Negro camp. In the Negro cantonments, especially those in the South, there was a great deal of discrimination and threats of mob violence. As the war wore on, much bitterness was aroused by the treatment of Negro troops in France, and the attitude of white officers toward black officers.

The government did considerable to counteract these difficulties. It called together the editors of the Negro press; it appointed a representative of the Negroes to consult with the Secretary of War. He had no power but he could bring things directly to the ears of the Secretary. There was even a plan to put one or more Negro officers in the Intelligence Service, but sudden caution stopped this. On the whole, however, the conduct of Negroes led mainly by the N.A.A.C.P. and other organizations, resulted in giving the Negro a better status during the war, with black officers over his troops and with some chance to show his prowess. It was, however, in his services as laborer that he did the greatest work in the war. His stevedore units made extraordinary records in the movements of goods and did brave work behind the lines.

These matters occupied the attention of Negro leaders, but beneath all this there were vast changes in the economic condition of Negroes to which they gave but passing notice. First came the northward migration. Before 1914, not more than 10,000 Negroes a year were going North because of the competition of foreign emigrants. The addition of emigrants from abroad each year for 10 years preceding the war was equal to the entire Negro population of the North and this fact made the Negroes unimportant to trade unions who kept them out. Since 1820, 36,000,000 European immigrants had come to the North and industries had absorbed this common labor. In 10 years, from 1900–1910, over 7,000,000 immigrants arrived. The World War brought sudden change. Immigration was checked and new industries established because of the demand of war. Later, legislation restricted immigration to a 3% quota and finally to a 2% quota based on the census of 1890. As a result, Italy, Austria, Hungary and Russia, which in 1910 were sending 600,000 a year, were reduced to less than 6,000.

Ira De A. Reid says:

> The demand for labor was high and the Negro was most available. Labor agents began to bring Negro workers into Northern industries in great numbers. Unskilled workers were especially in demand in the steel and iron industries and building construction, in the stock yards and for road maintenance and construction on railroads. In many cases, these men were brought in as strikebreakers and between 1915 and 1928, 1,200,000 Negroes came from the South to the North. Now for the first time, the Negro had to be considered in the problems of Northern capital and labor. The United States Department of Labor reported a 34% increase in skilled labor among Negroes and in some cases this increase went to 186%. In Pittsburgh, Negro steel and iron workers were 100 in 1910 and 16,900 in 23 plants in 1923. The Ford Automobile plant employed 11,000 Negro workers. Chicago employed Negroes in iron and steel and in the packing industries.

The first result was physical conflict. White workers threatened to quit if Negroes were employed and many did. Southern whites were imported to Northern mills as foremen. Many trade unions began to seek Negro members, but Negroes were not always willing to join. There was much discussion as to the efficiency of Negro labor. Came the bitter year, 1919.

> Serious mob outbreaks against Negroes and clashes between the races were reported from 26 cities. The most spectacular of these outbreaks and riots were those occurring in Washington, D.C.; Chicago; Omaha, Nebraska; Knoxville, Tennessee (the latter two were in reality attempts at lynching which precipitated the race riots which followed); Longview, Texas (also an outgrowth of a lynching); and the widely heralded "uprising against whites" at Elaine, Phillips County, Arkansas. Serious riots occurred also at Charleston, S.C.; Norfolk, Va.; Philadelphia and Bisbee, Arizona.
>
> Six persons were killed outright in the Washington riots, from July 19 to July 23. These riots were begun and carried on by uniformed soldiers and sailors. Fifty persons were seriously injured and a hundred or more less seriously wounded. Order was restored only by the intervention of United States troops. (*Tenth Annual Report* of the National Association for the Advancement of Colored People, 1919, p. 34.)

During the war, union labor was triumphant. The President of the American Federation of Labor was on the Council of Defense and the War Labor Board. He pledged the co-operation of the unions to win the war. While, on the one hand, the unions promised not to strike, on the other hand, the government gave recognition to collective bargaining, the 8-hour day and a high standard of living. Union membership increased between 1917 and 1920 by almost 2,000,000.

Union labor had not welcomed Negro workers since the collapse of the Knights of Labor. The new American Federation of Labor passed through this evolution: in 1881, it declared "the working people must unite and organize irrespective of creed, color, sex, nationality or politics." This was re-affirmed in 1897, after opposition; but in 1902, it was voted that separate charters might be issued to Central Labor Unions, local unions or Federal Labor Unions composed exclusively of colored members. This, in fact, recognized the legality of excluding Negroes from local unions and City Central Labor bodies.

From 1910–1914, the Federation allowed organizations which excluded Negroes to affiliate with them, but hired three Negro organizers and proceeded to organize separate local and Federal unions. When Negro workers in the North began to increase between 1916–1920, the matter of organizing was pushed in the conventions of the A.F. of L., but no machinery was provided. As a result of all this, the A.F. of L. had before the depression less power and influence among the Negro group than it did at any other time.

Most Negro union members are in the Hod-Carriers' Union, the carpenters, the bricklayers and masons, the plasterers, the longshoremen, the international seamen, the United Mine Workers and the Ladies' Garment Workers. Reid reports 3,523 Negro members in American trade unions in 1890; 32,769 in 1900; 57,662 in 1910; 61,032 in 1926–1928. To this last number, if we add independent Negro unions and organized Negro workers, the total would be 81,658. Reid says: "Today 24 national unions exclude us from their ranks and proscribe us in our employment."

Monroe N. Work shows that the World War sharply divides Negro population trends. In the period before the World War, the trend of the Negro population was determined mainly by the demand in the South for labor in the production of staple crops. In the period since the World War and up to the present depression, the trend of Negro population has been mainly determined by demands by industry for Negro labor, particularly in the North.

As a result of this, the black belt areas—that is, counties in which half or more of the population was Negroes—increased from 244 in 1860 to 300 in 1880 and then decreased to 189 in 1930. With this has come an extraordinary urbanization of population; 80% of the Negro population was rural in 1890; 73% in 1910 and only 56% in 1930. In nine main metropolitan regions in the North, over 2,000,000 Negroes were living; 1,500,000 more in metropolitan districts of the South. In occupation, the change has been great. During slavery, the Negro was chiefly engaged in agriculture and in domestic and personal service. As late as 1890, of the Negro population 10 years of age and over,

56% were in agriculture and 31.2% in domestic and personal service. On the other hand, in 1930, 36.7% were in agriculture, 28.6% in domestic and personal service, 29.2% in manufacturing and mechanical industries and trade and transportation.

This indicates almost an economic revolution. The most striking changes are the decrease of the farmers and servants, the increase of those in the professions, trade, transportation, manufacturing and in mechanical industries. If we take up the manufacturing and mechanical industries, we find that the increase in building trades from 1890–1930 was over 500% and the cloth and allied industries 270%. The food and allied industries 473%, lumber and furniture industries, 418%, and the metal industry over 1,000%.

The building trades and the metal industries showed the largest relative increase. The increased effort to earn is shown by the percentage of population 10 years of age and over who are gainfully occupied. For the entire population of the United States this percentage changed but slightly between 1890–1930. For the Negroes, it increased from 57.6% to 59.2%.

When the war was over, the government largely withdrew its support of labor. There were a number of strikes and employers began to push for the open shop. They began to undermine the labor unions by company unions, stock sales to employees and profit-sharing. In the steel and coal strikes, public opinion upheld the steel trust and the failure to organize Negroes in the industry helped to break the strike. In the coal strike, court injunctions were used to break down the resistance of labor although in this strike numbers of Negroes were members of the unions. By 1923, therefore, labor had lost most of its war gains.

Rising business prosperity, due to an extraordinary profits psychology, took place, which swept up to 1929, but labor did not gain equally. Even at the peak of prosperity, there were many workers who had lost their jobs because of new machinery and efficiency schemes. Membership in the unions declined and almost disappeared in the steel and automobile industry and the textile industry. The miners' union was torn with internal strife. Then came the depression with its vast unemployment, reduction of wages and of standards of living. Masses of men were competing for the few jobs that remained.

Certain basic difficulties had appeared before the war. The machine in the great industries, like coal, petroleum, steel, textiles, automobiles and railroads which are the chief industries of America, was replacing human labor, not only skilled labor, but even that of digging and lifting. The coal industry was collapsing from waste, exploitation and competition. The oil wells were run largely by machines. The automobile industry, especially the Ford plant, began to use Negro labor and Negroes got into the steel mills, both South and North, as semi-skilled and skilled laborers. But the Southern textile industry was practically monopolized by whites, a part of the tacit understanding which was one of the earliest results of the Booker Washington compromise.

Occasionally the struggle against Negro labor took the form of intimidation and, in some cases, of actual violence. The most notable recent illustration was a series of assassinations of Negro locomotive firemen in Mississippi and Louisiana, evidently with the purpose of running all Negro trainmen off their jobs. Idleness on the part of both races has been conducive to unrest, ill temper, crimes against property and other irritating conditions. Certain efforts to lead Negroes to revolutionary violence have fomented mutual distrust, fear and potential hostility and have developed a number of threatening situations.

From the time of Emancipation down until the World War, the Negro had a monopoly on certain jobs in the South that were poorly paid and involved menial service. As Alexander says, it used to be true that "A Southern white man will curry a mule but he will not brush a gentleman's coat. He will drive an ox wagon, but he will not act as coachman." These so-called Negro jobs were the jobs of servants and laborers, but they were fairly permanent and the workers received certain perquisites in food, in clothes and had personal relations with employers that gave them a degree of legal and social protection. The money which built homes and churches for Negroes, educated Negro children and saved sums for capital investment, came largely out of this wage.

Gradually, however, toward the time of the World War and markedly thereafter, this situation changed. In most Southern hotels, the sons of poor whites are today the bell boys and their daughters the waitresses. This class has pressed into the cities and competes with the Negro as a porter, a garbage mover, a newsboy, and a day laborer. It became more and more definitely believed that no Negro should have a job as long as a white man was unemployed and the division of labor by race almost completely disappeared.

The white laboring class in the South was competing for Negro jobs and pushing Negroes from nearly all lines of work, except farming and domestic service. There was severe competition in agriculture and Negro migration to cities was holding down wages and increasing the opposition of white labor.

On the other hand, the change in industrial techniques, the widespread use of machines and mass production, made the effort of the industrial schools to train skilled labor among Negroes extremely difficult, while the situation of the farmer, both white and black, in the presence of new problems of labor, machinery and markets, made the advance of the Negro farmer almost impossible. It was thus that by the time of the World War, the Washington program for the economic emancipation of the Negro had met insuperable difficulties. The small black capitalist or capable college graduate found no place or welcome to the vast machine which controlled capital and credit and directed industry. He could only hover on this fringe of exploitation which the whites neglected, using color discrimination as a sort of protective tariff for his lack of capital and training.

In the South, white organizations, like the Blue Shirts of Jacksonville, Florida, the "Black Shirts of Alabama," and the revived Ku Klux Klan and "Sons of Justice" of Georgia, tried to drive Negroes out of jobs.

A basic difficulty which Negroes encountered was impossibility of promotion to any positions of authority or supervision and the practical impossibility of technically trained Negroes in the higher lines of engineering getting any work. The engineering schools themselves discouraged Negroes from taking the courses because of this. In business, Negroes made repeated efforts, but there again the great concentration of capital and credit, the severe competition brought by chain stores and similar enterprises, the tremendous cost of advertising, was the undoing of most Negro enterprises. Taking advantage of the discrimination against Negro risks, several large Negro insurance companies were started, but the depression brought the failure of two of the largest and while the others are maintaining themselves and in some cases, with considerable success, they are more or less at the mercy of white investment concerns. Twenty-one Negro companies had in force in 1930 policies aggregating $260,000,000 and assets amounting to $18,445,000.

These difficulties were particularly illustrated in the case of the banks; the Binga Bank of Chicago was a strong institution, but when the pressure came, it was among the 200 small banks which the larger banks of Chicago crushed and it was more easy to sweep away this colored bank than most of the white banks. An effort was made to start a Negro chain of grocery stores, but it began at a time when it had to depend upon wholesale dealers who were themselves being pushed to the wall by the larger chains. It was impossible during the depression for this Colored Merchants Association chain to break through this cordon of competition.

In education, Negro colleges increased in number and stability. In ten years, the enrollment had increased from 5,000 to 20,000, and the total income of these colleges was in 1931, $9,317,764. On the other hand, the public schools and high schools which were the basis of this pyramid, are not strong. Rural schools have been closed or cut seriously. The crass discrimination in teachers' wages and buildings and equipments as between whites and blacks has continued and even widened.

The whole economic situation of American Negroes has, thus, been greatly complicated by the present depression. In almost every city in the country, the rate of unemployment and the amount of dependency among Negroes has, for the past three years, been greater than among white people. This has meant the loss of homes, disappearance of savings, bankruptcy of Negro business and further handicaps all along the line. When better conditions come, the masses of Negroes will face the task of beginning again to lay foundations for their economic life.

Discussion and Reading

1. Should the American Negro have fought in the World War?
2. Should he have submitted to a separate draft and separate camp for officers?
3. How was the Negro soldier and stevedore treated?
   (Consult Emmett Scott, *The American Negro in the World War*; Hunton and Johnson, *Two Colored Women with the A.E.F.*; Heywood, *Negro Combat Troops*; Niles, *Singing Soldiers*; *10th Annual Report* of the National Association for the Advancement of Colored People, 1919.)

CHAPTER VII   THE BLACK FARMER

The most vital matter which the New Deal has touched so far as the Negro is concerned is the agricultural situation. More teaching and propaganda have been used to encourage and force the Negro into agriculture than in any other matter. It was the chief burden of Mr. Washington's program. It was long the chief object of Hampton and Tuskegee and the various state agricultural schools. It has been encouraged by the national government and by all of the philanthropic agencies.

On the other hand, the Negro farmer has been terribly handicapped. He was emancipated practically without land and capital. The little land actually given him was all taken away after an astonishing breach of faith on the part of the government, for the attempt to make the Negro a peasant-proprietor by giving each Negro family 40 acres was defeated by the greed of Southern planters and the stinginess of Northern manufacturers.

Notwithstanding this, by thrift and private effort, landholding among Negroes increased and the farm attained some prosperity. But these gains were cancelled out not only by the world-wide subjection of agriculture to industry, but also by lynching and lawlessness, especially in the small towns which dominated the country districts.

Negro landholding reached its peak in 1910 when there were 218,467 Negro (including other colored) landholders in the South owning about 16,000,000 acres of land. The number of owners dropped a little in 1920, and in 1930 to 182,019 holding 11,478,898 acres. In 1935, Negroes lost another million acres and the value of their holdings between 1930–1935 decreased from $339,242,651 to $207,932,597. In 1920, nearly 24% of the colored farmers owned land, and in 1930, this had dropped to a little over 20%.

The Agricultural Adjustment Administration by its cotton crop control program closed foreign markets to this greatest export crop and gave it over to cotton producers in other lands. On the other hand, it increased the misery of the sharecroppers and led to bloodshed in Arkansas and elsewhere, because the planters dominated the execution of its policies in the South and the Secretary of Agriculture was so afraid of the Southern contingent in Congress that he suppressed one report of his own investigator.

A government spokesman says:

> Probably the most difficult governmental service, to analyze from the viewpoint of the Negro, is that of agricultural adjustment. Negro farmers, of course, have had access to all of the benefits offered, but because of the larger proportion of Negro tenant farmers, many of these citizens have been deprived of their rights through unscrupulous landlords who have schemed to appropriate for themselves the benefits of land rental and reduced acreage to the exclusion of their tenants. This practice the government discourages and seeks to prevent. However, Negro farm owners generally have taken advantage of their privilege of securing agricultural loans and have cashed in on cotton acreage reduction in the same way that other farm owners have exercised their options. As a whole, government officials report that the credit record of the Negro farm owners has been highly commendable.

A Commission of Three, consisting of W. W. Alexander, Charles S. Johnson and Edwin R. Embree, has for the past year been working on problems of the Negro in the emergency and the recovery programs, financed by a special grant from one of the New York foundations. One of the major efforts of this Commission was to explore the Southern farm problem. Starting from interest in the plight of the rural Negroes, their study led directly into the general question of tenants and sharecroppers regardless of race.

From these studies, it becomes clear that the depression brought Southern agriculture very near to complete collapse and that the AAA program, necessary and useful as it was to farm economy as a whole, has made the plight of the tenant still more desperate. Pegging the cotton price and payments for crop reduction, it saved the land owner, but decimated the ranks of the tenant-croppers. Owners found naturally that they did not need so many worker families on the reduced acreage. Furthermore with cash in hand, they began to hire labor simply for the active months and to discontinue the system of supplies to tenants through the year. The result was that tens of thousands of families, both white and colored, who heretofore had been getting a living, however meager, were thrown off the plantations and [onto] relief. These families will probably never be taken back as tenants or croppers, as the owners have found a new and cheaper way of working their cotton through temporary hiring of cheap labor during the active work season, some three or four months a year. The movement away from dependent living on farms into the ranks of casual labor and relief has already involved probably three hundred thousand to four hundred thousand families and is steadily continuing. Of course it will not wipe out all or probably even a majority of the tenants and croppers. But it may easily run to six hundred thousand families in the Southern states, or to about thirty per cent of this dependent farm population.

Unfortunately, because of the old race bugaboo, the South is peculiarly incapable of handling problems of disrupted economic systems and floating populations or casual workers. Great bands of Negroes unattached to the soil, unaccountable to regular bosses, are a new and unmanageable problem. These Negro hordes, competing with poor whites for such casual labor as appears, competing with whites for relief while it lasts, possibly raiding fields or stores if they begin to starve—all this may easily lead to hysteria, terrorizing, lynchings and race riots of unprecedented scope and violence.

An effort is being made to correct these evils by re-distributing land among peasant owners. This was the basic thought of the Bankhead Bill, which has not yet been passed, and of the Resettlement Division in the WPA. Some work has been done along these lines, but the whole future of the New Deal and the funds at its disposal, are at present too uncertain to begin a broad, definite program.

Discussion and Reading

1. What is the future of the Negro farmer?
2. Should Negroes buy land?
3. How can the rural Negro be assured of law and order?
   (Consult Johnson, Embree and Alexander, *Collapse of Cotton Tenancy*; Johnson, *Shadow of the Plantation*.)

CHAPTER VIII   THE NEGRO ADVISERS, 1934

At the Inter-Racial Conference held in Washington in May, 1933, a Negro representative in the New Deal was proposed. A committee went to the Secretary of the Interior and asked for the appointment of a Negro Adviser in his department. They recommended three candidates: two white and one colored. The Secretary chose Clark Foreman, a white man, from Atlanta, Georgia. He was "attached to the Interior Department where his duties entail special attention to the manner and extent to which Negroes are sharing in the results of the operation of the National Recovery Act."

The first appointee aroused a great deal of criticism because a Southern white man was to represent the American Negroes in the Administration instead of a colored man. Foreman's salary was met from philanthropic sources and he had a difficult time between the fire of the blacks on the one hand and the reluctance of the officers of administration on the other hand, to touch the delicate subject of Negro leadership. After a while, however, as the fire of general criticism increased, colored appointees were added and eventually in 1935 Foreman was replaced by Robert C. Weaver, a colored Ph.D. of Harvard, while he himself was promoted to a higher position in the Interior Department.

The status and work of this Adviser are thus outlined by Dr. Weaver:

> The Adviser on the Economic Status of Negroes in the Department of the Interior is responsible to the Secretary. His duties are to acquaint the Secretary with the effect of the agencies of the Department upon Negroes, to suggest measures intended to increase the benefits to Negroes under the various programs administered by the Secretary and to integrate Negroes into the activities of the Department and the Public Works Administration. In doing these things, he is in constant touch with the Divisions of the Department of the Interior and with the Office of the Secretary. The Adviser is also a consultant to the Housing Division of the Public Administration.

In September, 1933, a conference of 10 prominent Negroes was called together by the Secretary of Commerce, Daniel C. Roper, to advise with him on the action which might be taken by the Federal Government to advance the economic life of the Negro.

As a result of this, on November 1, the office of Adviser on Negro Affairs to the Secretary of Commerce, was established and E. K. Jones, head of the National Urban League, was appointed to that office.

Pressure still continued for appointment of Negroes as administrators and especially as investigators to learn the real truth about conditions. A meeting was held September 18 of what was said to be the "Special Industrial Recovery Board." There were present Secretary Ickes, chairman of the Board, Secretary Perkins, General Hugh Johnson, Judge Stephens, Dr. Ezekiel and Dr. Dickinson. What was said and done has never been officially reported, but an alleged transcript of the remarks was published which we reproduce in part without vouching for its absolute accuracy:

> Secretary Perkins: Are you all so situated that every day brings demands from a group of Negroes to be appointed to something or other?
> Chairman Ickes: I do not see how we can appoint them as Negroes. If we did that we would have to appoint women as women, and nationalities as nationalities.
> Secretary Perkins: I do think there should be in my department a division studying the problems of Negroes.
> Chairman Ickes: Has Mr. Foreman been up to see you yet?
> Secretary Perkins: Yes, sir. I have eight or ten others. These Negroes

do not agree with each other.

Chairman Ickes: I was criticized for appointing Foreman. It seems to me that he will give them better service than a Negro would in his position.

Secretary Perkins: You have to watch your assignments very closely.

Chairman Ickes: I think Negroes have to be dealt with as individuals.

Secretary Perkins: The Negroes are treated differently as workers than any other group of people and it is just possible that one who has [not]¹ experienced discrimination against Negroes and who has the necessary training in other fields is not qualified to follow up their complaints. Other things being equal, a Negro investigator sent out would be able to bring back the facts better than anybody else.

General Johnson: If the Board thought well of it, we could appoint a Negro Advisory Committee. They are becoming very clamorous.

Secretary Perkins: A Negro (John P. Davis) made a good statement of the case. He pointed out that for the most part in the South where Negroes are not factory workers, they were domestics and that the domestics' wages are not increasing and that there is no likelihood of a code for domestics. I agreed with him that there would not be. He explained that in the meantime they are being paid $2.00 a week wages with no chance of raising them and that the price levels are increasing perhaps by only small fractions, but still sufficient to make it difficult for those getting only $2.00 a week to get along.

Dr. Dickinson: Might I say that the units of the NRA—the Research Unit, I believe—was about to send down into the South a colored female research worker, who comes from Oregon, I believe; and who has done very competent work at the University of Chicago; but the thought is that the selection of the research worker from the Negro race to go down and make that investigation would perhaps meet with difficulties that would not be met by a research worker of some other race, and that if it were desired to win the confidence of the Negroes in the result of a research investigation, that purpose could be accomplished in a more tactful way which would be, instead of sending a research worker from their race, to put the investigation in the hands of some outstanding Negro, like Mr. Moton, or somebody of that kind; and then if he wanted, to let him employ the research worker. That was my suggestion, but the point here is whether this research worker shall be given her ticket and sent down there this afternoon.

General Johnson: I stopped that. I think it was very unwise.

Dr. Ezekiel: We would be playing with fire to send a Northern trained Negro to the South and certainly anyone trained in Chicago.

1. This word seems inadvertently to have been omitted in the original.

All this complaint and agitation brought further efforts by Negroes. First of all, a number of Negro organizations united under two young men in Washington and formed a Joint Committee on National Recovery which proceeded to agitate for better conditions and to interrogate leaders of the NRA. This committee, formed in July, 1933, included twenty-four member organizations.

Of these organizations, ten were religious, four academic fraternities and sororities, one, a fraternal order, one an organization for agitation and reform, four, organizations for professional men, one, an organization for club work and three, industrial organizations.

If we divide these organizations according to their outlook on economics and industry, we find that half are reactionary in outlook or believe in the essential soundness of the present capitalistic system. Of the other twelve, eight may be classed as liberal in their economic outlook, while two are distinctly labor organizations and two organizations of capitalists. Under these circumstances, it was naturally impossible that the Joint Committee should attempt to lay down any guiding program.

There was only one matter on which all the organizations could agree, and that was that in the administration of the recovery program there should be as little color discrimination as possible. But as to the program itself, its general objectives and measures, it had nothing to say and it certainly had no desire to consider or lay down a distinct program for the guidance and protection of the Negro race in industry.

The Urban League did not join the Joint Committee, but attempted to set up an Emergency Advisory Council. T. Arnold Hill, acting executive secretary, in sending out an open letter to Negro workers urging them to organize Workers' Councils, wrote in part:

> For fourteen months we have been witnessing in the United States a most unprecedented effort at economic stabilization. The cause of labor is riding "high, wide and handsome," with the possibility for attaining many desirable goals. Yet the cause of Negro workers has not been one with labor's general aims. The appeals of social organizations in your behalf to the National Recovery Administration, the American Federation of Labor, independent labor organizations and many persons of influence and prestige, while partially successful, have fallen far short of the desired goal. These shortcomings have convinced us that the position of Negro workers will strengthen only if they themselves realize the necessity for action.

Apparently this proposed organization has never actually functioned, and the Secretary, E. J. Jones, Adviser in the Department of Commerce, seems to have turned to the movement for fully restored capitalism. On the other hand, the NRA, stirred by the investigator's complaints and pitiless publicity of John P. Davis and Robert Weaver, who headed the Joint Committee, executed an adroit flank movement and invited Dr. Weaver to join Clark Foreman as Adviser on Negroes in the Department of the Interior. Davis and others protested against Weaver's acceptance, but nevertheless, he eventually accepted.

August 9, 1933, the FERA authorized funds to be used for the hiring of unemployed teachers. Dr. Ambrose Caliver, from the Office of Education in the Department of the Interior, was put in charge of Educational Relief for Negroes in December, 1933.

When conditions got worse in October, 1933, the FERA inaugurated a Civil Works program, November, 1933. This was to provide work at once for 4,000,000 unemployed persons on short-time public projects and $400,000,000 was allocated to finance this plan.

A Negro, Forrester Washington of the School of Social Work in Atlanta, Georgia, was appointed as Director of Negro Work in the FERA. He selected a tentative body of welfare workers to help him, but after a few months, resigned, because he found he was to be given no real power. His assistant was named as his successor, but instead of being designated as "Director of Negro Work," he was called the "Colored Assistant in the Correspondence Division." He received complaints from Negroes concerning the administration of relief funds by local authorities and communicated with the state administrator.

The Farm Credit Administration was created by Executive Order and is under a Governor appointed by the President. The purpose is to provide a complete and coordinate credit system for agriculture. One colored man, Henry Hunt, is assistant to the Governor and has an office with a secretary and stenographer. He receives complaints from the colored farmers and makes every effort to remedy injustices placed upon Negroes in the administration of the funds. He has no administrative responsibility, but makes observation tours and inquiries at the offices of the Federal Land Banks.

Among the Negro appointments eventually made in the New Deal administration, were two in the Department of Labor, nine in the Department of the Interior, including the re-assignment of Ambrose Caliver from his office as Specialist in Negro Education to Specialist in Educational Relief among Negroes under the FERA, three in the Federal Emergency Relief Administration, one of whom resigned after seven months' experience, one publicity man who filled Negro newspapers with rosy reports about the New Deal and was reassigned to the FERA, one in the Farm Credit Administration, one in the Public Health service, one in the Bureau of the Census, an old employee who was given work as Specialist on Negro Statistics, one in the Department of Commerce and also one appointee to the Consumers' Advisory Board, but he soon resigned. Beside these appointees, there are many subordinate and clerical appointees, as for instance, some twenty in the FERA.

The result, then, of Negro criticism was a corps of Negro advisers and a few Negroes in subordinate, administrative and clerical positions. The adviser could exercise much influence or none, according to his own training, ability and personality and according to the character of the administrative official whose case he has. A subservient Negro and an official disposed to ignore or merely pacify Negroes rendered the system ineffectual and this was true in the case of several appointees. On the other hand, a conscientious cabinet officer who could depend on the knowledge, courage and tact of his Negro adviser could accomplish much and this was proven in at least two cases.

CHAPTER IX   THE PROMISE OF RESTORED CAPITALISM

Reaction against the effort of the New Deal radically to reorganize the basis of American industry has now set in due to the decisions of the Supreme Court and will probably swell to an increasing if not irresistible current. While something will doubtless remain of the effort to compel by Federal action the conduct of industry for the public benefit rather than for private profit, it does not seem at present as though these efforts were going to be widespread or fundamental.

If, now, instead of reform in industry, we are going to have the restoration of the capitalistic regime, what hope in that restoration is there for the American Negro? One gets an idea of what is in the mind of capital by studying the efforts of the Department of Commerce. The Department of Commerce has definitely conceived itself as the organ of American business and the present secretary, Daniel C. Roper, has been devoting something of his time to the situation of the American Negro. In a nation-wide broadcast September 23, Mr. Roper called attention to Negro business and some of its accomplishments.

> From my study of the Federal Census statistics as they reveal the Negro's progress in business, I cite one significant feature, seldom stressed. I refer to your successful commercial ventures in the larger urban communities. Negro merchants, operating retail stores in fifteen of our largest cities, are said to thus serve about two million people. There are in these fifteen cities over 5,700 retail stores with approximately 10,000 colored proprietors and employees. The net sales of these retail stores have run as high in a given year as $27,000,000. This appreciable expansion in business indicates the vast potentialities for future developments in this field. I feel that this feature in business for Negroes should be stressed along with agricultural pursuits, dentistry, medicine and such other industrial and professional lines as are required for complete service to

the race by representatives of the race when and if desired by colored people.

One of the most important objectives to be attained by the colored race today is the establishment of the Negro business man in his rightful place in our economic system, thus enabling him to operate his business efficiently, multiply his resources and earnings and expand his buying power to such an extent that it will be of even greater help and influence upon himself and the economic life of our country....

The result of Mr. Roper's activity was the appointment of E. K. Jones of the Urban League as the Adviser on Negro Affairs, November 1, 1933. Mr. Jones has prepared a bibliography on Negro business; has furnished information to persons planning to go into business; has held conferences with the Farm Credit Administration and Federal Housing Administration. In many cases, he has acted as liaison between Negro business and the Department of Commerce, and encouraged lecturers and writers. Work has been secured for a thousand or more trained Negroes.

Here, we have clear vision of a return to the earlier ideas of Mr. Washington and the long stressed program of the National Negro Business League. Is this a real way of escape for American Negroes? It is not. In the first place, the old idea of accumulating small capital by thrift and going into business is largely unreal today. Capital is concentrated in immense amounts and the credit agencies monopolize its division and allocation. This means that the small business man is being largely forced out of business.

The individual grocery store cannot maintain competition with the chain store, particularly when the chain store becomes a vertical organization, buying its own raw material and manufacturing and preparing its goods. The small bank will be more and more forced to be part of a large chain. The small insurance organization will not be able to stand up in resources or guarantees of security against the great aggregation of capital in the larger associations. There may be limits beyond which this concentration and monopoly of capital will not go, and many persons expect by use of the vote and political power, not to displace the private ownership and control of capital, but to supplement them by careful public control. This is the program of the greater nations in the world,—the United States, Great Britain and France. It is not a program, however, that seems to promise success. The utmost that it is apparently able to do is to produce a series of cycles of prosperity and depression with the well-grounded fear that the length and time between depressions will increase and the eras of prosperity will not really restore and rebuild the economic organization.

But whatever the facts may be so far as these nations are concerned, when it comes to a minority and disadvantaged group like that of the American Negro, a restoration of the full power of the capitalistic system in the United

States can mean to them little more than a restoration of their former unfortunate condition. They may be restored as small landholders and farm tenants, but with the control over machines and markets which capital has in the United States, there is no real prosperity for the Negro farmer. They may retain their place as servants in low-paid positions with the social stigma which menial service carries. The place which they secure in industry will depend upon their relation to the labor movement and to the plans of the leaders of organized labor.

There is, therefore, only one real opening and real plan in the restoration of complete capitalism for the Negro and that is the old plan which seeks to admit to the ranks of capitalists enough of the Negro bourgeoisie to enable them to share in the exploitation chiefly of Negro labor and to some extent of white labor. So far as the attitude of white capitalists is concerned, it is very doubtful if they will be more minded tomorrow than today to admit the Negro capitalists, save to small, outlying fields where the chances of success are very small.

This means that young men who have received in Northern and Southern colleges the prevailing economic training will be forced by severe competition to resort in the future, as they have to some extent in the past, to all of the worst fears of exploitation. They will incur, therefore, the resentment and hatred of their own labor classes and any hope of solidarity in the fight of American Negroes against race prejudice or for their own material advancement will be gone. Furthermore, the laboring classes which the colored business man can exploit will be those receiving the least wages and working under the worst conditions. The possibility of exploiting them will depend upon unfair laws and administration and inevitably the class interests of colored business men will be thrown with those very elements that today make capitalistic methods disreputable and harmful. In the South, particularly, the methods of taxation, the fines and penalties, the laws for the collection of debts, the system of installment paying, the irresponsible advertising, the agents and collectors, who swarm in Negro homes, all those must inevitably have back of them the support of Negro business; who will either resort to these methods themselves or fail. There is, then, under ordinary and probable circumstances, no chance for an ultimate economic emancipation of Negroes through the ordinary working of Negro business.

Discussion and Reading

1. Can Negro business develop in competition with white business?
2. Will the philanthropy of the wealthy solve the Negro problem?
3. Does the depression emphasize or disprove the theories of Booker T. Washington?

(Consult Harris, *Black Capitalism*; United States Bureau of the Census, "Negroes in the United States, 1920–1932.")

CHAPTER X   THE PROMISE OF LABOR ALLIANCE

Because of the facts marshalled in the last chapter, it has been the growing
hope of many thinking American Negroes that the future Negro advance
must be an alliance with the labor movement in the United States. This is a
revolution in thought from the earlier generations. The legacy of slavery
was an abject admiration of aristocracy, wealth and power. The ordinary
descendant of Negro slaves had the ambition to be rich and powerful and
gain his livelihood through the hiring and use of laborers. It has taken hard
experience and careful thought for a considerable number of American
Negroes to see that they are an integral part of the labor movement of the
world, logically, if not actually.

If, corresponding to this, there had been the feeling on the part of white
labor in the United States that Negroes did belong in the organized labor
movement and if Negroes had been welcomed into it and given their chance
to work at a decent wage, the history of the United States would have been
different. Far from this being so, the experience of the Negro laborer confirms
him in the belief of the Negro bourgeois; namely, that capital is his friend
and organized labor his enemy.

Personal experiences of laborers emphasize this attitude far beyond the
actual facts. The employer who dangerously foments race prejudice and uses
its results to cut down the wages of labor and make the conditions of work
administer to his greater profits, can easily hide behind anonymity, pursue his
aims through agents or even accomplish the results unconsciously. But the
laborer who hates Negroes or fears their competition or the undercutting
of wages, works personally and openly by means of strikes, mobs and violence.
Thus the Negro worker in the United States cannot forget the attitude of
organized labor toward him for well-nigh two centuries.

It happens, however, that today the labor movement is bringing changes in
the attitude of organized labor. The movement toward shop unions and vertical
unionization within the factories and the so-called left-wing unions, all these
have worked to break down the Color Line and to admit Negro labor where
the Negroes apply and are willing to abide by union rules. But this movement is still small as compared with the craft unions represented by the
American Federation of Labor. There comes, therefore, a practical matter
of policy. How far can Negro labor unite with a minority of white laborers
and work with them toward the emancipation of labor regardless of race?
Manifestly, so far as the labor movement in the United States is working
toward the goal of increasing wages and limiting profits; of maintaining the
political power of the labor vote and using it for such reorganization of industry
as will limit exploitation and divide the national income on some basis of
reason and desert rather than by chance and uncurbed power—so far as this is

true, the Negro must more and more become a part of the labor movement if he expects to be a modern citizen of a modern country.

If we include agriculture, the wage earners of the United States in 1930 were 10 9/10 per cent organized as compared with an organization of 35% which Germany used to have and an even higher percentage in Great Britain. Even if we exclude agriculture and domestic service and clerks, labor in the United States is only 1/5 organized. Further than this, 4/5 of this organized labor is in craft unions which are seeking the advance of small groups of skilled labor without regard for the situation of the mass laborers.

The conscious labor movement in the United States which is seeking the uplift of the laboring classes, consists of half a million workers to whom may be added, however, those in the American Federation of Labor who are rebelling against the craft organization system. These rebels have been increasing in number and power, but they are still considerably in the minority. In practically all the craft unions, with a few exceptions, Negroes are excluded, either by constitutional provision or by the invariable vote of local unions and even those Negroes in the union are liable to discrimination and refusal of recognition. Here, manifestly, there is as yet only a small basis of opportunity for the Negro to co-operate with the union labor movement. A practical labor alliance in his real mass interests is not at present available to the Negro.

Suppose, now, that the Negro turns to the promise of socialism whither I have long looked for salvation. I was once a member of the celebrated Local No. I. in New York. I am convinced of the essential truth of the Marxian philosophy and believe that eventually land, machines and materials must belong to the state, that private profit must be abolished, that the system of exploiting labor must disappear, that people who work must have essentially equal income and that in their hands the political rulership of the state must eventually rest.

But notwithstanding the fact that I believe that this is the truth and that this truth is being gradually exemplified by the Russian experiment, I must nevertheless ask myself seriously, as must every American Negro: "Is there any automatic power in socialism to override and suppress race prejudice?" This has not been proven in America. The analogy of the Jews in Russia does not parallel our case and may easily be misleading.

On the other hand, the tendency of the radical labor movement is not to stop with the socialistic outline, but to embrace communism and that extreme form of it which believes in revolution as the only solution of our present problems. There can be no doubt of the great contribution which Karl Marx has made to civilization; of his indefatigable industry, his broad knowledge and insight into the ills of the economic world. But along with this went his transformation of Hegelian philosophy into a complete system of economic determinism, and an integral part of this system as laid down by the celebrated "Communist Manifesto" was that the breaking up of the capitalistic system must come by inevitable revolution through which the exploited proletariat would violently take complete charge of the state and conduct it in its own interests.

Most American communists have become dogmatic exponents of the inspired word of Karl Marx as they read it. They believe, apparently, in immediate, violent and bloody revolution and make it one of their main objectives. This is a silly program even for white men. For American colored men, it is suicidal.

In the first place, its logical basis is by no means sound. The great and fundamental change in the organization of industry which Karl Marx foresaw must, to be sure, be brought about by revolution; but whether in all times and places and under all circumstances that revolution is going to involve violence, war and bloodshed, is a question which every sincere follower of Marx has a right to doubt.

Here, then, is the chance for two points of view. Liberals and Socialists may agree with Marx in his terrific arraignment of capitalistic exploitation. They may believe firmly that the industrial organization which divides society into two main classes—one of laborers without capital who must sell their labor, and the other of the owners of machines and materials who get their chief income not from their work, but from ownership of the products of labor—is wrong. They may firmly believe that this system must be changed into a state where the political power is in the hands of the masses and the state is conducted in the interests of those who work and not in the interests of the owners of capital. But these same persons may not believe that this development is coming by inevitable violence. They may, on the contrary, insist that great and fateful economic changes have come in the world since 1848. Increased concentration of capital has not brought universal poverty and despair among laborers, but higher wages and better standards of life. Universal suffrage, including that of women, is widely exercised. While these great changes do not essentially alter the basic conflict they do make it possible to believe fundamental reform may be brought about by methods of peace and reason, if the masses interested work for this end.

In any real social revolution, every step that saves violence is to the glory of the great end. We should not forget that revolution is not the objective of socialism or communism rightly conceived; the real objective is social justice, and if haply the world can find that justice without blood, the world is the infinite gainer.

Leaving out for the moment the grave question whether or not with the race hate now prevalent, the Negro in the case of a violent social revolution might not stand between the two factions as buffer and victim, it is clearly the part of wisdom for the American Negro to make social justice and not revolution the objective of his social effort and loyalty. The first duty of workers is not to fight but to convince themselves that union of workers, class solidarity, is better than force and a substitute for it.

The real problem, then, is this concert of the workers. The real emphasis today should be not on revolution but on class consciousness, and labor's uplift. This is the job of socialism, and the first proof of conversion is the abolition of color and race prejudice among the laboring class.

Discussion and Reading

1. Should Negroes join trade unions?
2. Should Negroes become strikebreakers?
3. Is white labor the enemy of Negro labor?
   (Consult Spero and Harris, *The Black Worker*; Wesley, *Negro Labor*.)

CHAPTER XI   CONSUMER'S ORGANIZATION

Growing industrialization and the unfair use of the Negro as a poorly paid and irregularly employed labor reserve checked the economic possibilities of Booker Washington's plan. The attitude of labor leaders, lack of education and vision among the laboring classes and the monopoly of certain lines of employment made possible by excluding Negro labor ruined the chances of raising Negro labor through trade union organization. The present radical and revolutionary program lacks both the logic and power to emancipate the Negro.

The gravity of the Negro's condition is shown in the small success of the current reconstruction efforts of the Federal Government. Wherever relief is to be administered by state and local agencies, wherever work is to be allocated, wherever codes are to be administered, the Negro must depend absolutely upon the good-will of his white neighbors and unless public opinion is unusually favorable, relief will come to him after everyone else has been served; jobs will be given him after all others are at work; and his wages will be held at the lowest point.

This situation cannot last forever. The labor movement will see sooner or later that the black worker is absolutely essential to its success. Radical communists will learn that the Negro has too much sense to become the shock troops of its revolution. But meantime, while the nation is regaining its balance on new foundations, and while the labor movement is ridding itself of caste, the Negro is compelled to live and work, and his efforts should begin with the undoubted power of the Negro as a consumer. Two million eight hundred thousand Negro families must spend at least two billion dollars a year. There can be no reasonable doubt but that proper adult education and economic organization among intelligent American Negroes can so direct this spending as gradually to accomplish the following results:

1. More effective spending so as to secure better goods and services for less money, releasing some surplus for a higher plane of living and for increased social effort.

2. An organization of spending power so as to increase the employment of those Negroes who already produce goods and services which Negro consumers use, thus making Negro employment more secure.

3. A plan to induce Negroes of the requisite training to furnish other goods and services beside what they are now furnishing, backed by a definite organization of Negro consumers who would guarantee the sale of such goods and services regularly; thus expanding Negro production.

4. Continued effort to compete with national industry only in those lines and under those circumstances where the level of Negro efficiency is so raised that the total effect upon national welfare would be to increase and not diminish it.

5. Continued effort to integrate this organization of consumers' co-operation with the efforts of white consumers and producers where no Color Line is drawn and to the extent that integration of the Negro with industry under the best industrial conditions is allowed and encouraged.

These are the general outlines for a sound recovery of Negro industry, or perhaps one would better say, of initiation of the Negro into modern industry, with intelligent comprehension of the industrial process and a plane of living properly enabling him to become an integral part of the national life and of modern human culture.

There are those who insist that the American Negro must stand or fall by his alliance with white Americans; that separation in any degree, physical or social, is impossible and that either, therefore, the Negro must take his stand with exploiting capitalists or with the craft unions or with the communists. To such people it is not convincing to point out that a poor group, like the American Negroes, cannot gain any effective admission to the ranks of capitalism, even though they wish to and thought it was the wisest thing; and secondly, that they cannot co-operate with such craft unions as will not admit them to membership; and that it is suicidal for them to try to lead violent revolution in the United States. Moreover, and in addition to this, whether Negroes can act separately or not is settled by the fact that in so large a measure they already do.

We hardly need to remind ourselves of the degree to which we form ourselves today a separate nation within a nation. Most of us are in separate churches and separate schools; we live largely in separate parts of the city and country districts; we marry almost entirely within our own group and have our own social activities; we get at least a part of our news from our own newspapers and attend our own theaters and entertainments, even if white men run them.

In our economic life, the separation is not so complete and yet it is considerable and much more thorough-going than we are apt to remember. I pointed out in 1907 [in the Atlanta University Studies] what I then called the "Group Economy" among American Negroes. It consists of such an arrangement of industries and services within the Negro group that the group tends to become a closed economic circle somewhat independent of the surrounding white world. The recognition of this fact explains many of the anomalies which puzzle the student of the Negro American.

> You used to see numbers of colored barbers; you are tempted to think they are all gone—yet today there are more Negro barbers in the United States than ever before, but also at the same time a larger number than ever before cater solely to colored trade where they have a monopoly. Because the Negro lawyer, physician and teacher serve almost exclusively a colored clientage, their very existence is half forgotten. The new Negro business men are not successors of the old; there used to be Negro business men in New York, Philadelphia and Baltimore catering to white trade. The new Negro business man caters largely to Negro trade. So far has this gone that today in every city of the United States with a considerable Negro population, the colored group is serving itself with religious ministration, medical care, legal advice and education of children: and to a growing degree with food, houses, books and newspapers. So extraordinary has this development been that it forms a large and growing part in the economy in the case of fully one-half of the Negroes of the United States.

What was true in 1907 is even more true in 1935. A great deal of this segregation is not only unnecessary but harmful and all of it ought sometime to disappear. But it will not disappear immediately, not in our day; and it looks distinctly to me as though we will see more race segregation in the United States in the near future than in the past.

It has long been the object of Negro organizations to get rid of this segregation by agitation, appeal, recourse to the courts, new legislation and even direct action. After the Reconstruction Acts and for fifty years up until the New York Civil Rights Bill, we united to put upon the statute books bills which would forbid this kind of segregation and discrimination in public places. Charles Sumner, perhaps our greatest friend, died pleading for this civil emancipation. The movement failed, yet, it did not all fail. We have today [an] appreciably wider range of civil rights than we had fifty years ago; nevertheless, we still are discriminated against in school and church, in travel and theater, in parks and playgrounds, in work and wage. We recognize from this experience, that back of law must lie public opinion. It was the basic thought that lay back of the Niagara movement and the N.A.A.C.P. that if once we could bring the facts of our desert and suffering before influential portions of the American public, that we would receive enough co-operation and sympathy to break down the main lines of segregation.

We have worked at that program for a quarter of a century, more continuously and assiduously and with larger expenditures of money than the Negro ever before put into one line of reform action. The result has not been complete failure. The legal defense work has a splendid record of accomplishment; the agitation has made millions listen; but we cannot point to substantial and undoubted advance against the general policy of race discrimination in this land. The work, of course, ought to go on. There never ought to be a time when in the United States, both by organized effort and by individual protest, we should not continue to say to this nation that a separation of men simply by race and color is not only illogical but a distinct slap in the face of civilization.

But our program in the future cannot be confined to this. It has got to be changed from one mainly of agitation and appeal to one of inner organization for self-defense. Not for offense, not for blind chauvinism, but for sheer existence. If we were today earning a living; if we had average incomes which would support life on a plane that meant health, education and the essentials of culture, we could sit down before the ramparts of race hate and continue our slow, determined, unceasing undermining of the walls. But we are on the edge of starvation and we do not need to be. Most persons writing concerning the present depression seem to regard the Negro as utterly helpless; and even in normal times the current philosophy is that both in the United States and elsewhere, we are absolutely at the mercy of the surrounding economic organization. This assumption arises from the fact that we believe that no group can approach economic independence or a position of self-sustaining inter-dependence unless it is organized as a nation with law-making powers, armies and police.

On the other hand, we should remember that the American Negro numbers about 12,000,000 and thus we are much larger than either Denmark, Greece, Hungary, the Netherlands, Norway, Portugal or Sweden and very nearly the size of Egypt, half the size of Spain, and one-third the size of Brazil. This surely indicates that we must have great economic power. This power is curtailed by the fact that we have no decisive economic place in production or transportation, in commerce or credit, or in government; we sell our labor and farm produce at prices determined by a market in which we have little influence; and we must buy what is offered to us at prices determined by others.

Here is food for thought. The economic process today does not logically begin with production, but with consumption. We do not consume in order to produce. We produce in order to consume. We are misled as to this basic fact, because for two centuries emphasis has been put upon the production of goods and their transportation and their sale. In the next few centuries this is going to be changed and we are going to look more toward the welfare and power of the buyer. As a buyer, the Negro spends something like two thousand million dollars each year. How much exercise of judgment has he in this buying? At first, it may seem that he has a little. However, in fact, he has a great deal. He has a wide choice of stores which he will patronize. He has a wide choice of articles of food and clothing. He has some choice in the selection of housing material. In fact, in nearly everything that he buys, either of goods or services, he has a power which today is not organized and which he does not use.

Recently, we have had some intimation of what he can do. The American Negro can, to a large extent, confine his patronage to such retail stores as employ colored people and treat colored customers with honesty and courtesy. This was shown by campaigns in Chicago, Washington, and New York. The net result in actual employment has not been large, but the total effort has been limited and spasmodic. There can be little doubt but that the five million Negroes living in cities could by quiet mass pressure compel the employment of ten to fifteen thousand Negroes next year in the retail stores where they buy goods.

In the matter of public service agencies, like telegraph, telephone, electric power, railroads and the like, the Negro, through his political power and his power as a consumer, can compel a wider employment of colored people and greater courtesy and consideration in the treatment of colored customers. This has already been shown by increased use in instances of colored collectors, messengers, ticket-takers and ushers. The possibilities here reach into many tens of thousands, once Negroes realize their power.

Such mass and racial demands have, of course, difficulties and invite retaliation. The campaign of the *Chicago Whip* to put Negro clerks into Southside chain stores led to the collapse of the paper through withdrawal of advertising. Conceivably a racial demand for employment might lead to discharge of colored workers in concerns with a white clientele. But surely Negro papers cannot be independent and rely on inimical advertising; and white concerns hiring Negroes are after all, thinking of profits and not of race.

There is a vast field for the organization of mutual services among Negroes which has been almost untouched. Negroes raise and prepare food; they buy it and eat it. Much of the food which they buy and eat is raised and prepared by Negroes. Much more might be. Much of the raw material raised on Negro farms and prepared by Negro workers is consumed by Negro buyers. In addition to this, many services which are rendered Negroes by white people and many services which are rendered to white people could by thought, training and organization be rendered to Negroes, thus inducing more sympathetic service and more regular employment. By group buying at wholesale instead of retail, by organized and country-wide effort instead of by single stores, and by turning the profits back to the buyer to secure his interest and educate him in economics, a great deal could be saved and many Negroes lucratively employed.

The people who can buy, build and maintain church edifices to the value of $60,000,000 could do the same thing with regard to homes and tenements, if they were organized and trained to do it. In fine, by co-operative effort in doing their own laundry, making their own bread, preparing most of their food, making a considerable part of their clothes, doing their own repairing of all sorts, printing their own papers and books and in hundreds of other ways, the colored people of the United States, if they put their minds to it and secured the proper training, could spend a considerable part of two thousand million dollars each year in hiring themselves at decent wages to perform services which the Negro group needs; and they could do this without antagonism to the white group, without any essential change of law and without a national organization involving army and police. They could even do it without the help of a protective tariff because color prejudice and race loyalty furnishes a certain amount of the same kind of protection to the Negro which the tariff furnishes manufacturers.

Of course, we believe in the ultimate uniting of mankind and in a unified American nation with economic classes and racial barriers leveled; but we believe that this ideal is to be realized only by such intensified class and race consciousness as will bring irresistible force rather than mere sentimental and moral appeal to bear on the motives and actions of men for justice and equality.

The peculiar situation of Negroes in America offers an unusual chance. Negroes cast today probably two million votes in a total of 40 million and their vote will increase. This gives them, particularly in Northern cities and at critical times, a chance to hold a very considerable balance of power and the mere threat of this being used intelligently and with determination may often mean much. Again, the consuming power of 2,800,000 Negro families has recently been estimated at 166 million dollars a month—a tremendous power when intelligently directed. Their man-power as laborers probably equals that of Mexico or Yugoslavia. Their illiteracy is much lower than that of Spain or Italy. Their estimated per capital wealth ($215 according to the *Tuskegee Year Book*) about equals that of Japan (£44 according to the *Encyclopedia Britannica*).

For a nation with this start in culture and efficiency to sit down and await the salvation of a white God is idiotic. With the use of their political power, their power as consumers and their brains, added to that chance of personal appeal which proximity and neighborhood always gives to human beings, Negroes can develop in the United States an economic nation within a nation, able to work through inner co-operation, to found its own institutions, to educate its genius and at the same time, without mob violence or extremes of race hatred, to keep in helpful touch and large co-operation with the mass of the nation. This has happened more often than most people realize, in the case of groups not so obviously separated from the mass of people as American Negroes are. It must happen in our case, or there is no hope for the Negro in America.

Any such program is today hindered by the absurd Negro philosophy of "*Scatter, Suppress, Wait, Escape*." That is—many even of our educated young leaders think that because the Negro problem is not in evidence where there are few or no Negroes this indicates a way out! They think that the problem of race can be settled by ignoring it and suppressing all reference to it. They think that we have only silently to wait for the white people to settle the problem for us; and finally and predominantly, they think that the problem of 12 million Negro people, mostly poor, ignorant workers, is going to be settled by having their more educated and wealthy classes gradually and continually escape from their race into the mass of American people, leaving the dregs to sink, suffer and die.

Such persons claim with much right, that the plight of the Negro masses is not the fault of the Talented Tenth; that the slavery and exploitation which has reduced Negroes to their present level or at any rate hindered them from rising, is the fault of the white world; and that the age-long process of raising a group is through the escape of its upper class into welcome fellowship with risen peoples; that for the intelligentsia among Negroes to bend their backs to the task of lifting the mass of people would mean their own ultimate submergence. There is logic in this answer, but futile logic.

If the leading Negro classes cannot assume and bear the uplift of their own proletariat, they are doomed for time and eternity. It is not a case of ethics; it's a plain case of must.

And the method by which this may be done is, first, for the American Negro to achieve a new economic solidarity. This is not turning back to the older program of Booker T. Washington, although Mr. Washington envisaged something of this in collusion with the capitalist system and with its philanthropic cooperation. He thought Negro capitalists would gain the opportunity to exploit their own masses and that the mutual interests of capital would integrate these black masters of industry into the group of the ruling captains of industry throughout the nation. This plan failed and can never be restored. But just as the Jews in the dawning of the new capitalism had a chance to enter the new organization of industry and become entrenched there before the masses of the world foresaw the trend, just so today there is a chance for the Negro to organize in fact the co-operative and socialistic state within his own group by letting his farmers feed his artisans and his technicians guide his home industries and his thinkers plan this integration of cooperation, while his artists dramatize and beautify the struggle to achieve economic independence. To doubt that this is possible is to doubt the essential humanity and the quality of brains which American Negroes possess.

No sooner is this proposed, however, than a great fear sweeps over the older group of Negroes. They cry "No Segregation, no further yielding to prejudice and race separation." It is true that such effort at group planning for the benefit of American Negroes does imply organized and deliberate self-segregation. And there are plenty of people in the United States who would be only too willing to make a plan of this sort an excuse to increase such legal and customary segregation between the races as already exists. This threat which many Negroes see is no mere mirage. What of it? It must be faced. If the salvation, economic and spiritual, of the American Negro calls for an increase in American race segregation and prejudice, then increase must come. Notwithstanding this, American Negroes have got to plan for their economic salvation and this social survival of colored folk in America means in a real sense the survival of colored folk in the world and the building of a full humanity instead of a petty white tyranny.

The immediate reaction of most white and colored people to this suggestion will be that the thing cannot be done. Negro scholars have from time to time emphasized the fact that no nation within a nation can be built because of the attitude of the dominant majority and because all legal and police powers are out of our hands and because large industries, like steel and electric power, are organized on a national basis and impenetrable by small groups. White folk, on the other hand, simply say that granting certain obvious possibilities, the American Negro has not the ability to engineer so delicate a social operation calling for such self-restraint, careful organization and ingenious leadership. In answer to both these groups, it may be said that this matter of a nation within a nation has already been partially accomplished in the organization of a Negro church, the Negro school and retail Negro business; and with all the justly due criticism, the result has been astonishing.

It is becoming clearer to larger groups of American Negroes that, through voluntary and increased segregation, by careful autonomy and planned economic organization, we can build so strong and efficient a group of 12 million men that no hostile group can continue to refuse them fellowship and equality.

In round numbers, American Negroes were thus employed in 1930:

2,000,000 farmers
1,500,000 common laborers
1,000,000 servants
  800,000 skilled and semi-skilled workers
  150,000 in public and professional service
   50,000 in commercial employment

Only the 800,000 skilled and semi-skilled laborers—the miners, steel-workers, automobile workers, tobacco workers and the like—are integrated in basic industry and could not easily find support otherwise. But the farmers and farmer laborers, the common laborers and most of the servants are ready and eager for any work which guarantees a living wage, continuous employment and decent treatment. Any subtraction from the mass of half employed and exploited workers, any new line of work for 50,000 or 500,000 of these marginal workers would not only directly save them but indirectly raise the wage and thus better the treatment of all other Negro workers. Is it really impossible for us to employ 500,000 in ministering directly to our own needs? The Negro professional and business men are already so employed for the most part and some of the builders and mechanics.

Never before since the abolition of slavery have the Negroes of the United States had such motives for uniting in a desperate effort to save themselves. If they have the guidance of educated thought and of honest character, there are certain things that they can do as easily as they can eat and sleep and perhaps in these days more easily. The Negroes who eat food can arrange to buy a large part of it from those Negroes who raise food on their farms; the Negroes who use towels and sheets can buy them of Negroes who raise cotton and spin and weave it on machines which can be bought at public sale; the Negroes who wear clothes can have those clothes made, not by individual tailors and dressmakers, but by Negro members of the various clothing unions which have welcomed them and this effective demand can supply the necessary sewing and cutting machines; the Negroes who wear shoes can make those shoes on machines of the United Shoe Machinery just as easily as white workmen can make them; the homes that Negroes live in can be built by Negro carpenters and masons; and so on. This list could be carried out almost endlessly and in most cases, the actual exchanges of goods and services thus indicated are already to some degree being carried out among Negroes; but the chief difficulty, now, is that the work has not been systematized, the advantages of the new highway transportation have not been taken into account, and the whole arrangement has been accidental and spasmodic rather than a carefully thought out and planned racial economy.

But, there is even a greater drawback and cause of failure than this lack of organization. It is that such co-operation as we have carried out within the race has been carried out in accordance with the private profit idea; that is, we have tried to make the incentive success and the enriching of our own owners of capital. What I propose is a complete revolution in that attitude; that we begin the process of training for socialism which must be done in every labor group in the world and in every country in the world, by organizing a nationwide collective system on a nonprofit basis with the ideal that the consumer is the center and the beginning of the organization; and that to him all profits over the cost of production shall be returned.

In these costs of production, however, we should provide not for starvation wages, not for the waste of advertising and not for goods that are merely cheap; we should be able to say to the man who pays at a Negro co-operative

$1 instead of the 95 cents, which he might pay at the white chain store,—we could say to him: that small difference which you have paid insures the employment of Negroes at a decent living wage throughout the country; it insures you getting standard goods and pays for popular education of the people in the meaning and expansion of co-operation.

The real difficulty of any such organization would be the competition and undermining retaliation of surrounding capitalism, and above all, the question of brains and character among the Negroes who organize it. Of the competition of capital there can be no doubt. It would consist not simply in underselling, but in deception, in propaganda, in unjust laws and mob violence. In the end, it could only be counteracted by unusual race loyalty and by such combining of political power with the laboring classes of America as they could be made to agree to.

The education of the leaders in the economic re-building of the American Negro group is also difficult. You cannot get honest business with dishonest men; you cannot get social planning with every person struggling for his own advancement. This matter of character is difficult. A generation ago, character, honesty, straight-dealing, was emphasized in Negro schools and in public. But for twenty-five years and more, we have said little about it. Following the lead of white America and of the white world, we have put the stress upon intellectual sharpness; upon accomplishment regardless of methods; upon efficiency, even though it was immoral and destructive. We have got to turn about and while it is much easier to say this than to show how it can be done, the necessity of doing it is absolutely prerequisite to any plan for the rescue of American Negroes under any circumstances.

Unless the present generation of Negroes can have their path lighted by some vast vision of unselfish accomplishment, our planning will be in vain. There is no doubt of the fact that those Negroes who have learned their economics in Northern institutions and those who are learning them today in most Negro institutions, are imbibing a reactionary capitalistic way of thinking which is directly opposed to the interests of American Negroes and of the laboring class in general. They come out of college knowing nothing of the issues of the modern crisis, knowing nothing of the labor movement, lightly criticizing Marx, Russia and communism. The process of securing among these men and among other persons who have the knowledge and the courage to teach a new system of Negro economics, is I admit, a discouraging one, but, I believe nevertheless that in the near future we are going to have a body of economic leadership in the United States that can undertake the organization of the consumers' power among American Negroes and lead them to success.

The attitude of our professional group must be changed. Already they are the center of a larger co-operative movement. But they seek to monopolize this for private profit. We need socialized medicine, law and dentistry designed to preserve group health and prevent disease, and sustained by regular fees and limited and adequate salaries.

Especially must come planning for Negro health. The general medical practitioner among American Negroes, running an individual enterprise for private profit, must make way for the medical social worker and the nursing home. We must have health surveys, visiting nurses and hospitalization, and if we cannot get admission and decent treatment in public hospitals we must have our own hospitals. Disease and death cannot wait for justice.

There is a further suggestion which I cannot refrain from making. It will be asked immediately: what social units or beginnings of organization can undertake this vaster regimentation of consumers' power? I answer: it can begin with the Negro church, which is the most complete and oldest and in some respects the most effective Negro institution. Without it, Negro business would be largely helpless and the connection between the church and the school is historic. But the Negro church today has come upon difficult days. Its theology and creed are no longer compelling; the training of its ministers is poor and ill-adapted to the function of the church. The housing of the church is often elaborate beyond its necessary social function; and to put it baldly, the Negro church needs something to do and someone to do it.

But why would it not be possible for the Negro church to add to its organization a business manager: a man trained in business methods, particularly in a knowledge of non-profit business methods, who had studied the work of consumers' co-operation throughout Europe and in the United States? If the church today furnishes recreation and information to its members, there is no reason why tomorrow it should not furnish coal, food, houses, and clothes. A trained business manager, either running an organization under the auspices of the church, or taking charge of the whole business of the church, could accomplish this and eliminate the private profit motive from Negro economic organization. This would leave a chance for the Negro minister to be an ethical leader and source of intellectual information for his people, just as the Jewish rabbi is today in the reformed Jewish church. But, of course, it would mean also a new type of pastor. It would mean young men of high character and brains going to theological schools where the whole course of study would be changed. There would be an end to liturgics, homiletics, exegesis, and Hebrew; and a stressing of economics, sociology, history, modern languages, music and art. Such young, vivid and honest men, freed from the necessity of these endless collections from the poverty of the poor, could talk about things that they were interested in on this earth, instead of confining themselves to heaven and hell.

I know how difficult and seemingly impossible this program appears in the mere stating. It would involve the elimination from the present church organization just as far as possible, of theology and supernaturalism. It would relegate miracles to the lore of fairy tales and prayer would become earnest and purposeful effort. Nevertheless, the Negro church and even the white church, faces grim alternatives: either it becomes a great social organ with ethical ideals based on a reorganized economics, or it becomes a futile and mouthy excrescence on society which will always be a refuge for reaction and superstition. Yet this change need be nothing revolutionary or sudden. The co-operative enterprise could be grafted on the church in the same way that organized charity and the visiting of the sick are a part of its present program. It could gradually be incorporated into the church organization and the business manager become the manager of the church along with the minister as ethical leader. This method would save a great deal of expense and difficulty of an entire new organization, in expenditure for housing, group organization and propaganda.

On the other hand, if the Negro church cannot do this, co-operatives can and must be set up as organizations entirely distinct from it, which means that they would have to compete in a way that would eat into the church organization even more than the fraternal lodges have, since the program of the co-operatives would be more vital and the results more satisfactory.

While we are organizing for our own industrial development largely along segregated lines, there is no reason for giving up our fight for equality. On the contrary, the fight against discrimination must be emphasized, but at the same time nationalized. We must provide for immediate and long-term programs, for programs that can be reasonably attained in a decade and for other programs which may take centuries to obtain, but nevertheless must be continually followed.

The short-term program must concentrate upon the education of Negro children and the discovery and support of Negro ability and genius. The children must be educated whether this is done in the public schools or in separate Negro schools: the object being not to use the school as a base of operation for or against segregation, but to use the school as a means of education and to oppose any system which ruins and discourages our children, even though it is called an unsegregated school. But above all, the immediate program must begin with the economic foundation of Negro work through the organization of their consuming power.

With this must go a long-distance program,—the training of children and adults in race relations along the lines of the program so finely worked out by Rachel Davis DuBois in "The Service Bureau of Human Relations" and so inexplicably neglected by American Negroes. This is an attempt to make all children, youth and adults calmly face the facts of race discrimination, study the results, get some acquaintance with the history of races, and then leave them to work out in their own minds and souls the line of action which they think is decent and just. In the same way, a much more careful plan for bringing the question of Negro citizenship and political power before the higher courts must be laid out. We must not for a moment be discouraged by one adverse decision, like that in the Texas Primary case, disappointing as that may be. Even a reactionary body of old men can in the long run be made subservient to the demands of poverty and right. Repeated and carefully planned attacks all along the line, including the "Jim-Crow" cars and discrimination in school funds, must be carried on despite their great expense and long-drawn-out litigation. The Board of Legal Strategy which does this must be headed by men of nationwide ability and by men who have the confidence and trust of the nation.

At present, American philanthropy stands almost check-mated before the Negro problem. The task is so enormous that philanthropy simply cannot attack it. It cannot undertake to put idle Negroes to work so long as white employers will not hire them and white laborers will not work beside them. It cannot support Negro schools, when states and cities and even the Federal government, deliberately and openly neglect these schools and discriminate against them. Even a New Deal cannot relieve Negro distress and starvation if it has to work through local and prejudiced agents.

Control of their own education, which is the logical and inevitable end of separate schools, would not be an unmixed ill for Negroes; it might prove a supreme good. Once Negro schools meant poor schools. They need not today; they must not tomorrow. Separate Negro sections will increase race antagonism, but they will also increase economic co-operation, organized self-defense and necessary self-confidence. Of course, the extreme development of this might even lead to complete separation or expulsion. What of it? Better stand in isolation or leave as men, or die as fighters, or be kicked out by superior power, than live as willing slaves and affable, spineless peons.

It is by no means certain that we shall be alone and unaided in such a constructive program. There was a time when the American Negroes thought of themselves simply in relation to the people of the United States and it was then that we argued that there could be but two methods of settling the Negro problem; either the Negro [would] be absorbed physically into the nation, or else he would die out by violence or neglect. Since the World War, this attitude has changed. Not only do we realize that the majority of the peoples of the world are colored, but we also realize that the unquestioned supremacy of the white race over these colored people has passed forever. Europe will not dominate Asia; torn as China is by internal strife, she will not accept Western domination; certainly not in political lines and not even in economic lines, whenever she is able to escape the rule of Western capitalism. Japan has chosen and so far is following ruthlessly the path of domination laid down by Europe, but it is following this path for the hegemony of Asia and of the yellow race. It will take time for India to assert its political and economic independence, but that time will be spent on achieving inner unity rather than in fighting English domination. That unity once achieved, India will go free. In Africa, one easily forgets that Africa is held under the dominance of Europe mainly by black African troops; that the black and brown regiments of France, England, Belgium, Spain and even Italy, are indispensable to the continued domination of that land. It is, then, in the long run, only a question of knowledge and realization to make the continued white domination of Africa impossible.

If American Negroes, taking the path of organizing their consumers' power, should be able to raise their working classes to dominate within their own group and to such a command of income and resources that they would not be objects of charity and dole, they can not only ally themselves with the white laboring classes in the United States and in Europe, but equally well with the black laborers of the West Indies and South America and of Africa; and with the colored laborers of India, China and Japan; and if this union could be cemented by mutual interests, by co-operative exchange of commodities made possible by lowering of the American tariff and the revision of the commercial rules which hamper British colonies, all this might lead to so strong an economic nexus between colored and white labor that the day of industrial imperialism would be over. It is a far-fetched dream, but it is worth the contemplation.

No cause of human uplift can be completely gained in one unhesitating assault. There must always be some choice of essentials; some compromises which involve comparative values. The only single and unyielding principle is that the great ideal be brought nearer by every move. During the World War, I once sat in the office of the Secretary of War and complained to him bitterly of discrimination against Negro officers and soldiers. Secretary Baker answered bleakly: "In this conflict I am not trying to settle the Negro problem." "No," I answered, "but you are trying to settle as much of the Negro problem as interferes with the winning of the war." So today, if we move back to increased segregation it is for the sake of added strength to abolish race discrimination; if we move back to racial pride and loyalty, it is that eventually we may move forward to a great ideal of humanity and a patriotism that spans the world.

What we need today is not fighting, but that basis of economic security which will permit us to fight. What we need is not vociferous complaint but such victory over threatened starvation as will give us stamina to back our future complaints with power. We know from bitter experience the futility of asking an administration which bases its power on a political foundation of fifty congressional votes stolen from Negroes, for an effective anti-lynching bill which in many cases would hang a very considerable number of their constituents; or to ask the New Deal for an exercise of Federal power which would really distribute Federal funds with justice, when we know perfectly well that any such honest attempt would wreck the administration in a month.

Not being utter fools and knowing that momentarily the greater plans of the Niagara Movement and the N.A.A.C.P. for the emancipation of the American Negro cannot be realized because of the depression, and especially because white America is not ready to have them realized, we are compelled to subŝtitute a program of economic power; we are forced to put back of the demands of twelve million people not mere sentiment and appeal, but power. That power must be the power that labor gives to the laborers when it is intelligently directed and when its fruits are justly distributed. For this new racial production and reasoned distribution, we must unite every unit of our own forces no matter how much we segregate our spiritual and social life, so long as we never lose sight of one great aim: the making of American Negroes into a real force for economic justice to all men.

Discussion and Reading

1. Is the Negro movement toward consumers' cooperation feasible?
2. Comparing the United States and Sweden, what advantages and disadvantages are there here for consumers' cooperatives?
3. What can the Negro learn from Denmark?
   (Consult, Child's *Sweden: The Middle Way;* Warbasse, *What Is Co-Operation?;* Kress, *Capitalism, Co-Operation and Communism.*)

LIST OF WORKS CITED

Brawley, Benjamin. *Social History of the Negro.* New York: 1921.

Childs, Marquis. *Sweden: The Middle Way.* 1932. Reprint. New Haven, Conn.: Yale University Press, 1961.

Du Bois, W.E.B. *Black Reconstruction: An Essay toward a History of the Part Which Black Folk Played in the Attempt to Reconstruct Democracy in America, 1860–1880.* New York: Harcourt, Brace and Co., 1935.

———. *The Souls of Black Folk: Essays and Sketches.* Chicago: A. C. McClurg and Co., 1903.

Edwards, Bryan. *The History, Civil and Commercial, of the British Colonies in the West Indies.* 5 vols. London, 1819. Reprint. New York: AMS Press, 1970.

Harris, Abram. *The Negro as Capitalist: A Study of Banking and Business among American Negroes.* Philadelphia: 1936.

Helps, Arthur. *The Spanish Conquest in America and Its Relation to the History of Slavery and to the Government of the Colonies.* 4 vols. London, 1856–58. Reprint. New York: AMS Press, 1964.

Heywood, Chester D. *Negro Combat Troops in the World War: The Story of the 371st Infantry*. Worcester, Mass.: 1928.

Hunton, Addie W., and Kathryn M. Johnson. *Two Colored Women with the A.E.F.* Brooklyn, N.Y.: 1920.

Johnson, Charles S. *The Negro in American Civilization*. New York. 1931.

––––––. *Shadow of the Plantation*. Chicago: 1934.

Johnson, C. S., Edwin Embree, and W. W. Alexander. *The Collapse of Cotton Tenancy*. Chapel Hill: University of North Carolina Press, 1935.

Kress, Andrew J. *Capitalism, Co-Operation and Communism*. Washington, D.C.: 1932.

Merriam, George S. *The Negro and the Nation: A History of American Slavery and Enfranchisement*. New York, 1906.

Miller, Herbert. *Races, Nations and Classes: The Psychology of Domination and Freedom*. Philadelphia, 1924.

Niles, John J. *Singing Soldiers*. New York, 1927.

Nowlin, William F. *The Negro in American National Politics*. New York, 1931.

Scott, Emmett. *The American Negro in the World War*. New York, 1919. Reprint. New York: Arno Press, 1969.

Skaggs, William H. *The Southern Oligarchy*. New York, 1924.

Spero, Sterling, and Abram Harris. *The Black Worker: The Negro and the Labor Movement*. New York, 1931.

Stephenson, Gilbert T. *Race Distinction in American Law*. New York, 1910.

Steward, Theophilus G. *The Haitian Revolution, 1791–1804; or, Sidelights on the French Revolution*. New York, 1914.

Wesley, Charles H. *Negro Labor in the United States, 1850–1925*. New York, 1927.

Woodson, Carter G. *The Negro in Our History*. 4th ed. Washington, D.C., 1927.

––––––. *The Story of the Negro Retold*. Washington, D.C., 1928.

Young, Donald. *American Minority Peoples*. New York, 1932.

1937-1944

Memorandums on the Proposed Encyclopedia
of the Negro (1937 and 1939?)

*Du Bois projected the idea of an Encyclopedia of the Negro no later than
1909, but it was not until 1931 that Anson Phelps Stokes, head of the fund
established by his family, expressed interest in helping to bring this work into
being. The 1930s saw the establishment of an editorial board, at first headed
by Du Bois and Professor Robert E. Park of the University of Chicago; the
latter was replaced in 1937 by Professor Guy B. Johnson of the University
of North Carolina. Throughout, the driving force in this effort was Du Bois,
assisted mainly by Irene Diggs, Rayford Logan, and L. D. Reddick.*

*Sufficient funding never was obtained in the United States; the only pub-
lished result while Du Bois lived was the* Preparatory Volume to an Encyclopedia of the Negro, *issued by the fund in 1945 in a 205-page edition and in
a revised, slightly expanded 217-page version in 1946.*

*When Du Bois went to Ghana, at President Nkrumah's suggestion, in 1961,
an essential purpose was the setting up of an Encyclopedia Africana, to be
headed by him with Dr. Alphaeus Hunton as his main assistant. Some progress
was made, but Du Bois's death in August 1963 and the reactionary coup in
1966 stopped work.*

Two volumes of a projected twenty of The Encyclopedia Africana: Dic-
tionary of African Biography, *edited by L. H. Ofosu-Appiah, were published
in 1977 and 1979 by Reference Publications. The editor's introduction in the
first volume notes the seminal work of Du Bois and Hunton, but Du Bois's
concept had not limited the encyclopedia to biography.*

*Two memorandums to Anson Phelps Stokes concerning the encyclopedia
project are published below. The first was sent from Atlanta University
on 15 March 1937. The second is marked in ink, in Du Bois's handwriting,
"Not sent," and it is undated. It is likely, however, that it was written sometime in 1939, for Du Bois states that he had first conceived of such an encyclopedia "thirty years ago." Why this memorandum was not sent is unexplained.*

CONFIDENTIAL MEMORANDUM REGARDING
THE SIGNIFICANCE OF THE PROPOSED
Encyclopaedia of the Negro

In presenting a plan for the proposed Encyclopaedia of the Negro to the
various Foundations in order to secure proper financial support, I suggest
emphasis on the following points:

First, Timeliness of such an Encyclopaedia. Interest in the facts concerning
the past and present development of the Negro races has been greatly stimulated
in the last twenty-five years. Studies have been made and published and
others are in the making. It is fair to say that the old attitude of the scientific
world toward the Negro race has largely changed during this time. For this
reason it is essential to make available to the ordinary reader the present
status of knowledge concerning the Negro. This is not because this knowledge
is anywhere near complete, but is necessary because we shall go forward
more surely toward better scientific work and understanding if we can make
it clear to the ordinary man, and particularly to the student, just what is
already known today. Our casual knowledge always tends to lag behind
scientific accomplishment, and it is still possible today to make and reiterate
the most reactionary statements concerning Negroes which science has long
disproved.

If, for instance, one wishes to make a reasonable and authentic statement
concerning the Negroes in Africa, in North America, or the West Indies and
Latin America, or concerning distinguished men of Negro descent, where
would one look today in order to have reasonable authority for such statements and not find one's self flatly contradicted by current gossip and
exaggeration? It is imperative today that present knowledge of this branch
of the human family should be set down and made available in temperate,
balanced exposition, for the use of the mass of those who would know and
who seek further enlightenment. If in any line of knowledge one waits for
definitive information no encyclopaedia would ever be written.

In my judgment as to the necessity of an Encyclopaedia today I have been
strengthened by personal interviews during the last year with the leaders of
thought in history, anthropology, and sociology in various parts of the world.
I have consulted large numbers of such persons in the United States and
published their judgments. More lately I have talked with scientists in England,
France, Belgium, Germany, Austria, and Japan. I have found practically
unanimous opinion that such an Encyclopaedia is demanded and feasible in
the present state of scientific knowledge.

Second, Who should carry out such a plan? Manifestly the leading scientists
of the world who know the social sciences, and the development of the
Negro race, should make the contributions to such an Encyclopaedia. The

leadership in such an enterprise should be in the hands of those who look upon the Negro race as an integral branch of humanity, worthy of the same scientific attention and sympathetic study that other branches have received. If the work were done entirely under the auspices of Negroes there might be danger that they would not be able to furnish the scientific equipment and knowledge on all points that would be necessary; and they would naturally be tempted to make the study a brief for a long disadvantaged race, rather than a carefully balanced scientific statement. On the other hand, if the work were put entirely in the hands of white scientists, there would be equal danger and their lack of personal contact with the Negro and knowledge of his problems would lead to a serious error in appraisement and understanding. There might easily be wide gaps in the actual field study and quite naturally there would obtrude itself here and there the old and widespread assumption of the sub-humanity of the Negro race. For this reason it would be wise to have a collaboration between white and Negro scientific workers such as would include as far as possible the best available minds of the world, and at the same time, the widest and most sympathetic knowledge which could be had. No scientific work done by living, feeling men and dealing with humanity can be wholly impartial. Man must sympathize with misfortune, deplore evil, hope for good, recognize human fellowship. All that social science can do is so to limit natural human feeling by ascertained facts as to approach a fair statement of truth.

For this reason I have tried to gather into a cooperating group: first, the best known white scientists of America and Europe and, secondly, the best equipped scientists of Negro descent in America, the West Indies, South America, and Africa; in this latter case I have especially sought the younger men who have had the latest and best training. As a result I have, so far as Negroes are concerned, the large majority of the doctors of philosophy in history, sociology, and economics, trained in the best institutions of the United States and Europe during the last twenty-five years; among white scientists I have the promise of the widest and most interested cooperation from the leading anthropologists, sociologists, and historians of Europe, Africa, and Asia. The letters substantiating this statement are on file in this office.

There is another somewhat subtle but real reason for inter-racial cooperation. Young colored men of this generation are showing conspicuous ability in many lines of work. They are pressing hard against the gates of opportunity and these gates are opening less easily and widely than ability is asserting itself. The result is a widespread feeling that white America is determined not to recognize the Negro even when he excels, and the very presence of this feeling increases the unrest even in the case of Negroes who have not worked hard and do not possess real power to achieve. Particularly does this feeling exist in fields of science where the reluctance to give Negro scholars opportunity in laboratories and as research assistants makes them suspect the color

Board of Directors of the Encyclopedia of the Negro *at Howard University, Washington, D.C., May 1936.* Left to right, front row: *Otelia Cromwell, professor of English, Miner Teachers' College; Monroe N. Work, director, Department of Records and Research, Tuskegee Institute; Charles H. Wesley, professor of history, Howard University; Benjamin Brawley, professor of English and history, Howard University; Du Bois; Eugene Kinckle Jones, director, National Urban League.*

Center: *Willis D. Weatherford, head, Department of Religion and Humanities, Fisk University; James Weldon Johnson, professor of creative literature, Fisk University; Charles T. Loram, Sterling Professor of Education and chairman, Department of Race Relations, Yale University; Alain Locke, professor of philosophy, Howard University; Waldo G. Leland, director, American Council of Learned Societies.*

Rear: *Arthur A. Schomburg, founder, Schomburg Collection, New York Public Library; Joel E. Spingarn, professor of comparative literature, Columbia University, and president,* NAACP; *Clarence S. Marsh, vice-president, American Council on Education; Anson Phelps Stokes, president, Phelps-Stokes Fund; William A. Aery, dean of instruction, Hampton Institute; James H. Dillard, former president, Jeanes Foundation and Slater Fund; Florence Read, president, Spelman College; Mordecai W. Johnson, president, Howard University.*

line even when it is not there. If now we could have at this particular time
a conspicuous example of inter-racial fellowship in scientific work, with
generous opportunity and recognition for the work of young scientists in the
Negro race and collaboration between them and white scientists of both
America and Europe, it would be an unusually fine thing in itself and a
singularly wise proof that although the way of the black scholar may be
difficult, it is by no means blocked. It would prove that the Foundations and
philanthropy are willing not only to subsidize Negro work when it is segregated,
but just as eager to help Negro scientific work of the highest grade and in
conjunction with the world's best scientists if it is known that they can hold
their own on the highest planes of endeavor. Also the value to Negro scholars
of such unusual opportunity for associating with the world's best would be
incalculable.

Third, Editorial procedure. The practical problem is how to bring these
persons who are willing to cooperate, and who have the best knowledge of the
subject, into such joint effort as will evolve the sort of Encyclopaedia that we
wish. In order to facilitate this I have attempted certain preliminary work.
In a way these attempts have involved a certain presumption and apparent one
man effort, but I think the object attained has justified this method. I first
sat down to make, with clerical and scientific assistance, an outline of the
possible scope of an Encyclopaedia of the Negro race. This was primarily to
impress upon those who had not given much attention to the subject, how large
a field of interesting knowledge and exploration lay open for inclusion in such
an Encyclopaedia. The possible subjects for treatment in this Encyclopaedia
made up mimeographed pamphlets of one hundred and fifty pages, and this I
sent out to a number of scientists and interested persons and asked for their
criticism. Naturally, most of them had time only for very general criticism;
quite a number made detailed criticism of certain parts; a few like Professor
Westerman of the University of Berlin voluntarily prepared a simplified list of
subjects on Africa. From these criticisms and offers we shall have ready in
this office in the late spring a dummy of four volumes indicating allocation of
space to each of the proposed lists of subjects which an Encyclopaedia of the
Negro might treat.

This will be, of course, by no means a final list. It will be simply a survey of
the field which a board of editors can more carefully delimit and make practical.
It will, however, save a lot of preliminary and costly speculation and confront
the editorial board with a fairly clear idea of the field which might be covered.

In addition to this two editors-in-chief have been selected: A Negro and a
white man, both of whom have given a life time to the study of the Negro
race. They are both elderly men, selected because of their experience and
because their selection symbolized racial cooperation in this work. It is proposed
that they should be surrounded by a small group of younger editorial assistants,
both colored and white, who should form the working nucleus of an efficient,

well-trained editorial board, and in case either or both chief-editors should find it necessary to retire before the work is finished they could easily be replaced by younger men. Around this smaller editorial group would be a larger group of consultants and advisers, and a still wider group of actual contributors.

Fourth, The Cost. The experience in the making of encyclopaedias, especially during recent years, has naturally made Foundations and contributors afraid of the large cost involved. An encyclopaedia well done is without doubt a costly enterprise. But on the other hand, there have been certain obvious wastes, and a certain lack of planning in many enterprises which can guide the present attempt. Usually, the first idea in the mind of those who plan an encyclopaedia is to cover the field with scientific thoroughness, making the matter of cost a secondary consideration. In the case of an encyclopaedia which seeks to exhaust a world field of knowledge this idea must be made paramount. But for an encyclopaedia which covers a special field like this, it is possible as it seems to me to take advantage of the experience of the past and budget the cost and then keep strenuously within the limit of that budget. I should say, for instance, in the Encyclopaedia of the Negro, our task would be not to exhaust the field of information but to set down the plan frankly as an attempt to see within a given expense how complete a picture and scientific statement of the past and present of the Negro race could be made, knowing that this limitation of cost would put necessary boundaries to the extent of the information that could be gathered and printed.

I would suggest, therefore, if the proposed budget in the memorandum totalling $200,000.00 does not seem satisfactory to the Foundations, the Editors consult further with persons formerly connected with other encyclopaedias recently published. The Trustees would, of course, be delighted, should the Foundations so desire, to have them represented on such a committee. This committee could carefully guide and allocate expenditures during the preparation and manufacture of the Encyclopaedia so that the cost would fall within the limit of the budget.

It seems to me that with this practical limitation of cost, and with the large scientific cooperation which has been secured, we may be able to make an epoch making contribution to three things: the establishment of truth concerning the Negro race, the cooperation of science regardless of race difference, the limitation of expense according to available funds.

ON THE SCIENTIFIC OBJECTIVITY OF THE PROPOSED
Encyclopedia of the Negro AND ON SAFEGUARDS
AGAINST THE INTRUSION OF PROPAGANDA

There is no final assurance that scientific work in the social sciences will be unbiased or rigidly objective in its aim to attain truth, save in the character and ability of the persons in charge. Reasonable checks and arrangements for consultation and criticism can and should be made; but no editorial machine can proceed by majority vote and no consistent and reasonable interpretation of ascertained fact, and indeed no search for such facts, can be obtained by seeking to balance extreme and opposing opinions in final decisions, and to get conclusions by veto rather than by consistent and open-minded reason.

The bodies then who are considering the wisdom of aiding the proposed Encyclopedia of the Negro, must first of all be satisfied that under my editorial leadership there will emerge a body of organized knowledge which will gain the recognition of the scientific world as a fair reflection of the present consensus of its best opinion.

That will be no easy task for anyone. Fifty years ago, perhaps even twenty-five years ago, the field would have been too violently torn by bitter controversy to expect scientific calm and balanced judgment with regard to the Negro race. But so much of understanding and research have been accomplished lately that it is well worth an attempt to put it on record, not simply as an established body of fact and logical deduction, but even more as an agreed basis from which further advance can be made, steadied by an intelligent public opinion, instead of being threatened by increased lag between racial science and racial folk-lore.

Of the subjects set down for treatment in this encyclopedia, I think it is fair to say that nine-tenths of them are matters of fact, to be ascertained by accuracy of scholarship: the number and distribution of Negro peoples; their history; [their] physical characteristics; their health and death rate; their labor and occupations; their relations to their environment, social and physical;—all these matters today are known, not completely, but accurately enough to draw an approximate picture of the truth.

There is a remaining tenth of the possible subjects which would still raise wide differences of opinion and prophecy. This is not peculiar to this subject but is inevitable in attempts to codify and systematize any branch of knowledge which deals with human action, wish, and will. In the treatment of such matters, complete detachment is impossible. No one, for instance, would expect an Encyclopaedia Britannica to be anti-British; or a Jewish Encyclopaedia to be pro-Hitler; or a Catholic Encyclopaedia to agree with the Protestant estimate of Martin Luther. Nevertheless we would insist upon such allegiance to the spirit of modern science and such regard for exact truth as would not allow in any such works, deliberate falsification even of unpleasant truth; or any method or conclusion which the common judgment of the world of science would consider unfair, partial or designedly incomplete.

An editorial board under my leadership would, of course, make certain assumptions concerning Negroes which a number of honest minds still regard as unproven. These assumptions would revolve around the belief that black folk are human beings, with reactions essentially the same as those of other human beings. But beyond this basic assumption we would be willing and eager to face the ascertained truth unwaveringly and to interpret all facts in the light of science. Where there are still areas of irreconcilable controversy we would certainly indicate these and see that the contentions of both parties were fairly stated.

All of this however depends on two matters; the possibility of gathering today a body of scientists, largely from the Negro race, with sufficient training and scientific spirit to carry out this hard and delicate task. It also involves the rather peculiar problem of the willingness of white scientists to collaborate with such Colored men as fellow workers in a common task.

When, thirty years ago, I first envisaged such an encyclopedia, it did not for a moment occur to me that such collaboration would be possible. I hoped only for scientific advice from white men to guide the few Colored scholars whom I knew and whose training was admittedly inadequate in many fields. Today in contrast, I have no doubt of adequate Negro scholarship in a large number of the fields which we propose to touch.

There is as yet between white and Colored scientific workers in this country no such complete and illuminating fellowship as enables a white man at all times to know the Colored men in his own field. No matter what his ability, no Colored scholar has more than one chance in a hundred for appointment on a white college faculty in the United States. Recently in recommending highly a young economist to Atlanta University, a Harvard head professor said, "Frankly, we gladly would appoint this man here if he were not Colored." Despite this attitude we have had in the last two decades Colored instructors and assistant professors in Harvard, Boston, Chicago, Pennsylvania, Northwestern and several other institutions. The fine work of Negroes in many branches has received national and sometimes international recognition although often the racial identity was unknown or forgotten.

While then casual investigation may easily fail to realize our scientific material, because it was so scattered and hidden and sometimes too self-conscious and retiring, nevertheless a careful search convinces me that in history, psychology, sociology and economics we have first class scientific and editorial ability, recognized by high degrees from the best educational insti-tutions in the nation. Even as recently I was doubtful about anthropology I came across the work of a Harvard and Chicago fellow, former student of London, and quoted as an authority in Huxley and Haddon's "We Europeans." [1]

I have been especially gratified to see among white scholars in England,

1. Du Bois is referring to Allison Davis, coauthor with John Dollard of *Children of Bondage* (1940). On p. 100 of *We Europeans*, by Julian Huxley and Alfred Haddon (1936), there is a reference to an Allison Davis, author of an article on race in the *Sociological Review* (London). This article appeared in 1905, however, and the Davis Du Bois has in mind was not born until 1902.

France, Belgium, Austria, Germany and Japan, not only approval of this project but the utmost apparent willingness to co-operate in every way. From South Africa I have had letters from nearly every one of the white students of native life. In the United States there seems no reason to doubt that white scientists of standing are willing to work side by side with Negroes in an encyclopedia of this nature.

This however, brings to my mind a danger and warning. I believe it would be fatal to the high object of this interpretation, if its inter-racial character over-shadowed and diverted its scientific aim. What we propose is a modern, accurate, well-written encyclopedia, and not merely an exercise in inter-racial comity. If this object can be well done and can at the same time include good race relations as a means, this will be ideal. But the set up of the encyclopedia must not be made with the idea of balancing race representation and checking excesses of prejudice on one side by excess on the other.

I want as colleagues men of science seeking the truth. I shall be gratified if a goodly number of them are white men, but it is not the color of their skins but the caliber and quality of their minds that is to me important. I would not for a moment accept the position of editor if my co-editor was selected simply because he was white and not primarily because he was interested in a good scientific job.

As I have said then, the character of this encyclopedia cannot be insured by any mechanical system of checks or by any merely racial balance. It must in the end depend on the character and scholarship of the editors. My own experience in that line is, I presume, well-known. I started in 1897 as assistant instructor in the University of Pennsylvania with the aim of making a scientific study of the Negro in Philadelphia and eventually in America. Going then to Atlanta University, I worked from 1898 to 1910 for the elaboration of this plan. I was finally compelled to drop it because we could not obtain support even to the extent of $5,000 a year to carry on the only systematic study of the American Negro being made anywhere in America or perhaps anywhere in the world.

I turned then, for a quarter of a century, to the work of agitating for these basic human rights without which no science or art is possible. At the end of my years I have returned to the dream of completing in some way my original scientific program. I can point to these works as specially illustrating my work in this line:

"The Suppression of the African Slave Trade," the first volume of the Harvard Historical Series.

"The Philadelphia Negro."

Fourteen annual studies of the American Negro made at Atlanta University.

A volume on "The Negro" in the Home University Library.

A biography of John Brown.

A study of reconstruction called, "Black Reconstruction."

Four or five special investigations made for the United States Bureau of Labor.

A monograph in the Ninth United States Census.

Various articles in the *American Historical Review, Foreign Affairs*, the *North American Review*, the *Atlantic Monthly* and in several English, French and German periodicals.

On these works all judgment of my editorial ability and aptitude must rest.

Finally, may I call attention to one aspect of this enterprise: whatever temptation there might be for Colored editors to make this encyclopedia a defense of the Negro race would be tempered by the much more important possibility of writing and publishing a statement concerning the Negro race so temperate and accurate and so well done, as to merit the approval of the scientific world. I cannot emphasize too much the fact that this would be the great ideal of those willing to work with me on this project.

On the Roots of *Phylon* (1937)

Du Bois was the founder and for the first four years of its existence (1940–44) the chief editor of Phylon, *the scholarly quarterly still published at Atlanta University. By the early 1930s Du Bois's views were more and more at odds with those of the dominant leadership of the* NAACP; *he formally resigned from it and from his editorship of the* Crisis *in the summer of 1934, but by the previous summer he had accepted an invitation from his very dear friend John Hope, president of Atlanta University, to return to his teaching efforts there.*

One of Du Bois's hopes was that with such a position, he would be able to help establish a first-rate quarterly. This goal was set back when Hope died in 1936. Du Bois, with much reduced support at his own university, continued the effort to establish the journal first by seeking to interest other universities—originally Fisk—in the idea and second by trying to obtain funds from the General Education Board. Neither effort succeeded, but finally in 1940, with a very modest—and grudging—grant from the trustees of Atlanta University, Phylon *was launched.**

Illustrative of the efforts at Fisk and those aimed at the board are the documents that follow.

* Letters relevant to *Phylon's* history are printed in the *Correspondence*, vol. 2.

PERSONAL AND CONFIDENTIAL
MEMO OF THE CONFERENCE

Dr. Charles Johnson, Mr. Ira De A. Reid, Dr. Rayford Logan, and Dr. W.E.B. Du Bois met in Nashville May 8, 1937, in the Social Science building of Fisk University. The purpose of the meeting was to consider preliminary plans toward cooperation between Atlanta University and Fisk University and their departments covering the social sciences, more particularly in the joint publication of a quarterly journal. At this conference and in a further conference in Dr. Johnson's home Sunday, May 9, the following matters were discussed:

1. the need of a journal
2. the possibility of cooperation between Atlanta University and Fisk University
3. the editorship of the journal, and the editorial board
4. the name of the journal
5. the character of the contents
6. the probable cost and its allocation

While no final decisions were made there was frank and interesting discussion which resulted in unanimity of opinion essentially along the following lines:

First, that the time was ripe for a journal of this sort. There is a great deal of scholarly work being done by Negroes and others, and further work being planned in the field of the social sciences which touches the interest of the Negro and the colored races and interracial relations with the whites. The volume of the work could be notably increased if there was encouragement and a reasonable chance for publication.

Second, that it would be an excellent thing if Atlanta and Fisk Universities in particular and other colored institutions should initiate scientific research in the social sciences by generous and wide cooperation; and that it would be practical to issue such a journal as we have in mind by united effort; and that it would be for the distinct advantage of both institutions, and of other institutions, or individuals connected with them willing to join us.

Third, it was suggested that we proceed to inaugurate a journal treating the social sciences in fields in which the Negro and other races were interested; and that this be issued quarterly beginning with an initial number for January, 1938, under the joint editorship of two persons representing Fisk and Atlanta Universities, and of an editorial board representing these Universities and selected persons from some other institutions. Mr. Du Bois and Mr. Johnson were suggested as editors and the following persons on the editorial board: from Fisk University: Mr. James Weldon Johnson, Mr. Watkins, Mr. Doyle.

From Atlanta University: Mr. Ira De A. Reid, Mr. W. Stanley Braithwaite, Dr. Logan. From other institutions the following names were suggested tentatively: E. Franklin Frazier, Howard University; Horace Mann Bond, Dillard University; Ralph J. Bunche, Howard University. It was suggested that this board be made a real editorial board with responsibilities and contributions.

Several names were suggested like "Journal of Negro Sociology," "Negro Journal of Social Science," and others; but it was finally agreed that a good name would be "Race and Culture."

As to the contents there were the following suggestions:

a. special scientific studies and monographs
b. short book notices and long comprehensive and careful review of important books
c. a carefully selected and annotated chronicle of happenings touching races and interracial relations and forming a continuous, reliable, and comprehensive history of such developments
d. illustrations and photographs designed to make clear social and historic development
e. the possibility of carefully selected poetry

It was agreed that the magazine ought to be well printed so as to make a dignified and impressive appearance.

It was suggested that an appropriation of one thousand dollars each be sought from Atlanta and Fisk Universities, and that this two thousand dollars each be matched by a donation from outside sources. It was thought that four thousand dollars would pay the annual deficit assuming that the Universities furnished the services of the editors free with some clerical assistance. It was hoped that it would be possible to pay contributors a small but a set sum.

The conference ended with the promise on the part of the conferees to consider these matters further and especially the question of editorial and business offices, and the various problems due to the joint cooperation of separated institutions.

A PROPOSED OUTLINE OF A PETITION TO THE GENERAL
EDUCATION BOARD FOR A SUBVENTION TOWARD THE
PUBLICATION OF A JOURNAL OF SOCIAL SCIENCES

The always vague, often sentimental, and generally academic discussion of the subject of race in the United States is gradually giving way to a better conception and a more trustworthy technique. Scientific investigation and beginnings of measurement are showing that group culture and so-called race are conceptions easily confounded; and that much that we have called race problems are really problems of culture. This point of view puts the matter of the study of race on a much more practical basis. Instead of investigating intangible and almost unreachable ultimate human distinctions we are led to study, certainly for the most part, measurable facts of human culture and culture groups; and we shall be in the future increasingly able to apply definite and reliable terms and measurements to this study.

In such a study American Negroes should share largely; not only [because] their natural interest impels them to such study, but also because the very existence of such interest calls for careful guidance and direction through scientific method. There is need of harnessing and guiding and sternly limiting natural race interest for the sake of a real discovery of truth and scientific fact beneath the so-called race problems.

There are ready for this work an increasing number of young Negro scholars. The latest compilation made by Harry W. Greene of West Virginia Collegiate Institute (1937) shows that since 1876, one hundred forty-eight men and women of Negro descent have received the degree of doctor of philosophy from American and foreign universities. One hundred and nine of these degrees have been awarded since 1928. Of the persons receiving the degrees six are known to be dead. The leading institutions conferring these degrees are: University of Chicago, Harvard, Columbia, Cornell, and Pennsylvania. And the leading fields covered by them are in order of their importance: education, sociology, chemistry, history, and English. There are, therefore, available today for scientific work in the social sciences with the best modern training some twenty-five or thirty young Negro scholars; and in addition to that a considerable number who have not yet finished their course, and others who while they have not taken degrees are nevertheless capable of thoroughly scientific work.

In a part of the field of the social sciences there are already journals edited by Negroes: the *Journal of Negro History* edited since 1916 by Carter G. Woodson has been a notable accomplishment. The *Journal of Negro Education* edited by Charles H. Thompson since 1931 is also doing first class work. There is a small quarterly journal published at Florida Colored A and M College; a *Journal of Negro Higher Education* at Johnson C. Smith in North Carolina; and a new *Arts Quarterly* at Dillard. This still leaves a very considerable field of the social sciences particularly as they relate to the Negroes uncovered. The white sociological journals in the South like *Social Forces* and others have been generous in allotting space to subjects of interest to the Negro. Nevertheless, there is a distinct and large field of research and publication still uncovered.

Two institutions among Negroes stand out as worthy of consideration in pursuing the development of Negro social science. Atlanta University was the first institution in the United States to attempt a scientific study of the Negro problem and for thirteen years from 1897 to 1910 made annual studies of certain aspects of the Negro problem, and published reports. The work was limited in field and imperfect in method but it was a distinct and noteworthy beginning. After a lapse of some years Atlanta University in 1933 re-established a department in sociology in the graduate school and is taking renewed interest in the development of this department. Fisk University, under Charles S. Johnson and his co-workers, has developed a department of social science which is without doubt the best equipped among Negro colleges; and has issued directly and indirectly in the last few years a number of notable studies.

President John Hope in asking for proposals in which the work of the department of sociology in Atlanta University could be forwarded entertained seriously a proposition made by Dr. Du Bois and Mr. Ira De A. Reid for a quarterly journal of sociology. His illness and death precluded any action in the matter. In 1937, thirteen professors and instructors of Atlanta University in the departments of history, economics, sociology, French, English, and Education united in a petition to the Board of Trustees of Atlanta University to establish such a quarterly journal; but the Board while expressing sympathy was unable to finance the venture at present. Meantime it seemed to the instructors in the departments of Atlanta University that the cooperation of Fisk University should be asked because of the preeminence of her work in the social sciences. They, therefore, had various consultations with Mr. Johnson with the result that the teachers in social science in these institutions have united this year in a project for a journal of *Race and Culture* to be started in the year 1938 and to cover the following fields:

a. special scientific studies and monographs
b. short book notices and long comprehensive and careful review of important books
c. a carefully selected and annotated chronicle of happenings touching races and interracial relations and forming a continuous, reliable, and comprehensive history of such developments
d. illustrations and photographs designed to make clear social and historical development
e. the possibility of carefully selected poetry.

The estimated cost of such a journal would, we think, be between $3,000 and $5,000 a year. This would be the cost of paper and printing without any allowance for editorial work which would for the first years be entirely voluntary. It is planned to begin the journal as the private enterprise of groups of teachers in these institutions and then appeal to the institutions to take over the publication of the journal and be thereafter responsible for it. Such a proposal will be submitted to the two universities at the next meeting of their boards of trustees. In the meantime we are asking from the General Education Board a subvention of $5,000 for five years. In case we can get such help the taking over of the magazine would be without financial responsibility for the two institutions during the first five years and after that it is possible that $1,000 or $2,000 on the part of each would supplement any discrepancy between the cost and income of the established journal. We are, for the reasons given above, asking that the General Education Board consider favorably this proposition.

The Future of Africa in America (April 1942)

While Du Bois was head of the Sociology Department at Atlanta University and editor of Phylon, *he was invited to speak at Vassar College. The text of his lecture follows here.*

Of the social problems that must be faced anew, reconsidered and restated there is none of greater importance than that of the presence on the American continent of thirty millions of persons of Negro descent. Of these perhaps fifteen millions have no visible intermixture of white blood, while the rest are of mixed European, Negro and American Indian descent. There are many other millions, perhaps thirty, who are in fact of Negro descent but with so large an infiltration of white blood that the Negro blood is not in evidence and sometimes quite unknown.

Two considerations set this body of American immigrants apart: their visibility,—the fact that more easily than in the case of any other body of immigrants they can be recognized; and secondly, and closely aligned with this, the fact that the overwhelming majority were forcibly transported as chattel slaves and consequently are only a generation or two removed from the lowest social status. The union of color and status, therefore, has fixed in the minds of men a psychological reaction which must be taken into account. One could hardly be born in America, North or South, and not subconsciously regard color and low social status as inevitably connected. But there would be a difference in rationalizing this fact; in the United States color would [be] assume[d] to be the cause of the status of blacks; while in South America status would include Negroes and Indians for social and historical causes. In the West Indies white descent largely determines status while caste applies usually to unmixed Negro blood.

It has been the fashion in practically every American nation to attempt to ignore the Negro-American as a problem. Even when this population affects other social problems, the situation is often considered and treated as though the Negro element were not there and did not greatly modify the conditions of the problem. For instance many books on immigration to the United States ignore entirely the Negro immigrant. When foreign immigrants are considered often the Negro is regarded neither as an immigrant nor as a native American. (Compare [Louis] Adamic's *Two Way Passage*.) When restriction of immigration into the United States was debated between 1917 and 1927, the basis gradually was changed from the proportion of the foreign born of different origin to consideration of the original racial stocks as the standard for future incomers. But at the beginning of the Nineteenth Century, 19 per cent of the inhabitants of America were of Negro descent. It took some adroit wording of the law and administration of its provisions to avoid this uncomfortable fact, but it was avoided. Visitors to the West Indies, especially if they are from the United States, are surprised and intrigued at the fact that the West Indies are predominantly Negroid, but they say little about it. Thereafter they leave the West Indies out of their consideration of democracy and equality; of general progress and development; without the openly stated reason, but with the reserve judgment that such development is either impossible or undesirable in a land of Negroes. Thus the West Indies and Central America tend to become a sort of international slum to be exploited by foreign capital and tourists.

On the other hand, it is increasingly evident that we must in the future give more notice to this element among the nations of the Americas. When after this second World War we come to consider the pressing social problems before us, the Negro is going to be an element in this problem, not simply because of his actual social condition, but because of the psychological reaction of his fellow citizens toward him. In the matter of poverty, for instance, which we are going to face after the war, not as an inevitable curse, but as something which will yield to remedial measures, we will have to remember and take account of the past. We will recall that the plight of labor in South America and the West Indies, makes poverty a pressing and immediate problem and that the condition of labor there finds its greatest and most convincing excuse in the fact that the labor of these countries is largely Negro and Indian. That Negroes and Indians will always be poor, is accepted as both probable and bearable and the only solution will lie in their becoming white by absorption and white immigration. Until that time, former philosophy has assumed that poverty, disease and inefficiency must characterize the laboring class. Imported capital will thrive on low wage and servile conditions, while labor laws and unions will be few. In the same way in the United States the whole labor movement, especially in its attempt to fight poverty by unionization, has long been faced and frustrated by the fact that perhaps an eighth of that labor is of Negro descent and unless unionized, can be and has been widely used to break down the living standards and keep down wages of white labor. Skilled labor enclaves, like the locomotive engineers and the machinists, have maintained a purely racial exclusion from these unions; but where mass production has superseded special skills, the Negro worker competes as in the automobile industry. On the other hand, white labor because of inherited cultural patterns and surrounding public opinion is unwilling to recognize Negro laborers as fellow human beings. Often this resentment flares in riot and mob rule.

Out of this situation arise, as children of poverty, disease and crime: a widespread incidence of communicable and dangerous disease, a great loss of time through sickness, the death of millions of people in the prime of life. And also a great amount of crime evidenced, as crime always is, among the young, by stealing and fighting and low sex mores; and leading to bitter reprisals and large expense of police and courts; and to the continuous manufacture of a distinct criminal element not only in Harlem but over the land.

What now is going to be said of a frontal attack on poverty after this war if this attack is to include not only the Southern United States and the Negro slums of New York and Chicago, but also Cuba, Puerto Rico, Honduras and Bahia? Will not the ready reply be: Impossible! Inconceivable! and would not the cost include dearer sugar and cocoa and a lower return on investment? Finally, there would be the one unanswerable reason against any action: Race. The alternative would be to attack poverty among white workers only but this cannot be done in America today.

Stepping beyond this, we face even greater post-war difficulty, when we come to the problem of applying something of what we have been newly preaching and even screaming about democracy, after two wars to defend democracy have been fought. Long before these wars, there was the deliberate exclusion of the great majority of Negroes from political rights by reason of poverty and ignorance, in the West Indies and South America; the attempt to realize anything that could really be called democracy involves equality; equality of status based at least on approach to equality of income. So far as Negroes are not regarded as equals, there can be no real conception of a democracy which includes them. In the United States most Negroes have been disfranchised no matter what their social and intellectual status might be.

Historically Americans have sought three ways out of this impasse: religious conversion: climatic extinction and biologic inferiority. The conscience of England and New England based excuse for slavery on heathenism, from which the Society for the Propagation of the Gospel proposed wholesale conversion. Invested capital in the colonies resisted this effort first by obstructing the instruction of slaves and finally by declaring openly with Virginia in 1667: "Baptism doth not alter the condition of the person as to his bondage or freedom, in order that diverse masters freed from this doubt may more carefully endeavor the propagation of Christianity."

There is no doubt of the large public opinion which historically turned to one solution of this problem and that was the question of how to be rid of these people by natural death; how by physical removal or social pressure so to reduce the number of proportion of persons of Negro descent that the residue could be absorbed without noticeable difficulty. It is interesting to reflect how sincerely we have hoped in the past for some such solution. When for instance, the fathers of the American Revolution suppressed the slave trade they believed that they were not only curbing an unholy traffic, but also, by cutting off the artificial increase of the Negro population, they were going to leave the Negroes already in America to a fate of inevitable extinction. Relying on the evidence of the slave trade in the West Indies and in some parts of the United States, they believed that from climatic reasons and biologic differences, the Negro could not survive, unassisted by foreign immigration. Jamaica, for instance, had in 1690, 40,000 Negroes. Between 1620 and 1820, 800,000 more were imported. Yet in 1820 there were only 340,000 Negroes on the island. The supporters of the colonization movement were of many minds; some wished simply to transport free Negroes. But numbers hoped to assist nature by starting Negro emigration, which would gradually so grow in volume as to reduce the Negro population and leave the residue to self-extinction, through the very hopelessness of their situation.

After the American Civil War this hope was reborn. Governor Sharkey of Mississippi sat before a congressional committee in 1866 and assured them with tears in his eyes that the emancipated Negroes were bound to die out. "My expectation concerning them is that they are destined to extinction, beyond all doubt. We must judge of the future by the past. I could tell you a great many circumstances to that effect; I am sorry I did not come prepared with means to state the percentage of deaths among them. It is alarming, appalling. I think they will gradually die out. Some of them will become thrifty and prosperous; but as a general thing, I think they are destined to extinction. I may be mistaken; I hope I am; but that is my impression." The census of 1870 seemed to confirm this; showing an increase of less than 10 per cent for Negroes in the decade; but when in 1880 there came a census more accurately and more scientifically taken, the whole nation was aghast at an apparent Negro increase of 35 per cent. The nation, we might say, was bitterly disappointed because the Negro race in America was surviving; and was only partially appeased when these official figures were officially "revised" to increases of 21 per cent and 22 per cent respectively.

In somewhat similar ways, in the West Indies after emancipation there was a more or less tacit thought that England and France and Denmark might profitably wait and let matters go as they would, until the Negroes of those most beautiful parts of America were so decimated by laziness and disease that they could be replaced by white immigration. The Negro refused to die.

In South America the same problem was faced in a different way: there was no question of letting the chief labor force die out; let it live and work;

but let it become a real part of the state only as it was physically absorbed into the white race. Brazil, with eighteen million Negroes and mulattoes out of fifty million inhabitants in 1940, was never particularly worried as to whether the Negro died out or not, so long as he remained a fairly submissive laborer and was gradually absorbed into the nation leaving white culture dominant.

Realizing at last more or less clearly and after the lapse of long years, that the Negro physically is a fixture in America, without the slightest hope that he is going to decrease in numbers, we are faced by the question as to how far force, either the social force of caste or actual physical force in other guise, can be used to settle this problem of black folk in America. Of course the greatest hindrance here is the ethical problem. After all, America represents the part of the world where the Christian religion has shown in some respects its highest development and most efficient organization. It was possible so to twist the tenets of that religion as at first to excuse the slave trade and afterward to condone slavery; but it was more difficult for Christians to face the problem of caste restriction and social suppression.

Deliberate and planned suppression of a group of human beings could only be defended if it were based on religious dogma or on accepted scientific proof of an inborn and unchangeable inferiority that no wish nor act could change and which put the sacred duty of self defense on white civilization.

The attempt of the Christian church, Catholic and Protestant, to build a foundation of religious dogma and biblical sanction beneath Negro slavery is one of the most curious and disreputable incidents of organized religion. As Bishop Hopkins of Vermont solemnly voiced it: "The Almighty, foreseeing this total degradation of the race, ordained them to servitude or slavery under the descendants of Shem and Japheth, doubtless because he judged it to be their fittest condition. And all history proves how accurately the prediction has been accomplished, even to the present day."

Gradually appeal was made to science in place of theology. It is astonishing with what bitter, almost missionary zeal, the attempt to prove the biological inferiority of the Negro was carried on for over a hundred years and still persists in wide circles. It began with the Cotton Kingdom and the attempt to defend its income by proving Negroes were natural and eternal slaves. Religion, and philanthropy were forced into subserviency to this dogma. And even today when science has rebelled and regained its independence and self-respect, the belief in Negro inferiority widely persists.

The argument against Negro equality began with an appeal to history and observable facts; the white race alone was civilized and the inventors and spreaders of civilization; the yellow race had contributed a little; the black race nothing. Then came the Darwinian "survival of the fittest": Africa was a land of slavery because Negroes were fit slaves, and white men, fit masters; when biology began to question race distinctions, measurements of head form and brain weight were appealed to. When the results of such studies yielded further confusion there was widespread appeal to psychological reactions which were supposed at first to measure "native" intelligence.

With this went a series of historical and social studies designed to disclose the ignorance and inefficiency of emancipated Negroes. The leading universities of the United States united to show that the worst result of the Civil War was the enfranchisement of Negroes and that the emancipated slave was worse off than his fathers.

Despite this desperate and ruthless crusade backed by fiction and art, the experience of Brazil, the West Indies and the United States emphasizes the fact that a considerable and growing proportion of Negroes and mulattoes are modern civilized men, with every prospect of becoming increasingly efficient and creative. The contrast between the white and dark populations of America can no longer for a moment be considered a contrast between cultivated and the uncultivated. The most we can say is that, if one compares the two groups of white and black one will find at the bottom a larger proportion of Negroes and Indians than whites; but in both groups these lower classes share the same human characteristics. On the other hand, at the head of both these groups you will find a small but undeniable proportion of Negroes and Indians side by side with the larger proportion of whites and with no essential differences in ability and creativeness.

The social average of the Negro group is at present considerably lower than that of the white group; but there are Negroes, and many of them, quite as cultivated as the corresponding classes of whites, just as there are whites quite as hopeless as the lowest class of Negroes. It is the unquestioned truth of facts like these that, in spite of all the accumulated race fiction, has swept the foundations away from modern theories of race and especially of race distinctions based on the color line. There is no scientist of repute today who for a moment would declare that biological differences between white folk and black consign an individual of either race inevitably to a lower status. Consequently the whole argument for a different treatment and a different fate to be meted out for Negroes can no longer be based upon the biological or evolutionary argument. We must face the Negro problem as a series of cultural facts.

We have, of course, the right to believe that under other circumstances it would have been wiser, and we would have preferred, to keep peoples of different cultural backgrounds and different physical appearance in the parts of the world where they were first developed or at least to make contacts under happier conditions. This may or may not have been advisable; probably not, when we consider the cultural values of race and group contact under any conditions. In any case we must remember that it was the greed and adventure of the white race that in modern days disturbed the ancient distribution of mankind and that Europeans did this primarily for their own

selfish purposes. Moreover, we have no right to say that because other generations were guilty of the African slave trade and the domination of Asia,
that present peoples have no part in the blame. They are heirs of their success,
if success it may be called. They are heirs to the enormous prosperity of
the Sugar Empire and the Cotton Kingdom and of the capitalistic methods of
production which Negro slavery in America was primarily responsible in
upbuilding in England and Europe. America could not have been America,
without the African slave trade and African slavery. If, therefore, Americans
are the heirs of an ancient error, so long as they insist upon grasping and
holding the advantages of that error, they must pay for it.

In the United States we have gone far enough to know that the ability which
can be developed among persons of Negro descent, is of the widest range;
that in physical, intellectual and artistic lines, the Negro is not only in
evidence but if it were not for deliberate hindrance to his development he
would doubtless make even better showing. We know that his health and
crime can be adequately explained by his poverty, and that increased income
and education can without reasonable doubt raise the mass of the Negro
people to or above the average level of their white neighbors.

But these very facts disclose a problem which the nation and the white world
are unwilling to face. Even with present barriers, if the Negro continues to
develop in the United States and Latin America, there is not a single door
of human progress and of social recognition at which he is not going to knock
in the future with increasingly bitter violence. On the other hand, if the
barriers are done away with, the Negro race in America is going to reach
within a calculable time a level of efficiency which will challenge the whole
assumption of the natural superiority of the white race. It will take more and
more deliberate effort on the part of whites to enforce caste restrictions.

What do we propose to do about this after the world war? Are we going
to see that the Negroes of the Southern United States are admitted to the
ballot on the same terms as white folk? Are we going to insist that the England
which we have helped rescue at fabulous expenditure of treasure, installs
democratic forms of government to control capital and investment in her
colonies and especially in the West Indies? Are the states of South America
like Venezuela, Brazil and Colombia going to see to it that through education
and social uplift, a foundation of real democratic government is built upon
this Negro and Indian Labor? Are we going to continue to let North American
influence in South America emphasize and even insist on white supremacy
and color discrimination, while all South America and Central American
countries who wish capital and tourists respond to this pressure?

In answer to these queries we may note today four centers of solution for
future relations between black people and white on the American continent:
the policy of racial absorption especially in Brazil; the policy of absorption

with Negro suppression through the domination of capital as in Jamaica and Cuba; the policy of racial segregation illustrated by Haiti; and the policy of legal caste shown in the Southern states of the United States.

We have grown used to being told the settlement of the Negro problem in Brazil is merely a matter of time and absorption: that if we shut our eyes long enough, a white Brazil and white Venezuela and Colombia will emerge and Africa in South America disappear. The United States has made a wry face at such a process and tried to blame most of the political and social ills of American regions south of us to this miscegenation. Many of our unfortunate relationships with our continental neighbors have arisen because of this racial prejudice. We have established ourselves as missionaries of white supremacy and refused personal relationships with South Americans who show too evidently Negro and Indian blood. We are willing to accent the white result, but hate the colored means.

Backed by the tremendous power of our capital and tourist wealth, this attitude has unduly influenced race relations, and when added to the equally strict but more carefully expressed attitude of England, countries like Brazil, Chile, Peru, Colombia and Venezuela have striven to be "white" nations and make the process of the absorption of Indians and Negro involve the gradual disappearance of these people.

Biologically such absorption is difficult because of the numbers involved. Fully half of the fifty million population of Brazil today is of acknowledged Negro and Indian descent and this proportion of whites has only been maintained by large Portuguese and Italian immigration. Of the fifteen million people in Ecuador, Colombia and Venezuela not more than 20 per cent are white; perhaps only 10 percent of Peru's six and one-half millions. This means that biological absorption into a "white" race will be difficult without greatly increased white immigration. Such immigration is hard to procure because Indians and Negro form a chief laboring proletariat with whom white labor cannot compete. And if the status of the Negroes and Indians deliberately is raised, white immigration will further decrease. The result already is a noticeable darkening of the white group in most of these countries with a distinct Indian or Negroid mixture.

In addition to this, and of far greater importance is the question of cultural blending. The Negro brought to America strongly developed cultural patterns which even slavery could not entirely efface. With emancipation came his frantic efforts to adopt white European culture, and the net result has been a cultural blending which has deeply stamped South America in music, dance, art and literature. So much so that in the deeper currents of thought a new race is envisioned in which the strong Negro and Indian element is frankly recognized.

On the other hand, the economic trend is away from this. No South American country wishes to be regarded as "colored" in a world organized in industry and politics for white peoples. In diplomatic and social intercourse usually with Europe, always with North America, South America suppresses color, and in this policy the Negroids usually consent and cooperate. A dark Brazilian might occupy a high office of state but he would never be ambassador to St. James. And even domestic industry using English and United States capital would tend to keep the black worker "in his place" and withhold authority from mulattoes. There are only occasional signs of revolt against this pattern of action on the part of blacks and mulattoes, although this may increase.

The racial absorption in Brazil therefore is not simple and has not had altogether happy results. With the avoidance of racial friction and the open color bar which Brazil has accomplished, there has come the economic class line, when color combined with poverty has kept a large class of dark laborers in a depressed condition; and which consequently makes it unlikely that a Brazilian would care to boast of his African ancestry as openly as he would assert his descent from white Europeans. Unless, therefore, racial absorption in Brazil is going to be accompanied by economic emancipation and a real democracy of equals, the solution of the Brazilian problem of African and American cannot be really accomplished. Moreover such amalgamation, as many see, will not leave Brazil "white." Negro and Indian blood will produce a new race, undeniably "colored."

In the West Indies the pattern again changes. Of the 13 million inhabitants, probably 12 millions are of Negro descent. This means that the so-called whites are largely mulattoes. In Cuba for instance, competent authorities maintain that 60 per cent are of Negro descent although the census admits less than 40 per cent. Manifestly, the white minority cannot absorb the black majority of West Indies. The partial absorption dating from the sixteenth century has established a powerful class of mulattoes who for the most part are distinctly white in mores and often white in color. Every economic and social incentive drives these folk to escape into the white race. It is this that leads the colored Dominican Republican to welcome Jews and bar black immigration.

On the other hand, the blacks, both in culture and blood, dominate this beautiful, rich and intriguing part of the world and are held by the unyielding color bar especially of England and America. United States capital and English investment in Jamaica, Cuba, Puerto Rico, Haiti and the Dominican Republic, rule like tyrants, to establish color caste, keep down wages and deny labor the right to organize. Political power is mainly in the hands of the whites and the property-holding mulattoes. In Cuba and Puerto Rico where the dark proletariat has some power and is trying to exercise it, the whole power of property and foreign investment is holding them in check.

In most of these islands, one sees a frantic rush of black folk to be included in the privileged status of the whites. Most Negroes seek to accomplish this not so much by cultural progress as by breeding white at any social sacrifice.

The cost of this to family life, normal contacts and political action is too great. Always you have left a poverty-stricken peasantry who can be deprived of real political power and social advantage because they are a depressed economic class, in addition to being Negroes. American capital comes in to strengthen and perpetuate this class and caste.

In the case of Haiti one has the solution of separation: a black republic with a mulatto elite but with the African cultural background distinctly recognized. Instead of that being a solution, it makes Haiti at distinct disadvantage in her whole intercourse with the white world. She not only suffered immense economic injustice in her brave effort to make herself free from France, but she has suffered the same injustice in her intercourse with England, the United States and South America. She has become a sort of pariah of the Western Hemisphere, excluded largely from cultural contact, from economic cooperation and from recognition in the society of nations.

In her inner social development Haiti occupies a peculiar place. Her land belongs primarily to her illiterate peasants which means that the weapon of land monopoly has been denied to Haitian aristocrats. The Haitian elite, therefore, has not become like the East Indian elite and the white overlords of Cuba, a rich oligarchy. On the other hand, they are, on the whole poor men but educated and cultured. If there can be built up between this leading aristocracy and the Haitian peasantry a nexus of leadership and direction, without slavery of labor which has in the past and in so many places characterized this leadership, Haiti may give to the world an extraordinary example of economic and social development. There are some signs of this: there are an educational movement among the younger educated people and an interest in Haitian folklore and African cultural survival which are encouraging. Perhaps no other part of the West Indies, or even of South America, has so rare a chance for social experiment.

Haiti's prolonged and determined fight for recognition is one of the finest the modern world has seen. She rightly claims, as her greatest statesman said at the recent American Conference of National Commissions of Intellectual Cooperation at Havana, to be the center of French culture in America. Haitian art and literature is no small part of French art. But far more than this, Haiti represents Africa. Nearly all the chief African tribes have left their cultural imprint and this is being to a degree consciously developed. Alone of American peoples, Haiti is not ashamed to be black.

In the United States our whole social advance has been continually frustrated and made paradoxical by our attitude toward Negroes. We declared all men free and equal when we owned 750,000 black slaves. We fought for a Union of white men and could get it only after using a half million black soldiers and laborers and emancipating four million slaves as a desperate but only possible bid for victory. We cannot today discuss democracy; we cannot carry through a draft for war; we cannot hold an election; we cannot establish hospitals; we cannot raise wages; or do any one of the thousand things that social uplift calls for, without running across a discrimination with regard to Negroes that either blocks or weakens our best efforts or convicts us as hypocrites. With all our tumult and shouting and pious rage against Hitler, we are perfectly aware that his race philosophy and methods are but extreme development and application of our own save that he is drawing his race lines in somewhat different places.

It is ridiculous for an intelligent nation to allow this to go on. In order to preserve our intellectual honesty and ethical pretensions, this question must come in for frank discussion and decision. We cannot permit the Southern United States to be a social back-water in order to hold the Negro "in his place." Neither can we allow the West Indies and Central America to be made deliberate slums for the profits and vacation activities of the whites. In South America we have long pretended to see a possible solution in the gradual amalgamation of whites, Indians and blacks. But this amalgamation does not in our mind envisage any decrease of power and prestige among whites as compared with Indians, Negroes and mixed bloods; if it did and so far as it may, it will result in a new mulatto culture not a white. A white culture means an inclusion within the so-called white group of a considerable infiltration of dark blood, while at the same time maintaining the economic exploitation and consequent political disfranchisement of dark blood as such. We have thus the spectacle of the Dominican Republic, Cuba, Puerto Rico and even Jamaica trying desperately and doggedly to be "white" in spite of the fact that the majority of the white group is of Negro or Indian descent. The success of such an effort spells prolonged poverty, disease and crime.

Before everything today in our thought must stand the question of the induction of the Negro in the whole Western Hemisphere into the democratic status. Democracy cannot have a rebirth in the world unless it firmly establishes itself in America. It cannot establish itself in America if the majority of Negroes in the United States are disfranchised despite intelligence and property; if property barriers and administrative oligarchy reduce Negroes to serfs in the West Indies; and if there is in South America no determined attempt through education and social uplift to make the Negro and the Indian and the mixed blood an intelligent, modern citizen. Denial of steps like these, is simply conspiracy of industrial exploitation, the rule of political oligarchies and the encouragement of future economic and race war.

This problem of the African in America cannot be avoided. He is not dying out; and he is not likely to die out. His sudden physical absorption without planned social effort would result in a distinct lowering of the level of culture over wide areas. His slow absorption if accompanied by curbing and extinction of his genius is but worship of white domination. On the other hand, the attempt to raise culture among the whites and lower or even retard it among the Negroes and mulattoes, is a task inexcusable if not impossible.

There is needed, therefore, in the Western world widespread consultation and planning, backed by united effort, first to decide just how far we are willing to treat Negroes and mulattoes as human beings, and if not, what tenable justification we have for denying it. If we are going to break down the barriers and at great cost in wealth and effort gradually raise this depressed class to the level of culture of which they are capable, we must frankly understand that this does not involve the continued domination of white world, in the future; in fact, it is the beginning of the end of such domination. There is no moral question facing the Americas of greater and more pressing importance than this question of racial tolerance in the Western Hemisphere.

We are only deceiving ourselves if we try to think that the solution of the problem of these millions of black folk in America is going to cost us nothing. That simply by a polite waving of the hands and judicious propaganda the problem will disappear. No. If we want to realize humanity and world peace, this can only be done at the cost of so thorough and drastic an overturning of our inherited fixations and cultural patterns as will shake the Western World. In the first place it will call for a stern attitude toward Europe and especially the British Empire. The British Empire is predominantly colored: black, brown and yellow people form the overwhelming majority of its folk. It has never been a democratic organization and does not today propose to be one, because its white minority is supporting itself in luxury from the depressed wage and cheap raw material which they are extracting from colored folk through their organized and dominant military power and industrial technique.

Not only has this got to be overthrown, but the means of its overthrowing is a firm conviction on the part of white America that a change in the present organization of the world is best for the world. And that only by recognition and conviction, and action following such conviction, can the world come to a place where it recognizes human beings as essentially equal and works toward the actual equality which may be accomplished.

There are many people in the Americas and especially in the United States who would rather die than see any such world or equal white and colored people. They must be made to realize that this is the ultimate price which they are going to pay for the solution of the Negro problem. That otherwise they are setting before the world a vision of continual struggle, of continual recurrence of war after war, the end of which no living man can see.

The Future of Europe in Africa (April 1942)

The trip north during which Du Bois spoke at Vassar also included a stop at Yale University to present an address.

Two great world movements in modern times have had to do with the relation of Africa to the rest of the world; the first was the African slave trade which established capitalism in England and the Sugar Empire and the Cotton Kingdom in America. The second was the partitioning of Africa which was foreshadowed in the Congress of Berlin in 1878 and planned in detail in the Berlin Conference of 1884.

Since this partitioning there has been invested in Africa a sum estimated at six thousand five hundred million dollars which is a sum larger than the total gold reserves of the British Empire and France in 1939. As a result of this investment, there were exported from Africa in 1935, seven hundred million dollars worth of exports consisting of gold, diamonds, copper, wool, corn, cotton, palm products, cocoa, rubber and ground nuts. Since 1900, the total capital owned by the United States in Africa has increased from five hundred millions to fifteen hundred millions and is nearly equal to British investment.

One would think that a continent which was so integral a part of the world trade and world industrial organization, inhabited as it is by at least one hundred fifty million of people, would be carefully considered in any plans for post-war reconstruction. This is not the case. If we consider the proposed peace plans we find that Africa is practically unmentioned or referred to only vaguely in general phrases which have the same intent and connotation. In President Roosevelt's four freedoms, May 1941, he manifestly was not thinking of Africa when he mentioned freedom of speech, freedom from want and freedom from terror. When Pope Pius XII spoke in June 1941, on peace and the changing social order, his only reference which could have been to Africa was "The more favorable distribution of men on the earth's surface."

The British Christian leaders in May 1941, made ten proposals for a lasting peace. The tenth reference was to the resources of the earth which "should be used as God's gifts to the whole human race." The American Friends Services Committee in June 1941 asked that all nations be assured "equitable access to markets." The eight points of the Atlantic Charter were so obviously aimed at European and North American conditions, that Churchill frankly affirmed this to be the case although he was afterward contradicted by President Roosevelt. Later have come the proposals of Streit and Luce which propose a domination of the world by English-speaking peoples, that is, by the peoples who have led in fostering the slave trade and color caste.

One can see in all these proposals the persistence of old patterns; the need of raw materials from Africa and the assumption that this raw material must be made cheap by land monopoly and low wage; and that the object of the whole organization of Africa must remain primarily the economic advantage of Europe. Yet it is clear that these old patterns of thought and action will be changed if not entirely swept away by the two world wars.

Looking toward such a result, it would be well for thinkers of the modern world to realize much more clearly than they do, just what Africa means. In the first place there is no one Africa. There is in Africa no such unity of physical characteristics; of cultural development; of historical experiences; or of racial identity, that can possibly allow us to look upon the continent as a unity. We may distinguish today at least ten Africas: North Africa with Tunis and Algeria which are in reality a part of Europe; there is French West Africa, a vast and loosely integrated region, where in one small part a splendid educational and cultural development of the natives has gone on together with some economic progress. There is Egypt whose history is well-known and which is still a satellite in the British Empire. From this has been arbitrarily cut off the Anglo-Egyptian Sudan, forming a different problem, a different economy and facing a different destiny. There is Ethiopia only recently discovered by the United States.

Turning westward again we have French Equatorial Africa, an economic echo of the Belgian Congo, the seat in the past of terrible exploitation and in the present of a curious military movement. There is British West Africa consisting of four colonies representing the most advanced possibilities of the Negro race in Africa but held in check by a denial of all real democracy and by carefully organized exploitation. There is the Belgian Congo whose astonishing history is known to all.

British East Africa, consisting of Uganda, Kenya and Tanganyika, combines an advanced native state with the European land-aggression in Kenya and the spoil of German Africa in Tanganyika. There is Portuguese Africa torn in two by the British and dependent upon British economic organization and yet individual and different. And finally, there is South Africa and the Rhodesias where three million white people are holding ten million natives in economic slavery while they rape the land of its priceless gold, jewels, and metals.

There is an extraordinary amount of misinformation and contradiction current concerning this continent, despite the scientific study recently carried on. First of all and most fundamental, is perhaps this singular paradox that African colonies, and indeed all colonies, are never profitable to the mother country and thus represent a sort of philanthropic enterprise, which is to be commended for whatever education and social service it has given, and not to be blamed if these services are miserably inadequate as compared to the need. Directly contradictory to this kind of assertion is the well-known fact that modern colonial imperialism has been a source of immense profit and power to Great Britain, France, Germany and other countries.

The truth of the matter is, that so far as government investment is concerned the money which Great Britain and France and Germany have invested in Africa has yielded small direct returns in taxes and revenue. But on the other hand this governmental investment has been the basis upon which private investors have builded being thus furnished free capital by home taxation; and while the mass of people in the mother country have been taxed heavily for this governmental gift abroad, the private capitalist investors in the colonies have reaped not only interest from their own investment but returns from investments which they did not make protected by armies and navies which they do not support. And in addition, immense sums from raw material and labor whose price is kept at a minimum and sold in the mother country as processed goods at the highest monopoly prices. The net return, therefore, of the white races, for their investment in colored labor and material in Africa has been immense and this, with similar returns from Asia and other parts of the world, has been the cause of the high standard of living, the luxury expenditure and the consumption for show which characterizes modern civilization. This is the basis of the indictment which Africa has against the modern world and this indictment must be answered by the present war or by wars which are bound to come.

The question as to what we want the future of the African people to be; and what they themselves want, must be clearly envisaged. Do we want them simply for their use to Europe, or do we look forward to a time when they are to be deliberately trained for their usefulness to themselves and for their own development? The academic discussion as to the capabilities of Africans for a long time obscured these fundamental questions. So long as Christian moralists and modern scientists considered the Africans in the main were less than men and suited primarily for slavery and domestic service, manifestly any question as to their wants and desires could be avoided. But we know today that this whole argument was initiated by the gain which it gave to men through slavery, and the temptation of considering that a civilization built on the degradation of millions of men was the natural reward of white superiority. There is no question today of the capabilities of native Africans that need for a moment restrain us from considering honestly and sincerely the needs and desires of black folk.

In 1923, the white masters of Kenya who have seized most of the cultivable land in the territory and confined three million natives to fifty thousand square miles of the poorest lands—these whites argued that Europe must give up Asia but cling to Africa with white domination. They said:

> It has been shown that the Black Race possesses imitative but lacks constructive powers, characteristics which justify Lugard's judgment that for the native African "the era of complete independence is not yet visible on the horizon of time." The Controlling Powers may, therefore, aim at advancing the Black Race as far along the road of progress as its capacity allows, without misgivings that the success of their endeavours will lead to a demand for their withdrawal, entailing loss of prestige and trade.

Judging from the experience of missionaries, travelers and government agents it would be clearly possible today to place four centers of education in Africa which would in less than a generation train an intelligentsia capable eventually of taking complete charge of social development of the continent. There are beginnings of such training today at Fort Hare, South Africa, Achimota, and Fourah Bay, West Africa, and Makerere, Uganda. Social development for the welfare of the African would certainly interfere with the private profits of foreign investment and ultimately change entirely the relation of Africa to the modern world. The question is, do we really want this, or desire a world dominated by Anglo-Saxons, or at least by white Europe? Do we want to keep Africa in subjection just as long as it is physically possible? If we do, are we not planting right here inevitable seeds of future hatred, struggle and war?

There is no denying that in such training intellectually and technically of an African intelligentsia we face most difficult problems: the problem of preserving rather than violently destroying the native cultural patterns; all the problems of new inexperienced social leadership. The point is that the decision in these matters must not be left to profiteers, to colonial imperialists or alone to white people. It must become the work of an international mandate with the intelligence of Africa represented on the guiding boards, in cooperation with the half-dead social conscience of Europe. It will mean a new scientific and cultural crusade which might be the greatest result of the two world wars and put reality and decency into the whole Christian missionary crusade, which in the nineteenth century was used not so much to raise the heathen from savagery to civilization as to make safe the investments of white people in African serfdom.

Even if this problem is not frankly faced, the African is bound to be trained increasingly as a fighter and a modern soldier. Black soldiers conquered German Africa during the first World War and helped subdue Italian Africa in the second World War. They were used in Asia in the first World War and their descendants have gone as far as Australia in this war. There is no more dangerous thing in the world than thus setting fire to this potential dynamite. Moreover, to the trite truth that a nation cannot exist half slave and half free, or a culture cannot survive half democratic and half totalitarian, we must add the much more practical and obvious dictum that the modern world cannot survive with attempted democracy among white Europeans and colonial imperialism rampant in Asia and Africa; and that this is true not simply from the point of view of the good of the colored peoples, but from the fact that any attempt at democracy among Europeans will be overthrown if the more powerful classes within the democracy are supported by streams of wealth which come out of the low wage and cheap materials from over more than half the earth. This war cannot end without wide economic revolution in the leading nations of the world. Such revolution can never be satisfactory or complete if the new economy rests on African poverty and Asiatic subjugation.

It is of singular interest to note how we have inevitably moved toward this logic during the present war. Eight basic objects may be discerned as the war progressed.

1. Defense of smaller nations
2. Self-determination in all nations
3. Higher wage for white labor; security and freedom from want
4. Political democracy in the State
5. State control of capital
6. Freedom for "our way of life"
7. Open door for white nations to raw material in Colonial areas occupied largely by colored folk
8. Disarmament and World Police by white folk.

Defense and self-determination were our heritage from the First World War, and were echoed in the Atlantic Charter. That Charter added higher wage and freedom from want for Europe and America; and the open door to raw material which was a concession to the German demand for the "return" of African colonies. The insistence on democracy as an object of the war was by way of answer to dictatorship and state control of capital. "Freedom" for "our way of life," meant continuance of the established system of private profit without essential change.

For a time it looked as though the governments with democratic political methods under the control of private industry, would be aligned in death struggles against political dictatorship and state-controlled industry and capital. However the break between Germany and Russia, even though anticipated, suddenly changed this; throwing British and American democracy allied with Russian Communism, in opposition to German, and Italian dictatorship. Logical justification for this alignment was difficult to furnish. But Hitler and Hess sought to inject the logic by a re-arranged crusade against Communism. They had sympathizers both in England and America, but organized Anglo-Saxon capital feared National Socialism and Fascism almost as much as Communism. Many shared Mr. Moore-Brabazon's secret hope that both "pests" might destroy each other.

Japan was also in the background but was considered as bluffing even when she made peace with Russia. When against all precedent and prophecy she suddenly met the prolonged social insult and open economic war of America with the unannounced attack at Pearl Harbor, the face of World War II was changed. As in a kaleidoscope the whole pattern changed and changed so absolutely that few seem yet to have the courage to re-draw the pattern of this conflict and say for what who are fighting. While before December seventh, Japan had been a shadowy factor in the war, none took her world role seriously. Her attempted conquest of China was looked on as a belated and eastern copy of British and French imperialism.

The attack at Pearl Harbor, the capture of Manila, fall of Singapore, and capture of the Dutch Indies and threat to India put a new face on the war. The United States now openly entered war. For what purpose? For the defense of Poland, Greece and China? For democracy in Germany and India? For state control of capital in Europe, Africa and Asia? For the open door to colonial wealth? For disarmament? The very statement of such aims is curiously contradictory.

There can be little doubt but that the United States with the help of the white portions of the British Commonwealth of Nations; with the neutrality of South America; the silence of Africa and the cooperation or helplessness of most of Asia, can in the end crush and conquer both Germany, Italy, and Japan, especially if Russia continues to cooperate. The cost to the world in wealth and human beings in this struggle will reach fantastic proportions. The loss to art, literature and civilization will be incalculable. Nevertheless, so far as one can now predict, Germany, Italy, and Japan can be conquered by England and the United States.

The eventual attitude of Russia cannot be forecast with complete confidence. Russia has more reason to resent past aggression on the part of England and America than on the part of Japan. Her accord with China was not with Chiang Kai-Shek, but with his bitter communist opponents, whom he once tried to destroy by wholesale assassination and whom he now endures because he must. Russia's clear duty to herself is to smash Hitler. After that, what? The choice of her then joining England and America in crushing Japan depends on the Anglo-Saxon program in Africa and Asia.

What now can we say is the object of the Anglo-Saxon world in its conquest of Asia? It must have an object beyond justifiable anger for the sudden and ill-advised onslaught of Japan on Hawaii. It is too late in the history of the world to enter upon a war of this kind and fight simply for revenge. On the other hand, can we say, or do we want to say, that we are fighting for democracy in Asia? If we are fighting to make it possible for the people of China to establish a real republic upon the foundations of the ancient and magnificent Chinese culture, are we also fighting to free India from British domination, so that by her own will and by democratic methods she may become a modern commonwealth? Are we fighting to make the Dutch Indies not simply a peaceful center of cheap and politically quiescent labor with enough of education and self-government to keep down discontent, but a real modern country with educated folk and well-paid labor? Are we fighting to break down the indefensible monopoly of the great continents of Australia and New Zealand, opening the doors to all men who can reach a reasonable standard of economic and cultural efficiency and not confining citizenship and even residence only to people with a certain color of skin? Are we ready to admit to the United States and Canada colored men who are fit for residence and citizenship?

If these are our objects, they are worthy of every effort of mankind. They are worth all the blood that will be spilled and all the treasure that will be spent. But on the other hand, if we have such high objects as this, why do we not express them? Why does not that great English leader, whose expenditure in cigars for a month probably approaches in cost the income of an Indian peasant family for a year ($25.00), join Franklin Roosevelt and openly declare these objects? At present they do not agree. Churchill has said that the Atlantic Charter applies only to Europe. Roosevelt declares: "The Atlantic Charter applies not only to the parts of the world that border the Atlantic, but to the whole world; disarmament of aggressors, self-determination of nations and peoples, and the four freedoms."

Is there no increasing danger that we revert to the age-old method of preparing a nation for war? The discredited method of whipping people to insensate hate and deifying cruelty into unheard of valor; and designating the majority of the people of the world as "yellow bastards"? Moreover with all European and American power and their ability to conquer Japan, what about our ability to hold Japan and Asia conquered in continued tribute, to our industrial empire? Can we count on India, China, Java and the Philippines to continue to fight for "white prestige" in Asia? Are we not set to plunge the world eventually into a vast race war?

I wrote in 1920 [in *Darkwater*]: "What of this darker world? ... Most men belong to this world. With Negro and Negroid, East Indian, Chinese, and Japanese they form two-thirds of the population of the world. A belief in humanity is a belief in colored men. If the uplift of mankind must be done by men, then the destinies of this world will rest ultimately in the hands of darker nations.

"What, then, is this dark world thinking? It is thinking that as wild and awful as this shameful war was, it is nothing to compare with that fight for freedom which black and brown and yellow men must and will make unless their oppression and humiliation and insult at the hands of the White World cease. The Dark World is going to submit to its present treatment just as long as it must and not one moment longer!"

Where in a day like this is the militant and vociferant Christianity of the modern world? Why does not the church, Catholic and Protestant, with the religion of Mohammed join the faint efforts of the Buddha in India, in a more practical effort to achieve peace, decency and civilization than Gandhi has been able to accomplish, by simply saying: we are fighting for Peace and Universal Peace; we are fighting for Democracy and for a democracy which will include all men of all colors and all nations; we are fighting to apply peace, democracy and economic justice to the Negro tribes of Africa despite the reaction of Dutch Boers and English investors; to the people of

the Dutch Indies despite all the wealth that Holland has squeezed out of
these dark islands; and to the people of Japan in spite of the fact that we
fear the power and possibilities of the Japanese nation as rivals in the upbuilding
of civilization?

Here is a magnificent opportunity in the midst of the worst catastrophe
which the world has seen, to turn degradation into cultural triumph.

In the meantime today what is happening in Africa? The propaganda of
directed telegram service in the world, would lead us to think that Africa
had no thought nor stake in the present war and that after the war all Africa
will return to normality. On the contrary there has been serious upheaval
in South Africa. A movement among the Dutch to disfranchise both British
and blacks; a resultant effort among the British to draw closer to the Africans
through military combination and promises for the future. A determined
effort to keep down the strong movement for democratic reform in black
West Africa. The organization of the virtual independence of French
Equatorial Africa, under a black governor, with the free French who have
helped in the conquest of Libya. And then finally the extraordinary driving
of the Italians out of Ethiopia.

Here propaganda has reached an extraordinary height in the United States.
In the final conquest of Ethiopia an agreement was formed between the
Emperor of Ethiopia and the British. It was not a treaty. It was an "agreement"
for two years and yet this astonishing agreement virtually makes Ethiopia
a protectorate of the British Empire while the British advertise that "Ethiopia
is now free and independent"!

By this agreement the British minister takes precedence over all foreign
representatives accredited to Ethiopia. The British and no others appoint
advisers to the Emperor, including police and judges. Britain lends Ethiopia
two and a half million pounds to be expended as the British advisers permit.
Currency is under British control. Italian prisoners are under the control of
the British and not of the Ethiopians. And Great Britain controls the army
and has a monopoly of civil and military air service in Ethiopia; and takes
full charge of the one railway.

Worse than this the Italians made investments and staked out monopolies
and claims in Ethiopia; the claims covering practically the whole mining
prospects in the country. These claims are going to be settled by England,
as she puts it, in accordance "with international usage"; which means that
Ethiopia is probably going to be made to pay for her conquest by European
monopoly of her natural resources under the control of Great Britain and
in the name of democracy!

May I illustrate further what I am saying by the case of the first National
Congress of British West Africa which met in Accra, capital of the Gold
Coast colony, in mid-March, 1920. The congress was composed of delegates
from Nigeria, the Gold Coast, Sierra Leone and Gambia. The chairman of

the Congress in his inaugural address said "it is important to note that each
one of these delegates is an African belonging to a distinctive African
family and thereby commanding the rights of property and other interests
either in his own right or in the right of the family to which he belongs.
It follows from this that apart from the delegates to the conference, being
the natural leaders of the people of their several communities, they have in
themselves the right to appeal to His Majesty's Government for such constitutional reforms as in their judgment are necessary."

The Congress then drafted a memorial to His Majesty the King which is a
worthy and remarkable document:

> In presenting the case for the franchise for the different colonies
> composing British West Africa, namely, The Gambia, Sierra Leone,
> the Gold Coast and Nigeria, it is important to remember that each of
> these colonies is at present governed under the Crown Colony System.
> By that is meant that the power of selecting members for the legislative
> councils is in the Governor of each colony and not dependent upon the
> will of the people through an elective system.
>
> Up to the beginning of the present year (1920), there had been no
> improvement in the situation with the result that in March 1920, a
> Conference of Africans of British West Africa was held at Accra, the
> Capital of the Gold Coast Colony, at which were present the represen-
> tatives of each of the four colonies composing British West Africa....
>
> It will be noticed that the first resolution deals with legislative (includ-
> ing municipal) reforms and the granting of the franchise and administrative
> reforms with particular reference to equal rights and opportunities....
>
> In the demand for the franchise by the people of British West Africa,
> it is not to be supposed that they are asking to be allowed to copy a
> foreign institution. On the contrary, it is important to notice that the
> principle of electing representatives to local councils and bodies is
> inherent in all the systems of British West Africa. According to African
> institutions every member of a community belongs to a given family
> with its duly accredited head, who represents that family in the village
> council, naturally composed of the heads of the several families. Similarly
> in a district council the different representatives of each village or town
> would be appointed by the different villages and towns, and so with
> the Provincial Council until, by the same process, we arrive at the
> Supreme Council, namely, the State Council, presided over by the
> Paramount Chief....
>
> The Congress presses for the appointment of duly qualified and
> experienced legal men to judicial appointments in British West Africa
> no matter how high the emolument might be. It also presses for the
> appointment of African Barristers of experience, many of whom as jurists

and legislative Councillors are found along the West Coast, to appointments on the judicial bench as well as other judicial appointments. The Congress contends that there are African legal men of experience capable of holding any judicial office in British West Africa. It may be mentioned that in Sierra Leone years ago the late Hon. Sir Samuel Lewis, Knight, C.M.G., an African, held the appointment of Acting Chief Justice; the late Mr. J. Renner Maxwell of Oxford University, an African, held the office of Chief Magistrate of the Gambia, which was equivalent then to the office of Chief Justice; that His Honour the late Mr. Justice Francis Smith, an African, was the Senior Puisne Judge of the Gold Coast, and on several occasions held the appointment of Acting Chief Justice; that the late Mr. James A. McCarthy, an African, was for many years the Queen's Advocate of Sierra Leone, which was then equivalent to the post of Attorney General, and on many occasions acted as Chief Justice of that Colony. Subsequently he became the Solicitor General of the Gold Coast and acted as Puisne Judge on several occasions in that Colony. Further, the late Sir Conrad Reeves, an African, was Chief Justice of Jamaica for many years. Therefore it is no new thing to suggest that worthy Africans should be admitted to the highest judicial offices in the judicial service of British West Africa. It is worthy of note that so renowned is the forensic ability of the African legal practitioner, generally a barrister of one of the Inns of Court in London, that they usually control all the practice in British West Africa and the percentage of European practitioners is hardly three.

It must be remembered that this clear and concise demand for elementary democratic rights among black people of British West Africa was drafted by native born Africans of Negro descent. Some attention was paid to it by granting an elective element in the governor's councils, still retaining however for the governor a majority of the council so as to enable him to pass any legislation which he might wish; and in addition to this in these same councils, in all the colonies, sat men representing business and industry directly; that is, voting in the name [of] and for foreign investors which added to the power which those investors had as English subjects and voters in England.

The future significance of Africa in the modern world will grow. These same white inhabitants of Kenya said in 1923:

> The development of British territories in Africa opens up a vista of commercial expansion so endless that calculated description is difficult. The bare facts are that the area of these territories is 4,000,000 square miles, as compared with India's 1,900,000; that India's overseas trade is about 350,000,000, and British Africa's (excluding Egypt) is about 292,000,000; that the non-self-governing territories, whose total area is 2,628,498 square miles, already produce an overseas trade of 76,500,000,

although their development can hardly be said to have begun; that the average fertility and mineral wealth of their soil are at least equal to those of any other great land mass; that they hold an intelligent fast-breeding native population of about 6 million, waiting for guidance to engage in the production of the raw materials of industry and food stuffs; and that white settlement co-operating with the native populations does stimulate production many hundreds of times, and does bring about a demand for manufactured articles out of all proportion to its numerical strength.

The development of Africa from 1923 to 1939 justifies this forecast. Nevertheless after the war Ethiopia will be a British or Italian protectorate ready for ruthless exploitation. French Africa and the Belgian Congo are going to belong to Germany or to England; Portuguese Africa is already a pawn to the English investor and there is in all Africa no single English colony where democratic methods of control over government or industry will be recognized. American investment will make our ownership of land and labor in Africa equal to the British. When one realizes this, the future of Africa stands out in clear and dangerous outline.

I have been meeting recently with a committee that proposed to lay down certain post-war plans for the continent of Africa.[1] There are represented in that committee a number of missionary and educational foundations and indirectly there is represented the industrial organization of America, that is, the various bodies receiving their chief support from philanthropy and this philanthropy has its original source in the profits made out of industrial enterprise in this country, in Africa and Asia. The question is how free is this committee going to feel in the planning for the ultimate emancipation of Africa? To guide the committee I have offered to them the following post-war plan in the shape of a statement. Frankly, I do not believe the committee is going to adopt it, but I am convinced that unless something like this is adopted, believed in and adhered to, the troubles of the world today are not going to end in Asia. They are going to begin there and spread to Africa.

Looking forward to the World Peace which must eventually follow World War, certain basic principles governing our thought and action in regard to the people of Africa, seem clear.

---

1. Du Bois is referring to a Committee of Forty, from England and the United States, appointed late in 1941 to study the relationship of Africa to the war. In 1942 this committee issued a book, *The Atlantic Charter and Africa from an American Viewpoint*. Du Bois's critical review of this book appeared in the Sunday book section of the *New York Herald Tribune* on 10 January 1943.

1. We have no warrant for assuming that there are a few large groups of mankind, called Races, whose hereditary differences, as shown by color, hair and measurements of the bony skeleton, fix forever their relations to each other, and indicate their possibilities. There is no proof that persons and groups in Africa are not as capable of useful lives and effective progress, as peoples in Europe and America.

2. The great problem facing the World, is to achieve such wide contact of human cultures and mutually beneficent intercourse of human beings as will gradually by inspiration, comparison and wise selection, evolve the best civilization for the largest number of human beings.

3. To accomplish this, there is need of a great crusade, a religious mission, guided by the proven conclusions of science, the object of which shall be the continuous progress of mankind, regardless of race and color.

4. It must be clearly recognized that the main hindrance to such a movement, is today the more or less conscious feeling, wide-spread among the white peoples of the world, that other folk exist not for themselves, but for their uses to Europe; that white Europe and America have the right to invade the territory of colored peoples, to force them to work and to interfere at will with their cultural patterns, while demanding for whites themselves a preferred status. On the other hand, colored folk have their contacts with other and higher cultures seriously and arbitrarily restricted.

5. The most dangerous excuse for this situation is the relation between European capital and colored labor involving high profit, low wages and cheap raw material. The strong motive of private profit is thus placed in the foreground of our interracial relations, while the greater objects of cultural understanding and moral uplift lurk in the background.

6. So long as broad scientific philanthropy is thus hobbled by greed, the results will be and have been slavery, cultural disintegration, disease, death and war.

7. We are slowly but surely recognizing facts analogous to these within the confines of the advanced countries themselves. Here we are curbing and guiding the activities of industry and limiting the profits of private enterprise in the interest of the laboring masses. Not so in colonies and in quasi-colonial areas. There, for the most part, we are tending to repeat and perpetuate the errors of the worst days of capitalistic exploitation in Europe. This hurts not only the backward peoples by restricting their initiative, by ruining their best culture and substituting no adequate cultural patterns; but also this colonial economy frustrates and nullifies much of the reform effort within the more progressive lands which own and control colonies.

8. It seems clear, therefore, that our future attitude toward Africa should be based upon principles something like these:

A. The land and natural resources of Africa should be regarded as belonging primarily to the native inhabitants, to be administered for their advancement and well being. Where land has already been alienated, it should be eventually restored. Industry in Africa should be directed primarily toward the consumption needs of the inhabitants and only secondarily to the European demand for raw material. The necessary capital, instead of being imported quickly and at high cost, should be gradually and increasingly raised from the savings of the Natives.

B. In ascertaining the legitimate wants of the native African, his own wishes must be taken into account and allowed the broadest possible sway under the guidance of carefully ascertained scientific principles and well-tried cultural standards; and without the interference of religious dogma or the brute force of modern wage slavery. Especially must an educated class among the natives be systematically and increasingly trained according to modern standards and its opinion given due voice and weight, instead of being, as at present, largely excluded by careless misrepresentation and deliberate design.

C. Political control must be taken from commercial and business interests owned and conducted in the foreign nations dominating the colonies and vested provisionally in an international Mandates Commission. This commission must be controlled by recognized statesmen and philanthropists of the highest character, with the collaboration of unprejudiced and rigorously tested science. Its rule should be carried out with the increasing participation of such educated persons as share the blood and culture of the persons affected; to the end that gradually the systematic increase of democratic methods will transfer political power to the mass of the native people as that people gains in intelligence and civilization.

D. There need be no minimizing of the extreme difficulties, frustrations and mistakes that will inevitably accompany the attempt to understand, change and improve the cultural status of any people through contact with people of higher culture and through educational effort and moral teaching. But these difficulties instead of being regarded either as negligible or as insurmountable must be faced as the real kernel of the problem of human uplift and humanitarian effort.

E. Within such [a] vast framework, the real work of civilizing the world can proceed, and a new crusade of real religion and a new modern abolition of slavery will begin to build a world-wide system of culture on the trained knowledge and free will of all men regardless of race and color.

As I look upon the world in revolution today, I can well believe that the Democracy which will crown the twentieth century will, in contrast to the nineteenth, involve the social control of the masses of men over the methods of producing goods and of distributing wealth and services. And the freedom

which this abolition of poverty will involve, will be freedom of thought
and not freedom for private profit-making. For this reason, the colonial and
quasi-colonial peoples will be more ready to achieve and accept this Democracy
of industry, than the misled people of Europe whose conception of democracy has been industrial anarchy with the spirit of man in chains. Anarchy
of the Spirit alone is the true Freedom.[2]

The Release of Earl Browder (May 1942)

*Late in 1940, when anti-Communist feeling was high, the United States
government indicted Earl Browder, general secretary of the U.S. Communist
party, for passport fraud. Browder, in the course of his party activities—
visiting lands where such activities were prohibited—had used a passport
bearing an assumed name. He was convicted early in 1941 and given the
extremely severe sentence of four years in prison.*

Du Bois, in his weekly column in the Amsterdam News *(New York City),
noted on 9 November 1940 that certain leading intellectuals, including the
economist Wesley Mitchell and the anthropologist Franz Boas, had objected
to the indictment; he added that he agreed with this protest because the
facts against Browder had been known for years and his present prosecution
was in reality an attack on freedom of speech.*

*After Browder was convicted and sent to prison, Du Bois objected, again
in his* Amsterdam News *column (5 April 1941): "Browder is sent to jail not
for lying but for being a Communist. We may disagree with his beliefs but
it is cowardly evasion to call it crime."*

*With the Soviet Union as an ally of the United States after Hitler's attack
of 22 June 1941, the movement to free Browder grew. President Roosevelt
was persuaded to release him in May 1942, and Du Bois very soon thereafter
analyzed this step.*

It is not my purpose to discuss to any length the question of the guilt of
Earl Browder in breaking passport regulations. It is admitted that he broke
the law and for this he has suffered punishment. On the other hand, it is
also quite clear that the punishment which he underwent was more than
sufficient to expiate the offense in the light of precedents; and that his further
incarceration would have been unwise and unfair.

2. Du Bois devoted his weekly column in the *Amsterdam News*, 16 May 1942, to
a fairly detailed account of the circumstances surrounding his Vassar and Yale
appearances.

The question which I wish to bring before you, is why under such circumstances, there was continued hesitation at restoring Browder to freedom. This reason is not often openly discussed and yet it is on the minds of every American. The reason is that a large number of American citizens believe that it is dangerous to discuss Communism; and especially dangerous if that discussion is led by a man of intelligence whose good character in general is unquestioned. And, therefore, despite the injustice of carrying out Browder's extreme sentence, that his release would involve danger to American institutions.

How can free discussion imperil a nation? If the doctrine advocated is false, it carries the seeds of its own destruction among honest and intelligent people. If a doctrine is true it cannot in a progressive age be long suppressed. Extreme cases may to be sure occur: where falsehood is stealthy and underground and not easily answered; where people are ignorant and bitter and ready for any change, good or bad. But in a land of normal intelligence, the openly expressed beliefs of honest, frank men even though wrong or partially wrong are not nearly as dangerous as enforced silence or imprisoned convictions.

I do not know Mr. Browder personally. I am not a Communist. I do not believe that the institutions which have been set up in Soviet Russia can be or ought to be bodily transferred to the United States. I do not believe in revolution as an inevitable method of social reform. I admit that there have been in the past revolutions which have resulted in the uplift of mankind: one that freed the United States from English domination; one that released the great middle classes of France from the rule of a decadent nobility; but I also believe that we have reached a stage where today such methods are no longer necessary and that the terrible cost of forcible upheaval of institutions, of murder of men, destruction of wealth and overthrow of culture can be succeeded by gradual but equally determined change.

On the other hand, I have seen Russia twice. I sometimes boast that I am the only American who has spent six weeks in Russia and not written a book about it. Nevertheless I have had a glimpse of that vast land. I have had some opportunity of comparing Russia with most modern civilized countries and I am firmly convinced that there is no country in the world today whose chance for settling and settling fairly the greatest problem of our era is as good as in Russia. I have never seen elsewhere a nation where the mass of laboring people, as I saw them in 1926 to 1936, from one end of Russia to the other; from Leningrad to Odessa, from Moscow to Otpur, seemed so inspired and so full of hope despite desperate difficulties and continuous struggle.

In the light of this faith of Russia, I am trying to face fairly the problems which are forcing the world today into unprecedented upheaval. This war, which began as a war against dictatorships, is gradually changing into a War for Race Equality. This is not a conscious change, but it seems inevitable. Just as the Civil War in the United States began as a war for federal unity and ended as a war for the emancipation of black slaves; just as the Thirty Years War began in dynastic rivalries, changed to efforts at national expansion, only to end in a vast step toward freedom of religious belief; just so today our fight against dictatorship is slowly resolving itself into a fight against the imperial domination of the world by so-called superior races. Further than that, I am certain that even this struggle is not the end of the story; that the end of the story like its beginning, is the problem of Poverty; not only the poverty of the white working classes, but the depression of the mass of colored workers to depths even below the low standard of living of the working classes in Europe and America.

This seems to me both cause and excuse for the doctrine of racial inequality which has swept across the world; and that just as before the beginning of this war, the problem of poverty was pushing itself forward as the main problem of human culture, in the same way after this war, no matter how it ends, we must return to this basic human problem.

Moreover, the curious thing today is that we are facing the problem, trying to understand it, and beginning to settle it, even in the midst of war. And the great value of Russia to the civilized world, is not necessarily the fact that Russia may have discovered the real answer to the problem of poverty, but rather that it has dared to face the problem. Nearly every other modern country, and especially the great democracies, has tried to evade the matter or reduce the question of production and distribution, wage and income, to the level of mechanical necessity or unchangeable social law, which could not be reached by statutes, sentiment or philanthropy.

Russia seized upon a doctrine, which was not necessarily the whole truth, but which certainly emphasized the fact that poverty was not a human necessity but a human choice; and that the will of the people had a right to seek to change this choice; that men could by organization and legislation, by religious belief and hard work, make it impossible that the majority of mankind or any considerable minority should have less food and shelter than is necessary for health or decency or should have their opportunity for education and happiness so cut down as to make life not worth living.

I believe that the influence of Russia or perhaps I would better say the influence of that long line of philosophers whose thinking Russia has followed, has changed the outlook toward industry and wage in every modern country. Today in England and America, not to mention France, Germany and Italy, the state is one of the largest owners of capital; the state rules and directs capital; the state is increasingly determining wages; the state is undertaking housing and relief, and more and more is planning the course of industry. No intelligent observer today expects that there is going to be any fundamental change in this progress toward the socialization of wealth and work or a return to individual initiative and free enterprise in industry. On the other hand, there are plenty of us who are not at all sure as to what the final answer is to be; how eventually industry will be organized and controlled; and how far our present progress toward state socialism is going to mean the elimination of private industry and private property and private profit. What we all want on this subject is Light, a real knowledge of the facts, a realization of the condition of the mass of working people, a realization of the dangers of great accumulations of individual wealth, and the possibility of evolving a commonwealth where there shall be no poor people, no slums, a minimum of sickness and a maximum of individual freedom. This does not involve hatred and envy, destruction and revolution; it is not so much a matter of individual guilt as of widespread ignorance.

I doubt if many persons would accept high profits at the price of starvation wages if they knew the filth, squalor and shame which such wages involve. Suppose one could never see the charm and urbanity of English aristocratic life save against an equally clear background of black half-human slaves toiling for diamonds in the dark damp bowels of the Transvaal. Light, more light, is what the world of industry needs today. There is a connection between poverty and luxury and there must be no shrinking of delicacy or prejudice in making this connection clear.

This is where real democracy enters. Democracy is not, as so many of us are prone to think, simply the right of electing our rulers. It is not simply, as others think, the right of working people to have a voice in the conduct of industry. It is much more than this; it is a vaster and more inclusive ideal; it is the right to accumulate and use a great reservoir of human thought and experience, out of which a people may choose, not simply men and methods, but the wisest and best policies of government and conduct and have their choice all the more valuable because the sum of human knowledge is open freely to their understanding and inspection. It is here, in thought and concept, that real freedom lies. Freedom is not a mere matter of physical movement; that may be curtailed by geography. It is not just a matter of the election of officials; that may easily be frustrated by lack of candidates. It is not even economic freedom; for economic processes are to a degree subject to physical conditions. But there is a freedom of thought and planning, by which the world, if it has a broad basis of fact and knowledge of experience, can slowly and laboriously work out a way of life for the mass of men.

In free discussion and free investigation with the requisite intelligence to understand, lies the hope and the excuse of democracy. There must not be allowed to stand in the way of this freedom, either the Fear of the Satisfied or the Fury of the Distressed. It is natural that those people who are today living reasonably pleasant lives, under the present organization of industry, should be afraid even to discuss change, lest such change involve their disaster. It is perhaps even more reasonable that people whose lives by any standards of judgment are today not worth living; whose food is too little for health; whose shelter is too curtailed for decency; whose intelligence has had no adequate chance for development; that these in their fury should often want to tear down all that is, in the conviction that nothing could be worse than present conditions for millions upon millions of human beings.

Neither of these attitudes can be yielded to. The only thing that civilization can do is to investigate and know and discuss and then plan and achieve. There has been much of this during the twentieth century; there will be more during the twenty-first. And in this planning of human life, one fact stands out with curious clarity today; and that is that the unity and unshakeable determination of Russia is the rock on which rests apparently the salvation of the best culture of our day. This would be inconceivable to a man like Lothrop Stoddard who once wrote a book to call the Russian Revolution the "Revolt against Civilization"; it would be inconceivable to such a man that at this hour Russia should be the bulwark against which the most sinister and powerful foe of modern civilization is hurling itself in vain. The reasons for this may be various and yet we cannot deny that the frank and open way in which Russia has attacked the question of work and wealth is a part of that reason.

Since then America is staking her future upon the death struggle of Soviet Russia against Hitler, it was a fine gesture, in deference to this ally that we released Earl Browder from prison, not simply because we know that he has been sufficiently punished for breaking our laws, but more especially because we are not afraid to discuss the social and economic reform which has built Soviet Russia. We do this not because we agree entirely with Earl Browder or Josef Stalin, but we are willing to discuss with them or with anyone else the ills of our world in the hope that in open free discussion we are going to achieve that intellectual democracy and that possibility of world-wide planning which is based on freedom of thought.

This is a great and strong nation. Its realization of the democratic ideal is the broadest ever attempted by man. Its standard of living for the working class is the highest in the world. Its economic and industrial technic is miraculous, yet our very accomplishment should make us neither foolish nor afraid. We know our own failures. Born in liberty we deliberately nourished slavery until it all but strangled us; we stood for human equality and let ourselves become a center of race prejudice and discrimination; we established free democratic elections and allowed them to degenerate into rule by one race, by political bosses and by great corporations. All this and more; but we know our faults and are going to correct them, lest government by the people and for the people perish from the earth. We are not afraid of criticism. We welcome discussion and we are not going to imprison any man of honest conviction because we fear the Truth. For this reason we rejoice at the freedom of Earl Browder.

Replies to Queries from the Southern Correspondent
of the *New York Times* (6 November 1942)

In October 1942 Julian LaRose Harris, the southern correspondent for the
New York Times, *visited Du Bois, who was then teaching at Atlanta University.*
On 22 October he thanked Du Bois for "a delightful visit" and submitted a
list of fourteen mimeographed questions relevant to race relations upon which
he desired Du Bois's opinion. Du Bois's answers make the content of the
questions clear. No reference to the exchange appeared in the Times.

1. The Negro in the South has not received just treatment politically, economically or in his housing and environment. This fact has made the unjust
treatment of the poor whites easier.

2. In the change of folkways I recognize no absolutely unyieldable point.
Race and color segregation and separation in educational facilities will have
to yield in the South. It may take much longer for yielding to come on these
points than many others. Other steps toward breaking-down unjust folkways
should include the right to vote for everybody on equal terms; the breaking-
down of racial discrimination in wages and salaries; the broadening of opportunities for employment according to ability and regardless of race; the
widening of natural opportunities for human intercourse in lectures, concerts,
debates, public celebrations and places of public interest; the yielding to
colored people of titles of respect particularly in documents like telephone
directories, school reports and the public press.

3. I believe in the Negro's right to vote on identical terms with the whites
and I believe that the abrogation of the poll tax is a step toward the enfranchisement of the Negro and the poor white; especially federal elections should
be under federal control.

4. There is no excuse in law or political morality for a white primary. In any
primary Democratic, Republican or otherwise, all of the Negroes who qualify
should be permitted to vote.

5. Equality of pay for identical work is the foundation of economic justice.
Segregation of workers by race, sex or other differences is uneconomic and
simply emphasizes the idea of segregation. Negroes objected to the Sun Shipyard experiment [in Pennsylvania] because, as they said, if this shipyard hires
men simply because they are black it would give another shipyard the excuse
to hire others just because they are skilled and not because they differ in color.
If, of course, the folkway is so set and temporarily so unchanging that white
and black people must work separately in certain lines of work or in certain
places it is better to have vertical separation than horizontal separation which
would confine Negroes to the lowest and worst paid jobs.

6. One of the greatest crimes against the Negro has been the failure to give him good educational facilities. Russia has shown us that illiteracy can be done away with in a single generation. Today, particularly in the South, the opportunities for Negroes to get even good elementary education are so limited that the persistent per cent of sheer ignorance has been lowered but little despite our inaccurate census reports. It is becoming more and more admitted that the state should be responsible for furnishing opportunities for higher education to those of its citizens who have the ability. To discriminate against colored students here is to discriminate against ability.

7. The organization of laborers in unions which fight for better wages and better conditions of work is one of the greatest pathways toward real democracy. Inevitably the union must break down racial discrimination or fail in its objectives. The school, the labor union, cooperatives and the uplift of the tenant farmer are the four great paths to Negro emancipation.

8. There are numbers of racial goodwill incidents and also numbers of incidents of race friction. It is a little difficult to judge the net results but on the whole I think that the relations between races in the South, despite the upheaval of war, are better than they were twenty-five years ago and probably better than ten years ago.

9. Negroes do not usually serve on juries in Georgia. There are exceptions once in awhile.

10. There is a great deal of friction on street cars and buses. It is chiefly avoided in Atlanta by some of the street cars being given up almost entirely to Negro patrons. On the other hand the bus situation is bad and seems to be growing worse in the present difficulties of transportation.

11. In general the white South does not like the idea of Negro soldiers. So far in Georgia I do not think the presence of soldiers or the presence of Northern Negro soldiers has led to very great difficulties of racial contact but there are possibilities. There is a tendency to greater and more complete separation between white and Negro soldiers than there was when the number of Negroes was smaller.

12. While the Negro turns to the federal government for bringing to bear upon his problems a broader outlook and a more advanced legal and humanitarian stand, it must also be remembered that the white South has turned to the federal government for economic aid and help in social uplift. For this reason it is hardly likely that the white South would be willing to give up federal aid for roads, relief and various federal projects simply because the Negro evoked federal aid for political rights and education.

13. It is quite possible that as the Negro gains greater political and economic rights that racial tension, especially in certain localities and at certain times,

would be increased. It seems to me almost inevitable that in the long run the result of greater political and economic equality would be the fading away of racial discrimination.

14. Race relations are on the whole better than they were ten years ago.

An Analysis of *Up from Slavery* (1943)

Early in 1943, probably in March, Du Bois participated in an "Invitation to Learning" radio program of the Columbia Broadcasting System, originating in New York City. The ediphone-transcribed copy of his remarks that was subsequently sent to him is presented here.

As I read *Up From Slavery* again after a lapse of a quarter century I seem to see certain clear threads: one, there is the classic statement of the effect of poverty on a growing boy and his striving against it. Two, there is the Hampton-Tuskegee theory of education: Learn by doing. The object of education being not so much what is learned as the discipline of labor. This is illustrated by the night school. Work is regarded as a good in itself and especially common labor and agriculture and work with animals. Latin and Greek are useless. Three, labor. Washington worked in a salt furnace, was a miner, a servant, a janitor. He emphasizes labor but has no sympathy with laborers. He condemns spending for pleasure. He believes that merit is always recognized. Correlative to this is his almost reverent attitude toward the rich and toward businessmen. He believes that their wealth is the result of hard work and that their giving it up would be disastrous. Five, there is his desperate attempt to appease the South. This was forced upon him by the situation at Tuskegee and by lynching and Jim Crow. He met it graciously but over-did it. He made every effort to praise the South and seldom criticized it. He declared that he had never been personally insulted. Finally, Washington was undoubtedly a great orator. His four speeches at Madison, Wisconsin, at Atlanta, at the Shaw Monument and after the Spanish War at Chicago are great efforts. The one at Atlanta epitomizes his philosophy: Cast down your buckets where you are. Begin at the bottom and not at the top. In all things purely social we can be as separate as the five fingers. Glorify common labor. Employ Negroes rather than foreigners and thus avoid strikes and labor war. Deserve privileges rather than demand them. With all this as a sort of sixth thread is his deep reverence for Samuel Armstrong.

A Social Program for Black and White Americans (31 May 1943)

In 1943 Du Bois delivered the commencement address at Florida A. and M. College in Tallahassee.

The close of the Civil War left in the South two groups with irreconcilable social programs: the one believed in the status of slavery for the mass of Negroes; with some limitation of the slave trade; some shifting of control from the owner to the state and a certain minimum of civil rights, including ownership of property and at least a nominal wage system. This was the thought of the defeated planters, the professional class and the merchants; and of those poor white laborers and farmers who wanted to escape the competition of slave labor. Many Negroes, born in slavery and shrinking from the unknown responsibilities of a free labor system, agreed tacitly or openly with this program.

On the other hand, the mass of ex-slaves, the free Negroes, North and South; the Abolitionists of the North and many of them who had come South as soldiers, teachers and merchants and a few White Southerners laid down an entirely different program for Negroes: personal freedom, a wage system, land and education for black and white, universal suffrage and equality in civil rights.

It goes without saying that these two programs were utterly irreconcilable; and the last seventy-five years have been devoted to a more or less conscious effort to find some workable basis of accommodation between these two points of view. In the actual practice of everyday life, the programs had to be reconciled, albeit with wide regional differences, much lawlessness and a disastrous contradiction of ideals. I need hardly rehearse the varied steps in this history, which form the story of the South and of the Negro problem for three quarters of a century.

Usually such divergences of opinion are settled by sheer force with its resultant reactions. If, however, the disagreement takes place inside a larger community, then the results depend on public opinion in the larger surrounding group. In the case of the American Negro the enveloping group was the nation of which the South was a part, and also the surrounding world of European culture to which America belonged. The North was more liberal toward Negro aspirations than the South, but it never went as far as the Negro and his Abolitionist friends wished. On the whole it tended, from 1876 to 1900, to yield increasingly to the Southern position. It finally consented to the nearly complete disfranchisement of the Southern Negro and to the establishment of legal caste conditions.

On the other hand, throughout the European world, the white laborer gained political power and civil equality. But outside Europe and in the continents and islands inhabited by colored races but increasingly dominated by European industry and commerce, a color bar arose which excluded colored peoples from political, economic and most civil rights. Here then for many years the white American South received wide world support in its attitude toward Negroes. On the other hand, throughout the world, and particularly since the first World War, when colored troops helped preserve European culture, the idea of democracy as applied to the colored peoples began to spread and found a strong ally in the new social sciences. American slavery, for instance, after Darwin and Gobineau, had based its argument not only on the Curse of Canaan, but on the alleged inferiority of the darker races. With the advance of biology, anthropology and a more critical historical method, this dogma began to yield to a new scientific belief in the fundamental equality of the great groups of mankind. After the first quarter of the twentieth century, it was generally conceded by intelligent men that the differences between groups of men, instead of being in-born biological traits, were in the main, differences of climate and nutrition, physical health, education, income and human contacts.

No stronger support of this new doctrine could be presented, than the history of the American Negro. Despite widespread disfranchisement and a system of caste which kept down his income, limited his educational opportunity, segregated him from contact with the higher patterns of culture and made him feel inferior, he has since 1860 increased his numbers from less than four and one-half to nearly thirteen millions, most of whom can read and write, and a million of whom have a high school or college education; and who are an integral part of increasing importance in American industry. They have made their mark on American literature and art. This does not deny that as a mass, the American Negro is poverty-stricken, ignorant and diseased, with strong criminal tendencies; but he is nevertheless comparable to the laboring masses of white Europe.

Moreover, it is undeniable that his condition might be vastly superior to what it is if his efforts to advance had not met so many deliberate efforts to retard them. This partly deliberate, partly instinctive effort to hold back a large part of its working class, has made the South, what the President has called the nation's Economic Problem Number One. Not only is the Negro today faced with the necessity of increasing his income, combating his disease, raising the level of his intelligence and fighting his crime, but the white South must realize that it is just as much interested in raising Negro wages, giving him physicians and hospitals, increasing the efficiency of Negro schools and preventing rather than encouraging crime, as is the Negro. In fact right here lie two attitudes which hinder understanding in the South: one, that it is to the advantage of the white South or any part of it to have Negroes poor, sick, ignorant and shiftless; the other that the advance of the Negro by his own effort is absolutely impossible. These are the two heresies of the present South.

For a long time the post–Civil War South was diverted from reality by the dream that it could settle its race problem eventually by the forcible and complete removal of the Negro from America. Today this is seen to be unthinkable, not solely on account of the size and inevitable cost of the job, but because we realize in this war, that the future of this world does not and cannot lie in increasing segregation of its races; but rather in the increasing ability of human beings to live together in cooperation and common aims. Europe cannot live as it would without Asia; nor Asia without Europe; Africa and the islands of the sea need America no more than America needs them—their brawn, their products, their art and their cultural ideals.

This draws our attention anew to our American racial scene. Can we reach here and today in the South, as wide agreement as to the common aims and efforts of the two races, as to reduce social friction to the minimum and give a maximum of effort to the advancement of this whole region? We must first of all admit that this is not simply a local Southern problem. Among the elements to be recognized are the Negroes of the North. Of the Negro population of the nation, nearly three million now live in the North and West. By history, tradition and actual status, this group wields an influence beyond its numbers and must be listened to. Many of these Negroes have a tradition of freedom and independence running back two or more generations; some are well-to-do and make good income from honorable occupations; their opportunities as an urban population give them better schools and a higher level of intelligence than the mass of Southern Negroes. They all have and exercise the right to vote. This does not say that their condition is satisfactory; most of them are recent immigrants from the South; the severe competition of the North and race prejudice make it difficult for them to earn a living; they are still largely victims of poverty with its concomitant sickness and crime. Their right to vote is limited by their need to eat, and is as often for sale to venal politicians as to the demand for good government and self-protection. Nevertheless they have a right to their opinions and a right to assume that the battle they have put up for equality and freedom has earned them a voice in its defense. They cannot on the other hand speak as those who have won their own battle. They have not. They have been partially but not wholly successful. A Negro in New York or Chicago suffers from discrimination in employment and promotion, in the courts of the law and in personal contacts—not as much surely as in Jacksonville or Atlanta. But he is not a free American citizen. He has had a taste of freedom and he is fighting hard and ceaselessly for complete equality. For this he deserves commendation.

What now do Northern Negroes demand; or rather what must they demand if they would keep up their fight for freedom? Their demands represent the ideal toward which every intelligent man, white or black, must aim today, and are in accord with an unrealized but steadily approaching world democracy. The words of the "March on Washington" Movement, encouraged and driven left by the extreme Socialists and militant Communists, express these radical demands as follows:

A. The right to vote and to hold office.
B. The removal of all legal restrictions based on race or color.
C. No segregation by race of any sort. Free social intercourse, and intermarriage for such individuals as personally desire it for themselves.
D. Work for all without discrimination, with social security and without fear of unemployment; a wage equal to that of other Americans, continuously rising so as to support increasingly higher standards of living.
E. Democratization of industry, with promotion to places of authority, according to ability for Negroes as for whites; in government, social guidance, technical management, and leadership in teaching, in science and art.
F. A recognition of interracial cooperation and understanding among various physical, national and cultural groups of America as the greatest step toward world democracy and international control.

The first reaction from this frank and clear statement is rage on the part of many white Southerners and fear on the part of Negroes. Neither attitude is justified. This is a statement which is believed not only by three million Northern Negroes but by the majority of the peoples of the world. On the other hand, nine million Negroes in the South know that as a present practical program it is quite impossible of achievement. It is, however, deserving of study and comparison with other programs.

Rightly to estimate the practicability of this program, let us turn to the extreme white Southern view:

This can be illustrated by recent statements made by ex-Governor Eugene Talmadge of Georgia, ex-Governor Frank M. Dixon of Alabama and ex-Senator Bilbo of Mississippi. It is on the whole a program of stabilizing present caste conditions and even of reaction to former conditions during the slavery regime. As Talmadge has recently expressed it "race prejudice is divine." It may be summarized as follows:

A. The disfranchisement of Negroes and their exclusion from office-holding and service on juries.
B. Legal horizontal caste; that is, laws against intermarriage and against equality in political and civil rights.
C. Social vertical segregation including separation in travel, in residential areas, in education, in recreation, and in public and cultural facilities.
D. Public stigma: the refusal to accord Negroes titles of courtesy; the use of

their given names and the general assumption that Negroes are not an integral part of the body politic.

E. A curtailment of the right to work by setting aside certain kinds of menial work and unskilled labor as Negro jobs, and paying all Negroes in any kind of work lower wages than whites in the same work would receive. The refusal to admit Negroes to labor unions or if admission is permitted, into separate unions with curtailed rights of voting and representation.

F. A refusal to enter any international cooperation or comity which involves a recognition of racial equality.

These sentiments are not held by a single homogeneous group, and certainly not by the white South as a whole. They represent a cultural heritage from the Old South of slavery and have been received uncritically and often almost unconsciously by large numbers of white Southerners; beside these are ranged a large number of employers, who are interested, or who think they are, in cheap, ignorant and docile labor and whose profit depends on keeping the Negro "in his place." To these we must add millions of Southern white housewives who think that cheap ignorant domestic help has no social cost beyond its pitiful wage. In addition to these and even more dangerous, are the politicians who capitalize on this race antipathy. In the past we had Tillman and Vardaman; today we have Bilbo and Talmadge. And standing part-way between the demagogue and the investor are leaders like Dixon of Alabama and Jones of Louisiana. The program of these heterogeneous elements is reactionary to the extreme and absolutely unacceptable to any self-respecting Negro, North or South. Not only that, it is also irritating to the liberal white South.

Liberalism in the South from the beginning of our history has had a hard row to hoe because it has come into increasing competition with expanding economic interests. There was a time in the late eighteenth century when opposition to slavery had some forceful and noble advocates in the South. In fact most of the great Southern leaders of that day were fundamentally against slavery: men like Washington, Jefferson, Madison, Monroe and others were frank to say that slavery was wrong and its long continuance unthinkable; admitting the educability of the Negro, they only hesitated as to practical methods of emancipation. Then while they and their successors were hesitating and groping for a way to fulfill the program which began with the abolition of the slave trade, the Cotton Kingdom arose and slave labor became its foundation.

The new agricultural and industrial leaders, North and South, saw such increasing profit in Negro slave labor, that it was easy for them to persuade themselves that this was almost a divine institution based upon a natural inequality. John S. Calhoun said in 1850:

"We of the South will not, cannot, surrender our institutions. To maintain the existing relations between the two races, inhabiting that section of the Union, is indispensable to the peace and happiness of both. It cannot be subverted without drenching the country in blood, and extirpating one or the other of the races. Be it good or bad, it has grown up with our society and institutions, and is so interwoven with them, that to destroy it would be to destroy us as a people. But let me not be understood as admitting, even by implication, that the existing relations between the two races in the slave-holding States is an evil: far otherwise; I hold it to be a good, as it has thus far proved itself to be to both, and will continue to prove so if not disturbed by the fell spirit of abolition."

Even then in the middle of the nineteenth century there persisted among a considerable group of Southerners the idea of recognizing exceptional Negroes and giving them a chance through manumission and other opportunities. But the Cotton Kingdom grew, the profits rose and by 1860 there was a widespread dream of slave empire sweeping from the Potomac to the Amazon, bound up with the British and French empires by strong economic bonds and destined to play a dominant part in the later nineteenth and twentieth centuries. It was this dream that stopped manumission, degraded the free Negro, sought to annex new slave territory and re-open the slave trade and finally led to Civil War.

After the Civil War and Reconstruction, Southern liberalism was definitely restricted by bitter memories, impoverishment, death and suffering. Some Southern liberals like General Longstreet accepted Negro suffrage and civil equality but most of the white South fought desperately for complete disfranchisement of Negroes, caste and serfdom. When caste and disfranchisement became legal between 1876 and 1900, a new white liberalism began to grow. It grew slowly with many setbacks. But lynching and mob-law; cheating and injustice gradually affronted the conscience of the South. Today this liberal spirit is not triumphant but it is widespread. It is not too much to say that the majority of the younger, white, intelligent South disagrees radically with the reactionary Southern program. The new liberalism has been expressed by younger men like John Temple Graves and Virginius Dabney, by older men like Frank Graham and Mark Ethridge; and by increasing numbers of teachers, writers and ministers throughout the South. These liberals do not agree on a program but perhaps their attitude can best be seen by noting a recent speech by Mark Ethridge of the Louisville *Courier-Journal* who was the first chairman of the President's Fair Employment Practices Committee. This speech made at Birmingham may be summarized as follows:

A. Negroes should be allowed to vote on the same terms as other American citizens. They should have the right to hold office and should serve on juries and be regarded as a part of the body politic.
B. There should be vertical separation of the white and Negro races in travel and education, but equal facilities provided; and equality in civil rights and the enjoyment of public accommodations should be maintained.
C. Segregation should be maintained in social intercourse but there should be no public insult involved nor imputation of inevitable inferiority of all Negroes to all whites.
D. Negroes should be given work according to ability and be paid on the same terms as white workers.

This liberal attitude has been a challenge to Southern Negroes. They do not disagree with the pronouncements of Northern Negroes nor with their demands; but the nine million black men living in the South realize that their future is largely dependent upon Southern conditions and that facing the facts of Southern laws and beliefs they must make every attempt to accommodate themselves especially in the face of the liberal Southern attitude. In accordance with this thought, there met in Durham, North Carolina, in October 1942, a conference called by Gordon B. Hancock, professor in Virginia Union University, which issued "a statement of purpose and basis for interracial cooperation and development in the South." This statement may be condensed as follows:

"We are fundamentally opposed to the principle and practice of compulsory segregation in our American society, whether of races or classes or creeds; however, we regard it as both sensible and timely to address ourselves now to the current problems of racial discrimination and neglect and to ways in which we may cooperate in the advancement of programs aimed at the sound improvement of race relations within the democratic framework.

"We regard it as unfortunate that the simple effort to correct obvious social and economic injustices continues, with such considerable popular support, to be interpreted as the predatory ambition of irresponsible Negroes to invade the privacy of family life.

"We have the courage and faith to believe, however, that it is possible to evolve in the South a way of life, consistent with the principles for which we as a Nation are fighting throughout the world, that will free us all, white and Negro alike, from want, and from throttling fears....

"We regard the ballot as a safeguard of democracy....

"We therefore record ourselves as urging now: a. The abolition of the poll tax as a prerequisite to voting. b. The abolition of the white primary.... Exclusion of Negroes from jury service because of race has been repeatedly declared unconstitutional....

"Where segregation of the races is currently made mandatory by law as well as by established custom, it is the duty of Negro and white citizens to insist that these provisions be equal in kind and quality and in character of maintenance....

"The only tenable basis of economic survival and development for Negroes is inclusion in unskilled, semi-skilled and skilled branches of work in the industries or occupations of the region to the extent that they are equally capable....

"There should be the same pay for the same work.

"It is imperative that every measure possible be taken to insure an equality of education to Negroes, and, indeed to all underprivileged peoples....

"It is a wicked notion that the struggle of the Negro for citizenship is a struggle against the best interests of the Nation. To urge such a doctrine, as many are doing, is to preach disunity and to deny the most elementary principles of American life and government."

In reply to this statement, one hundred white liberals recently met in Atlanta and said, in part:

White leaders, conferring in Atlanta, emphasized their opinion that the program must be one of "evolution and not revolution."...

These Negro leaders rightly placed emphasis in their statement on discrimination in the administration of our laws on purely racial grounds. We are sensitive to this charge and admit that it is essentially just....

The only justification offered for those laws which have for their purpose the separation of the races is that they are intended to minister to the welfare and integrity of both races. There has been widespread and inexcusable discrimination in the administration of these laws....

In the economic field, unquestionably procedures should be undertaken to establish fully the right to receive equal pay for equal work....

All men who believe in justice, who love peace and who believe in the meaning of this country are under the necessity of working together to draw off from the body of human society the poison of racial antagonism....

We agree with the Durham conference that it is "unfortunate that the simple efforts to correct obvious social and economic injustices continue, with such considerable popular support, to be interpreted as the predatory ambition of irresponsible Negroes to invade the privacy of family life."...

It is futile to imagine or to assert that the problem will solve itself. The need is for a positive program arrived at in an atmosphere of understanding, cooperation and a mutual respect.

Before such difference of opinion and to some extent actual contradiction, what can the thoughtful citizen, colored and white, say and do? Manifestly the two radical programs may be set aside, but for quite different reasons: a demand today for the complete abolition of discrimination against race in American life is right in the sense that it is the ideal toward which the whole world is slowly striving. The progress is and has been slow and will be, because of two world wars, perhaps even slower. But manifestly every thoughtful human being looks forward to a world of essentially free and equal human beings.

On the other hand, the statement that human beings today are not free and equal is unassailable and too there is the additional fact that no matter what scientists may believe and philanthropists assert, there is in the United States, both North and South, a hard nucleus of opinion which believes that Negroes are inferior; that their advance is a threat not simply to the domination of the white race but to civilization itself. Now no matter what we may think of this widespread feeling, it is a fact that we must face. We cannot either ignore it or ridicule it or even legislate it out of existence. Deep-seated cultural patterns of this sort are eradicated only by time and effort: time which gives the slowly working nerve mechanism of human beliefs the sheer physical chance to change; and effort which through education, discussion and scientific investigation faces the human reason with an increasing body of incontro-vertible fact and makes men face fact. If every law discriminating against the Negro were swept away from the statute books of the South tomorrow, the difference in status treatment so far as Negroes were concerned, would scarcely be changed an iota, simply because public opinion is the basis of law and while law in the long run may change public opinion it does so slowly with difficulty. And vice versa while public opinion may change the law, it must itself change first.

In comparing, therefore, these programs we may set aside the radical program of the Northern Negro and the reactionary program of the conser-vative South. The last being too patently reactionary for the development of real democracy in the United States and the world. The first being too idealistic to fit the facts of the present situation.

This leaves us to compare the program of white liberal Southerners and Southern conservative Negroes and to ask if there is between these a basis of accommodation which will on the one hand take into account the inherited prejudices of the South and on the other the natural aspirations of a rising race.

There are certain points on which there is practical agreement between these programs. These points are:

A. the right to vote and hold office
B. equality of civil rights, including education, social services, etc.

C. employment and equal wage

D. interracial courtesy.

On the other hand, there are certain matters of disagreement which center around racial segregation in:

1. Marriage
2. Private social intercourse
3. Public social intercourse (hotels, restaurants, theatres and concerts, public meetings, churches, parks, burial grounds, asylums, jails)
4. Schools
5. Travel
6. Residence

In these cases, if the rights and accommodations for each race are substantially equal, such separation can only be objected to because of its social waste; and on the other hand can be agreed to because of the right which persons have to follow their tastes and preferences in association. If, however, race segregation is practically impossible without forcing one race to accept inferior accommodations or to be deprived of cultural opportunities and public facilities this would seem to be a point upon which the advocates of segregation would have to yield or retreat to undemocratic caste repression.

In the matter of social intercourse, which both programs approach gingerly, it must certainly be admitted that the essence of democracy demands freedom for personal tastes and preferences so long as no social injury results. If, for instance, the overwhelming majority of white people in the South and in America would prefer not to intermarry with persons of Negro descent or with Asiatics or other physically and culturally different people, they should have the right to exercise this preference. On the other hand, if there are some few people who desire such intermarriage and social intermingling the attempt to interpose legal barriers to such preferences may lead to more evil than it seeks to correct. However, this whole matter is at present theoretical rather than of practical moment. If every law restricting marriage between races in the United States were repealed tomorrow there would be no appreciable increase in intermarriage. What American Negroes must admit is that white people have the right to exercise their taste as to marriage alliance. The family is an intimate center of cultural development and must be guided and protected according to intelligent choice. On the other hand, white people must admit that if intermarriage is condemned on the ground that Negroes are sub-human, unusually diseased or criminal; or if racial intermarriage can only be warded off by unscientific propaganda, the end does not justify the means. Cannot a basis of accommodation be found in the admission on the one hand by whites that Negroes are human beings of possibilities quite equal to whites and by Negroes by acknowledging that whites have a perfect right to exercise their taste in the choice of marriage companions?

With regard to general private and public intercourse, it is manifest that democratic methods in government and the promotion of human equality cannot be attained if lines of social segregation are so drawn that human beings cannot come into mutually helpful social contact. It must be candidly acknowledged by Negroes that they are at present on the average culturally inferior to white Americans. They have a right to say that this inferiority is not greater nor even as great as their history and social difficulties in America justify. Nevertheless, they must admit that it is a fact and that the poverty, sickness and crime prevalent among American Negroes can be seized upon not only as justification for discrimination and segregation, but in the minds of many honest people may stand as actual proof of inborn inferiority.

While the Negroes are demanding equal treatment in order to rid themselves of these handicaps they must themselves as a matter of sheer self-defense make every effort to remove these handicaps. They must especially recognize their power as producers and consumers to improve their economic situation. They must themselves apply among their own folk the various accepted methods of social uplift. The temptation to lag in these efforts because such internal organization may give excuse for segregation or retaliation should not act for a moment to inhibit thoughtful, careful and scientifically directed planning by Negroes to eliminate poverty, to get rid of disease and to curb crime.

Also the whites must resist the temptation to let Negro social degradation persist, lest its disappearance remove the chief excuse for racial discrimination. For instance the "Jim-Crow" car cannot long survive essential equality of social status between Negroes and whites; and too, compulsory Negro poverty and ignorance will justify the "Jim-Crow" car much longer than necessary. Here is a call for intelligent sacrifice: on the part of those Negroes who are already equal to whites in social status; and on the part of whites who are asked at great cost to give opportunities to peoples and races in whose abilities they do not honestly believe.

Here then centers the most difficult problem facing interracial understanding today: how far can different elements in the United States and in the world, including whites, Negroes and Asiatics, work together, think together and know each other, without infringement upon the right of each to choose his close companions and his family mates?

Finally, and probably of more pressing importance than anything else, is the question of work and wage: if there is to be set up in the world a hierarchy of people some of whom rule and receive large income while others work and live in poverty, then the future of the world is going to be a future of war and struggle. If on the other hand, in a great nation like

America, we are going after this war to try to keep all people at work who
are able to work; and increasingly to distribute these workers in accordance
with their gifts; and to pay them so as to raise the average of the national
standards of living; then we can lead the world into an attempt to do something
similar in international and interracial relations.

The question then comes: can we reach substantial agreement on the matter
admittedly in dispute; or if not agreement at least working compromise and
tolerance? In that case what are the next steps on which white and black
people in the United States can unite in order to insure progress in race
relations? Possibly these steps might be indicated as follows:

1. Legislation. Legislation against lynching and restriction of the right
to vote; legislation which should insure the elimination of illiteracy in the
quickest possible time. Legislation which should decrease the friction due to
segregation laws which cannot be equitably enforced and serve only to
hurt and inflame; and especially laws which if enforced, increase ignorance
and degradation.

2. The abolition of discrimination in membership by labor unions; and in
work by employers.

3. A crusade to stop systematic insult and unscientific depreciation of
Negroes in newspapers, in moving pictures, in textbooks, on the radio and
by secret underground propaganda.

4. An effort to make public conventions of scientists, social students and
artists free of discrimination so far as hotels and meetings are concerned.

5. The opening of cultural facilities such as churches, theatres and concerts
to all persons who are interested and who wish to avail themselves of such
facilities.

With all this must come conscious, determined and wide-reaching organization within the Negro Race to accomplish their social advance despite
discrimination and segregation. As a matter of fact we already have a great
deal of this in organized religion, in education, in community life, very largely
in work and partially in economic organization, in literature and art. We
form in the United States a separate and distinct group, but our group efforts
take place in such an atmosphere of resentment and disappointment as tend
to retard them and lead to short term compromise rather than long term
planning; our efforts become far less effective than they ought to be and the
argument against their development is that the very success of segregated
social effort among us will increase and excuse segregation.

This is probably a mistake and a grave one because it excuses us from
a great mass of social effort which might in itself remove just causes of dislike
for our group and fear of its eventful influence. To take an extreme case
there is, for instance, very little organized effort among American Negroes
to meet the problem of Negro crime. The reason is clear: the police and

the courts, especially in the South, increase crime among Negroes, sometimes deliberately, and we have restricted influence to counteract this. Nevertheless, in sheer self-defense we must do it. We ought by long term planning to defend our youth from contact with crime, from anti-social actions and social degradation. We ought to make organized effort to defend the accused in court. We ought to turn a large part of the thought and action which we put into religion into a fight against crime among our own people.

Beyond this our economic organization ought to be more carefully and completely thought out by means of consumers' co-operation and even consumers' production. The thirteen million American Negroes could arrange to spend their three billion dollars of annual income in such a way as considerably to reduce unemployment and raise wages among themselves. If it is the job of the white South to change its cultural pattern so as to recognize the possibility of democracy and equal treatment for the colored races of the world, equally it is the job of the American Negroes to make the white man's program easier of acceptance by reducing their crime to a minimum and raising their standard of living to a civilized level.

Our attitude and actions on these matters will determine the future of race relations in the United States and to some extent in the world. There are we must realize three possibilities: complete vertical racial separation; complete horizontal subordination of one race to the other; gradual cultural assimilation. It would seem that a policy of complete separation would be dangerous in the present situation of the modern world. If races and nations are to look forward to such separation there is danger of recurrent disagreement and war. The democratic program cannot contemplate the complete subordination of one race to another. Complete assimilation does not necessarily begin with biological assimilation or even end there; physical differences of race may persist indefinitely; but assimilation does include cultural tolerance, and eventual cultural equality and unity of democratic ideal.

To this must be added one set of considerations which the new psychology makes important. While cultural patterns are changing and while social conditions are shifting, the great and important thing is to keep the spiritual balance of the persons involved. Oppression, discrimination, poverty are powerless to kill a people who believe in themselves and in their destiny. And on the other hand, a group which despite its superiority and power, knows and realizes that it is doing wrong and standing in opposition to the great lines of human advancement may easily fail in its very triumph. The danger of the white South today is that it tends in its action to deny the Christianity and democracy which it openly and blatantly advertises. The danger of the black South is that it blames the white world for a social degradation which is partly its own fault. If American Negroes can continue to believe in themselves, their progress and their ultimate destiny, despite present facts, are certain; and if Southern whites can become increasingly dissatisfied with a religion that preaches equality and practices caste, then the future of America and of the world is secure.

A Program of Organization for Realizing Democracy in the United States by Securing to Americans of Negro Descent the Full Rights of Citizens (19 March 1944)

While still on the faculty at Atlanta University, Du Bois was invited to submit a statement of his views to a national Conference on Race Relations held at the University of Chicago, 22 March 1944. His statement was read at the conference.

The Negro Problem is a complex of social problems which can be solved by no one organization nor one course of action, and yet calls for understanding and cooperation among many agencies.

The essence of the problem is the cultural lag of the descendants of slaves behind the average of culture in this land; coupled with widespread determination among many of their neighbors to prevent attempts to bridge this gap and even to deny normal human rights to that large and rapidly increasing number of Negroes who equal and in some cases surpass the average cultural levels of the nation.

Efforts for solution must therefore fall into two main divisions: efforts to raise the average cultural level of Negroes and efforts to alter the attitudes of their white neighbors.

A. The low average cultural level of Negroes is shown by their poverty, ignorance and disease, and by the consequent crime caused largely by these hindrances.

1. There is need for a movement to increase the income of Negroes by giving them opportunity to work according to ability and to receive higher wages for their work. Labor unionization, trade apprenticeship, together with consumer organization will help here. But the decisive aid will come as Negroes are integrated in a new organization of industry, which discarding the assumption that unrestrained private initiative and private profit always make for the public welfare, demands that the public welfare be the first object of industry and that individual income neither rise above nor fall below the interests of the public good.

2. There is need for a new crusade of education, involving a much larger outlay of funds and guaranteeing equal opportunity to all children for thorough elementary education, under well trained teachers and adminis-

Du Bois with Senator Emile St. Lot, while on lecture tour in Haiti in 1944.

Du Bois in about 1948, scanning an early issue of the Crisis.

Du Bois with Paul Robeson, around 1949.

Formal portrait of the candidate for the U.S. Senate from the state of New York on the American Labor party ticket, 1950.

Marriage ceremony with Shirley Graham, 27 February 1951.

trators with state and federal support for high schools and colleges, and effective continuation of training for adults. No separation of schools by race or class must be permitted which involves any limitation of educational opportunity for anyone.

3. Social medicine and public hospitalization, on a national scale with security against age, sickness and unemployment, is a third imperative need.

B. So far as the low cultural level of Negroes is caused, increased and prolonged by their white fellow-citizens, there must be organization and movements to counteract this, for it is culturally dangerous and ethically indefensible.

1. Organizations are needed to work for full equality, in law and custom, for all persons regardless of race, color and social class. This program is difficult but feasible in most parts of the north and west, where Negroes have political power, better opportunity for education and greater economic security.

2. The Border States and the South present for the most part a special national problem. For historic reasons, the betterment of race relations there is not entirely a matter of reason and ethics but is made difficult by long-standing and sub-conscious patterns of thoughts and action, often frozen into legal caste, which threaten domestic tranquility and economic order. The contagion of intolerance; the illusions of superiority in the midst of ignorance and poverty, threaten personal integrity, national democracy and world peace. There must be organized earnest effort here to work for amelioration of conditions according to widely differing local levels of culture and *among both white and blacks.*

All the organizations and movements necessary for the ends indicated should cooperate in sympathetic understanding, but not necessarily in agreement as to methods, as to estimates of the time involved, nor as to the exact form of ultimate solution. Some must work by appeal, palliative and compromise; others must fight directly for ideal aims, abstract right and final goals. All must agree that present conditions are dangerous; putting an intolerable strain on all men of good will and calling for earnest and immediate effort toward betterment and toward ultimate democratic equality.

A Farewell Message to the Alumni of Atlanta University (Summer 1944)

In November 1943 Du Bois was suddenly notified by President Rufus Clement of Atlanta University of his dismissal as professor and head of the Department of Sociology, effective 30 June 1944. As a result of nationwide protests, *many coming from alumni of the university, Du Bois was retired as professor emeritus and given his full salary ($4,500) for 1945; from 1945 to 1950 he was to receive $1,800 annually and from 1950 to his demise $1,200 a year.*

Fisk, Howard, and North Carolina College for Negroes were among institutions offering him employment, and in May 1944 the NAACP invited him to rejoin as director of Special Research. It was the latter offer that Du Bois chose to accept. He left for New York City in June, and at a meeting with officials of the association on 28 June 1944, it was agreed that his duties with the NAACP were to begin on 1 September.

Sometime that summer the annual dinner of the Atlanta University Alumni was held. Du Bois's message for the occasion, which was read in his absence, follows here.

I am sorry that I cannot be with you tonight; and because of that fact, I have asked Mrs. Louie Davis Shivery, who has been my student, helper and friend for forty years, to read to you this last word.[1]

Against my wish and will, and in direct contravention to the clear understanding which I had when, at the repeated request of John Hope, I returned to this institution, I was retired by vote of the Trustees last November, without consultation, without notice and without being given a hearing.

A committee consisting of the President and two Southern white men were appointed to pass upon the question as to whether I should be given a pension. At first in sheer astonishment, I was silent. Then I appealed to you. The result was the most arresting thing that has happened in my long career. From all over this land, at your request and protest, there poured in letters upon the Trustees of this institution, until in lieu of proper notification they gave me a year's salary and also granted me a small pension.

But that was not all. From two universities, two colleges, and two National associations, I have been offered work and asylum with security of income and freedom of effort, for the rest of my working days. I am now in the astonishing position of having at the age of 76 to apologize to several of those institutions at not being able to accept their courteous and thoughtful offers.[2]

I had hoped to finish my life work here at Atlanta University, where virtually I began it fifty years ago. There was no earthly reason why this wish of mine should not have been granted and applauded. Especially, since I was just bringing to Atlanta University an opportunity for scientific leadership

1. Letters exchanged between a daughter of the Shivery family and Du Bois, her godfather, are printed in the *Correspondence*, 2:8–10, 45–47.
2. For the details of Du Bois's dismissal from Atlanta University, see ibid., pp. 390–409, and the *Autobiography*, pp. 321–24.

of the South, which will now go to Fisk or Howard.[3] I have not stooped to answer the attack on my integrity as a teacher nor to refute the allegation that I gave up a life-time job for a one-year appointment here. In bowing to the decision of the Board of Trustees, I leave this institution with the knowledge that what I have done and what the world is offering me, has not been the result of flattery or boot-licking; but of straightforward effort to accomplish the things that were for the good of this institution and of the world.

I have attended these dinners since 1897 with the exception of the 23 years that I was absent in New York. They have always been a source of inspiration and triumphant hope. I want to greet the Alumni this year with special confidence. You have grave tasks which no other body can perform. I trust you are going to face them with firm faith and determination. Since my long association with the families which you represent, you are in a sense children of my efforts to make straight the Way of the Lord. I lay on your shoulders the hard duty of making this institution a real university, which it is not today. It will call for sacrifice and work, but what you have done in the past, you can do in the future; and in the unwavering prosecution of that effort, I bid you goodbye and God-speed.

3. In 1943 Du Bois had persuaded twenty Black land-grant colleges to join Atlanta, Fisk, and Howard Universities in renewing the Atlanta University Conference to Study the Negro Problems, begun in 1896. Full details will be found in the *Report of the First Conference of Negro Land-Grant Colleges for Co-Ordinating a Program of Cooperative Social Studies*, Atlanta University Publications, no. 22 (Atlanta, 1943), edited by Du Bois.

1944-1961

Colonialism, Democracy, and Peace after the War (Summer 1944)

At the invitation of the Haitian government, and with the encouragement of the U.S. State Department, Du Bois participated in several scholarly and cultural activities in Haiti during the summer of 1944. Two of his papers given at this time were published in French.* Two other papers offered at that time, also prepared in French, are translated here; they anticipate in concentrated form Du Bois's subsequent Color and Democracy: Colonies and Peace *(New York: Harcourt, Brace and Co., 1945).*

THE COLONIAL GROUPS IN THE POSTWAR WORLD

In the lectures which I am planning to deliver in Haiti, I want to examine with you the prospective status of the colonial groups in the world after the conclusion of this war and in the organization of peace for the future. You will I am sure bear with my imperfect French in this intricate and difficult task.

First of all I am deliberately using the word "colonial" in a much broader sense than is usually given it. A colony, strictly speaking, is a country which belongs to another country, forms a part of the mother country's industrial organization, and exercises such powers of government, and such civic and cultural freedom, as the dominant country allows. But beyond this narrower definition, there are manifestly groups of people, countries and nations, which while not colonies in the strict sense of the word, yet so approach the colonial status as to merit the designation semicolonial. The classic example of this status has long been China. There are other groups, like the Negroes of the United States, who do not form a separate nation and yet who resemble in their economic and political condition a distinctly colonial status. It was a governor of the state of Georgia [Ellis G. Arnall] who said in the recent Democratic nominating convention in Chicago: "We cannot continue as a nation to treat thirteen millions of our citizens as semi-colonials." Then, too, there are a number of nations whose political independence is undisputed

---

* "La Conception de l'éducation," *Cahiers d'Haiti* (Port-au-Prince) 2 (September 1944): 14–19, 22–25, 32; "Message du Dr. Du Bois," ibid. 2 (October 1944): 28. These are reprinted in *Writing by Du Bois in Periodicals Edited by Others,* ed. H. Aptheker, 4 vols. (Millwood, N.Y.: Kraus-Thomson, 1982), 3:193–210, 215.

and who have a certain cultural unity; and yet by reason of their economic ties with the great industrial and capital-exporting countries, find themselves severely limited in their freedom of action and opportunity for cultural development. They are in a sense the economic colonies of the owners of a closely knit world of global industry. The Balkan countries and those of South and Central America, and the Caribbean area occupy in varying degrees this sort of semicolonial status.

Looking therefore upon this colonial and semicolonial world, I wish first to ask what common characteristics we may discern; how these characteristics exhibit themselves in the different groups, and how these groups suffer common disabilities and hindrances with social classes in the more advanced lands of the world; and finally, what place these colonies should and will occupy in the democracy which we hope will gradually inherit the earth.

There are in the first place certain characteristics of colonial peoples, which are so common and obvious that we seldom discuss them and often actually forget them; colonial and quasi-colonial peoples are as a mass, poverty-stricken, with the lowest standards of living; they are for the most part illiterate and unacquainted with the systematized knowledge of modern science; and they have little or no voice in their own government, with a consequent lack of freedom of development. Naturally these characteristics vary widely among different groups and nations; so that before we generalize, make comparisons and seek remedies, we must stop to examine certain specific types of colonial countries. This examination, I shall make in very general terms in this lecture. Later I hope to treat in more detail various selected lands.

Let us first consider the colonies proper: the countries of America, Africa and Asia which we usually designate as colonies. In America, we have the British West Indies, the French islands, the American acquisitions. All of these conform to a well-known type: at the top, a group of varying size, consisting mainly of whites and mulattoes; they are in income, often well-to-do and sometimes rich; they are literate and in some cases highly cultured, and they have some voice in government. Below this group, and composing from seventy-five to ninety percent, are a mass of people, predominantly of direct African descent, illiterate largely, and making a decent living with difficulty; subject to disease, with high infant mortality, and having for the most part no voice in government, and with restricted personal freedom.

Discussion of this situation in the past and largely today, confines itself to the persisting disabilities of the elite, to questions of their political power and cultural recognition. There can be no question but that these matters are of grave concern and call for remedy. But our preoccupation with these problems which in so many cases are peculiarly personal, must no longer blind us to the much vaster problem: as to how far it is necessary that in the most beautiful part of the New World, the overwhelming mass of the inhabitants be precluded by poverty, ignorance, disease and disfranchisement from taking any effective part in modern civilization. White citizens of the United States and most Englishmen find nothing unusual or alarming in this situation. They have argued from the days of the slave trade that not more than a tenth of the Caribbean peoples are capable of modern civilization or conceivable participants in political and cultural democracy. Without any profound dissent, many of the colored folk themselves have accepted this dictum without question and confined their protest against social conditions to the situation of the élite, which certainly and justly demands betterment.

But how has it been decided, and who has decided, that the social distribution of the Caribbean is normal and inevitable? We are led to question the conclusion all the more, when we remember that it is not long since when the overwhelming proportion of the populations of most European countries was as poor and ignorant as modern colonial peoples. In answer to this reflection, the nineteenth century posed the question of "Race," of the existence of such inborn and ineradicable difference between stocks of human beings as made the proportion of civilizable people vastly different in Europe and America, and between the lighter and darker folk. I need not remind you how fierce a controversy arose over this theory of race, and how that pseudo-science long hindered not simply remedy for the degradation of colonials, but even conception of the possibility of remedy. Today as we stand near halfway through a century which has proven the biological theories of unchangeable race differences manifestly false, what difference of action does this call for on our part?

First of all it calls our attention to the fact that so far as science is concerned, there is no earthly reason why the elite of Haiti, Jamaica, Martinique and Cuba should not comprise nine-tenths instead of one-tenth of the population. If this be true, what hinders steps toward its realization? Such steps must begin with knowledge; with concerted effort such as I am indicating in this lecture, to study colonial and quasi-colonial status in various parts of the world. Turning to the colonies of Africa, we find certain differences and contrasts with the West Indies. In the colonies of West Africa and East Africa, the emerging group of the elite as a recognizable class is largely missing. There are out-standing personalities, and social movements, but instead of conforming to the European class pattern, they link themselves to another and a different social heritage. The tradition of a strong and ancient organization persists—an organization that linked the mass of the people directly to the chief through an intricate nobility; in this society the tribe became an integral state in which the interests of no individual were neglected.

There has recently been published a most thoroughgoing study of the Kingdom of Nupe in Nigeria. Any person, white or black, who has a lingering conception that Africa evolved no political state, should read this book. But in this case as in most African colonies, there has cut across this ancient pattern, changing, spoiling and even partially obliterating it, the modern colonial system, born in the West Indies and transferred to the source of the developed slave trade. This system substitutes for the local, home-born and home-developed elite, foreign control, represented by a mere handful of more or less temporary representatives, who govern the tribe or state. The objects of this government determine the character of the colony. The earlier African colonies were for purposes of trade, and all government was directed toward facilitating trade. Outside that, the colony conducted its own affairs in its own way.

Then certain valuable articles of trade came into greater demand and pressure was brought to bear to increase the supply. Slave trade and slavery resulted overseas, but on the African mainland, gold, vegetable oils, copper and diamonds, became more valuable than slaves in the West Indies, and the tribal organization was partially or wholly disrupted to supply regular labor. The value of these new products undermined the foundations of slavery in the new world. Slavery, therefore, disappeared from the New World especially when Toussaint and others used force to accelerate this development. On the other hand, the African colony became therefore a vast business organization to reap profit for European investors out of the invested capital and forced labor of Africa. Across this cut the efforts of missionaries and philanthropists and West Indian and American Free Negroes. The result today is a series of African colonies, conducted for profit, and yet with their policy modified so as to recognize in varying degree the development and progress of the native. With all the advance made, it is fair to say that the investment motive is still supreme in West and East Africa. It is less powerful in French Senegal, but in the Belgian Congo, while changed materially from the disgraces of Leopold, it is still an investment far more than a philanthropy. In South Africa, strong tribal organization met modern industrial exploitation and finance capital, head-on. The result is the most complicated race problem on earth, with retrogression and reaction fighting against almost every forward movement of the native proletariat and opposed by a small but growing philanthropy on the part of the whites.

Turning now to Asia, we face the problem of India, the largest colony in the world and the one that poses the greatest colonial problem. In India we have an ancient culture, an intricate political history, and a long economic development. On this fell the power of the West and East: the East with organized military power; the West, first with the religious might of organized Mohammedanism, meeting the spiritual seeds of indigenous Buddhism. On this was thrown in the century before the widest growth of the African slave trade, the newly organized power of the new capitalism, which American slavery had given birth to in England. The loot of India by European political adventurers and merchants established modern capitalism in Europe and with the accompanying technical and scientific inventions, gave Europe mastery of the world. Capitalism was a great and beneficent method of satisfying human wants, without which the world would have lingered on the edge of starvation. But like all invention, the results depend upon how it is used and for whose benefit. Capitalism has benefited mankind, but not in equal proportions. It has enormously raised the standard of living in Europe and even more in North America. But in the parts of the world where human toil and natural resources have made the greatest contribution to the accumulation of wealth, such parts of the earth, curiously enough, have benefited least from the new commerce and industry. This is shown by the plight of Africa and India today. To be sure Africans and Indians have benefited by modern capital. In education, limited though it be; in curbing of disease, slow and incomplete as it is; in the beginning of the use of machines and labor technique; and in the spread of law and order, both Negroes and Hindus have greatly benefited; but as compared with what might have been done; and what in justice and right should have been accomplished, the result is not only pitiful, but so wrong and dangerous as already to have helped cause two of the most destructive wars in human history, and is today threatening further human death and disaster.

To realize this, look at India today. No one has ever tried to prove that its vast horde of three hundred and fifty million people are not normal human beings and as gifted as the Europeans. No one denies that Indians have worked hard and long, have been cunning in technique, profound in thought and lofty in religious ideal. Yet this land after three hundred years' subjection to European political control and industrial domination, is poverty-stricken to an inconceivable degree, is ninety percent illiterate, is diseased and famine-cursed, and has limited voice in its own government. It is for instance in this war not by its own consent but by declaration of Great Britain. Thousands of its leaders who have dared peacefully to protest against this situation are today in jail.

Dutch and French India approach, with some modifications and variations, the British Indian pattern; in other words, India, while a partner in the development of modern capitalistic civilization, and while sharing some of its benefits, has received so small and inadequate a share as compared with Europe that its present plight is a disgrace to the world. And this is because the modern world under the guidance of Europe and North America has become used to thinking that the plight of the human millions of Asia and Africa is normal, essentially right and unchangeable except after long periods of evolution if even then.

Let us now turn to certain states which are not colonies but which for various reasons approximate the colonial status. Some of these are China, many of the countries of South America and groups like the Negroes in the United States and the Indians of the Americas. To these may be added the majority of the Balkan states, the states of the Near East, and the independent Negro countries, Liberia, Haiti and Ethiopia. In these cases there is recognized political independence, and a cultural heritage of varying strength and persistence. But on the other hand in all these cases, the economic dependence of the country on

European and North American industrial organization, in commerce, in sale of raw materials and especially in obtaining the use of capital in the shape of machinery and manufactured material—this dependence on world industry makes the country largely dependent on financial interests and cultural ideals quite outside the land itself. There have been many cases where this partnership between a land of labor and material, and a land of wealth, technical efficiency and accumulated capital goods, has worked advantageously for both. But in most modern instances, the wealthy country is thinking in terms of profit, and is obsessed with the long-ingrained conviction that the needs of the weaker country are few and its capacity for development narrow or nonexistent.

In that case, this economic partnership works to the distinct disadvantage of the weaker country. The terms of sale for raw materials, the prices of goods and rent of capital; even the wages of labor are dictated by the stronger partner, backed by economic pressure and military power.

The case of China is well known. The seat of the oldest civilization surviving in the world, China was compelled at gunpoint to trade with Europe. This procedure was justified as leading to the Christianization and economic uplift of this great land. The results justified this method only in part. For the most part the colonial pattern prevailed: a mass of poverty-stricken people, illiterate and diseased, with their political autonomy partially nullified; until when native resentment revolted in the late nineteenth century, Europe planned to divide the country into colonies. This was delayed by the rise of Japan as a major power and her insistence on sharing the spoils. From this point the path to World War was straight and clear.

The Indian and Negro group in America have paused on a threshold, leading by one door to complete integration with the countries where they reside; and by another door leading to the organization of a sort of nation within a nation, which approaches colonial status on the one hand and eventual incorporation on the other. The Indians have taken one path, and the Negroes of the United States the other. The eventual result is not clear, and depends to a degree on the development of the colonial status among other peoples of the world. In the case of the Balkans and the Near East, a strong cultural tradition, urges them toward independent nationhood, while the elite of their own people, especially the great landlords, the new manufacturers and home capitalists, stand in such close alliance with and dependence on the European industrial and financial organization, that most of these countries remain bound hand and foot by a web of their own weaving. This is peculiarly true of Poland, Hungary, Bulgaria and Rumania. In South America, the pattern changes, because the cultural heritage and bond is weaker, and the social conditions in Europe become guide and ideal for the independent American colony. The normal situation, with poverty, ignorance, disease and disfranchisement seems in the eternal nature of things and nearly all effective effort is expended on raising an elite which shall be recognized by Europe and share the privileges of Europeans. Only in comparatively recent days, has an ideal arisen in lands like Chile, Peru and Brazil, of a spiritually independent South America, with a people of white, red and black blood intermingled, and with a laboring class as high in standards of living and political rights as the best of European lands.

The independent Negro nations, Haiti, Liberia and Ethiopia, suffer first from the widespread assumption of the nineteenth century, that Africa and the black race were not an integral part of the human picture and consequently could not and must not be allowed to try to develop like other nations along the lines of economic uplift, social development and political independence. We Negroes who in the last half century have convinced ourselves of our equality with mankind and our ability to share modern culture, scarcely realize how high a wall of prejudice based on color we have still to surmount today. This makes us all the more eager to force recognition of our worth, and too often forgetful of how the burden rests on us as on all peoples, to increase and increase rapidly and widely among the masses of people within our group who are still depressed in poverty, ignorance, and disease, and incapable of adding to the total of the emerged classes, the ability, physical strength and spiritual wealth, of which they are possessed. The studied and bitter attack on Liberia because of alleged slave raiding was of minor importance so far as the facts were concerned. Britain, France, Spain, Belgium and other countries had been pursuing and still were pursuing in some cases in Africa identical methods of labor recruitment as Liberia.

But beyond the bare facts was the allegation that Liberia was using against her own people the methods which she protested when used by whites. Even this was not really true, but it had enough semblance of truth, to hurt Liberia deeply. The same tactics used against Ethiopia almost fixed the charge of slavery upon this land at the very time she was making hard effort to abolish the slave status. I need not remind you how often and persistently the charge of voodooism brought against you has so twisted the clear truth as to emphasize the denial of cultural equality to a land which has in so many instances led America in cultural development. Yet here the truth is that your cultural elite, with all its fine accomplishment, is not anywhere near as large as wealth, education and health might raise up from your peasantry.

Now let me sum up this preliminary survey of the colonial problem: the depressed peoples and classes of the world form the vast majority of mankind today in the era of the highest civilization the world has known. The majority of human beings do not today have enough to eat and wear or sufficient shelter for decent existence; the majority of the world's peoples do not understand what the world is, what it has been and what the laws of its growth and development are; and they are unable to read the record of this history. Most human beings suffer and die years before this is necessary and most babies die before they ever really live. And the human mind with all its visions and possibilities is today deliberately distorted and denied freedom of development by people who actually imagine that such freedom would endanger civilization. Most of these disinherited folk are colored, not because there is any essential significance in skin color, but because most people in the world are colored.

What now can be done about this, in this day of crisis, when with the end of a horrible and disgraceful war in sight, we contemplate Peace and Democracy? What has Democracy to do with Colonies and what has skin-color to do with Peace?

DEMOCRACY AND PEACE

In my last lecture I talked to you about the general situation of colonies and quasi-colonies in the world and tried to indicate that because the vast majority of the people in the world came under a colonial or semicolonial status that, therefore, the future of colonies was of vast importance to the future of the world.

I want to indicate today that because of the colonial situation, democracy is not being practiced among most people; and without worldwide democracy applied to the majority of people, it is going to be impossible to establish a universal peace. Peace in the long run must be based upon contentment and the world is not content with the colonial status. To illustrate this I want to take up the main difficulty with colonies, which I have touched upon before but which now I emphasize again: and that is poverty.

Poverty has always been a social problem and always will be. But when this is said, its real meaning and implications depend on our definition of poverty. I was born in a small town in New England, where most of the people could fairly be described as poor. The average income was small. The wage of laborers was a dollar a day for ten hours' work. Servants received two to three dollars a week. Yet in that town there was almost no distress or suffering from poverty. Everyone had enough to eat. There were some poor homes that were not weatherproof, but for the most part the community was comfortably housed. Nine-tenths of the people could read and write; all adults usually attended town meetings and helped elect officials; nearly all children attended good schools nine months in the year. There was little disease, crime or disorder. There was some drunkenness but on the whole poverty in New England in the last quarter of the nineteenth century did not mean distress or acute discomfort and certainly not suffering; it meant that most of us worked regularly for plain living, without luxuries or extravagance. We had thrift and frugality dinned in our ears; but no one ever starved.

On the other hand, in colonies and quasi-colonial regions today, there is a degree of poverty that is frightful. We read of the recent famine in India with a shudder of disgust; and all the more because we realize that most human beings today are too poor to enjoy life, to have sufficient to eat and drink, to keep healthy or even to refrain from stealing and crime. Exact figures as to income the world over are lacking, and this makes intelligent discussion difficult. Nevertheless, we do know with fair certainty, that the annual income of an Indian family averages twenty-five dollars; that black miners in Africa receive from fifty to seventy-five cents a day; that the schools for natives in South Africa cost one-tenth of what is spent on white children and only thirty percent of the native children are attending their poorly equipped and poorly taught schools. As compared with the people of Europe and North America, colonial peoples have a standard of living so low that they cannot be expected to compete with the modern world in physical or mental development.

Why is this and how far is it necessary? For if extreme poverty is the inevitable lot of most people in the world, then improvement in health and intelligence must lag. In such case, the realization of Democracy and world peace in any near future must not be expected. Democracy is an irrefutable postulate of logic. But it calls for intelligence. As it is today in our leading democracies, the ignorance and stupidity of many voters is appalling. I know something of the working of democracy in the modern world. I grew up in the part of the United States where democratic government was most successful. I saw the growth of Social Democracy in Germany in the last decade of the nineteenth century; I have seen government in France, Russia and Japan. And everywhere the democratic process limps and hesitates and goes insane, primarily because the average voter is not intelligent enough to realize just what he is doing. The ultimate triumph of the democratic process, therefore, depends primarily on more thorough and complete education, not only for children but for adults. But education costs time and money. The United States spends immense sums for the training of youth, but that expenditure is not enough. I am this term reluctantly withdrawing my granddaughter from the public school of Baltimore because the schools are so crowded and inefficient. But if this is true in the rich United States; and if similar failures in education are troubling England, what prospect is there that the mass of the world's inhabitants, now festering in ignorance, will in any reasonable time receive enough training to make them intelligent supporters of democracy?

It is questions like this which have fostered Fascism; which have led intelligent men to despair of democracy and depend upon uncontrolled tyranny of dictators. It is thus true that in a day when intelligent comprehension of the world's problems is needed as never before, so many of good will are saying: most men must remain ignorant because education costs too much; with three-fourths of mankind ignorant, we must have continued disease and crime and democratic control is unthinkable. But without democracy, what hope is there of Peace?

When such a logical impasse as this is reached, it is time for us to retrace our steps and ask: is it really necessary that most men be poor? Our greatest hope and inspiration here is the world's experience in the recent past. The world, and the most advanced parts of the world, are still ignorant; but when we compare the ignorance of the average Englishman in the twentieth century with that of the average Englishman in the seventeenth century, the improvement is enormous. The average American is today not rich or even well-to-do. But the American laborer today has comforts that were denied Roman emperors and that the leaders of the Renaissance would have called miraculous. What we need to realize today is that poor and ignorant as the advanced countries are today, their advance in the last millenium gives hope not only for them in the near future, but also for the masses of the earth's disinherited who are now no more hopeless than was the European of the seventeenth century.

What then keeps the colonies poor and so conspicuously more poverty-stricken than the peoples of Europe and North America? Is it their inborn lack of ability and application, or is our whole colonial system, and the ideals upon which it is built, so serious a mistake as to threaten world democracy, world peace, and the development of human intelligence? It is this latter thesis that I am defending.

Colonies, I have said, are for the most part investments, the main object of which is the profit of the investing country. It is difficult to prove this by detailed and accurate figures. Complete data are not published, and the information available is often ill-adapted to outlining a true picture. Moreover, as has often been pointed out, colonies have in many cases reaped much benefit by their connection with the mother country. The abolition of slavery and the slave trade in Africa owed much to Englishmen, and the French Amis de Noirs helped the freedom of Haiti. Nevertheless, it stands clearly to reason that the commercial interests of no modern country would endure the burden of colonial administration unless the profit on the venture lured them. West Africa, South Africa, the Belgian Congo, the Rhodesias have been of enormous financial gain to Europe during the nineteenth and twentieth centuries. But despite this the standard of living for the natives in these lands remains wretched and so far beneath the standards current in the mother country that they are a standing threat to those standards. It is argued that the mother countries cannot afford the high cost of modern wages, hospital and medical services, and complete schooling for natives. This is true, if the current rates of investment profits are maintained in colonies. Investment in gold, diamonds, copper, vegetable oils, tin and many other products of Africa have yielded Europe fabulous returns in the last century. The cost of native uplift might easily have been subtracted from this total and still left a fair return for the real effort involved. But so long as the main object is the high profit, the native is not only not uplifted but often degraded, while the inordinate profit leads to European rivalry, waste and war. If colonial exploitation has been a prime cause of the last two world wars, not to mention other conflicts, who can doubt that this cost of war could easily have uplifted the colonial and quasi-colonial world to a status where it could begin to take intelligent part in modern democracy?

To illustrate what I mean, let us glance at the social history of West Africa. West Africa has had an extraordinary and intriguing history. As late as the fifteenth century trained observers could discern no such difference in culture and ability between black Africa south of the Sahara, and Western Europe as would warrant any prediction that Europe would in five centuries far surpass Africa in civilization. Nor was the eventual discrepancy due to the fact that Africa chose the wrong path to culture, and Europe the right. They, to be sure, chose paths that diverged widely, but neither path was absolutely right or wrong; both paths had certain clear advantages. Africa recognized no private property in land or the main products of the earth. Her clans or families knit the community into vertical units instead of the European pattern of horizontal social classes. Industry was state-planned and regulated, and the wage contract was unknown. The encouragement to individual initiative in accumulation was lacking, but the artistic impulse had time and strength to develop because there could be no fear of want as long as there was food for any one in the tribe.

The weakness of this organization was the small size of the state and city units and their helplessness before power and greed. Exquisite bits of local culture arose here and there, in the Congo, on the Atlantic coast, about the great lakes, only to be swept away by marauding bands sweeping east, west and south. But the greatest marauder was the swiftly rising Europe armed with new weapons, wide trade, new money and accumulated capital. Gradually organized African culture was partially obliterated, and nothing new from Europe wholly replaced it. The Africans received some education and knowledge of the European world; they became a part of a vast industrial machine whose objects they did not understand; and they were thrust into the modern wage system with its wants, disease and helplessness; and lost the security of the ancient African family without any opportunity to acquire the thrift and initiative of the new status.

All over the world, the organized economic power of Europe driven by the new capitalism and implemented by the new science and technique, fell upon ancient static cultures, ripped them apart, left them in helpless ruin and built a mass of poverty, ignorance and disease, that contrasted so painfully with what Europe was accomplishing, that Europe not unnaturally concluded that everything European was right and progressive, and everything Asiatic and African was decadent and barbaric. Then it was that gradually Europe, despite her bitter struggle not to admit it, began to realize that much which she had ruined or distorted was necessary to real civilization; and that while Asia and Africa were at present too prone and helpless to reform an ailing world, nevertheless Europe was like to commit suicide after all her magnificent effort, unless she proceeded to rid herself of the worst of the consequences which she had herself evoked.

Europe today with an accumulation of knowledge of this universe, built up laboriously and triumphantly over five long centuries, is unable to redeem mankind because most men, bound mind and body in the shackles of European profit, are too ignorant to appreciate and help preserve and extend this price-less treasure. Rolling in unprecedented wealth and capable by her miraculous technique, of indefinitely extending and multiplying this wealth, Europe finds herself bankrupt because of wars waged to defend this wealth and make more; and weighed down in every part of the world by an array of sheer sordid poverty on the part of the very people, whose work rightly directed, would give every human being a decent living. With a knowledge of the human brain and body capable of prolonging life twenty years beyond the biblical three-score-and-ten, Europe faces a world swept by preventable disease among colonial millions; her own birthrate declining because of luxury and indulgence, followed by the deliberate murder of ten million of her most promising young men in desperate effort to save that world which she has created.

We do not here have a simple case of right and wrong, of good and evil. We have a complicated intricate pattern of human life which through no one fault, and no one mistake has gone grievously astray. The modern world's mistakes need not necessarily be fatal, but certainly every hour lost in righting wrong, piles up enormous cost.

What then must be done? It is natural for us who belong to the disinherited of modern culture, to think that all initiative toward righting the world must come from those who now so largely own and rule the world. I want to point out that while without cooperation from the white world, the present colored world cannot successfully undertake the whole program of reform, yet there is not only an opportunity but a duty for the colored world today to lead in reform. In the past much which has gone to the credit of the white philan-thropist was initiated by Negroes. American Negroes were prominent in the abolition crusade; what man did more to make American slavery impossible than Toussaint L'Ouverture? So today, certain movements in black and colored groups are pointing the way to world peace and democratic government. On the Gold Coast, British West Africa, the agitation for civil rights and economic independence has long been carried on. The Congress of West Africa which met after the first World War initiated a movement which gained Negroes for the first time elected representation in the governing councils of five colonies. This gain was not solely an act of grace on the part of the British Empire, but was forced by a union of effort on the part of the Africans, which united the old cultural organization headed by the chiefs, with young Oxford grad-uates. It was a fusing of old and new cultures which was epoch-making. Sometime you should get hold of and read the demand for democratic rule which these Africans wrote: "We are not asking," they said, "to imitate Europe, but demanding restoration of ancient African rights which our fathers were promised when they admitted Great Britain to joint ownership of our state."

So in economic lines the Gold Coast stands out. In the middle of the nineteenth century the great cocoa firms of England determined to wrest control of raising cocoa from the Portuguese and turn it over to the British. The excuse alleged for this was that Portugal was winking at virtual slavery in the cocoa islands of San Thome and Principe. This was probably true; but also motives of increased profit lured the British. It was planned to establish large plantations and hired labor in West Africa, which would have meant the usual pattern of low wages, disrupted families, meager schools and a high death rate. But the black Gold Coast was too smart. The people had tenaciously held onto their old African land ownership and on their own lands they introduced cocoa raising. The result was that the Gold Coast is today the greatest cocoa-raising area in the world and the crop is raised by black proprietors on land which they own. It is the first instance in modern history of a crop in world demand raised by natives without the intervention of the white exploiter.

In the United States the efforts of the Negro to achieve citizenship and, thereby, to become a part of American democracy are fairly well known. The attempts fall into three periods: the colonial period when well-to-do free Negroes became voters, not only in certain Northern colonies but in most of the colonies of the South. Then slavery succeeded in disfranchising not only slaves but free Negroes in the South and in the North except in Pennsylvania and a few other states. The second period came when the Negroes, taking successful part in the Civil War, secured the Thirteenth, Fourteenth and Fifteenth Amendments and became legal citizens of the United States. Reconstruction was a prolonged battle to deprive American Negroes of their right to vote. After ten years the Negro was practically disfranchised again until after the first World War when the power of the Negro vote began to be felt in the North and now during the second World War, it is beginning to be felt in the South. When now after the second World War we look forward to universal peace, it is not only desirable but absolutely compulsory if we are going to save civilization.

•   •   •

What have we got to do in order to insure democratic government among most people? Before we answer this question let us set ourselves straight on certain underlying principles. There is a deep-seated feeling in the world, all the more powerful because it is not altogether conscious and reasoned, a feeling that ability is scarce and that the culture based upon human ability is of such an order that if it is shared it is lessened and cheapened. You find this attitude in the most unexpected places. Here is a nation; people say it has fine culture,

a high civilization. What they mean as a matter of fact is that in this country
there is a smaller or larger number of people who are cultivated or civilized.
Little or nothing is said of the fact that most of the people, often an overwhelming majority, are not cultivated. Notwithstanding this the feeling in that
country is that if we try to raise the level of culture among the mass of people
we will not only fail but we will ruin what culture we have. Thus when you
consider the age of Louis XIV in France you think of its magnificence and
splendor; of the high level of thought and discussion; of the cultivated society;
of the beautiful furniture; of the lovely chateaus. You do not think of the
France which consisted of ignorance, of dirty and poverty-stricken peasants.
When it was suggested in the eighteenth century that the mass of the people
of France ought to share in the privilege of the nobility, the answer was it was
impossible to let them share unless you ruined the civilization of the Grand
Monarch. And yet what happened? In the nineteenth and twentieth centuries
you had a France where millions of people shared in the civilization which
formerly was confined to a few hundred thousand. And while in certain
matters of delicate finish and exquisite special attainment, French civilization
may have suffered; yet on the whole the France of the twentieth century
meant infinitely more to human culture than the France of the seventeenth
century.

In other words the level of culture in the world has got to be raised if we
are going to have the possibility of democracy and if that democracy is
going to bring universal peace because it spells universal contentment. Most
persons would immediately admit that if the abolition of extreme poverty were
possible, it would be the greatest boon to mankind imaginable; it would make
ignorance rare, curable disease nonexistent and crime at a minimum. They
doubt the possibility of the abolition of poverty because of the cost. I am
pointing out that modern miracles of technique make a world without poverty
possible if industry is carried on not simply for private profit but primarily
for public welfare.

Beyond this when it comes to democracy, the placing of political power in
the hands of the mass of intelligent people, there are many who regard this
step as philanthropy and withal dangerous philanthropy. They think of the
right to vote as a concession from the cultured elite to the inexperienced
and irresponsible mass, with the threat of slowing up or even attacking
civilization. Such retrogression has occurred and may occur in the progress
of democracy; but the vaster possibility and the real promise of democracy
is adding to human capacities and culture from hitherto untapped sources of
cultural variety and power. Democracy is tapping the great possibilities of
mankind from unused and unsuspected reservoirs of human greatness. Instead
of envying and seeking desperately outer and foreign sources of civilization,
you may find in these magnificent mountains a genius and variety of human
culture, which once released from poverty, ignorance and disease, will help

guide the world. Once the human soul is thus freed, then and only then is peace possible. There will be no need to fight for food, for healthy homes, for free speech; for these will not depend on force, but increasingly on knowledge, reason and art.

The first answer to such a proposition will be: all this is impossible. To raise the level of culture means in the first place that you have got to educate the masses. Now education costs money. The United States spends much per capita upon the education of its youth and yet for satisfactory results the appropriation for education ought to be doubled tomorrow. Even more is this true in England, on the continent of Europe, in all the Americas, in Haiti. The people say that with the widespread poverty of the world, civilization cannot pay for the education of the masses. Without education you are going to continue to have preventable disease and as a result of poverty, ignorance and disease you are going to have crime.

Directly opposed to this statement is a counter-statement: unless you curb crime by treating sickness; unless you have large enough income not only to educate the masses but to raise the standards of living; unless these things are done, democracy is impossible and without democracy you are going to have the world ruled by and for a larger or smaller minority of people; and this almost of necessity means that the world will be ruled not only by these people but for the benefit of the minority and not of the majority. If now modern civilization is going to be ruled for the benefit of the minority you will not have democracy, and peace for any long time will be utterly impossible. This is the paradox which faces the world and it centers itself in this question: is poverty inevitable and therefore because of poverty must we endure ignorance, sickness, crime and periodic wars?

I can easily see that in the tenth century, in the fifteenth and even in the eighteenth the prospect of the abolition of poverty seemed beyond human possibility. But today because of the very things of which we boast, the possibility of the out-and-out attack upon poverty lies in our hands. It is the consensus of scientific opinion that the technical mastery over the forces of the world can be used not simply for profit or for war but for making poverty a thing of the past. If we can do this then we can make this a world of educated men who include not simply men of leisure, lawyers, physicians, writers and artists but also, and in far larger numbers, highly trained farmers, mechanics, engineers, homemakers and laborers equally well paid and respected.

•   •   •

Before you dismiss a picture of this sort as a mere dream, stop and study what agriculture has accomplished and can accomplish, what chemistry is able to do, the immense and incalculable power which lies in the physical forces about us, and above all how much we now spend in waste and war which

might be spent in education, clothes, food and medicine. I maintain that this
is the outlook for peace, made certain through permitting the mass of men
to have a voice in their own government; that any attempt to accomplish
this aim simply through political organization, or organized force, or technical
superiority of one group over another, is absolutely hopeless and will be simply
a prolongation of the blood, sweat and tears which mark the path of attempted
world progress.

Haiti (1944)

*Sometime after his return from Haiti—probably early in the fall of 1944—
Du Bois sent to* Collier's, *then a widely read weekly magazine, an essay
summing up his impressions. It is worth noting that in this piece Du Bois
projects the idea that slave uprisings helped motivate revolutionary and
democratizing efforts in Europe in the latter half of the eighteenth century—
one of the themes proposed in Eugene Genovese's* From Rebellion to Revolution *(1979). Du Bois's final paragraph here reads like a publicity release
from the Kennedy administration for its Alliance for Progress.*

Perhaps it is unnecessary to add that Collier's *rejected this essay with an
undated and unsigned form.*

People, naturally, see in strange places and lands what they expect to see;
what they have been taught that they will see. To most lands we thus carry
in our thoughts and memories as much or even more than we receive from
the new impressions of the visit—the more so if our visit is brief. Americans
especially have definite expectations in Haiti: a land of "Negroes" with all
that the name connotes; with poverty and disease and exploitation by a small
group of mulattoes aping whites; especially Voodoo: weird, decadent African
rites, hidden in the mountains, vigorously denied but evidenced clearly by
the drums that echo of Saturday nights; and by twice-told tales; on the whole
a "funny" land seeking the impossible, the abnormal. This is what most
white visitors to Haiti expect to see and naturally this is about what they
do see, although here and there and lately a visitor may have a word of
appreciation for the well-educated and cultivated persons with whom he
comes in contact; or he may conceive some revision of his older idea of
"Voodoo" rites.

But if one visits Haiti with the minimum of pre-judgment and with open
ears and eyes capable of new and fresh impressions, he is struck first by the
singular physical beauty of the "land of mountains" as the name means.
Port-au-Prince lies like a white pearl between the enfolding arms of the

mountain ranges which jut into the sea; clean, simple, quaint and lovely, with its white public buildings, its villas, its rows of narrow homes. Above and behind, range on range of mountains roll upward and eastward leaving high valleys here and there where the great plantations of old used to stand; with little towns and cities which seem quiet and peaceful, with palms, cotton-wood and oaks shading them. Especially, always passing in stream of silent, dark humanity, are the busy straight-backed, hard-working peasants. Their thatched huts nestle, almost hidden from the casual eye, on mountain side and in secret valley—each one its own tiny homestead of land. Compared with Europe and North America, the standard of living for the peasants and for the middle classes is low. Compared with Spain, Italy and eastern Europe, extreme poverty is not conspicuous. There is sickness, malaria and tuberculosis. Wages are meager but crime is low. But above all there is a singularly urbane elite, handsome, well-mannered; men and women with culture and traditions who know how to live graciously on comparatively low income. There are lovely homes, with flowers and foliage beneath great palms; there are clubs and restaurants; and the ceremonials of marriage and death are absorbing; early marriage and many children are widely the rule. Five lively daily papers feed Port-au-Prince alone.

There is a national crop, coffee, and coffee of high grade which formerly only France bought and used; but now America is learning its rich flavor. There is cacao, logwood, cotton, sugar, rum, hard woods and new crops like sisal. There are some small industries like wood-carving and weaving.

There is effort at education, not only with the new university just set up by combining the older schools of medicine and law with new efforts in engineering and liberal arts; but the city high schools and the few country schools that can be reached by road and foot path. There is effort to encourage agriculture through the new school at Damien and its branches whose young trained teachers come from Cornell, Ames and other American schools. All this is but a drop in the bucket but it is effort based on older and long-standing institutions.

In government there is law and order. The cabinet of the president is composed of quite young men, men in their forties, many of them American-trained, some of them trained in France and Germany. The civil service is large and poorly paid, and the economic outlook is curiously inhibited and strained. Here lies the meat of the cocoanut. This is because there is in Haiti a cultural tradition coming straight down from eighteenth century France and now with twentieth century American influence. Life is suave, kindly, conventional. There is still prejudice and church influence against educating girls; development of theatre and dance is hindered by ideas of the role of "jeunes filles." Almost unconsciously, however, Haitian life is built upon a preexisting African cultural pattern. It is this cultural pattern, loosely described in some of its superficial phases as "voodoo," which vicious and ignorant white criticism of the nineteenth century caricatured and led Haiti to try in vain to suppress and repudiate. It survives today not only as an ethical basis for standards of peasant living but as a growing incentive to art and literature.

Here then is the curious situation: a cultivated conventional leading class founded on French eighteenth century culture, a peasantry of three millions whose culture harks back to seventeenth century West Africa with its intricately organized cultural patterns. The slow imperfect interaction of these two cultures; French peasant land-holding, building and education from Christophe and Petion; religion, family life and government from Africa; language from both; now at last, technique and public schools from America; music, literature and art from Africa. But the crux and center of all is technique, industry; work and wage, earning a living.

One-fourth of the wealth made by hardworking Haitians is going today to pay debts to North America. Haiti must operate and extend its government with all the multitudinous things which need to be done on 5½ million dollars a year. On the other hand, the legitimacy of these debts is a matter of treaty obligation and not of justice. Haiti rescued her country from pawn after the American Occupation by acceding to practically all the claims set up by various exploiting persons and corporations, just as in previous years under Boyer, Haiti consented to pay France for recognition of her independence, a sum out of all proportion to her ability to pay. But it seemed the only way to regain political independence from American Marines; and on the other hand it led in the past to internal stress and dissension.

Haiti, like so many undeveloped regions of the world, is a land of potential wealth; of water power that might be developed; of soil denuded but capable of fairly quick restoration; of forests of precious woods prematurely cut and yet yielding some woods now and capable of responding quickly to reforestation; and above all a peasantry, stubborn and independent but capable of efficient work if they can see results of that work. They differ from the usual peasantry, because the great and wise Christophe in his eager panting effort to build a nation in a moment, distributed lands to the Haitian peasants and thus gave them a unique position among the peasantry of the world. The peasant is able to live and sustain a family on three acres of land and thus has enough of economic independence to drive a real bargain with his would-be employer and to save from his toil leisure for enjoyment, festival and happiness. Thus with labor tied to the land, with a climate suited to rapid vegetable growth, with mineral wealth and water power, with simple needs in food and clothing and with guiding traditions from Europe, America and Africa, there are wide possibilities in Haiti.

So what! we may say. What is the significance of all this? What can one propose for Haiti's future? In the past, Haiti has been of deep meaning to the modern world: a meaning which the world does not acknowledge, chiefly because it does not realize it. Mercer Cook, the historical expert on Haiti, who guided me up to the greatest human monument of the New World, the Citadel of Christophe, said paradoxically, "Revolution did not come to Haiti from France; Revolution came to France from Haiti." He meant by this that repeated slave revolts in Haiti, the first and richest of modern colonies, the father of the colonial idea, influenced France in matters of income, liberal thought and labor revolt in the seventeenth and early eighteenth centuries. He reminded us how the Haitians had helped the American Revolution with money and troops. Millions of dollars were given to Washington and the American army by the Haitian planters and the money came through the hands not only of white but mulatto planters; and by whosoever's hands it came, it was wealth piled up by black slaves. Actually, Haiti landed troops on American soil and once saved the American army from annihilation at Savannah. Christophe was among them, and Petion. The Americans that lived and died that day did not sneer at these blacks and mulattoes.

When revolution came in France, Haiti sought to make it include all free people of the island, whether white or of Negro descent and this precipitated civil war in 1791, which was soon going against the mulattoes; then suddenly and to the world's astonishment, four hundred thousand black slaves rose, joined the revolt and seized the island and its property, under the great Toussaint. The world stood aghast. Europe and America were so frightened that even today their bitter resentment at successful slave revolt tinges and colors their whole thought of Haiti and Haitians. Reaction against revolution and class struggle came in Europe, led by Napoleon; and if he had succeeded in putting behind this reaction the might of an American empire, a different Europe might have emerged from the Napoleonic era.

The struggle of empire centered in Haiti: England sought to seize the island and use it against her most feared enemy, France; Spain sought to seize Haiti and rebuild her fallen empire; and France sent a great army to overthrow the impudent black rebel and build a new French empire in America. But Toussaint and his lieutenants and the fever beat them all and Haiti became autonomous. Then France tried treachery where she had failed by arms and killed Toussaint but the Haitian revolt was not a matter of one single leader: it was a people determined to be free; so that Dessalines made Haiti independent and Christophe and Petion organized the North and South. Napoleon in bitter chagrin tossed Louisiana as a gift to England's revolting colonies, turned his continental might on England and failed in 1815. Christophe defended Haiti with his mighty Citadel, its peasant land-ownership, its beginnings of education. Petion defended Haiti by education and by helping to free South America from Spain. Only yesterday Venezuela paid singular homage to the present president of Haiti as representative of Petion, the friend and savior of Bolivar.

Meantime the American slave power bolstered its falling fortunes by using the horrible example of Haitian slave revolt to retard the emancipation movement and bolster a new biological doctrine of race differences, which became the foundation of colonial aggression throughout the nineteenth and twentieth centuries. The result was the debt slavery of Haiti which made her a quasi-colony, bound in economic chains first to France and then to America, despite her political independence. Enforced and bitter poverty was at the bottom of the continued internal dissension and occasional anarchy which finally resulted in the American Occupation. The political power of the North American Negro coupled with peasant proprietorship and the stubborn refusal to cooperate on the part of Haiti's educated elite rescued Haiti from open political control by the United States but left subordination to American capital with such help from American technique which would insure Haiti's ability to pay her debt quite as much as willingness to develop a new and stable culture.

Now what? What can be done with this land? First, there is the primary need of getting rid of that fatalistic attitude toward Haiti which says that nothing can become of this entrancingly beautiful island rich in material resources and culture because its people are predominantly of Negro descent. This attitude of mind, more than any other fact, is Haiti's world handicap today. It has distorted her history; separated her deliberately from normal cultural contacts in America and Europe. If we ignore this attitude and refuse to let it divert us we can easily discern in this island, an extraordinary opportunity for human culture; for culture in microcosm rather than on world imperial scale. There is no reason why there should not arise in Haiti a new Afro-French-American culture which could in many respects set new ideals for the world. First of all the peasant land-ownership should be strengthened, confirmed and broadened. More land should be given each family and boundaries and records confirmed. Haiti and the world should learn that this settling of the land question can place Haiti in the van of economic progress, particularly if this individualism and security in ownership went hand in hand with socialized methods of cultivation, state aid in agricultural science and consumers' cooperation in marketing and buying. With this should go industrialization in town and city. This is beginning in small ways which are the chief remaining results of the American Occupation and of the guidance of European refugees: there are a sugar refinery, sisal plantations, attempts to raise rubber, wood carving and other corporate and individual efforts. There has not come to this land any considerable realization of the possibilities of socialized capital and consumers' cooperation; yet here is a peculiar chance successfully to introduce both and to build up internal and carefully grounded opposition to large industry, private profit for absentee investors, and local class exploitation.

To lead such a movement there is an established cultural class. North

America does not have in any of its other territories, a group of people better fitted for social leadership on a broad and gracious scale; who know as well how to live and enjoy life, who have more engaging manners and keener intellects. They have, however, been long culturally isolated, which has at once enriched and individualized their patterns and yet deepened them. They, therefore, today stand between the world-old temptation of becoming a ruling class existing for itself and its own enjoyment and set over against an exploited working peasantry [and], on the other hand, [the chance] of becoming as a class, masters of modern industrial technique and attacking the problem of a class joined to them by ties of blood and cultural history.

The peasants inherit an ancient cultural pattern coming down directly from Africa and of singular dignity and efficiency. Most modern countries have been built by smashing their cultural past, detaching themselves from it, despising it through ignorance, and seeking to build anew. Haiti far more than most modern lands has not yet accomplished this, in spite of contempt for "voodoo" and its rites, which sprung from white ignorance and was widely shared by the Haitian elite itself. This ancient cultural pattern has preserved the family life, guided work, set standards of right and wrong and of living and is today a most potent force in Haiti. It is beginning to be recognized by the elite as an art impulse, and if it can now be combined with scientific technique and economic progress a miracle might be accomplished.

Why could not America vary its blatant but sterile religious missionary effort with new missions not only of health but of economic reconstruction who would work in Haiti and other lands, not for the private profit of foreign investors but primarily and determinedly for the economic uplift of a small, self-contained, beautiful and historic land?

The Meaning of Education (1944?)

This succinct account of Du Bois's views on education in the latter half of his life was among the papers left in my care, but there was no indication of date or the circumstances of its delivery. It is my guess that this was a lecture, probably in 1944 or possibly 1945, at a class in some local educational institution.

You are of course aware that a new branch of learning has recently become popular which is called Semantics. Semantics has to do with the meaning of words and takes up the fact that very often we use the same word unconsciously with different meanings so that what is true of the word in one meaning is quite untrue in another meaning. I want to call your attention this morning to some differences of meaning in the word education. For some weeks you have been studying education and more or less unconsciously you have assumed that you mean by education always the same thing; but you do not. There are few words in modern use which vary so much.

In order to make clearer what I mean I want to go over first the meaning of education in my life. From the age of five through my twenty-sixth birthday, over twenty years, were spent almost entirely in receiving an education according to the preconceptions of the late nineteenth century. My course of education was as follows: first, I had long and rather severe discipline in the three Rs: in reading, writing and arithmetic, so that the spelling and grammar of the English language, the usage in phrase became deeply grounded and second nature to me at an early age.

Then I began to study what had happened in the past in this world: the history of the United States, of England and something of Europe. I began the discipline of languages, of ancient languages which had been used by civilizations now partially dead. I studied their literature and English literature by reading essays and books. I began to learn about the lives of certain men, most of them men of unusual ability and distinction who had left their imprint upon the world. Of the things which I had learned I began to write in essays and statements. Then I had courses in natural sciences, in chemical laboratories and physical; algebra and geometry, in studying rocks and stars. With this went a rather unusual amount of travel so that I had a chance of comparing people with people and land with land. I listened to lectures by distinguished students of science and history, I heard music in wide variety. I saw most of the leading examples of painting and sculpture throughout Europe.

Now at the end of these twenty years of study and travel which must have cost in the aggregate something like forty thousand dollars, I was not prepared to do any specific piece of work: I could not make a table or cook a meal or sew on a button. I could not carve nor paint; and the art of writing and revealing my thought had not been developed. On the other hand, I did have a rather firm grasp, and idea of what this world was, and how it had developed in the last thousand years. I knew something of the kind of human beings that were on earth, what they were thinking and what they were doing. I was able to reason rather accurately, and whatever there was that I had not been trained to do, the specific training that was necessary came rather easily because I had this general grasp.

Nevertheless, as I came into the twentieth century, I was aware of the widespread criticism of the sort of education which I had had, and the questioning in the minds of men as to how far that sort of education was really valuable and how far it could be applied to the youth of today. More especially during the present war, this criticism has been sharpened and emphasized in the United States. We have seen young people who had training in mechanics easily get jobs that paid wages almost fabulous.

In the great munitions factories hundreds of thousands of men, women and even children have been working at wages between five and fifteen dollars a day. There has been a special demand for people who knew how to apply the newly discovered laws of physics and electricity, for experts in radio, for people who could make and manipulate airplanes. Of all the different branches of knowledge perhaps chemistry has loomed largest. There has been the development of the combustion engine, the making of plastics; the substitution of new materials like nylon and synthetics for the older threads.

This has made the people say and doubtless you have had it emphasized here, that what education ought to do, is to prepare young people for doing work of this sort; and that it is a great waste of time to study what we used to call the humanities and art and literature, over periods which counted up into decades, rather than in a few years of intensive work made a man a capable workman in some trade or art where he could get an immediate and comfortable salary.

Now despite this, we look upon a curiously contradictory world. The technical advance of western European civilization in the last century has been the most marvelous thing which the world has seen. It can without exaggeration be called miraculous. Personally I never can get over the unreality of travel by airplane. When I was a boy we typified the impossible by comparing it to flying. Now we fly easily and with astonishing safety around the world. But not only that; we talk over immeasurable distances. We transport goods and ideas. We have a world whose technical perfection makes all things possible. And yet, on the other hand, this world is in chaos. It has been organized twice in the last quarter of a century for murder and destruction on a tremendous scale, not to mention continual minor wars. There is not only this physical disaster, there is the mental and moral tragedy which makes us at times despair of human culture.

Now when we compare the technical mastery which man has over the world, with the utter failure of that power to organize happiness, and peace in the world, then we know that something is wrong. Part of this wrong lies in our conception of education. There are two different things that we have in mind in education: one is training for mastery of technique; the other is training the man who is going to exercise the technique and for whom the technique exists. If, regardless of the man himself, we train his hands and his nervous system for accomplishing a certain technical job, after that work is done we still have the question as to why it is done, and for whom, and to what end. What is the work of the world for? Manifestly it is for the people who inhabit the world. But what kind of people are they? What they are depends upon the way in which they have been educated, that is, the way in which their possibilities have been developed and drawn out.

It is a misuse of the word education to think of it as technical training. Technical training is of immense importance. It characterizes civilization. But it is of secondary importance as compared with the people who are being civilized and who are enjoying civilization or who ought to enjoy it. Manifestly the civilized people of the world have got to be characterized by certain things; they must know this world, its history and the laws of its development. They must be able to reason carefully and accurately. Attention must be paid to human feelings and emotions which determine and guide this knowledge, and reason and action must follow a certain pattern of taste. These things: knowledge, reason, feeling and taste make up something which we designate as Character and this Character it is which makes the human being for which the world of technique is to be arranged and by whom it is to be guided.

Technique without character is chaos and war. Character without technique is labor and want. But when you have human beings who know the world and can grasp it; who have their feelings guided by ideals; then using technique at their hands they can get rid of the four great evils of human life. These four evils are ignorance, poverty, disease and crime. They flourish today in the midst of miraculous technique and in spite of our manifest ability to rid the world of them. They flourish because with all our technical training we do not have in sufficient quantity and for a long enough time the education of the human soul; the training of men to know and think and guide their feelings by science and art.

Now it is difficult to apply this broad and fundamental education. There is about it something intangible. It varies from individual to individual. Nevertheless it is the fundamental element in education. It can be handed on from teacher to pupil only in case the teacher himself has mastered the requisite knowledge, discipline of mind and organization of emotion. Without that fundamental endowment there can be no real teaching. No dexterity in technical manipulation can for a moment in school or in life become a substitute for the trained and disciplined mind which knows the world. I maintain, therefore, and this is the object of my talk, manual training is not education. Education is the development of the higher human abilities. Manual training, technical efficiency, are of tremendous importance in a civilized world, but only as they become tools in the hands of men who are educated and civilized. Otherwise they throw the world into disorganization and war.

For the Reelection of Franklin Delano Roosevelt (14 October 1944)

Sometime in the fall of 1944 Shirley Graham, author, close friend of Du Bois's, and six years later his wife, asked him for a contribution to the Independent, *a publication serving as an organ of the Independent Voters' Committee of the Arts and Sciences for Roosevelt.*

Du Bois sent the requested piece to Graham, but on 25 October the periodical's managing editor, Stella Rosales, rejected the manuscript, telling Du Bois frankly—in words that illuminate the history of the time—"Unfortunately, we could not use it for political reasons. As you perhaps know, many members of our Committee are Willkie Republicans and even our more liberal sponsors would take issue with your frankly socialistic point of view. Believe me, I would have liked to have printed your article, but I simply could not."

So much for the Independent *and the committee, whose members ranged from Albert Einstein to Bette Davis, from Eddie Cantor to Lillian Hellman, from Langston Hughes to Paul Muni, from Paul Robeson to John Dewey— and included Du Bois himself!*

The strongest argument in favor of the reelection of Franklin D. Roosevelt is to my mind one not sufficiently stressed in this campaign and glossed over by both parties. I am a socialist and have been for many years; that creed means to me that the wealth of a nation like this should be increasingly socialized; that the primary resources, the capital goods and machinery should to an increasing extent be owned by all the people and not by private persons for private profit; that the object of industry should be the common wealth and not the building up of enormous individual fortunes.

It seems to me that Franklin Roosevelt has pursued this goal in such vast undertakings as the TVA; in providing jobs for the unemployed during the depression, and seeking to aid works of art and literature which could not normally be undertaken as a matter of private profit. President Roosevelt has openly championed the cause and rights of union labor and fought race discrimination in employment. His housing program and efforts at land buying for farmers, rural credit and rural electrification are all in this line. He has at least begun regulation of stock-market gambling.

It seems to me that the Roosevelt administration has recognized that unless capitalism, as conducted in the United States, is more and more curbed by government action in the interest of consumers, that private initiative will disappear. Today individual effort, artistic taste and the higher ideals of living are curtailed by the action of great cartels and monopolies, by so-called big business both in farming and manufacture, so that the small shop and the individual worker have less and less opportunity for private initiative. I, there-fore, see Mr. Roosevelt as the distinct champion of the man who has an income sufficient for decent living and then can exercise his freedom to work, think and dream as he will, uncoerced by hunger and the threat of unem-ployment.

On the other hand, whatever Mr. Dewey may represent personally, and that I do not know and have been given few opportunities to find out, he certainly without contradiction represents that group of people in the United States who are determined to carry out after the war a program in this country different from that which is going to be followed by every other civilized land in the world which is free to act. While England is buying her mines, taxing her great fortunes, bringing democracy into her schools, estab-lishing a public health program, and especially so arranging her industry that unemployment will be impossible; while France has just voiced through De Gaulle a program of planned industry under government control; and while Russia is preeminently the example of a country with a completely socialized system of capital ownership; the group of people who are supporting Mr. Dewey are on the other hand determined to permit just as little govern-ment control of business as possible, just as little planning of industry as can be endured, and wish to allow individual corporations and persons to make as much profit out of monopoly and concentrated power as they are able to do under present conditions. My feeling is that this group of people are the ones who are stubbornly driving the United States toward disaster. I cannot see how intelligent persons having lived through the late depression and comprehending what the world is going through today can for a moment hesitate between Roosevelt and Dewey.

If Roosevelt is defeated it will be because of his championship of organized labor and the Negro. If Dewey triumphs it will be by grace of concentrated wealth and the Bourbon South as represented by Pappy Daniels of Texas and the lynching culture of Mississippi.

Flashes from Transcaucasia (24 November 1944)

In 1944 the University of North Carolina Press published What the Negro Wants, *edited by Rayford W. Logan. To this volume Du Bois contributed an essay, "My Evolving Program for Negro Freedom" (pp. 31–70). This book carries a quite remarkable foreword from the editor of the press, William T. Couch, which expresses sharp disagreement with its contents and, indeed, laments its publication. (It may be relevant to add that Couch left this press*

in 1945 and took a position as editor of the University of Chicago Press,
where he remained less than a year.)

   Among the Du Bois Papers were six single-spaced typed pages detailing
Couch's criticisms of Du Bois's contribution to the Logan volume, together
with Du Bois's reasons for rejecting them. As a result of this experience,
Du Bois penned the following brief commentary. (Transcaucasia is not on the
map; it is in the fourth dimension beyond the color line.)

The history of the publication of a recent book, *What the Negro Wants*, has
not been written. Persons carefully examining the book will find that its
authors are fourteen persons of Negro descent and its publisher the University of North Carolina. Usually the publisher advertises and commends his
book; but careful examination will reveal that in this case the publisher is
apologizing and trying to contradict everything essential which the book says.
What is the reason for this?

   The University of North Carolina has long had a reputation for a certain
liberalism on the Negro problem, a reputation which is already beginning
to fade. It had a department of publication which by help of large appropriations from the General Education Board has had some considerable success.
The business management is under a certain Mr. Couch. William Terry
Couch is a white Virginian who got his bachelor of arts from the University
of North Carolina in 1926. He has written a book[1] but is certainly no
expert in sociology.

   His acquaintanceship with Negro authors has led him to suppose that he
knows what the Negro wants and certainly what he should want. He, therefore, asked Rayford Logan (Phi Beta Kappa, Williams; Ph.D., Harvard;
Professor of History, Howard University) to edit a book on this matter. Logan
rushed to work and in a short time had the manuscript ready. When Couch
read the contributions, he hit the ceiling. He was angry clean through. He
said if that was what the Negro wants, the Negro must change his wants.
He slashed the manuscripts and criticized them savagely and finally declared
that he would not publish the book.

   Then Mr. Logan told him that he would either publish the book or face a
law suit for breach of contract. Mr. Couch had a change of heart. He published the book and none of the authors made any changes in his manuscript
but Couch inserted in the book as a publisher's note an apology to the White
South, an attack upon the Myrdal monumental study of the Negro in America

---

1. William T. Couch was editor of *Culture in the South* (Chapel Hill: University
of North Carolina Press, 1934), to which he contributed an introduction and an
essay, "The Negro in the South." He also was editor of *These Are Our Lives*, a
production of the Federal Writers Project published by the University of North
Carolina Press in 1939.

and his own firm conclusion as to the inferiority of the Negro. None of the contributors saw this preface before publication and the assent of the editor was not asked. Most people may neglect to read the preface but if they do they will miss the significance of the volume.

Meantime fourteen Negroes have thrown into Mr. Couch's face a statement of Negro wants which is quite worth reading. And meantime too the University of North Carolina may gradually be receding from its leadership of liberalism in the white South.

Memorandum to the Secretary for the NAACP Staff Conference (10 October 1946)

On request from Walter White, Du Bois submitted to the NAACP *the following memorandum, which was wanted in order—quoting White—to "appraise the situation ahead of us during the next few months and years both with relation to the objectives and methods of the Association and also in relation to the national and world picture."*

The views expressed here were basic to Du Bois's second dismissal from the association, at the end of 1947.

When the flow of progress in a land or age is strong, steady and unchallenged, a suppressed group has one clear objective: the abolition of discrimination, equality of opportunity to share in the national effort and its results. This was true of the American Negro at the end of the nineteenth century and the beginning of the twentieth.

But when, as in the first half of the twentieth century, progress fails and civilization is near collapse, then the suppressed group, especially if it has begun successfully to reduce discrimination and gain some integration into the national culture of America, must adopt something beyond the negative program of resistance to discrimination, and unite with the best elements of the nation in a positive constructive program for rebuilding civilization and reorienting progress.

This revised program in the case of American Negroes must give attention to:

1. Economic illiteracy
2. The colonial peoples, and more especially, Africans
3. Education
4. Health

5. Democracy
6. Politics

ECONOMIC ILLITERACY

The present breakdown of civilization is fundamentally Economic: the failure of human labor and sacrifice to bring happiness to the mass of men as rapidly as it increases the efficiency of labor. The leaders of two centuries have called attention to this threat to our industrial and economic organization; but the mass of people, even those of training, have not usually understood the increasingly complicated industrial structure of current society, and consequently have been in no condition radically to improve and rebuild it. Current education has permitted the man in the street to see industry as primarily a method of making individuals rich, and to regard freedom of individual initiative in business enterprise as the foundation for all progress. Again and again great thinkers have warned the world that this anarchy in industry would retain poverty, ignorance, disease and crime beyond possible reduction and culminate eventually in the suicide of war and destruction. This is what we see about us today.

To counteract this, prophets have demanded reform in industry based on curbing by government action the freedom of individual profit-making in the interest of social well-being. Such efforts have varied from palliatives like the New Deal to economic planning like T.V.A., to the O.P.A. and F.E.P.C., to English socialism and Russian Communism. Even Fascism recognized this necessity but placed the power to carry it out in the hands of irresponsible dictators and the object of its benefits was an oligarchy and not the working masses. The whole trend of the forward thinking world, before and since the war, is toward economic planning to abolish poverty, curb monopoly and the rule of wealth, spread education, insure health and practice democracy.

Here then the N.A.A.C.P. must take a stand. To do this intelligently, we must encourage study of economic organization by lectures and forums and lead the masses of Negroes and their children to clear comprehension of the problems of industry; we must not be diverted by witch-hunting for Communists, or by fear of the wealthy, or by the temptation ourselves to exploit labor, white and black, through business, gambling, or by industrial fascism.

COLONIES

We must look beyond the facade of luxurious cities, behind which modern civilization masquerades, and see and realize the poverty, squalor, slavery, ignorance, disease and despair under which the mass of men labor even today in our own slums, on our farms, and especially among the 200,000,000 colonial and semi-colonial peoples. Above all, we American Negroes should know that the center of the colonial problem is today in Africa; that until Africa is free, the descendants of Africa the world over cannot escape chains. We must believe Africans worthy of freedom, fit for survival and capable of civilization.

The N.A.A.C.P. should therefore put in the forefront of its program, the freedom of Africa in work and wage, education and health, the complete abolition of the colonial system. A world which is One industrially and politically cannot be narrowly national in social reform.

EDUCATION

From its founding in 1910, the N.A.A.C.P. has been curiously reticent on the matter of education. This was because, assuming that education of American Negroes was progressing satisfactorily, we saw at first our main duty in the task of fighting discrimination and segregation in the schools. Meantime education, especially the crucial elementary training in the three R's, has widely broken down in the world and particularly among Negroes in Africa and America. It is safe to say that today the average Negro child in the United States does not have a chance to learn to read, write and count accurately and correctly; of the army recruits, from 18 to 25, one-third of our young American Negroes could not read and write. This is simply appalling. Beyond this, higher education is deprived of adequately trained students and deterred from the facts and reform of industry.

Knowing that Democracy and social reform depend on intelligence, the N.A.A.C.P. should start a crusade for Negro education, and while not for a moment relaxing their fight on race segregation in schools, insist that segregation or no segregation, American Negro youth must be educated.

HEALTH

The health of American Negroes, of the Negroes of Africa and of the descendants of Africans throughout the world is seriously impaired and we lack physicians, nurses and hospitals to cope with this situation; we need too, teaching among the youth to curb excessive indulgence in alcohol, loss of sleep and gambling. Here again the N.A.A.C.P. has confined its activities hitherto mostly to fighting discrimination in medical schools, hospitals and public services and has accomplished much in this line. But we cannot be content to stop here. While continuing to contend for admission of Negro students to all medical schools and Negro patients to all hospitals, we ought to make redoubled effort to guard the health and cure the disease of Negroes the world over, by any method practical. Such planned effort should have immediate place on our national program.

DEMOCRACY

We, with the world, talk democracy and make small effort to practice it. We run our organizations from the top down, and do not believe any other method is practical. We have built in the N.A.A.C.P. a magnificent organization of several hundred thousand persons, but it is not yet a democratic organization, and in our hearts many of us do not believe it can be. We believe in a concentration of power and authority in the hands of a small tight group which issues directives to the mass of members who are expected to be glad to obey.

This is no new theory; it is as old as government. Always the leader wants to direct and command; but the difficulty is that he does not know enough; he cannot be experienced enough; he cannot possibly find time enough to master the details of a large group widely distributed. This has been the history of government, until men realized that the source of wisdom lies down among the masses because there alone is the endless experience which is complete Wisdom.

The problem—the always difficult and sometimes well-nigh insoluble problem—is how to tap this reservoir of wisdom and then find leadership to implement it.

This the N.A.A.C.P. has not adequately tried. It has regarded the demand of regions and branches for increased autonomy as revolt against the New York headquarters while in truth it has been a more or less crude attempt to teach New York the things New York must know in order to cooperate with Texas or California or New Jersey in the Advancement of Colored People.

The N.A.A.C.P. should set out to democratize the organization; to hand down and distribute authority to regions and branches and not to concentrate authority in one office or one officer; and then to assure progress by searching out intelligent, unselfish, resourceful local leaders of high character and honesty, instead of being content with the prominent and rich who are too often willing to let well-enough alone.

This securing of mass leadership of character and authority among young colored people of training and high ability can only be accomplished if we offer them not only adequate salaries, but even more, power, authority and a chance for initiative. This should begin right in the central office; the staff heads should be chosen not only to obey orders but to bear responsibility; the chief executive should be relieved of infinite details by distribution of real authority among his subordinates, reserving only broad matters of policy for himself and avoiding the paralysis of the whole office when he has no time personally to settle details. No one man can possibly attend to all details of an office like this and no assistant can work without power.

From such a top organism, power could flow down to the branches through chosen men armed with responsibility and power until it touches the mass of people themselves. All this is far easier said than done, but it is the essence of democracy and if it fails, Democracy fails.

Very soon a committee should be appointed to consider the reorganization of the New York office, with this in view. Such a committee, composed possibly of both office personnel and experts, should seek to consolidate and streamline the staff, reassign duties and powers, fix authority and responsibility and do away with overlapping. The office needs at least twice the space it now occupies to prevent unsanitary overcrowding and lack of privacy for work and consultation. Possibly the publishing, filing and more purely business functions might be physically separated from executive and research functions, or such a committee might seriously consider the removal of our head offices to the suburbs, to a building especially designed for this work with offices, archives, reference library, printing-plant and bindery, museum and art center, cafeteria, transient lodgings, large and small auditoriums and radio broadcasting facilities.

POLITICS

Finally, in our political program we should adopt two objectives—an immediate and a long term objective.

At present, realizing that party government in this nation has definitely and disastrously broken down, we should in future elections ignore entirely all party labels and vote for candidates solely on their records and categorical promises. Each state, each county, each election precinct, should find out for itself carefully and as completely as possible the record of each candidate and strive to elect or defeat him whether he be Democrat, Republican, Labor Party or Communist. This should be a continuous job and not merely a pre-election activity; and it cannot be done on a national scale; it is a local job.

But this is only preliminary; efficient democracy depends on parties; that is on groups united on programs for progress. We must in this land make such party government possible. Today it is impossible because of the premium put on disfranchisement by making population instead of actual voters the basis of representation in legislatures and Congress, and by failure to function of that separation between the Executive and the Legislature, which the Constitution tried to make. We must work for a constitutional amendment, concentrating both power and immediate popular responsibility on a Congress elected by popular vote, with membership based on the voting electors.

Today Congress is owned and directed by the great aggregations of Business —the Steel Trust, the Copper Syndicate, the Aluminum Monopoly, the Textile Industry, the Farming Capitalists and a dozen others, while the Consumers and mass of workers are only partially articulate and can enforce their demands only by votes which are largely ineffective; the great interests can compel action by offering legislators financial security, profitable employment and direct bribes.

The N.A.A.C.P. should lead in such political reform, all the more because no other American group has yet had the foresight or courage to advocate it.

A Petition to the Human Rights Commission of the Social and Economic Council of the United Nations; and to the General Assembly of the United Nations; and to the Several Delegations of the Member States of the United Nations (1949)

One of the more callous manifestations of racist injustice in the postwar United States involved a Black woman named Mrs. Rosa Lee Ingram. The details are stated in a petition drafted by Du Bois and signed by scores of Afro-American women. The death sentences meted out to Ingram and two of her teen-age sons were commuted to life imprisonment as a result of the world-wide campaign against this particularly flagrant instance of injustice.

The petition itself was presented to the United Nations by Mrs. Mary Church Terrell on 21 September 1949. In August 1959 Ingram and her sons were paroled; in 1964 the sentences were commuted with full restoration of rights.*

The signers of this petition wish to lay before the Assembly of the United Nations, a case of injustice done by the United States of America against its own citizens. We are bringing this case to your attention and begging you to give it your earnest thought and discussion, not because we are disloyal to this nation, but especially because we are citizens of this land and loyal to the freedom and democracy which it professes far and wide to observe.

This case of callous injustice is typical of the treatment which thousands of our fellows receive, who have slaved and toiled and fought for this country and yet are denied justice in its courts or consideration in its deeds.

In the state of Georgia alone, where this latest injustice is taking place, over 500 Negroes in the last sixty years have been publicly lynched, by mobs without trial; the latest victim being murdered this very year. Last year an election was held in the state in which the man elected governor[1] publicly promised to break the laws of this land and deprive a million black citizens in his state of the right to vote. In this state a legal caste system is in vogue which condemns American citizens to unequal education, unequal treatment for disease, segregates them in living quarters and discriminates against them in the right to work at decent wage. The governor promised to maintain this "race segregation" "at all hazards."

In this same state of Georgia, the following incidents occurred in 1947; a

---

*I am indebted to Professor Herbert Shapiro of the University of Cincinnati for much of this information.

1. In 1948 Herman Talmadge was elected governor of Georgia; he held the office until 1955.

Colored mother of 14 children, 12 of whom are living, lost her husband, Jackson Ingram, a share-cropper, who died in August.

With her children she tried to carry on the tilling of her farm in Schley county which was rented from C. M. Dillinger, a white man living in the town of Americus. Her neighbor was a white man named John Stratford, also a share-cropper. No fences were provided between the two farms or even between the farms and highway and often cattle strayed across the boundaries. On November 4, 1947 Stratford called the woman, cursed her and told her to drive her mules and pigs off his farm. She hurriedly left her washing and children and ran to his farm to find her stock. She found that her mules and pigs, and also stock belonging to her landlord, were on Stratford's place. As she entered his lot to drive them back, he met her, armed with a shotgun and began to pound her over the head with it. She begged him to stop and seized the gun. He kept beating her, until the blood ran, with a knife he tried unsuccessfully to open. Her two little sons 13 and 12 stood by crying and pleading, until at last a third son 16, ran from the house, seized the gun, struck Stratford over the head with it and Stratford died.

Mrs. Ingram immediately reported the death to the sheriff. She and her two oldest sons were arrested and put in jail, leaving the nine little children alone in the cottage. On January 26, 1948, she and her two sons were tried by a jury on which no Negro sat, and sentenced to be hanged for murder. Her landlord, Dillinger, seized all her stock, tools and growing crops. Colored people of the state and nation rallied to her defense and finally, April 5, the same court which sentenced her to death, changed the sentence to life imprisonment. This sentence the three are now serving.

This crucifixion of Mrs. Rosa Lee Ingram is of one piece with Georgia's treatment of Colored women. In 1946, twenty-five white lynchers in Walton county, Georgia killed two untried colored men, and then wantonly shot their wives to death because the women recognized the murderers. No one has ever been indicted or punished for this outrage.

Thus it is clear that the part of this nation which boasts its reverence for womanhood is the part where the women of Africa were slaves and concubines of white Americans for two and a half centuries; where their daughters in states like Virginia became human brood mares to raise domestic slaves when the African trade stopped; and where their granddaughters became mothers of millions of mulattoes.

Today these colored women and their children bear the chief burden of the share-cropping system, where Southern slavery still lingers. The women work the fields for endless hours and their children are driven from their poor schools into the cotton fields under labor contracts which disgrace humanity and debar them from all franchisement by poll taxes, and make the rural Negro family the most depressed in the world. It was such a family that

Mrs. Rosa Lee Ingram tried to defend and for this she toils for life in a Georgia prison camp.

Schley County has 3,000 colored and 2,000 white inhabitants, all native born and rural. Only 455 votes were cast in the county in 1942 and of these only 100 were colored. The colored people are almost totally disfranchised, hold no political offices of any kind, never share on juries, and work mostly as share-croppers on land owned by whites. Of the 750 farms 600 are worked by tenants. The money income of Negro families is probably less than $200 a year; their schools are poor and short in term. Twenty-four dollars per child is spent for white children and four dollars for colored, white school buildings are worth $1000 each and colored $600. Four Negroes have been lynched in this county without trial since 1900. It can be affirmed that in this county no Negro "has any rights which a white man is bound to respect."

In this case, we submit, every canon of law and decency, much less of justice has been violated. A boy of 16 struck an armed white man who was attacking his mother. They, mother and two teen-age sons, were tried by a jury of hostile whites, with no representative of their race. Their meager property was seized and the children are today subsisting on charity.

The federal government has made no move; the governor of Georgia has done nothing. The President of the United States, when approached by a delegation from 8 states, would not talk to them and through his secretary said he had never heard of the case. The Chief of the Civil Rights Division of the United States Department of Justice, A. A. Rosen, said: "This sort of thing is in the papers every week. It's shocking to me personally, but it is a matter to be settled internally by the State." He pleaded lack of jurisdiction and no available funds.

The formula upon which this nation rests in the ignoring and mishandling of cases like this, is the legal fiction that a sovereign government can if it will renounce all responsibility for securing justice to its citizens and leave such matters entirely in the hands of subordinate and irresponsible local corporations, even when such bodies openly transgress the law of the land. In the face of this, the United States of America declares its practice of democracy before the world and sits in the United Nations which has promised in its fundamental Charter to promote and encourage "respect for human rights and for fundamental freedoms for all without distinction as to race, sex, language or religion."

We are painfully aware that all matters of this sort, have by vote of the General Assembly been put under the jurisdiction of the Social and Economic Council; and that this Council has established the Commission on Human Rights to consider such cases. But the world knows what the Commission on Human Rights has done or rather has not done to fulfill its functions. We are nevertheless handing this petition to the Commission which in this case as in the past will either bluntly refuse us the right of petition, or will receive the document and hide it in its files as though it represented treason or revolution.

We will not rest with this attempt to conceal injustice and deny the right of petition. We charge that the Human Rights Commission under Eleanor Roosevelt its chairman and John Humphreys, its secretary, have consistently and deliberately ignored scientific procedure and just treatment to the hurt and hounded of the world. Instead of receiving complaints and giving them careful investigation and, when facts are ascertained, world publicity, they have buried the complaints and drowned themselves in a flood of generalities by seeking to re-write in verbal platitudes of tens of thousands of words, those statements on Human Rights which the American Declaration of Independence and the French Declaration of the Rights of Man set down a century and a half ago in imperishable phrase which no man can better today.

Hiding in this forest of verbiage, the Commission on Human Rights has worse than wasted three fatal years, until no sufferer has the slightest confidence in either its ability or honest intentions. It is not so much a question of the phraseology of a universal treaty on which all nations can agree, as the much more practical matter as to how far nations are living up to their own laws and professions. Even members of the Commission are becoming disgusted at the tactics of delay. Jonathan Daniels has recently said: "That if some means of grappling with the practical problem of petitions was not found, and the sub-Commission devoted itself only to theorizing in 'textbook style,' its members might just as well quit work and go home."

The sincere and scientific way to work out a Bill of Rights would be to examine carefully and thoroughly specific instances of injustice and from such basis of proven facts to build up methods of prevention and redress; instead of reverting to the outmoded scholasticism of seeking universal truth and eternal verities.

We appeal in this case to the Social and Economic Council and ask them to insist that the fundamental right of petition be affirmed and enforced in the Human Rights Commission. And further than this, we appeal to the General Assembly itself and to every member of it, to place on the agenda of its next meeting and publicly discuss, the relation of democracy in the United States of America to its citizens of Negro descent. We affirm that if the Assembly can and should discuss at length matters affecting the fifteen million Jews of the world, the thirteen millions of Czechoslovakia, the seven and a half million people of Greece, the ten millions of Arabia, the six millions of Austria, and the four million of Finland, it might find a half hour to discuss fifteen million of Negro Americans without disrupting the Charter of the United Nations or affronting the dignity and sovereignty of the United States.

Any nation has the right by law to curtail, for the greater good of the nation, the individual liberties of its citizens; but no country has the right to break faith with itself and deny its citizens rights which its own laws guarantee and its own declarations proclaim; and when it does this, is not this action a matter of International concern? Division of powers between nation and locality may satisfy the metaphysics of practical administration but it cannot divest a nation before the world of its responsibility for elementary justice to its citizens. This was admitted years ago when Louisiana lynched Italians and arrogantly refused punishment or reparation. The nation after years of vain quibbling was compelled by International law to pay damages to their kin.[2] The state of Georgia with its illiteracy and lawlessness is not a nation in the eyes of the United Nations, but the United States of America is a nation and as such bears sole responsibility for the miscarriage of justice in the case of Mrs. Rosa Lee Ingram.

It may seem a very little thing for 59 nations of the world to take note of the injustice done a poor colored woman in Georgia, when such vast problems confront them; and yet after all, is it in the end so small a thing to "do justly, to love mercy and walk humbly" in setting this mad world aright?

"Not by might, nor by power, but by my spirit" saith the Lord!

We Americans can send Communists to jail and drive honest citizens to suicide but can we stand before the world and defend the life imprisonment of Mrs. Rosa Lee Ingram as an example of democracy which the United Nations is teaching?

The undersigned colored women of the United States, legal citizens, voters, wives and mothers have commissioned Dr. W.E.B. Du Bois to draw up this petition,[3] because he has devoted much of his life to the cause of Negro equality. We endorse and subscribe to his words and urge action on the part of all nations who have signed the Charter of the United Nations.

Social Medicine (8 February 1950)

In 1950, during what used to be called Negro History Week, Du Bois delivered the following address in Chicago at the College of Medicine of the University of Illinois.

Freedom, the American way of life, private initiative, free enterprise and democracy are the slogans and catch words which are in familiar and constant

2. On 14 March 1891 eleven Italian-American men, held in jail in New Orleans in connection with the killing of a corrupt chief of police, were lynched by a mob of several thousand men. See Richard Gambino, *Vendetta* (Garden City, N.Y.: Doubleday and Co., 1977).

3. Among the women signing this petition—on which no action was taken—was Mrs. Geneva Rushin, daughter of the imprisoned woman.

use today. They appear axiomatic and self interpreting at first sight: we want to be free: we want to go where we please, when we please and do what we please; we do not like to have policemen ordering us about or chairmen stopping us from talking or governments loading us with laws. We want the right to make our plans, plan our own lives and set our own goals. We want avenues of advancement and accomplishment open to us and kept open. We want a voice in our own government; we want to elect the officials whom we favor and we want the way kept open to congress and the presidency. This is the American Way of Life. The difficulty with it is that it is not true and cannot be true and the sooner we face the facts we already know, the sooner we will talk like rational human beings and not like fools.

It is easy to see how historically these phrases arose and became imbedded in our cultural patterns. Americans of the 19th century were born in a vast land of unexampled wealth and variety of resource. There was rich land in abundance for the taking: there was remunerative work for everybody to do who was not sick or lazy: there was every variety of climate and kind of industry; every inducement of invention and technique; and if you did not like Massachusetts you could go to California, or move without let or hindrance from Chicago to New Orleans.

You know the sort of national character we evolved. We became bold, inventive and lawless. We explored, contrived, murdered, stole and lynched. Any man free, white and 21, was a law unto himself. It became axiomatic that an American could not and would not be held by ordinary restraints of law and order. Great Americans cheated their competitors, drove them to suicide and ruined their businesses and so became great and good that they could give the United Nations a site which no nation was able to afford. For thirty years between the Two World Wars, I drove a car, travelling off and on in nearly every state of the union. I used to tell my friends that I never saw a space marked "No Parking" where some car was not parked.

Of course, as a matter of fact, all Americans were not as Free, nor [as given to] initiative, nor so democratic as some were. It was only by ignoring the slaves, the poverty-stricken and the failures that we could keep up the illusion of this free successful land. And in the 20th century it began to dawn on many Americans, that in this land as in others, there were limits of freedom, individual enterprise and uncontrolled initiative which we must curb or perish. Of course we knew this before but somehow we hated to give up the illusion; moreover we had an idea that we could educate lustier and more virile children if we told them the falsehood that Americans were free and had a right to be freer than other human beings. I remember how as a boy I resented being expected to sing lustily about the "Land of the Noble, Free." I knew quite a few Americans who were not noble and I certainly was not free.

The learned professions in particular clung longest to the ideal of free and independent existence. The laborers, meeting time clocks and hard-faced men who hired and fired, began early to talk less about freedom and more about justice. The white-collar workers and civil servants long since realized that the treadmill into which their lot was cast was not properly described as private initiative or free enterprise; and they began to act accordingly. But lawyers, physicians, dentists, and clergymen long clung to the ideal of independence and freedom as the great attraction in these lines of occupation. I do not doubt but that concealed more or less successfully in back of the heads of most medical students is an alluring vision of a suite of offices on Park Avenue or Michigan [Avenue], where selected patrons are received by trim maids for quiet and interesting consultation; then after an hour or so in advice at the hospital with subservient interns a long sleek car whisks you to your books and conservatory. It is an alluring prospect, but not quite characteristic of most American physicians.

When I was in London in 1945, I stopped with a physician. Dr. Clarke was a charming man, born in the West Indies, educated at Cambridge, England, with an excellent and select practice in his office near the Elephant and Castle. He drove from there out to his pleasant new cottage in High Barnett where he had flowers, a little surgery, a well-trained butler and open fires. He enjoyed a leisurely but full life and liked to entertain friends from abroad. This winter rather unexpectedly he appeared in New York, on his way to Barbadoes which he had not visited for 30 years. He was not exactly unhappy, but decidely disconcerted. The British Labor Government had quite upset the normal complacency of his life. They took over his office and neat little surgery; they filled his office with a surging crowd of patients of all sorts and kinds and paid him a salary instead of fees. Of course they did give him a six-months' vacation with pay which he would never have given himself and he did not have to worry about his future. It was not that he was exactly worse off, but it was that he was certainly not free; he was not independent; he was a servant of the state and no longer a private practitioner. He did not exactly oppose the new socialized medicine of Britain, but it certainly could be improved; his real dismay lay in the plain fact that this revolution in the practice of medicine in Great Britain had come to stay. Not even the redoubtable and fearless Churchill would dare abolish it and go back to the days of Medical Freedom.

Why is this? The reason is quite plain: one man can be free; two men cannot. Just as soon as society grows in numbers and intricacy of organization just so soon individual freedom of action must be curtailed. The curtailment need not be slavery; it can and will lead to many compulsions. But in the end it can and must mean that individual effort will be curbed and conditioned for the common good. The individual must bow to the interests of society.

In no area of human activity is this necessity more evident than in the field of health. The advance of medical and surgical science during the 19th century has been phenomenal as you know much better than I. I know in my own case that had it not been for a certain technique becoming common about 1918,

I should have long been dead.[1] As a result of that experience, I tried preventive medicine. I went to an institute where they professed to lay stress upon investigation and advice. But I noticed that they still had the older point of view. Each year as I came, they asked solicitously "What is wrong?" "What are you suffering from?" And when I said that there was not anything wrong, so far as I knew and that I was not suffering, there was a certain lack of interest. After all, why should one come to a physician unless something was wrong? If instead of going to the institute, I went to any of my numberless friends who are physicians, they were all terribly busy; they had time only for acute cases and not for general advice. Moreover, incidentally, they could not charge adequately for advice, and they could charge for operations.

That means that there is a tremendous demand in this country for preventing disease,[2] which would not only save money, but save suffering. Again the young physicians, who are being trained in altogether too few numbers, naturally go to places like New York and Chicago, where life is easier and more interesting. As a result of this, you have our few physicans herded into the great centers while the mass of people living in country districts and sparsely populated parts of the nation, find it extremely difficult to get medical attention even in serious cases, much more to get regular advice.

I just had visiting me a friend from the West Indies who is younger than I am. But he lives on a far out-lying island. The result is that he is coming to New York to have attention given to his hearing, long neglected, and to have something done for his decaying teeth, which together with other difficulties, make him in appearance, much older than I. It was impossible where he lives and where he has been doing excellent social work for 25 years to get the professional attention which he ought to have.[3]

In the absence of advice as to health habits and for the prevention of disease, you have the tremendous and still growing sale of patent medicines and nostrums, increased now by advertisements over the radio, so that the majority of United States citizens are not only not given correct medical advice; they are having dangerous advice literally forced upon them. There is, therefore, clearly in the United States a wide and increasing demand for health service, for advice as to healthful habits, for prevention of disease, for hospitalization. And this demand must be filled.

We cannot depend upon the individual desires of medical students for the filling of this demand. Here is a social need and organization must see that the

1. In December 1916 and January 1917 Du Bois underwent operations which resulted in the removal of a kidney.
2. For Du Bois's very early advocacy of preventive medicine, see the *Medical Review of Reviews* (New York City) 23 (January 1917): 9.
3. The reference is to T. Albert Marryshow of Grenada, who from the early 1920s was a leader in the effort to end colonialism in the West Indies. Du Bois wrote of him in the *Crisis* 25 (February 1923): 153–54.

need is filled. Medical students must not only be trained for health work, but they must be assigned to districts where this health work is to be done. That interferes undoubtedly with individual initiative, it interferes with so-called freedom, but we have come to the time in the social organization of the world when need and not wish must prevail in larger and larger areas of life.

This is the result not simply of social organization; it is because we must bow to natural and biological law. It does not make any difference how free American citizens want to be, they have got to obey the law of gravitation. There are physical and chemical laws which must be obeyed and then in addition the enormous technique that has grown up, and the involved cultural patterns make our civilization so complicated, that individual wish or whim must be subordinated to the common good.

One thinks, of course, of social welfare as being logically in the hands of the state; but here in America we have been prejudiced against the state, because in the 18th century when the United States began as a nation, we were in the midst of days when curtailment of individual effort was most arbitrary and freedom in industrial life was looked upon as the one panacea for all ill. That freedom cry of the 18th century has got to succumb to the technique of the 19th century, and to the social welfare of the 20th century.

There are voluntary organizations for the care of the sick, for insurance against illness and operations. So far as they go, they are excellent, but they do not go far. They cover only a small part of the field. And whatever they do, should be done more completely by the state, if we have the sort of state which we ought to have. There is no reason for the prejudice in the United States against the state and its servants. A man does not become a scoundrel simply because he works for the United States instead of working for the Blue Cross or the Steel Trust; and the person working for Sears Roebuck could work just as efficiently and honestly for the state of Illinois, if he got as good wages, working conditions and security. There is no reason why the average of efficiency and character in the state employee should be lower than that among the employees of private organizations, except that those who work for private organizations are selected with greater care, are paid better wages and get more security.

But if the private organization can get that kind of service, the state organization can do the same thing. This means that the state has got to be taken much more seriously than we have taken it. It cannot be that democracy is mainly a way of selecting officials and making it possible for private organizations to increase their profit. If we begin to look upon the state as an organization for social welfare, then there is no reason in the world why the available ability of the country should not be hired and paid for by the state, made as secure in its tenure and as dignified in its work, as is possible with the private organization.

In other words, what we have to accomplish through democracy is a better state and that state has got to organize the demand for public service, not only in health, but in the procuring of justice, in the teaching in our schools, in planning and conducting certain industrial undertakings, in our literature and art. This means that we must revise in many ways our conception of the democratic method. We have looked upon it for a century or more as a matter of personal privilege, when in truth it is a matter of service and knowledge. Democracy is not so much a way of protecting ourselves from aggression as a way of getting the world's work done, and done in the best and most scientific way.

The experiences of the mass of men form a reservoir which is at the disposal of the state, if we know how to use it. The democratic method, through discussion and universal suffrage taps that reservoir, it ascertains through the experience of all what the needs of each are; and then proceeds with the best methods known, to secure for the State, the services of people who are going to put this knowledge into practice.

It is unfortunate that just now in the United States we are in a period when men of science, experience and knowledge hesitate to accept service in the government. We have had insult and persecution of unexampled and inexcusable variety visited upon persons in Government employ. We are slow in rewarding work of that kind and consequently at just the time in the history of the world when the work of government everywhere is expanding, when there are areas of service which no agency except government can undertake, we are persuading far fewer trained men to undertake this work than we must have.

When therefore, in the future we repeat these slogans of freedom and democracy, we have got to remember, as I have said before, that first of all, our individual freedom must be curtailed for the common welfare. And secondly that democracy is not simply a matter of election to office; it is a way of getting the world's work done by the very best methods.

We are always tempted to seek by-paths: to see if we cannot build up vast private agencies in insurance, in building, in the processing of necessary materials, in the transportation of goods, which will do the work which ought to be done by the State much better and more completely than any government is at present ready to do. But that means simply that governments must be made ready to do this work. That they must be organized for it, that the technique of the state must be so perfected that matters which are of national application and universal importance, and which can be accomplished only by an over-all organization, shall be done by such an organization, and that organization will be the State.

We need scarcely pile up arguments here. Practically all will admit that the necessary demand for medical service is not nearly met by present provisions: that the training and placement of practitioners cannot be left entirely to individual choice: that the social demand for human welfare in a world full not only of harsh natural forces, but with increasingly complicated techniques for processing and distributing goods and in addition, human thought and action set in intricate cultural patterns, that all this calls for over-head coordinating social mechanism to supply skills, distribute facilities and apportion human instruments on a scale which chance and individual choice can never provide.

The crucial question is what organ of social service can best do this? We can think of four sorts of organs:

1. Voluntary Organizations
2. Philanthropy
3. Business Enterprise
4. The city, state or nation

Voluntary organization can do much and in the future might do even more than now: but the total job is too big and calls for too much planning and executive action to be left to volunteers. If it is, it will tend to serve groups of selected persons rather than the mass of men. And above all it will lack the income necessary for a complete job. Philanthropy can be depended on for emergencies and at times of emotional strain, but it is neither sufficiently sustained nor powerful enough to conduct a social service like this. And in addition so long as philanthropy is a function of big business, it will serve industry first and humanity last. Large numbers of Americans turn naturally to business enterprise for any service or organization of magnitude. This is because we are children of the 19th century with its industrial revolution and free enterprise. The United States was born with the "Wealth of Nations," and has never passed out of the laissez-faire economic philosophy. We assume business organization and business methods are not only the best but the only way to carry on public service of any and all kinds. On the other hand and complementary to this idea, is the wide-spread belief that the state is incapable of anything but the simplest and roughest and least avoidable public service.

Most persons do not seem to realize what a contradiction these beliefs are to democracy. Most Americans are quite complacent over the admitted failure of democracy in this land and in most lands. Upon this basic disbelief Mussolini and Hitler built their totalitarian states; and because of this [dis]belief the citizens of the United States today submit without murmur to the control of this land by industrial enterprise not only in business but in government, news gathering, magazine and book writing, art and philanthropy. Let us not forget that unless democracy can cope with the broader services of public welfare it is idle to believe it can be trusted to govern the political state.

On the other hand, unless business enterprise is able to govern better in the future than it has in the past, then we must unfortunately conclude that human beings do not have sense enough to ensure their ultimate survival. For remember that business ruled the world during the 19th century. It was business methods which built the powerful British Empire, upon which the sun is rapidly setting; it was business which built and supported the dominance of the French language and canons of taste over most of the world. The Spanish and Portuguese, Dutch and Belgian dominions were built on successful business and these industrial powers reduced two thirds of humanity to slave labor in order to support in luxury a group of white super-men who owned and ruled the earth. Industrial enterprise, business methods, world commerce all marched into the 20th century "with colors gaily flying, with trumpet and with drum."

It was in 1900, the considered opinion of the leaders of white mankind that European technique, administered by white captains of industry, in accord with the basic principles of free enterprise and individual initiative and recognizing the unalterable inferiority of the vast majority of mankind, was destined to rule Asia, Africa, the islands of the Sea and in addition the laboring class of white nations for the benefit of British Nobility and Gentry, French artists in letters and gowns, and American millionaires.

What has been the result of this rule of business? We stand today in the midst of this century, with every great ideal for which the world ever stood in unexampled ruin. With "Peace on Earth, Good Will to Men," so unpopular and in such disrepute that we are prepared and eager to spend three-fourths of every dollar of our immense treasure to murder human beings, and not simply kill soldiers, but women, children, cripples and the old. We have fought two wars of such unexampled cruelty and destruction that they destroyed the very civilization they were declared to defend. Have you ever heard of the war for democracy? Well, it killed the democracy it defended.

The First World War was a war of big business against big business, of intrenched colonial imperialism in Britain and France against the imperialist appetite of New Germany. This war overthrew big business the world over, killed the world market, smashed the gold standard and landed the world in universal bankruptcy. Not satisfied with this triumph of free enterprise, big business determined to stop socialism, communism and colonial revolt and succeeded in a Second World War in starting a world upheaval, which may end anywhere, except in the restoration of the worship of private profit as the way of salvation. Either we put down the anarchy of free-for-all enterprise and make organized social striving the end of progress, or we perish.

Business has no alibi. It exercised practically universal rule from 1815 to 1915. If in that century, it could not establish peace and freedom; health and prosperity; education and faith, it cannot do so tomorrow amid the ruins which its overpowering greed brought on the world to drag it down to hell. We have tried the contradiction of universal selfishness; of gaining Wealth by letting everybody cheat everybody else; by testing all human value through the profit which can be dragged out of men by force or fraud. We have tried that method in every variation: now either the public weal, working through its highest expression, the State, will save civilization or it never can be saved. And that state will be a democratic state or it will be no state. Believe me, gentlemen and ladies, you are not entering a world to choose between socialism and some other way; there is no other way: you are not going to choose between democracy and some other way: there is no other way.

You will with justice now turn to me and say: look at the state; look at Washington. Glance at Springfield. And if your eyes are particularly strong peer at City Hall. And I answer, you are in none of these cases looking at democracy. You are not even looking at a good imitation. You are looking at what you and your fathers before you exchanged for democracy: you are doing exactly the same kind of thing which the founding fathers of this United States did when knowing that every fifth American whom they looked at was a Slave, nevertheless declared with perfectly straight faces: "We hold these truths to be self-evident: that all men are created equal; that they are endowed by their creator with certain unalienable rights; that among these are life, liberty, and the pursuit of happiness."

In the same way, we today are saying; we have in the United States a democratic form of government in which the people rule, expressing their will in open honest elections in which every citizen is free to express his will.

The result of this free democracy is that we dare not trust the planning and conduct of public health to this government because it is neither honest nor intelligent enough to conduct it. Instead we prefer to leave this work to the Metropolitan Life Insurance Company.

The reason we have not got a democratic government in this land capable of successfully dealing with health, education, transportation, communications, mining, manufacturing and heavy industry—the reason we have no such government—is because we do not want it; we have for three generations taught ourselves and our children that politics are nasty; that politicians are thieves; that democracy without corruption and manipulation is impossible and that our government, bad as it is, is the best on earth. Having made too true what we have declared is true, we are today fitting the capstone: we are asserting the right to accuse every public servant of being either a proven or potential spy. We are keeping out or kicking out of government service nearly every honest man of independent thought whom we can scare. And then we are saying: can a system of public health conservation and training, paying and distribution of physicians be entrusted into such government hands?

We of course answer the question when we ask it and the answer is no! But that does not end the questioning: is there any reason on God's earth why an intelligent nation of decent people cannot have a government capable of conducting socialized medicine, public education and such great industries as can only be run by monopoly and police force—is there any decent reason why that cannot be done? The answer again is no.

I know how easy it is to laud democracy and socialism by rounded periods which in themselves prove little: but I insist that if we can run this world with its intricate machinery of matter, force and mind for profit, then we can do it better for human welfare and avoid the disaster of universal selfishness and the contradictions of the present industrial system.

And the proof of this is that every country in the world with an ounce of vision, is trying to make just this change. Let no one tell you that the pending election in Britain is between Socialism and Free Enterprise: it is not: it turns entirely on the question of how quickly and by what steps inevitable socialism can be realized. France is a largely socialistic state: Scandinavia is markedly socialistic. Germany has been socialistic since Bismarck; Italy is socialistic despite the big landholder. Russia and China are socialistic and India and the rest of Asia have their eyes set toward this ultimate goal.

Only America, gorged with its billions and geared for war to a degree unexampled in the history of the world, is stubbornly trying to resist this world tide, even in the face of the facts.

I remember the collapse of 1929: I remember bringing my meager pay check up from Georgia to deposit it in the safe private coffers of the banks of New York, to find to my amazement these same banks of New York on their knees begging government to spare the poor business man a dime. I saw this country raised from poverty, distress and bankruptcy by the United States government in a series of socialist measures which included made work, state employment, flood control, wage floors, bank deposit insurance, control of profits and of big industry. It was socialism pure and simple no matter what we now call it nor how eager we are to repudiate its authors and leaders.

This argument of course is all unnecessary and beside the point. There is only one matter which Americans and Chicagoans are willing to argue about and that is Russia. This nation is straining every nerve and gathering every resource to see that Russia does not make Communism succeed. This is a strange crusade. I remember when George Kennan first revealed the tyranny of the Czars in the late 19th century: it did not cause a ripple in our complacency; I can remember when the misery and squalor of the Balkans were repeatedly revealed; but rich Americans were just as eager as ever to be appointed ministers to the squalid splendor of these tawdry courts. I remember when Russian peasants were coupled with American Negroes as the laziest and stupidest and most inefficient labor on earth. And I and a host [of] other Americans were uplifted when Russia threw off the shackles of the Czars and the Balkans kicked out their lazy princelings and staggered to their feet. What did we expect? Magnificent success? Quick and easy success? The wiping out in years of the oppression and exploitation of centuries in which we were just as eager to dabble as Britain, France and Germany? Surely we did not await this; but we did expect that we could make a neat profit out of Russia's new poverty and that was why a man who became president of the United States invested in eleven Russian oil wells and three timber concessions, which the leaders of the Soviet Revolution promptly repudiated. "Bolshevism," said Herbert Hoover, "is worse than war."

If ever a revolution was justified the Russian Revolt of 1917, certainly was. And how did Western Europe meet it? Within two years fourteen nations including the United States, invaded Russia without declaration of war and helped by men, arms and equipment set loose on the Russian people some of the worst butchering beasts of history. No sooner had Civil and Foreign war ceased than Hitler gave Trotsky two million gold marks to betray the Revolution. All over the world an international European attack on Russia financed by such millionaires as the founder of the Nobel Peace Prize was ready to overthrow Russia, when the bottom fell out of the industrial edifice of the European world in 1928 to 1931.

I am not defending Russia. I am explaining her attitude toward the United States and the world, and insisting that she has right to work out her destiny in her own way; and that the one fact in her condition which makes her to me the most hopeful country on earth, is that today after suffering more from one war than we have suffered from seven, she is spending more money on free, universal education of children than any country on Earth. She has 600,000 college students and last year published 800,000,000 copies of books. If intelligence does not solve her problems and ours, nothing will.

Once I landed in Kronstadt in 1926; it was a dead quiet and peaceful town. I went to Moscow and there with astonishment read in the *New York Times* that on the day I landed "Revolution has broken out in Kronstadt and the streets were running with blood."

I mention Russia not to defend her or justify her every act but only to insist that the use of that Bogey to halt socialism and the welfare state in this land, to hold up a national health program, a decent system of public schools; the control of industry in the interest of a welfare state instead of for the amassing of colossal fortunes to buy our newspapers, magazines and books; instead of such tactics coupled with the insane notion of world conquest, we should return to normalcy and common-sense. No matter what Russia, China, Asia and Africa do, we cannot stop them. We are a powerful people and perhaps in the words of that Great Brain which now presides over Columbia, "We can lick the world" [i.e., Dwight D. Eisenhower]. But we would better remember, that what we are doing now is licking ourselves into poverty, disease and ignorance by trying to mind everybody's business except our own.

Our problem is our democracy; the efficiency of our government: Law and order in our own land and particularly the use of our undoubted ability and knowledge in making this a land where the average citizen can get decent medical attention, whether he lives on the South or North side of Chicago, in New York or Mississippi, and earns a million a year or $1000. There is no question but what we can do this. Of the method by which it can best be done, I am not insisting, although personally I believe socialism is the only possible solution. But the means are less, far less important, than the Fact: and we sit and let the patient die while we discuss the best means of saving him and damn our neighbors for their diagnosis and technique. We have more students eager to heal men than we have facilities to train them: We are the richest nation on earth, if we build instead of fight. If we miss this great opportunity we are just plain stupid, if not criminal.

The Social Significance of These Three Cases (11 January 1951)

In 1950, in the midst of the McCarthy period, Du Bois ran as a candidate for the U.S. Senate on the Progressive party ticket in New York, and in 1950–51 he was indicted, tried, and acquitted of being "an unregistered foreign agent" in connection with his leadership in the effort to ban the A-bomb. In January 1951 he spoke by invitation at the Yale University Law School, at a meeting to celebrate three decisions issued in 1950 by the U.S. Supreme Court: Sweatt v. Painter (339 U.S. 629), holding that the plaintiff, a Black man, had to be admitted to the Law School at the University of Texas; McLaunin v. Oklahoma State Regents (339 U.S. 737), holding that the Black plaintiff, while a student at the Graduate School of the University of Oklahoma, must not be discriminated against; and Henderson v. U.S. Interstate Commerce Commission and Southern Railway (339 U.S. 816, 843), holding illegal segregation of diners aboard interstate railroads.

The recent election throws a side-light, on the cases we are examining here tonight. Almost the same number of persons voted for Republican and Democratic candidates, for Congressmen, in November—19 million 7 hundred thousand, on each side. Yet the Democrats elected 235 members of the House of Representatives, and the Republicans, 199. They were able to do this principally because most southern Negroes cannot vote. Yet their political power is exercised by southern Democrats. South Carolina and Connecticut had the same number of representatives, in Congress, in 1944. But South Carolina needed but 100,000 votes, to elect hers, while it took 800,000 to elect yours. Thus in the leading democracy of the world members of the Congress are not elected by majority vote. On January 3, the House of Representatives

decided 244 to 179 votes, not to allow the order and subject of its business
to be settled even by majority vote but to rest in the hands of a committee,
headed by Eugene Cox of Georgia.

Mr. Cox received [the] unanimous vote of 19,000 ballots in the November
election. It took 50,000 votes, in a total of 90,000, to defeat Vito Marcantonio
in New York. Mr. Cox has occupied his seat unopposed for 25 years. And
out of a voting population of 150,000, in his district two-thirds to five-sixths
never go to the polls. Evidently votes are more valuable in Georgia, and far
more influential, than here in New Haven, since it takes 45 of your votes,
to balance one in Georgia. As a reward for this disfranchisement of his
fellow-citizens, Cox is made chairman of the powerful Rules Committee, by
seniority, and he will make or stop national legislation for many years to
come in this democratic government.

This is not all. When the United States Senate was just organized the
majority leader, chosen by the Democrats, was Mr. McFarland of Arizona.
He will select, with advice of course, the majority membership of the powerful
Senate committees. Mr. McFarland is a southern Dixiecrat, whose every vote
has been reactionary and cast against civil rights, for free lynching, for the
poll tax, and against fair employment. He has helped filibuster on every such
proposal, which means he has denied even majority rule in the Senate. This
action as a Senator he has a legal right to take. But who made him Senator?
He received in 1948, a total of 80,000 votes in Arizona. I received last year,
in New York, 207,000 votes for Senator, and stood at the bottom of the list.
Senator Lehman received 2,600,000 votes, over 32 times the poll of McFarland,
to enable him to sit beside Senator McFarland, with only a fraction of
Mr. McFarland's power over legislation.

I mention these facts, first to remind you that no matter how fast we may
be accomplishing democracy in the United States, we are not yet in position
to do much boasting. You may object that this is emphasizing the color caste,
long characteristic of the United States, on the very occasion when we are
celebrating three important cases in which this caste has been broken. To
this I answer simply, that giving all due weight to the importance of
these decisions, and admitting in addition that more Negroes in this
country vote today than ever before, that nine out of 48 states, have fair
employment statutes, that lynching is disappearing, and segregation by race
is less frequent than 25 years ago—granting all this, it is also undeniable that
the present legal and customary discrimination against Americans of Negro
descent still renders them today the most suppressed and insulted group of
similar size and accomplishment in any modern civilized land. We can only
turn back to Czarist Russia and Hitler's Germany, to find a modern parallel.

Let us briefly face the facts: In the basic written constitutions of a majority
of the states, Negroes are specifically discriminated against with regard to
some fundamental liberties. By state legislation, a fourth to one half of the

states can for color alone annul marriages, interfere with travel, curtail recreation, deny public services, take away the right to vote, or to hold public office. States can for color alone interfere with property, hinder or deny education, designate Negroes with outward badges of inferiority, and make taxation without representation a general rule for them.

Throughout the South, regardless of law or gospel, no Negro has any rights which a white man cannot violate, without any penalty commensurate with the crime. Of the millions who have composed the mobs which have lynched 4000 Negroes during the last 75 years, not one hundred have received any punishment whatsoever, and none have been punished for murder. In the case of hundreds of thousands of Negro victims of mob violence, with millions in property damage, there has been little effort to recompense or restore. The majority of persons daily arrested in the south are Negroes whom no civilized tribunal would punish.

We are celebrating tonight three cases where Negro rights, have received recognition in our courts. But we are not considering the millions of cases where the mass of Negroes cannot get ordinary justice. Negro children in the south, and many in northern cities, are arrested and jailed not only with no adequate provision for their reform but with the calculated risk of making them criminals. Thirty per cent of all the felony prisoners in the United States are Negroes, and 53% of such prisoners in the south. Half of all Americans executed for capital crimes are Negroes, and of the women jailed in the south, 70% are colored.

In the south for 75 years crime has been a source of public income and private profit. The state of Georgia, between 1876 and 1904, made a million dollars profit on its prisoners. Does any honest American believe that these figures are a real measure of guilt, as between white and black folk? Of 1200 persons in military prisons, 250 are Negroes. Is this proof of Negro cowardice, or of military injustice?

The average black child today, in the southern south, has no adequate opportunity to learn to read and write. As one historian tells us, the south spent more in 1939 for trucks to transport white children, than for school-houses for Negro children. In 10 southern states, white pupils cost $40 a head a year, Negro children cost $13. The President complains of the extra-ordinary proportion of army recruits found sick and ignorant. But the proportion of young Negroes unable to read and write is often as high as a third. If we had educated Negroes to read and write as Russia educated peasants, there would be no illiterates among them today. But we turned the theory of industrial training into an attempt to retard Negro education. Charles Dudley Warner, who was at one time the direct mouthpiece of God in this valley, gave it as his considered opinion that Negroes as a race could not assimilate college education.

The nation needs more physicians, but the need of the Negro group is four times greater than that of the whites. Yet Negro students are still systematically kept out of medical schools, Negro physicians are usually denied hospital facilities, and only a single Negro has ever sat in the policy-making body of the American Medical Association, and that chiefly because he opposed social medicine.

Nowhere else in the world can it happen that annually great national meetings are held for science, religion, and athletics, at which members cannot fully participate, if they are colored. Despite much successful effort, it is still true that black folk have the greatest difficulty in finding work at jobs they are fitted to do, and at wages equal to those paid whites. The saga of the black locomotive firemen is the disgraceful story of exclusion by cheating and cold-blooded murder of honest workers at the hands of one of our oldest and most respectable trade unions.

Throughout the United States today systematic denial of opportunity to Negroes in study, in research, in science and in teaching is the rule. All that Ralph Bunche needed was opportunity and that was just what was long refused him. He could not teach in a first-rate college, he could not be more than a routine clerk in the Federal State Department and for that he must live in a Jim-Crow city. But when he became a part of the United Nations, a Scandinavian, from a socialist country which does not follow the American way of life, gave Bunche a job of policy-making, with authority over white people, an appointment which no American would have thought of. Bunche brought peace to the Middle East, when men of less ability and higher rank brought war in Asia. Then the United States applauded Ralph Bunche, generously, and Harvard offered him a professorship. But the opportunity for deserving this did not come from America, nor Harvard, nor Yale.

Here is a situation known to all who wish to know. Here is a caste system, still strong, far-reaching and cruel. Here and there, it shows hopeful signs of breaking, partly because of our higher cultural standards, partly because of world criticism, partly because it costs too much money to carry out, mainly because of the unceasing and unyielding push of 15 million human beings.

When thus by accident or good will, by cost or fear, the color-line yields a fraction, and a real fraction here and there, and now and then, in such cases we have evolved an extraordinary procedure. We go into a national snake dance, we sound the tom-toms and yell vociferously and call the attention of the world to the fact that the United States is now at last safe for democracy, and that the color line is disappearing so rapidly that it is good as gone.

We then proceed to work on the patriotism of American Negroes and ask them please if possible to yell louder than all the rest. Mrs. Edith Sampson swallowed this bait, and followed town halls all over Europe and Asia, telling of her people's freedom. When she came home the Carlton Hotel in Washington refused to let her eat at the celebrating banquet. The eminent pugilist

Sugar Ray Robinson, recently assured France that all American Negroes do not suffer discrimination. *The New York Times* hailed him in a Christmas editorial as our "Ambassador," who fittingly answered lying communists. But when Paul Robeson denounces the color line and praises the Soviet Union for abolition of race discrimination, he earns the near unanimous condemnation of America, and stern refusal to let him travel, talk or sing in Europe.

Negroes are not fond of posing before the world as step-children and outcasts in their native land. They welcome sincerely each sign of progress, but they are not called on to exaggerate each step beyond its meaning of significance in relation to the total picture. We can be hopeful without being ecstatic.

Ever since the United States conceived it the chief end of man to stop Russia from interfering with private profit, the world, the nation, and the Negro have been subjected to a steady barrage of propaganda to prove that Negro advance in this generation has virtually settled the Negro problem. There is no question but what American Negroes have accomplished much by the good will of their neighbors, and their own unremitting effort. They have been glad to testify to this. I sought to sum this up, in *The New York Times* five years ago.[1] But when another writer, in the same place, sounds the same note in 1950, but leaves out my qualifications and words of caution and warning which I then appended, I am forced to remember that relativity applies to the Negro problem here, and not simply to the sun and stars. These people have progressed but in the name of God never forget the distance they have still to go. And remember that the man who is climbing out of a well would best not waste too much time, celebrating, when first he sees light above.

Moreover, both white and black may easily exaggerate the meaning of instances like the three cases we are considering. They involve some subtle counter-costs. The decisions say, in effect, that states cannot deny professional education, and one necessary public service, to Negroes [or offer them] on different terms than offered whites. But back of these cases of discrimination lies a whole field of other discriminations, which if undisturbed, renders the social gain far less than it may seem. For instance, for 25 years Negroes have been compelled to build up an educational system topped by colleges and universities. We have often sneered at this effort. They used to joke in Booker T. Washington's day, at the Negro college man greeting a fellow with, "Is yo' done yo' Greek?" But it wasn't a joke; it built a nation within a nation, which today has the strength and will to survive.

1. It was three years earlier, not five. Du Bois's essay was published under the title "The Negro Since 1900: A Progress Report," *New York Times Magazine*, 21 November 1948, pp. 54–57. The editor's title distorted the article's contents.

To build colleges the Negroes begged alms, fought grafters, white and black, defied administrators, state and federal. They encouraged Negro scholars to seek training in the north and grit their teeth at insult and color discrimination, in order to fill teaching positions offered by Negro colleges in the south. There are today some twenty such colleges which are of higher grade than most New England colleges of the last century, with thousands of well-trained Negro teachers. Now suddenly Negroes in small number and under stress, are to be admitted to white colleges. The number will grow, even under insult and discrimination of every kind. The paradox is complete. The offer must be demanded and accepted or the whole fight against the color bar fails. A race cannot demand equality and then refuse it. But at the same time what becomes of all the Negro teachers? Of the field of work, open for Negro scholars? Of college life under civilized conditions, instead of studying as social outcasts? Judging from the experience at Yale, it will be at least fifty years, before a black professor appears. Here then is the perfect paradox without answer. Its effect must be subtracted from the rejoicing at these decisions. So too, equal travel can only be based, ultimately, on equal opportunity, work and wage. Of what interest is it to nine-tenths of American Negroes, that they can eat in Pullman dining cars if they cannot earn enough to pay for the meals?

The added danger today, beyond that of the past, is that color caste in the United States is strong and effective enough, despite all improvement, still to be reason for the failure of the democratic process in this land. And a prime cause why this land is heading toward a world war of races between the white world and Asia and Africa, with reckless willingness to risk civilization, rather than yield the right to exploit the darker world for the profit of American millionaires. This truth is clear and undeniable. It is the color prejudice, endemic in this nation for three centuries, which has lighted the path of our troops to Asia under the leadership of the wild man of Tokyo.

We embarked on war in Korea, and may soon in China, all the more gaily because these are colored nations. And we are born unconsciously to despise color. We dropped the first atom bomb on a colored nation, an unnecessary experiment, which we would not at the time have perpetrated on any white people. The reception of the late Chinese delegation, at Lake Success, reminded me vividly of the little delegation which fifty years ago colored Atlanta sent to the first public library opened there. The building had above the entrance a bust of Carnegie flanked by William Shakespeare. As citizens and taxpayers, we Negroes asked the same rights in that library as whites. I even ventured to point out that some of my own books were in the library, and I might want to borrow them. The disdain with which we were greeted was magnificent, and almost equal to Austin's desire to "summon" China to Lake Success, not to "invite" her.

We in Atlanta were duly punished and Negroes got no library rights for ten years.[2] The cost of repulsing us was little. But insulting Asia at Lake Success may cost more than 50,000 maimed and slaughtered American boys, with the end not yet. The price of the color line today comes high and may rise tomorrow. You can step on the faces of Negroes in America for 350 years without fatal results. But it may not be the greatest wisdom to try this game on 800 million Asiatics and 150 million black Africans.

There can be no question as to the effect which our continued refusal to face the Negro problem has had on our ability to reason, and our willingness to appeal to logic in our total cultural pattern. We stood 175 years ago, seeing every fifth American a slave, and yet declaring that all men were created equal. We fought against taxation without representation two centuries ago and ever since we have taxed most Negroes without giving them voice in government. We fought four years to maintain the right of states to enslave human beings, and then emancipated slaves from personal ownership into deliberate subjection to poverty, disease, and ignorance. We declared that the freedman must be educated and today three generations later, thirty per cent of young Negro army recruits cannot read or write. We have erected thousands of showy colleges and universities for the nation only to find that an astonishing number of our white graduate students cannot intelligently read, write or count.

We declare the United States a democracy based on free enterprise and individual initiative when we know perfectly well that this is not a democracy, never has been a democracy, and that no large body of leaders today intends, that it ever will be a democracy. That our industrial enterprise is dominated by vast monopolies and our freedom of thought increasingly chained by law, police spies and refusal to let anybody earn a decent living who does not think as he is told to think.

Every tendency displayed in this record has been helped, increased and guided by this basic habit of ours of refusing to face the facts with regard to our Negro population, of refusing honestly to right these wrongs and of continually excusing our mistakes by declaring to the world that we have already done that which we hope sometime to do.

It is again a background of such twisted logic that we do the most amazing things. How else will posterity explain that Yale University refused to listen to the music of one of the world's great masters because of his political beliefs? How is it that for 200 years Princeton refused to enroll a college student with a black face? How else can we put men in jail not for their deeds but for thoughts? How else can we declare all men traitors who ever wanted violently to overthrow the entrenched evil and greed of our civilization? Not reason but force, not logic but threat, rests at the present basis of much of our policy,

2. On this episode see Du Bois, "The Opening of the Library," *Independent* 54 (3 April 1902): 809–10.

and the most persistent ingredient of this frame of mind is the denial, exaggeration and deception which we have practiced with regard to American Negroes.

Today our rightful intelligentsia is curiously dumb and our political leadership, sunken to a low level. We seem unable to think, reason clearly or act with decision. To me, all this seems to trace itself directly back to the extraordinary color-complex into which this nation was born and still lives. Of all human distinctions it is the least logical, and yet and for that reason, has led to still wider lack of logic. We reconcile ourselves to college presidents leading armies and war propaganda, to a student body in this nation the most docile, hand-fed, and unquestioning of any similar group in the world, with no opinions, at least on this campus, not prescribed by the gospel, according to *Life*, *Time* and *Fortune*.

Address at American Labor Party Election Rally (27 October 1952)

In the 1952 election campaign the Republican candidates were Dwight D. Eisenhower and Richard M. Nixon; the Democratic were Adlai Stevenson and John Sparkman. The Progressive party (known as the American Labor party in New York) had as its candidates Vincent Hallinan, an attorney from San Francisco, and Charlotta Bass, a Black woman newspaper owner from Los Angeles. Its candidate for U.S. senator from New York was Dr. Corliss Lamont, author and teacher. Du Bois spoke as follows at Madison Square Garden in New York City on behalf of the Progressive party ticket.

While the American Legion was meeting recently in New York, I was returning from the sad funeral of a young veteran of World War II. My car was halted in front of the Pennsylvania Station, by gay young men forming for a parade. They were the "Young Rebels of Miami," and over them waved a Confederate flag.

During the whole Presidential campaign the Confederate flag and the Rebel yell have been in constant evidence. It was flown repeatedly at the Democratic National Convention, and when Eisenhower recently visited Atlanta, he was welcomed by the Governor waving a Confederate flag.

All this has been regarded as an amiable joke by most persons; others who know have met it with studied silence, and small mention has appeared in the press. I am sure, therefore, that most people forget for just what the Confederate flag once stood. *It stood for human slavery.* It was the flag of the slave states of the south, who fought against the free labor states of the north in a Civil War which was a rebellion against the power of the federal government to regulate land and labor. To me, naturally, the stars and bars of the Confederacy are more than insult, they are threat, because they signify the slavery of four million Negro slaves whose descendants number 15 million American second-class citizens today.

This Civil War, which killed nearly a half million Americans and maimed and wounded other hundreds of thousands, which destroyed millions [of dollars' worth] of property and disrupted the economy and cultural life of the United States and gave rule to corporate wealth, was caused by slavery. It is today the fashion to deny this and to assert that this unnecessary war was fought for "states' rights." People do not fight for abstract conceptions. They fight for money, power and fear; and in the minds of the people of the south who once marched behind the Confederate flag there was no doubt that they were fighting to keep four million black laborers working for them at the lowest possible wage in order that the masters should be comfortable, rich and powerful. On southern plantations millions of black laborers raised cotton, sugar and corn to pay for their living, luxuries and debts, while millions of unemployed poor whites starved. There are still historians who maintain that slavery represented the zenith of American civilization, and writers who rave over the jasmine and magnolias of the white-pillared mansions of the slave owners.

But not all white southerners were slave-owners; nor are all white southerners today waving the Confederate flag. Less than 10% of the whites owned slaves. But the slaveholders fought for slavery, and said so. Jefferson Davis, President of the Confederacy, said so. Alexander Stephens, Vice-President of the Confederacy, said so. A governor of South Carolina said, "God forbid that my descendants, in the remotest generations, should live in any other than a community having the institution of domestic slavery." The Confederate Constitution, which Stevenson admires, said in the 8th Section of its first article, that Congress shall pass no law, "denying or impairing the right of property in Negro slaves."

The Civil War resulted in emancipation for the slaves, not because the North or Abraham Lincoln fought for this, but because freedom for the slaves whose labor supported the South was the only way to win the war. The union of North and South must continue or Great Britain and France and the slave-holding South would lead modern industry.

The slaves themselves decided the war. As the armies advanced, the black workers deserted in increasing numbers to the Northern armies as laborers and spies, and finally as 250,000 armed soldiers, easily capable of expanding to a million. Lincoln had at last to say that four million black workers were "henceforward and forever free."

How free was the freedman? Not free enough for the Confederate flag to be furled. He had no clothes, tools or land. Thaddeus Stevens begged the government to give him a bit of the land which his blood had fertilized for 244 years. The nation jeered. Charles Sumner asked for the Negro the right to vote. The government yielded because only Negro votes could force the white south to consent to a high tariff and paying the public debt. This accomplished, that nation took away the Negro's vote and the vote of many poor whites went with it.

A fantastic economic development followed. Land, capital and labor are the founding stones of social life. In the South, the land was rich, and the climate mild; there was sun and rain for grain, fruit and fibre; there were natural resources in rivers, harbors and forests; in the bosom of the earth lay coal, iron, oil, sulphur and salt. All this was given by the government to the slaveholder, the landholder, the merchant and the employer. No part of it went to labor, black or white.

Capital was needed to develop this economic paradise. Government furnished most of this capital free to the landholder and employer. Railroads were subsidized, and rivers and harbors improved, and wealth escaped taxation. The North fattened on this and cheap immigrant labor, and poured private investments into the South. When labor lost its vote, landholders and capitalists voted in their stead and filled the legislatures and Congress with servants of exploitation and gave all the powerful chairmanships in Congress to the South. They gave the landlords and merchants millions to train soldiers for the First World War; during the depression, most of the southern relief went to landlords and not to labor. During and after the Second World War, the Southern industry moved into high gear. The Federal Government poured billions of grants-in-aid into the South. Southern Legislature vied with each other in bidding for industry, with free land, low taxes, and pliant police. Washington was lavish with certificates of necessity to build new factories and owners of oil wells were given tax rebates for depletion of the oil which God gave them; and today try to grab the oil underseas.

Above all, the South furnished and boasted of the largest pool of cheap, docile, unorganized labor, skilled and unskilled, in the civilized world. This mass of labor was first and historically split into white and black, each hating and fearing the other to a degree that persons unfamiliar with the region cannot begin to imagine. Then the whole labor group was divided into a group of organized laborers forming less than a third, and two-thirds of industrial labor unorganized, not to mention the agricultural serfs.

Here was a paradise for the investor, which the State improved: labor laws were lax and carelessly enforced; company towns arose under complete corporate control; the police and militia were organized against labor; race hate and fear and scab tactics were deliberately encouraged so as to make any complaint or effort at betterment liable to burst into riot, lynching or race war.

The result has been startling. In 1919, the South had less than a fifth of mining products; in 1946 it had nearly half. In value of manufactures it has

in 30 years risen from a tenth to nearly a fifth of the national total. Most of
the new and promising industries are seeking the south; and since World
War II have invested eleven billions in new industrial plants. The southeast
has already 80% of the cotton mills and all the new chemical fibre industry;
it is drawing the woollen and worsted mills, and the textile machinery mills
will soon follow. Paper and pulp mills and plastics represent millions of new
investment. The south-west is the fastest growing chemical empire in the world.

This newest South, turning back to its slave past, believes its present
prosperity can best be built on the poverty and ignorance of its disfranchised
lowest masses, and these low-paid workers now include not only Negroes,
but Mexicans, Puerto Ricans and the unskilled, unorganized whites. Southern
progress by means of this poverty is the creed of the present South and over
it floats the Confederate flag.

Where now is the American labor movement; what has it done; what is it
doing and what are its plans? The increasingly bitter and organized attack
on union labor in this nation is directly linked to the South and its past slavery
of Negroes and their long exclusion from the labor movement. The American
Labor movement, recovering partially with mass production from color and
skill discrimination, then allowed the employers to split them again with the
smear of "Communism." This fight against union labor today centers in the
South and builds itself upon that color line which once built black slavery and
now projects a new slavery of labor, black and white, North and South.

The Northern worker long went his way oblivious to what was happening
in the South. He awoke when the Black southern laborer began to come North
after the First World War and was welcomed by riots. Gradually the black
man has been integrated into the unions except those in whose crafts he was
not skilled and therefore could offer no competition. One of these was the
Textile Unions.

They built up a union movement which increased wages, improved conditions of work, and raised the standard of living. They excluded Negroes.
It would have been difficult to prove to them at that time that their attitude
toward Negroes was of any importance whatsoever. If Negro wages were low
in the South, what business was that of New England white labor?

Today the union man who looks about him sees that it was his business.
The factories, especially the textiles, are moving out of New England and the
North into the South. In the North 100,000 textile workers are idle; in the
South and in the world the workers are too poor to buy the textiles they
need and which machinery is more than able to make. Wages in the South
are twenty percent lower than in the North, and the Negro wages are set at
least 20% below white. This wage differential between North and South
represents increased profits of 4 to 5 billion dollars a year. Negro families in
the South get a median wage of less than a thousand a year; Southern whites
get $2000, and Northern whites $3000. Small wonder that Negro population in

Mississippi decreased 8% in the last decade, and that Negroes increased 55% in the North.

The carpet-baggers today are the vast Northern corporations which own the new Southern industry, and the scalawags are the Southern politicians whom they send to legislatures and Congress. The poor whites still ignorantly wave the Confederate flag, lynch or dynamite Negroes, and mob or kill union organizers.

Out of nine million industrial workers in the South considerably less than a third are unionized; last year 40,000 CIO Textile Workers, which excludes Negro members, struck in the South, and spent $1,250,000 in five weeks. They lost and their membership fell from 20% to 15% of the operatives.

Here looms the fight of the great corporations for cheap labor and disfranchisement, and this is what the new waving of the Confederacy flag means today. It means cheap labor and the progress of profitable industry by encouraging poverty among the lowest masses. Both the Republican and the Democratic party accept this significance of the Confederate flag. Both candidates court this newer South on its own terms. This is the Civil War, looking toward a new Emancipation Proclamation for the workers of the United States and the world.

The Confederate flag stood for black slavery in 1860; it stands today for slavery of black and white and it is ready to support slavery of black, white, brown and yellow, whenever and wherever the Lords of private profit call, in Europe, Africa or Asia. Both Eisenhower and Stevenson smile happily and joke beneath this flag, with its stars of wealth and the bars of slavery.

This then, is the problem of the newest South. Here is prosperity and here too, festers every one of the old problems of Capitalism in new and threatening form; poverty and disease, unjust courts, crime and barbarous punishment, graft and cheating, all excused by the presence of Negroes, all building a backlog for the flame of World War in which most of our military leaders are Southerners.

Who cares? Who studies the problem? What University, North or South, is bringing science to guide this new Leviathan? What church in a section which blisters with churches dares cry in the South today, "Thou shalt not kill?" Instead we wave the old flag of slavery and break the new labor unions.

The past is past; but today we vote in the future. What can Eisenhower and Stevenson do but kowtow to the new slavery and kiss its blood-stained feet? What can Sparkman and Nixon, the filibuster twins, offer but babble? What will Truman say but promise everything and do nothing? Or Taft, but promise nothing and disfranchise Ohio? All this is doing, while we dabble our hands in the blood of Korea.

Eisenhower, born in Texas, with neither broad educational background nor strong character, takes orders from big business and contradicts yesterday what he says tomorrow. Stevenson, who knows better, accepts from the same big business the most blood-thirsty and vulgar platform in our history, and becomes court jester of the campaign, courting the slave south and polishing rapiers whose phrases scratch but never cut.

It is amazing that these men can talk so much and say so little, until we remember that this is American mass production, using machines and smart young men with ears glued to the ground and brains for sale.

There is in this campaign only one true candidate and one platform of one word. Hallinan and peace. Not peace by war, nor peace for wealth, but peace, period! And for the rest, Charlotta Bass and Corliss Lamont. The ticket is complete.

If you want to throw away your vote, give it to Eisenhower or Stevenson. If you want to win, vote right, vote right and still vote right, if it takes a hundred years.

> *For right is right, if God is God*
> *And right the day shall win*
> *To doubt it would be blasphemy*
> *To falter would be sin.*[1]

In Memory of Joel Elias Spingarn (11 December 1953)

In 1953 Du Bois spoke at the dedication of the Joel Elias Spingarn Senior High School in Washington, D.C. Spingarn (1875–1939) taught comparative litera-ture at Columbia University (1899–1911) and was the author of several books in literary criticism, notably The New Criticism *(1911), and of collected poems. From 1913 to 1939 he held high office in the* NAACP. *Du Bois dedicated his* Dusk to Dawn *(1939) to the memory of Spingarn.*

In our day when the high places of the nation public and private are so largely occupied by men whom we all despise, I know of no one more fitting to remember than Joel Elias Spingarn who in vivid strength of his young man-hood seemed born to proclaim that oft-repeated word of James Russell Lowell:

> Let liars fear, let cowards shrink
> Let traitors turn away!
> Whatever we have *dared* to *think*
> That dare we also *say*.

1. This is from "On the Field" by Frederick William Faber (1814–63). Du Bois does not quote quite accurately, a fairly common practice of his. The original stanza reads: "For right is right, since God is God,/And right the day must win;/To doubt would be disloyalty,/To falter would be sin."

Du Bois at work in his office at the Council on African Affairs, New York City, 1954.

Du Bois giving his left-handed autograph to John T. McManus, Independent-Socialist candidate for governor of New York, 1958.

Du Bois receiving an honorary doctorate from his beloved Fisk University, spring 1958.

Du Bois speaking in Chicago at the celebration of his ninetieth birthday, 1958.

In defense of his unbending ideals the young Spingarn gave up Literature at Columbia University to vindicate a great man who had been wronged.[1] Turning, Spingarn threw his blazing energy into the least popular cause of his day. He did not stint nor compromise, nor pause when foe and friend alike advised and warned. He sought and found the firing line, made straight at the enemy and suffered almost joyfully the evil that beat upon him in return.

It is then our rare pleasure today here to revive his memory.

Honorary Degrees (1958–59)

During his ninetieth and ninety-first years, Du Bois traveled in Europe and Asia, visiting in particular Czechoslovakia, the German Democratic Republic, the Soviet Union, and the Chinese People's Republic. In the capitals of the first three, leading universities conferred upon him honorary doctorates, and in each case he offered fairly extended remarks. The event in Prague occurred on 23 October 1958, that in Berlin on 3 November 1958, and that in Moscow on 22 January 1959.

SPEECH IN ACCEPTANCE OF THE DEGREE
OF DOCTOR OF HISTORICAL SCIENCE, HONORIS
CAUSA, FROM CHARLES UNIVERSITY, PRAGUE

I am, gentlemen, deeply moved by the great honor done me today in a noted and ancient seat of learning, Charles University. I receive this honor in all humility holding it not so much personal but rather as an act of symbolism toward the race which I represent in America and on the continent of Africa. These are the people whose struggles today mean peace to the torn and distracted world or continuation of exploitation, theft and murder.

It may well be that many of my people do not today fully realize their vast responsibility to humanity. The fight against private capital and profit from investment in cheap labor and stolen land has been won in most of Asia, but it now centers in Africa. Britain, France, Belgium, Holland and America

---

1. Early in 1911 Professor Harry Thurston Peck, who had served for twenty-two years at Columbia, was summarily dismissed by the trustees. Spingarn's defense of him was so vehement that President Nicholas Murray Butler dismissed him, too, in March 1911. The cases created a sensation at the time; see B. Joyce Ross, *J. E. Spingarn and the Rise of the NAACP* (New York: Atheneum Publishers, 1972), pp. 7–9.

today stand on tip-toe, straining every muscle and using every device to induce black folk to sell themselves to the vast power of private capitalism in its final effort to rule this world.

For this failure among my people to see the struggle of the world clearly we cannot be too severely blamed. Science and religion have for five centuries united to deny the role of Africa in history and to teach Negroes submission instead of revolt. Even in America, where a modern slavery of the working class was established, even those blacks who finally overthrow it, today are unsure of their next step.

Too many of us are supporting the vast effort of the United States to bring on a third and last world war. I conceive it my duty to change this thought at least among my people and in Africa and the honor you have done me will inspire the last effort of my life.

Again, gentlemen, I thank you for what you have done today.

THE AMERICAN NEGRO AND COMMUNISM:
ADDRESS FOLLOWING THE INVESTMENT
CEREMONY, CHARLES UNIVERSITY

One hundred years ago, or in the time following the Communist Manifesto, those folk who were aware of the shortcomings and failures of civilization had various plans for improving the world through socialism; but they were not in agreement as to what plan would be best and above all they could point to no plan in modern life that had worked or was working. This was an almost fatal lack, and for near a century it held back much real advance toward socialism. We had socialist thinkers and planners, we had students culminating with the greatest worker in social research of modern times, Karl Marx; and we proceeded through the age of Lassalle and Plekhanov, Kingsley and Morris, the Chartists and the Fabians, but still had to acknowledge that socialism remained a dream or at best a series of unhappy and abortive efforts.

Today we have reached no millenium, but we can look about with a sincere rejoicing to see socialism over most of the world advancing and in much of the world triumphant. Our attitude toward this progress will be tempered by our own definition of socialism. When I was a student in a New England high school in 1885, we were warned against "socialism" and by that was meant mainly the intrusion of the government in private business. Today the town owns the waterworks, the state helps finance education and the federal government regulates the railroads, telephones and telegraph which serve the town.

But this is but a narrow definition of socialism. In a broader sense, socialism means the ownership of capital by the state; the regulation of all industry in the interests of citizens and not for private profit of the few; and the building of a welfare state where all men work according to ability and share income according to need. The complete socialism called communism has been reached by no nation; but the Soviet Union and China, with their 800,000,000 people, are within sight of this goal; Czechoslovakia, East Germany and Yugoslavia are striving toward it; while India, all West Europe and Scandinavia are adopting programs of government which are widely socialistic. In fine, most civilized states of the world today to a great extent regulate private industry and the use of property; own capital in railroads and communications; own some capital in industry; largely control education; direct and aid medicine and hospitalization; and profess that the welfare state is their ultimate object. Even in the United States, which is the most vocal enemy of socialism in the world, the advance toward socialism in the current century has been marked. We are still the only civilized state which does not own outright its railroads, telegraph, and telephones; nevertheless we strictly and increasingly regulate them; we own increasing capital in industry, in the shape of dams and waterways, forests, lands, and irrigation projects, vast stretches of highway, parks, public buildings and private homes; we engage in insurance, medical service, recreation and scientific research; and we process raw materials, manufacture goods, and engage in domestic and foreign trade. The world of my youth would undoubtedly have called this United States "socialistic" even before the New Deal and far on the road toward socialism after it. We can only call our present economy "private enterprise" today because in the last fifty years and especially since the Russian revolution our conception of the possibilities of public control has been so vastly widened by the phenomenal success of socialism in the Soviet Union and China.

If now we turn to the place which Americans of Negro descent must seek to occupy in the future, conclusions are difficult. Problems of race, class, income and education cross each other and complicate decisions. I have in the last fifty years found myself repeatedly changing my point of view, not so much because of the change in facts as in the importance of the facts and the consequent necessity for change of emphasis. For instance, as a boy under sixteen, my anxiety was to prove that in the past, despite the teaching of text books and despite then present surroundings, Negroes were folk like other folk. Then in my youth from about 17 to 25, I was intent to secure opportunity for black folk, despite color and poverty. In my working manhood from 25 to 45, I was fighting race discrimination in work, income and recreation and seeking legal and moral redress. It was not until after the Russian revolution that my main interest began to center in economic change as fundamental to the rise of American Negroes.

James Warbasse just died. He was little known but deserves never to be forgotten.[1] He was long the American champion of what was called consumers' co-operation (that is, of an economic approach to the problem of poverty which involved no violence and little change of law, but only united effort of intelligent people who bought and used goods).

In August, 1918, I held a meeting of those persons interested in the idea of consumers' co-operation and its spread and adoption among colored people. Among those present was B. M. Roddy of Memphis, Tennessee, who returned home and entered upon an active campaign for the introduction of co-operation throughout the south. By February, 1919, a charter of incorporation for the State of Tennessee was secured and a co-operative organization founded. Within ninety days after receiving the charter the organization had sold the entire $5,000 worth of stock and was obliged to amend the charter and capitalize anew at $15,000. By August 30, 1919, $10,000 worth of this stock had been sold and five grocery stores with meat markets were operating.

But in the end this and some fifty other efforts failed because they were tempted to turn into private investment enterprises and then big business froze them out or swallowed them. It is not true that the business man renders a public service. It is true that his private income and not his public service measures public esteem.

William Matney, who was teaching business in a Negro state school, organized a student co-operative. In 1927 he wrote:

> "The store is owned by student stockholders. The capital of the store was raised by selling stock in the co-operative society at a price less than one dollar per share. The store carries school books and school supplies, athletic goods, kodaks, toilet articles, some pastries made by the Domestic Science Department, confections and sundries, all of which are sold at the current prices in the city. Only stockholders participate in dividends. Dividends are paid out of net profits at the end of the fiscal period on the basis of the stockholder's purchases and not on the share of stock."

But the project failed. The whole consumers' cooperative movement, when it did not actually fail, in the U.S.A. eked out an existence which turned it it into an investment dependent on private profit or on alliance with big business. The difficulty with this brilliant and still valid idea was that without state support and protection it could not live nor develop. Or in other words, without a socialist state, consumers' co-operation fails; with socialism, consumers' co-operation can become the democratic tool of economic progress. The failure of consumers' co-operation in the United States spells the failure

---

1. James P. Warbasse, a surgeon and sociologist, was born in 1866 and died 22 February 1957. His autobiography, *Three Voyages,* appeared in 1956. Warbasse and Du Bois exchanged letters —see the *Correspondence,* 1:305–6.

of our socialism to advance more swiftly than it has. It shows how war and preparation for war is holding up the progress of the world.

Meanwhile, I began after the great depression to seek a way of advance for American Negroes. I repudiated the idea that Negroes were in danger of inner class division based on income and exploitation.

Here again I was wrong. Twenty years later, by 1950, I saw clearly that the great machine of big business was sweeping not only the mass of white Americans into a mad race for individual wealth made through private profit in any kind of legal and often illegal enterprise; it had also and quite naturally swept Negroes into the same maelstrom.

The outstanding fact about the Negro group in America, which has but lately gained notice, is that it is flying apart into opposing economic classes. Most people, including myself, long assumed that the American Negro, forced into social unity by color caste, would achieve economic unity as a result, and rise as a mass of laborers led by intelligent planning to a higher unity with the laboring classes of the world.

This has not happened. On the contrary, and quite logically, the American Negro is today developing a distinct bourgeoisie bound to and aping American acquisitive society and developing an employing and a laboring class. This division is only in embryo, but it can be sensed.

For instance: in New York the Negro families receiving an income of $5,000 and more a year form about 10 percent of the Negro population. That means that they possess at least $30,000 which puts some of them into the capitalist class. On the other hand, there are at least 50,000 Negro families in the city whose income is less than $1,000 a year, which is near pauperism. They are open to exploitation and crime.

The 300 or more Negro newspapers, with few exceptions, are mouthpieces of this bourgeoisie and bow to the dictates of big business which monopolizes newsprint, world news and credit facilities. Franklin Frazier, a leading Negro American sociologist, once President of the American Sociological Society, has recently emphasized the significance of this development:

"Negro public opinion is thus tied to current American thought either by reasons of security or sometimes by direct money bribery, especially during political campaigns. The dream among the intelligentsia of an independent Negro vote devoted to Negro progress, has therefore largely disappeared except under stress of some particular outrage like the Till murder.[2]

"Class differentiation in Negro organization is developing more slowly than in general life. In the church organizations there is a distinction between the

---

2. Emmett Till, a fourteen-year-old Black boy, was murdered in August 1955 in Mississippi for allegedly whistling at a white woman. The confessed killers were acquitted by an all-white jury.

churches of the very poor and ignorant and those of the well-to-do. But in the latter the main support comes from the workers and in control the physician often shares office and power with the janitor and porter.

"In a mass organization like the NAACP, the bulk of support from the beginning has come from the working class. Recently the well-to-do and rich have notably increased their contributions. It is still the dollars of the poor which support the organization and keep it a popular movement, except in some localities. The Negro control of the organization also is still the domain of the Negro intelligentsia rather than the businessman.

"Opposite the small Negro bourgeoisie is the great mass of black labor. It is at present only vaguely aware of its conflict of interest with the Negro businessman. This businessman employs a considerable number of Negroes and exploits them quite as much and often more than whites because of the limited jobs open to Negroes.

"As, however, the Negro laborer joins the white unions, he is drawn into the great labor movement and begins to recognize black business exploitation. But the main masses of American labor are at present in conservative unions under reactionaries like Meany. So far as these unions admit Negroes, the Negroes follow the reactionary philosophy of the white.

"Here the black, like the white, is restrained by charges of subversion and fear of loss of jobs." [3]

Thus it is clear today that the salvation of American Negroes lies in socialism. They should support all measures and men who favor the welfare state; they should vote for government ownership of capital in industry; they should favor strict regulation of corporations or their public ownership; they should vote to prevent monopoly from controlling the press and the publishing of opinions. They should favor public ownership and control of water, electric, and atomic power; they should stand for a clean ballot, the encouragement of third parties and independent candidates and the elimination of graft and gambling on television and even in churches.

The question of the method by which the socialist state can be achieved must be worked out by experiment and reason and not by dogma. Whether or not methods which were right and clear in Russia and China fit our circumstances is for our intelligence to decide. The atom bomb has revolutionized our thought. Peace is not only preferable today, it is increasingly inevitable.

3. Du Bois is quoting from chapter 8 of E. Franklin Frazier's *Black Bourgeoisie: The Rise of a New Middle Class in the United States,* originally published in Paris (in French) in 1955 and translated and published in New York by the Free Press in 1957.

HUMBOLDT UNIVERSITY AT BERLIN

Today you have fulfilled one of the highest ambitions of my young manhood.
In 1890, I received my degree of Bachelor of Arts at Harvard University, the
oldest college in the United States. I began in 1891 to study in the Graduate
School of Harvard for the doctorate. I wanted to finish my work at a German
University but I had no funds. By earning scholarships I staid two years at
Harvard and then applied to the Slater Fund for a scholarship to study in
Germany. This fund had been furnished by a rich American to educate
Negroes but most members of its board did not think any American Negroes
worthy of study abroad. I besieged them with such testimonials that they
finally surrendered and in 1892, I matriculated at the Friedrich Wilhelm
University at Berlin under Rektor Rudolf Virchow. I promised to pay back
half of the value of the scholarship and did so. I secured admission to the
seminars of Gustav Schmoller and Adolf Wagner for a staatswissenschaftlich—
statistical studies. I did not complete the university triennium but staid 3
semesters until my scholarship expired. Berlin would not count my residence
at Harvard and thus permit me to take the examination for the doctorate.
Schmoller tried to induce the faculty to make my case an exception, but the
Department of English made so strong an objection that the faculty refused.
I returned to the United States therefore, and eventually took my doctor's
degree at Harvard in 1895. However I had studied under some of your great
teachers like Wagner, Schmoller, Von Treitschke, Von Gneist and Lenz.
I had travelled by foot and train over much of Germany; I had listened to
music and drama. I had closely followed political life and social development.
However, I still regretted my failure to receive a German Doctorate. Today
by your kindness and I trust not prejudiced judgment, that ambition is fulfilled.
I am deeply thankful for myself, my wife and for my great-grandson, who
is 10 months old.

MOSCOW UNIVERSITY

Ten years ago I stood on this bare hill and looked down on Moscow. I was
told that here would rise in time a University to guard and guide the city
and the nation which fights poverty, ignorance and disease. Today I see that
University in stone and flesh, typifying the triumph of learning over life.
It has pleased you to honor me here with a degree, Honoris Causa. I am
grateful for this distinction and beg to thank you for myself and wife, Shirley
Graham: for my daughter and granddaughter and for my great grandson
who is thirteen months old today and who I hope will live to see a world
without war. My family has served the United States for eight generations,

yet I am not sure that my native land would wish to be represented by me here, since I am a descendant of the Negro race. But for that race now struggling to its feet in a world that for centuries has drunk its blood and tears, I can thank you and express my joy at standing here where the glory of your spire not only points to the stars, but actually reaches them.

Louis Burnham (28 April 1960)

Louis E. Burnham was an Afro-American activist in youth, labor, civil rights, and antiwar struggles, and a Communist. While speaking at a public meeting in Harlem, in April 1960, he suffered a fatal heart attack. At the time he was a writer on the weekly progressive newspaper the National Guardian, *published in New York City. A memorial meeting for him, sponsored by that paper, was held at Manhattan Center; Du Bois's remarks on the occasion follow here.*

I knew Louis Burnham for about 25 years. There are many matters of which I might speak concerning him; of the work he did; of the work he was doing at the time of his death; and of what he might yet have done had he lived. I might refer as all of you must to the future of his family and the education of his children. And above all none can forget his honesty and utter sacrifice.

I speak, however, only of one matter which seems to me of greatest moment to this audience. What I want to say has to do with the saving of lives like that of Louis Burnham; the stopping of the vast and reckless waste which goes on each year in this country and others, and deprives the world of irreplaceable help for the tasks which we have to do.

Here was a man of 44 at the beginning of what we regard as the prime of life. His education and apprenticeship had ended and his full life begun. Suddenly he is dead. Why? Let us take refuge in no mystical fatalism. He is dead because in his busy life he did not find sufficient time to attend to the needs of his body. He had a good body, not weak nor deformed, comely and normal. He had work to do, work of great moment but some of that work was neglected. The neglected work had to do with the preservation of the working mechanism which was his body.

This often is the fault of the individual. Some men abuse their bodies; others neglect them. But Louis Burnham was not that sort. If he neglected his health or overworked it was because of his absorption in what he saw as his duty, and because his friends neglected to warn him and the state of which he was citizen furnished no adequate code of health.

The human body is a marvelous instrument. It can be protected and strengthened. It can be misused and neglected. It has in its center an engine which beats in quiet regularity 38 million times a year. It has acres of tissue which need renewed sustenance and irrigation. It needs attention, much in some cases, less in most; nevertheless it must not be forgotten.

With heart and lungs, arteries and veins, teeth, bone and skin: with flesh and muscles; with senses centering in eyes, ears, and touch, these bodies of ours must be kept living and afire by eating and drinking and exercise and with all they must rest. The ceaseless functions must calm down. The repeating functions must ever and again stop. The body must sleep and sleep is a habit. It can be acquired. It can be lost. The body that is not allowed to sleep can forget how to sleep. And around the body must circulate air and water, rhythm and silence.

Happy the child that starts with a healthy rhythm of life. But when once he's grown the responsibility for preserving health falls on himself, his friends and the state. These three. But today increasingly the greatest responsibility is that of the state. We easily forget this. We blame a busy man for not resting but how can he rest when his work is not done, when his family may be in danger of starvation and when his friends do not sense this or warn him and the state does not furnish him facilities for good health.

We fall into the habit of going to a physician when we're sick, which is putting the cart before the horse. We should go to the physician before we are sick so as not to become sick. Our friends should feel it their duty to warn us when we are driving too hard and in the wrong direction. But above all the modern state should see to it that its workers rest, that they have recreation, that their work is done under healthy conditions and that there is an abundance of trained physicians and nurses, ten times as many hospitals as we have and services and medicines within easy reach of all.

Two years ago I was in London and was taken violently ill. I was treated for a week or ten days by an excellent physician and when I was well and asked for my bill I was told that there was no bill, that the British government paid for the physician's services and the cost of my medicines was less than $5. This was British social medicine which the American Medical Association has spent millions of dollars to prove is a failure.

About fifty years ago a group of physicians in the state of New York organized the life extension institute whose duty it would be for a small annual fee to advise clients just what the state of their health was and what they ought to do about it. I joined the organization in 1918, but gradually the state of New York so limited the work and functions of the life extension institute as to curtail most of its usefulness. They told me at last frankly, "Unless you have some specific ailment we really have no right nor facilities to advise you." And I had to reply: "It is just because I have no particular disease or complaint that I want the services of an organization like this."

The provisions for vacations, treatment, operations and hospitalization in the socialist and communist lands of the world go beyond that of social medicine in Britain. It is here in America, one of the wealthiest nations in the world, that health is grievously neglected. That there are far too few nurses and physicians and that the loss of life because of neglect and poverty is far greater than is necessary.

Most people give little thought to the health of their bodies. They are sure that the body's health is natural and they go on enjoying it. If they are taken ill they go to a physician. But to rush in upon any strange physician with a body already out of order is a crazy thing to do. The physician must learn what is the matter and that is not easy. He must become acquainted with the peculiarities of your particular body and that calls for time. The physician to whom you go should be your physician who already knows the condition of your body and the character of your work; and his business is not simply to see that you recover from a temporary illness, but rather to see that you do not get ill. Physicians should direct eating by advice and above all direct drinking. The present use of alcohol is not only unnecessary; it is idiotic. Alcohol is a useful and pleasant beverage, but it is not designed for continuous guzzling. Refraining from drinking liquids is if anything more dangerous. And the directing of a continual flow of smoke and gas over sensitive mucous membranes is neither reasonable nor in the end pleasant. I suppose that more than anything else one has to ask normal people today to stop trying to turn night into day and day into night in their work and play.

The greatest tribute that we can now pay to the life of Louis Burnham is to look around at our friends who are doing the world's work and pick out as we easily can those who are working too hard and trying to do too much and not getting enough rest nor medical advice of the right kind. Then we can take a further step which is so needed today and try to build up in the United States health services paid for by the state, from our taxes, and servants of health trained and paid by the state which will bring social medicine to the United States. Not simply to the young, not simply to the old, but especially to the great mass of people who are doing the world's work. We should vote for administrators and legislators who see this as their duty and against those who for any reason neglect this duty. We should try to bring to this nation something of the health services which can be found in the Soviet Union, in China, and in all socialist and communist states. There is no reason why the average normal human being should not live at least seventy years in happy useful life doing his share of work and being a joy and help for his fellows and not a burden.

For this is a beautiful world. We know its hurt and evil all too well. Yet we must never forget its beauty and possibilities. I have seen the high Alps blazing above Berne. The royal palms swaying in West Africa. The golden rain of Hawaii. I have seen 500,000 working people filling the Red Square before the Kremlin and thousands in the Place De La Concorde. I have

heard the babies laughing in the nurseries of Peking below the Great Wall
of China. This beauty can grow and men can see it if we but let them live,

> *And by contagion of the sun we may*
> *Catch at a spark from that primeval fire,*
> *And learn that we are better than our clay,*
> *And equal to the peaks of our desire.*

Socialism and the American Negro (May 1960)

*In 1960 Du Bois spoke as follows at the University of Wisconsin.**

Democracy has so disappeared in the United States that there are some subjects,
that cannot even be discussed. The essence of the democratic process is free
discussion. There was a time, when men were not allowed to talk of universal
suffrage, education for women, or freedom for Negro slaves. Today communism is the dirty word and socialism is suspect. I often refer to my
education in democracy. In the little New England town where I was born,
we had a high school of about 25 pupils. I entered it in 1880, at the age of
12. As I attended town-meeting, annually in the spring, there used regularly
to appear one of the dirtiest old men I ever saw. He was fat and greasy,
and every year he made a fierce attack on wasting his taxes on a high school.
I was always furious. I wondered why the citizens sat silent and let him rant,
but they did, and then quietly they voted money for the high school. There
I learned my lesson in democracy. Listen to the other side.

In this state, and in our time, occurred one of the worst blows to the
democratic process which our nation has suffered. Senator McCarthy succeeded
in making America afraid to discuss socialism, or to recognize communism
as aught but a conspiracy. And this, in the state of Robert LaFollette. I knew
LaFollette and his valiant wife. I voted for him for president in 1924, and
saw him give his life fighting monopolized wealth and asking world peace.
For a quarter of a century, I edited a little monthly magazine, *The Crisis*,
and despite opposition, I spoke plainly. I was criticized as being "bitter," as
seeking not simply political, but social equality for Negroes. For favoring
the teachings of Karl Marx, and for joining the socialist party. These accusations
were true, but largely as a result of my work, and the work of others, the
Negro made progress toward equal citizenship. Progress, but not complete
success.

* This speech is available on Folkways Record 1972 (FH 5514).

The collapse of the capitalist system after the first World War, brought poverty, unemployment and distress, worse than America had ever seen, and then came a surge toward socialism, called the "New Deal." The Nation relieved distress, built public works, helped agriculture and trade, encouraged literature and art. It joined the Soviet Union in overthrowing Hitler, Mussolini and Japan. And in forming the United Nations to avoid future war.

With the death of Roosevelt, came reaction. The United States not only stopped progress toward socialism, but ceased to discuss or study it and came to regard the object of socialism and communism as a crime. Especially American Negroes, still as a mass, poor, ignorant and sick, were given no opportunity to know the sort of progress the world was making to ameliorate the plight of the unfortunate working people, the world over, who were in [a] condition similar to ours. American Negroes were not socialists, nor did they know what communism was or was doing. But they knew that Negro education must be better; that Negroes must have better opportunity to work and to receive a wage which would let them enjoy a decent standard of life.

They were victims of disease, and drifting into crime. To remedy this, they sought to pattern their life after successful Americans. They must work hard, save money, become employers, and property owners and investors. This they thought would bring them recognition, as American citizens equal to others. But America has changed. There was still a chance for some to rise and get rich, but the working classes were no longer generally able to buy land. Their wages did not amount to what they in reality earned, and those handicapped by race prejudice had small chance to overcome poverty, ignorance and disease. A class structure began to arise within the Negro group which produced haves and have nots, and tended to encourage more successful Negroes to join the forces of monopoly and exploitation, and help victimize their own lower classes.

To remedy this situation, thinking Negroes still regarded their first step toward emancipation as being political power. They felt that their present plight was due to the fact that they had never become voting citizens of the country, and their first efforts were toward gaining the real right to vote.

The young colored men in 1905 emphasized this. The group meeting, at Niagara Falls, Canada, in June 1905, demanded freedom of speech and criticism, manhood suffrage, the abolition of all distinctions based on race. Recognition of basic principles of human brotherhood and respect for the working man. They called themselves the Niagara Movement and despite violent attack on all sides, met again at Harpers Ferry the next year. There they said: "In the past year the work of the Negro hater has flourished in the land. Step by step, the defenders of the rights of American citizens have retreated. The work of stealing the Black man's ballot has progressed and fifty and more representatives, of stolen votes, still sit in the nation's capital. Never before in the modern age has a great and civilized folk threatened to adopt so cowardly a creed in the treatment of its fellow-citizens, born and bred on its soil. Stripped of verbose subterfuge, and in its naked nastiness, the new American creed says: fear to let black men even try to rise, lest they become, the equals of the white. And this is the land, that professes to follow Jesus Christ. The blasphemy of such a course is only matched by its cowardice."

The NAACP, organized in 1909, added to the program of the Niagara Movement the realization that the fight for Negro freedom, could not be carried on by Negroes alone but by a national movement which united Negroes and whites. They emphasized the role which prejudice played, a prejudice often unconscious but nevertheless effective.

The NAACP made a nationwide fight against the horror of lynching and mob violence, and then more and more, it began to concentrate on the legal aspects of race discrimination, and the fact that the Negro was oppressed because the constitution of the United States was not being enforced. This fight had unprecedented success and culminated in 1954, in the unanimous decision of the Supreme Court against segregation.

But during all this struggle, we knew that something still was lacking. If we harked back, to the cry of the French Revolution, Liberty, equality and brotherhood, it was clear that there was not and could not be, *Liberty* of individual action, under the great industrial organization which was growing up in the world led by the United States. Production in industry and trade involved planning and planning curtailed liberty. Moreover our inequality was a matter of fact. Negroes with their ignorance, poverty and sickness, were distinctly below the average of those of their white neighbors who were educated, well-to-do and healthy.

Finally, despite all propaganda, we saw democracy failing in America. Fewer and fewer people went to the polls. It was increasingly difficult to know for whom, or for what, one was voting, and the cost of elections arose to suspicious heights. The election in which Abraham Lincoln became president of the United States cost about $100,000. The election which made Dwight Eisenhower president probably cost more than $100 million. Indeed it is possible that it cost twice that amount. Election expenses today include not only direct bribery, but indirect influences, monopoly, propaganda, and deception. Under these circumstances the appeal of socialism to all Americans increased. But the answer to the doctrines of Karl Marx, and the Utopias of Fourier and others, was that, with human nature as it is, socialism simply would not work.

To me, the obvious approach to socialism seemed consumers' cooperation. I tried to plan an organization among Negroes as consumers, which would furnish employment, help savings, and bring unity of action. But it was soon evident, as many of my fellow workers warned me from the beginning, that individual action alone, could not bring consumers' cooperation. That without the power of the government, it would fail, and with government cooperation it was socialism. My own training in this thought came from travel: my two years sojourn in Germany, at the end of the 19th century, where I saw the rise of the social democratic party. My repeated visits to England and France, in the first decade of this century. My visits to the Soviet Union, in 1926, 1936 and 1949. Then, as a peculiar aftermath of the two world wars, and my advocacy of peace, my travel abroad was stopped, from 1950 and 1958. In 1958, I was able to make a trip, covering eleven months, in which I visited western Europe, eastern Europe including the Soviet Union, and the Republic of China. This trip completely transformed my thinking. I started on it believing that socialism was a possible form of government, and economic organization, and was being carried on successfully in eastern Europe. That capitalism was also a successful form of organization, and while it might degenerate into fascism, and the rule of wealth, neverthe-less it could, as had been proven, by Franklin Roosevelt, become a progressive organization. I returned with completely changed ideas. I saw socialism as the most successful form of government today possible in the Soviet Union, and in the Chinese republic. I saw it evolving into communism, to an astonishingly successful degree. On the other hand, I was frightened and am still alarmed at the degeneracy of capitalism, and the possibility of it becoming a force so destructive, that it cannot be endured.

One of my first experiences was in England. I had in London a severe attack of intestinal disorder. A young physician, summoned at midnight came, and treated me. He made six or more visits, within the next few days, until he had me completely on my feet. When I asked for my bill, I was told that there was no charge. That his services were paid for by the British government. I reminded him that I was an American, and that in America we were repeatedly informed that socialized medicine in Great Britain was a failure. He smiled: the only cost of my illness, was the medicine which he prescribed, and that was less than $5.

On the other hand, I found Great Britain, France, Holland and Belgium countries which for past centuries, had built their comfort, prosperity and civilization mainly on the free land and materials, and cheap labor, partly of their own working class, but mainly of colored people overseas, whom they dominated, by their colonial empires. In 1958 it was clear that the end of this colonialism was in sight. Already most of the colonies of Holland had become independent. Britain had lost the empire of India, and France was fighting in vain to hold North Africa. Yet despite the fact that the colonial organization must end, these three great countries of western Europe, and others like Italy, West Germany, and Portugal, were depending for their future life on materials which they underpriced in the world market. On stolen land, and on labor wretchedly underpaid. The political power to carry on this process depended upon the laboring class in western Europe and America, and that laboring class was being bribed by political power and high wages which came, not so much out of the profits of the employers, as out of the low wages of colored labor. I did not sense in western Europe, and certainly I had not seen in America, any disposition so to improve the organization of work and the distribution of income as to make any essential change in the present capitalist system. On the other hand, I was astonished and encouraged by what I saw socialism doing. Not only did I see results of socialized medicine in England, progress in housing, health and workers, pensions in Sweden, Holland, Belgium and France, but in the Soviet Union, Czechoslovakia and East Germany, I saw a change of attitude which regarded the masses of people not as the wards and beneficiaries of the rulers of the nation, but as the main body, which itself owned the nation, and for which the nation existed; and as the reservoir, out of which were being recruited, those who were making civilization.

In China, it seemed to me that the process was going even further and that human nature was being so changed that instead of the self-seeking and class-hatred, which so characterized the West, there was coming a sense of partnership in a vast and growing nation, of willing cooperation and of a widespread content and happiness, which I had seen nowhere else in the world. All this was my deep and firm impression. I cannot prove it, particularly not to you, who have been poisoned by lies and distortion for ten years. After all, I saw these countries only partially and for brief visits. Yet I am a traveller of experience, and I know personally, the trials of the poor and despised. I was given unusual opportunity for observation and thus my conclusions are of value.

I saw the spread of socialism and communism. Today more than half the people of the world live under socialism, which is growing toward complete communism. In my mind, there is no doubt that the world of the 21st century, will be overwhelmingly communistic.

Returning now to the United States, I look again upon the scene. The legal fight led by the NAACP has been an astonishing success. But its very success shows the limitations of law, and law enforcement, unless it has an economic program; unless the mass of Negro people have not simply legal rights, but have such rights to work and wage that enable them to live decently. Here in the United States, we have had a stirring, in the Negro population, which emphasized these facts. In the slave south, Negroes impoverished and mistreated, have sought remedy by pouring into the cities of the south and especially the great cities of the north. There they have caused problems of housing and of crime, poverty and disease. It spells the damnation of youth, and death of children, and the degradation of women. Through this, the American Negro is passing. It emphasizes our national problem of gambling, prostitution, drug using, murder and suicide. On the other hand, the Negroes who have grown in intelligence and awareness of

Du Bois with Nikita Khrushchev in the Kremlin, early in 1959. Du Bois suggested the creation of an Institute of African Studies as part of the Academy of Sciences of the USSR; shortly thereafter his advice was taken.

Du Bois with Mao Tse-tung in the Lake Country, Central China, April 1959.

As the guests of President Azikiwe, Dr. and Mrs. Du Bois attend the ceremonies marking Nigeria's independence, October 1960.

Du Bois with Herbert Aptheker at Idlewild (now John F. Kennedy) Airport in October 1961. Du Bois was awaiting the plane that would take him to London and then to Ghana, at the invitation of President Nkrumah, to take up his duties as editor-in-chief of the Encyclopedia Africana. Courtesy of International Publishers, The Autobiography of W.E.B. Du Bois, *1968.*

President Nkrumah toasts Du Bois on his ninety-fifth birthday, 23 February 1963, in Accra, Ghana.

their handicaps have begun to fight back by the use of the boycott and passive resistance. The experience in Montgomery, the extraordinary uprising of the students, all over the south and beginning in the north, shows an awareness of our situation which is most encouraging. But it still does not reach the center of the problem. And that center is not simply the right of Americans to spend their money as they wish and according to law, but the chance for American Negroes to have money to spend, because of employment, in which they can make a decent wage. What then is the next step? It is for American Negroes in increasing numbers, and more and more widely, to insist upon the legal rights which are already theirs, and to add to that, increasingly a socialistic form of government, an insistence upon the welfare state, which denies the further carrying on of industry for the profit of those corporations which monopolize wealth and power. The stopping of a government of wealth for wealth, and by wealth, and a returning of governmental power to the individual voter, with all the freedom of action which can be preserved, along with an industry carefully organized for the good of the masses of people and not for the manufacture of millionaires. Does capitalism offer such a program? It does not. It offers war.

We have gone insane with the idea that we are going to rule the world by physical force. More than any other nation on earth, or in time, we are spending fantastic sums of money to prepare for war, and basing this necessity of war preparation on dislike, distrust and contempt for most of the human beings who inhabit the world. We have no peace movement in the United States that deserves the name. We have almost no men of intelligence and prestige who dare speak up for peace. Cowed and silent, we face immeasurable catastrophe and the first duty of Americans is to realize this fact.

To illustrate what I am trying to say, let me remind you of certain recent occurrences. On October 27, 1951, eight and half years ago, *Collier's Magazine*, a flamboyant pictorial with a circulation claimed to be a million and a half, published a number to which the leaders of American science and literature contributed. This at a time when few socialists in the United States dared open their mouths, and many were in jail, when economics and social science were being taught in our colleges with the utmost caution, and when I was being handcuffed, for advocating peace with the Soviet Union. This extraordinary magazine was on every newsstand, and on radio and television. It predicted and described in 130 pages, the aggressive war of the United States against the Soviet Union. The editors and contributors said that this year, 1960, would see the utter destruction of communism the world over and the victorious American troops walking the streets of Moscow.

Who wrote these words and made these prophecies? The editors say, "This historical report, was written by many of the West's top historians, political, economic and military experts, commentators and artists." Among them were Allan Nevins, "one of the foremost American historians," Stuart

Chase, Edward R. Murrow, Robert Sherwood, J. B. Priestley, and Margaret Chase Smith. Senator Smith wrote on "Russia's rebirth" which she pictured as being accomplished by American soldiers presumably like those then raping Korean women and burning Korean children alive and dropping disease germs on China.

For myself I knew that these writers were wrong. I had been in the Soviet Union in 1926 and 1936. In 1949, twenty-five Americans had been invited to attend, expenses paid, a Soviet Peace Congress. I was the only one who accepted. I addressed a cross-section of that great nation. I did not, as I would have been justified in doing, devote this opportunity to describing the plight of my people. On the contrary, I contended that I was speaking for those Americans who did not want war. And that they were a majority of the nation. No one visiting the Soviet Union, at that time could for a moment doubt its peaceful intentions. The reply to my thesis was this extraordinary article, which broke all rules of international decency, told lies and spread misinformation, and yet was received with applause in most quarters and unforgivable silence in others.

The year 1960 has come and is over a third gone. What has happened? *Collier's* Magazine has gone. Its vaunted million and a half readers have ceased to subscribe because the "reduced prices" which they charged for *Collier's* and a dozen other flashy periodicals which are thrust down our throats are not needed by the publishers, save as bait to advertisers who pay millions to make you buy their goods. The day will come, when *Life* and *Look* will pay their subscribers to allow the use of their names.

American troops are not in Moscow, and are not planning to be there. But the President of the United States is going, and we hope on an errand of peace to which he has been graciously invited, by the head of the Soviet State, in one of the greatest speeches of our day.

On the other hand, there are signs in this nation which should give us pause: there is stealing, cheating, poisoning, gambling and killing, to a frightening degree; our exports do not pay for our imports and we are settling the deficit by exporting $4 billion. Adulteration of food, and over-pricing of medicines, have reached alarming heights and the cost of living is continuously rising.

Perhaps our most unforgivable deed today, is our attitude toward China. Historically in America, "Chinks" have always rated below "Wops" and "Niggers." Negroes were lazy and jolly, and thus infuriated slave-drivers; but Chinese coolies worked like dumb, driven cattle. They were valuable, because they worked hard for almost nothing. During the nineteenth century, they were not only worked at home, but were transported in droves overseas like slaves to work for white folk. When they showed signs of rebellion in China, we began to steal their land, make them buy opium, and we planned to distribute the Chinese empire among the superior white nations. America willingly agreed so long as we got equal entry through this "open door." The Christian world sent droves of missionaries to make Chinese submission quick and easy. Then just as we were stretching our claws to pluck the rich fruit, of the "white man's burden," Sun Yat Sen led the last revolt. The Soviet Union helped, and Chiang Kai Shek assumed leadership. Our way was clear, despite the advice of our own General Stillwell. We bribed Chiang to betray and murder communists. We gave him money and arms, and yet with desperate determination, China won its independence, and drove the murderous traitor into the sea, where he still squats on an island, protected by our money and guns. We hate China. We propose never to forgive the Chinese. We count them outside humanity. We charge them with every crime we can invent. I was on the borders of Tibet, last year, when China saved Tibetan slaves, and we shed crocodile tears. We have sympathy and money for the slave-drivers who hold the Dalai Lama as prisoner; but for the prisoners in our own overcrowded jails, who rebel each day, and cry in vain for justice and mercy, our only remedy is more jails. This shows the increase in our religion. This shows why we tax Americans into crime, poverty and suicide, and spend ten times more for war than for education, health and social security. Our national debt for war is greater than possibly we ever will or can pay.

This nation tries to prove its prosperity by balancing the monopolized wealth of the owners of its great corporations against the poverty of our lower third. What does this call for? Not for a compulsory rush toward socialism. Many of us believe and hope that socialism will and must come to this land. We see no other way. But scores of others do not believe this, and that is their right. But they have no right to prevent the truth about socialism from being told. They have no right to prevent students from studying the remarkable philosophy of Karl Marx. They have no right to prevent Americans from travel in China. Especially Americans of eminence must stop the spreading of lies about the socialist world. A few years ago, I was invited to the Harvard Club of New York to hear a former president of Harvard lecture on Soviet education. I was loath to accept because no Harvard Club has ever admitted a Negro to membership. But it was my duty to go. Knowledge always costs something and this is the kind of currency I have often had to pay in order to know.

President Conant, former commissioner of Germany, and largely respon-sible for present conditions there, told his audience that after two visits to the Soviet Union he had been unable to learn on what basis of examination Russian students were graduated into the University. Now on his return to America, he had learned the truth: the communist party had refused to allow students to be examined in order to promote only followers of the party. He had hardly got his mouth closed before sputnik had crossed the heavens, and the back of the moon had been photographed, proving beyond doubt the leadership of a communist state in modern science. The superiority of the Soviet Union in the education of children became indisputable and her lead in industry seems soon inevitable.

America must let youth know. American students must dare study the Soviet Union and China as carefully as they study Great Britain and France. But especially American Negroes must know what is going on in the world today, and learn for themselves, what this has to teach them, in order that they may preserve their culture, get rid of poverty, ignorance and disease, and help America live up at least to a shadow of its vain boast as the land of the free and the home of the brave.

Remember how once Browning sang

"O to be in England, now that April's there!"

Today in Wisconsin one hears the winds of spring
But listen low and long: The wails we hear are not all spring
There moans beneath the swish of whips the lithe thongs of South Africa
Lashing civilization into Niggers: With drip of blood and roar of guns
And sob of mother and babies!
This is part of the system you defend
Americans have three hundred and fifty million invested in South Africa
It must make profit even as England's April does
For our profit the Blacks must work for what we offer. Chant Jew and
    Christian:
"Come unto me, all ye that labor and are heavy laden," and I will give you hell.
Take my yoke upon you or I will bash your Black faces in.
Listen to the winds
Hear the wail of death
And weep

Rabindranath Tagore (14 October 1960)

The Tagore Centenary Peace Festival was established in 1960 to help organize an international celebration of the birth of the great Indian writer (1861–1941), who had been awarded the Nobel Prize in 1913. The Indian writer Mulk Raj Anand, in a letter to Du Bois from Calcutta dated 30 September 1960, invited him to participate in the celebration. Du Bois responded with this message.

On his last visit to the United States I had the pleasure of meeting Rabindranath Tagore. Ordinarily American Negroes did not meet distinguished strangers and thus our visitors go home filled with what they are told about Negroes by white people, but having seen and known very few. It happened in this case that Tagore because of his color was insulted in our traditional way when he landed in San Francisco. There was discussion of the incident when he came East. I went to his hotel and talked with him. I was of course impressed by his striking presence and we found much in common to discuss concerning the color line which was growing in world importance.[1] I had heard of Gandhi and corresponded with him[2] so that my talk with Tagore increased my awareness of India and of its meaning to the world. Later I had long and close companionship with Lajput Rai while he was exiled in the United States and I knew of his martyrdom.[3]

Peculiar circumstances have kept Indians and American Negroes far apart. The Indians naturally recoiled from being mistaken for Negroes and having to share their disabilities. The Negroes thought of Indians as people ashamed of their race and color so that the two seldom met. My meeting with Tagore helped to change this attitude and today Negroes and Indians realize that both are fighting the same great battle against the assumption of superiority made so often by the white race.

A Scientific Study of Africa (December 1960)

During his 1958 visit to the Soviet Union, Du Bois had a two-hour discussion with Prime Minister Khrushchev on problems of peace, conditions of the Afro-American people, and developments in Africa. In the course of this meeting, Du Bois suggested that it would be useful to create an institute for the study of Africa as an integral part of the Soviet Union's Academy of Sciences. Later that same year he brought forward this idea in discussions with professors at Leningrad University.

Still later in 1958 Khrushchev appointed a committee to study this matter, and in October the establishment of an Institute on Africa as part of the Academy of Sciences was announced.

1. Details about Tagore's encounter with racism in the United States may be found in the *Crisis* 36 (October 1929): 333–34.
2. See the *Correspondence*, 1:402:3.
3. Du Bois and Rai spoke from the same platform in Long Island, N.Y., in September 1917 (see the *New York Evening Post*, September 22, 1917, p. 14), and Du Bois discussed one of Rai's books in the *Crisis* 36 (May 1929): 175. Rai's killing in India is noted in ibid. 36 (January 1929): 5.

A fragment of a paper enunciating Du Bois's ideas on the functioning of the institute is presented here.

Africa has just taken a decisive step toward independence and free cultural development. Its first efforts will be in economic and political lines. Education will receive some attention but not as much as is needed because of the limited resources and lack of teachers. I believe the Soviet Union can help the Africans in many ways and in a message to the late Congress at Accra I have stressed several of these ways and emphasized the necessity of African development toward Socialism.[1]

Another matter now comes to my mind: the scientific study of Africans and their continent is necessary for the guidance of their education and the organization of their culture. This is one of the many ways the progressing world can help its lagging parts and one with the fewest causes for friction and difference of interest.

I suggest therefor [that] an Institute of the Academy of Science establish a course of co-operative international and interracial study of Pan-African history, sociology, physiography, ethnography, anthropology and all cognate studies. This department of the Academy would aim at the promotion of scientific research into all the activities, past and present of the peoples of Africa, in their cultural, political and economic organizations; together with a simultaneous study of their physical, psychological and biological environment; their work in literature and art and in all human accomplishment.

This series of studies would be carried on with the central idea of the unity of the whole subject and the conviction that history is not separate from sociology or culture from biology, but that all research working together seek the one end of scientific knowledge.

While this enterprise should start in the Soviet Union and center there so long as this worked for its best success, it should from the first seek help, cooperation and assistance wherever in the world they can be found, so as to emphasize in this critical day the uses and practicability of world peace and friendly cooperation in the great ends of living.

From the first this Institute should seek the cooperation of Africans; of their states, schools and cultural organizations and particularly of their talent. For this end scholarships should be established for the promotion of study and research among Africans both at home and abroad.

The cooperation of all African organizations should be sought and welcomed and it should be the distinct object from the first to establish event- [the manuscript ends at this point].

1. Du Bois's message to the First All-Peoples' Conference, held in Accra, Ghana, on 9 December 1958, was read for him by his wife, Shirley Graham Du Bois; the full text is in her book *His Day Is Marching On: A Memoir of W.E.B. Du Bois* (Philadelphia: J. B. Lippincott, 1971), pp. 370–74.

A Petition to the Honorable John F. Kennedy (1961)

Among the papers left by Du Bois was the text of a proposed petition which he drafted early in 1961, probably in February. This does not seem to have gone much further than his own study. In a short time he was to leave the United States permanently to take up work as editor-in-chief of a projected Encyclopedia Africana, at the invitation of President Nkrumah of Ghana.

Dear Mr. President:

We come to you as Negro citizens conscious of our responsibility to add our contribution to the solution of the momentous problems confronting our country, conscious of our responsibility to ourselves, our children and to all those who comprise our great nation.

You, Mr. President, have said that our country has lost prestige in the councils of the world. We believe that this is true and that there is a definite relationship between this fact and the attitude of government toward us, its Negro nationals. Some of us cast our vote impelled by the hope your words generated, and guided by the fact that we cannot live as formerly.

Obstacles and racial barriers have been raised that not only prevent our enjoyment of rights and privileges without which none can give their best to the growth and development of our country but are as well an impeachment of our democracy, destructive of national morality and injurious to our integrity as a people.

We petition you, Mr. President:

Arouse the nation from the self-denying lethargy into which it has been cast through acceptance of the un-American, subversive and dehumanizing race relations. End the practice of gradualism. Use the Executive Order, the vast political powers which devolve upon you as Chief Executive decisively to change the policies of State and Federal governments in their relations with Negro citizens. Substitution of the doctrine of States' Rights for the Constitution in relations with Negro citizens must be stopped. American citizenship rights are paramount. Their priority must be respected. End segregation and jim-crow now.

Mr. President, use unsparingly the persuasive moral strength inherent in the office of President to end bias and prejudice in human relations. Use your great influence to bring respect for the inalienable rights of man. Mobilize science and the arts to render shattering blows to the myth of white superiority in every area of our cultural life.

Mr. President, order an end to discriminatory practices based on race, nationality, creed or color in the realm of employment and job tenure, voting, housing and education. These shameful features of our national life astound and shock the world. Their continued existence prevents the fulfillment of our obligations under the charter of the United Nations. It is impossible that they should not affect our prestige before the world.

Mr. President, the time is right for a new Emancipation Proclamation. President Abraham Lincoln showed the way. But the task was left unfinished. Our democracy must embrace all or it will embrace none.

Therefore, we petition you to:

1. Order an end to all practices and propagation of superiority based on race, nationality, creed or color enforced by legal and police powers of the Federal government.

2. Appoint a Negro to a new Cabinet post to be known as Secretary of Civil Rights to safeguard the rights of the Negro against encroachments by any state agencies under the guise of "states' rights" or the fiction of racial superiority.

3. Call a national "End Segregation Conference" now to be attended by Negro and white leaders of labor, the Church, education and culture to map out a moral code crusade against racist ideology.

4. Declare the Negro ghettoes that disgrace every metropolitan area distressed communities and formulate programs of relief and rehabilitation to eliminate the poverty, misery, illiteracy and chronic ill health.

5. Cut off all grants of federal funds to colleges and universities which practice or propagate segregation or discrimination based on race, creed or color.

6. Cancel all contracts with companies, corporations or individuals which apply any form of segregation or discrimination in their employment practices.

7. Establish the right of Negro citizens in every state to vote for any candidate for the Federal office of President, Vice-President, presidential elector, member of Senate or House of Representatives, or in any special or primary election held solely or in fact for the purpose of selecting any such candidate.

8. Order an appropriate bi-racial Federal Committee or Commission on Housing to be established in every city and state with a substantial non-white population to study racial problems in housing, receive and investigate complaints alleging discrimination.

9. Direct all Federal agencies to shape their policies and practices to make the maximum contribution to the achievement of this goal.

10. Direct that all the recommendations of the Civil Rights Commissions made to provide equality in housing and other sections of national life be immediately implemented and carried into action.

Yours is the hour of destiny, Mr. President. What we ask is within your power. We urge you to act now.

Henry Winston (7 September 1961)

Henry Winston, a leading Communist and an Afro-American, was convicted under the infamous Smith Act and sentenced to eight years in prison. Neglect in jail led to his loss of sight while in federal custody.

An international campaign resulted in Winston's release on 30 June 1961, and a banquet in his honor was held at the Hotel Theresa in Harlem in September. Du Bois was among the speakers. When the two men met (as Winston wrote to me on 12 February 1981), one of the things Du Bois said was, "There is hope in the world"—a reference to the campaign which had led to Winston's release.

The following month, I drove Dr. and Mrs. Du Bois to a New York City airport for their trip to Ghana. There Du Bois was to die on 27 August 1963, the very day when 250,000 people gathered in Washington to hear Martin Luther King speak of his dream. As Roy Wilkins told the massed throng at that time, when he announced Du Bois's death and asked for a moment of silence, "The man who wrote the slogans on our banners today passed away."

More than most men, Henry Winston has suffered for his determination to think and act in accord with what he believed was right. In this day of the coward and thief, the liar and murderer, it is a great honor to stand in the presence of this man, and beholding his wounded body and undaunted soul, to remember that great word of Emerson:

> *Though love repine and reason chafe,*
> *There came a voice without reply*
> *'Tis man's perdition to be safe*
> *When for the truth he ought to die.*[1]

1. This is from "Sacrifice."

Index